INTERPRETING CARNAP

Rudolf Carnap (1891–1970), one of the most important philosophers of the twentieth century, helped found logical positivism, was one of the originators of the field of philosophy of science, and was a leading contributor to semantics and inductive logic. This volume of new essays, written by leading international experts, places Carnap in his philosophical context and studies his topics, his interests, and the major stages of his thought. The essays reassess Carnap's place in the history of analytic philosophy through his approach to metaphysics, values, politics, epistemology, and philosophy of science. They delve into important topics of Carnap's mature thought, namely explication, naturalism, and his defense of analyticity; and they recover the logical and the linguistic components of philosophy and how they unfolded in the syntax–semantics relation, induction, and language-planning. The resulting interpretation of Carnap will be illuminating for both current and future research.

ALAN RICHARDSON is Professor of Philosophy at the University of British Columbia. He is the author of *Carnap's Construction of the World* (1998) and is on the editorial board of *The Collected Works of Rudolf Carnap* (2019).

ADAM TAMAS TUBOLY is Leader of the MTA Lendület Values and Science Research Group, at the HUN-REN Research Centre for the Humanities in Budapest, and Research Fellow at the ITD, Medical School, University of Pécs. He is coauthor (with Christopher Burke) of *Otto Neurath in Britain* (forthcoming).

INTERPRETING CARNAP

Critical Essays

EDITED BY

ALAN RICHARDSON
University of British Columbia

ADAM TAMAS TUBOLY
HUN-REN, Research Centre for the Humanities

Shaftesbury Road, Cambridge CB2 8EA, United Kingdom

One Liberty Plaza, 20th Floor, New York, NY 10006, USA

477 Williamstown Road, Port Melbourne, VIC 3207, Australia

314–321, 3rd Floor, Plot 3, Splendor Forum, Jasola District Centre, New Delhi – 110025, India

103 Penang Road, #05–06/07, Visioncrest Commercial, Singapore 238467

Cambridge University Press is part of Cambridge University Press & Assessment, a department of the University of Cambridge.

We share the University's mission to contribute to society through the pursuit of education, learning and research at the highest international levels of excellence.

www.cambridge.org
Information on this title: www.cambridge.org/9781009096874

DOI: 10.1017/9781009099080

© Cambridge University Press & Assessment 2024

This publication is in copyright. Subject to statutory exception and to the provisions of relevant collective licensing agreements, no reproduction of any part may take place without the written permission of Cambridge University Press & Assessment.

First published 2024
First paperback edition 2025

A catalogue record for this publication is available from the British Library

ISBN 978-1-009-09820-5   Hardback
ISBN 978-1-009-09687-4   Paperback

Cambridge University Press & Assessment has no responsibility for the persistence or accuracy of URLs for external or third-party internet websites referred to in this publication and does not guarantee that any content on such websites is, or will remain, accurate or appropriate.

Contents

List of Contributors   *page* vii
Acknowledgments   ix
List of Abbreviations   x

      Introduction: Carnap's Transformation of the Canon   1
      Alan Richardson and Adam Tamas Tuboly

PART I PHILOSOPHY IN NEW DRESS

1 Carnap's Noncognitivism: Paths and Influences   13
   Christian Damböck

2 Carnap Is Not against Metaphysics   32
   Vera Flocke

3 Interpreting Carnap's Construction of the World   50
   Christopher Pincock

4 Philosophy in a Collective Spirit as "Politics in Its
   Broadest Sense"   70
   Audrey Yap

PART II NATURALISM AND METHOD

5 Shades of Naturalism: Carnap and Quine   89
   André W. Carus

6 On Quine's Epistemological Objection to Carnap's Analyticity   106
   Joseph Bentley and Thomas Uebel

7 Carnapian Explication: Origins and Shifting Goals   127
   Erich H. Reck

PART III THE LOGICAL AND THE LINGUISTIC

8 Carnap's Approach to Semantics and Syntax: Relations and Tension   153
   Pierre Wagner

9 Carnap on the Formality of Logic and Mathematics   171
   Georg Schiemer

10 Carnap on Probability and Induction   192
   Sandy Zabell

11 Metaphysics, Tolerance, and Language Planning: Carnap on International Auxiliary Languages   214
   Başak Aray

PART IV SCIENCE AND THEORIES

12 Carnap on Theories and the Methods of Science   237
   Lydia Patton

13 Carnap on Unity of Science   252
   Bianca Crewe and Alan Richardson

14 Carnap on Determinism and Free Will   270
   Richard Creath

Bibliography   286
Index   308

Contributors

BAŞAK ARAY has a PhD in philosophy from the University Paris 1 Panthéon-Sorbonne and is an independent scholar.

JOSEPH BENTLEY is a lecturer in the Department of Philosophy at the University of Manchester.

ANDRÉ W. CARUS is a visiting fellow at the Munich Center for Mathematical Philosophy, Ludwig Maximilian University, Munich.

RICHARD CREATH is Professor in the School of Life Sciences, College of Liberal Arts and Sciences at Arizona State University.

BIANCA CREWE is a doctoral student in the Department of Philosophy at the University of British Columbia.

CHRISTIAN DAMBÖCK is a lecturer in the Philosophy Department at the University of Vienna.

VERA FLOCKE is Assistant Professor in the Department of Philosophy at Indiana University Bloomington.

LYDIA PATTON is Professor of Philosophy and Affiliate in the Department of Science, Technology, and Society at Virginia Tech.

CHRISTOPHER PINCOCK is Professor in the Department of Philosophy at The Ohio State University.

ERICH H. RECK is Professor in the College of Humanities, Arts, and Social Sciences at the University of California Riverside.

ALAN RICHARDSON is Professor in the Department of Philosophy at the University of British Columbia.

GEORG SCHIEMER is Professor in the Department of Philosophy and Head of Department of the Institute Vienna Circle at the University of Vienna.

ADAM TAMAS TUBOLY is Leader of the MTA Lendület Values and Science Research Group and Research Fellow at the Institute of Transdisciplinary Discoveries, Medical School, University of Pécs.

THOMAS UEBEL is Professor Emeritus in the Department of Philosophy at the University of Manchester.

PIERRE WAGNER is Professor in the Department of Philosophy at the University Paris 1 Panthéon-Sorbonne and a member of the Institute for the History and Philosophy of Science and Technology in Paris.

AUDREY YAP is Associate Professor in the Department of Philosophy at the University of Victoria.

SANDY ZABELL is Professor in the Department of Statistics and Data Science at Northwestern University.

Acknowledgments

During the editorial process, Adam Tamas Tuboly was supported by the MTA Lendület Values and Science Research Group at the HUN-REN Research Centre for the Humanities (Hungarian Academy of Sciences). Both editors are grateful to Hilary Gaskin for her kind support of the project and to all the reviewers and referees of the book and its chapters for their time and critical comments. All errors are, of course, our responsibility.

Abbreviations

Abbreviated Works of Carnap

Aufbau — *Der logische Aufbau der Welt.* Berlin-Schlachtensee: Weltkreis-Verlag, 1928. Quoted from the English translation, *The Logical Structure of the World.* Translated by Rolf A. George. Berkeley: University of California Press, 1967.

CIM — *The Continuum of Inductive Methods.* Chicago: University of Chicago Press, 1952.

CW1 — *The Collected Works of Rudolf Carnap, Volume 1: Early Writings.* Edited by A. W. Carus, M. Friedman, W. Kienzler, A. Richardson, and S. Schlotter. Oxford: Oxford University Press, 2019.

ESO — "Empiricism, Semantics, and Ontology." *Revue International de Philosophie* 4 (11) (1950): 20–40.

FLM — *Foundations of Logic and Mathematics.* Chicago: University of Chicago Press, 1939.

FoL — *Formalization of Logic.* Cambridge, MA: Harvard University Press, 1943.

IA — "Intellectual Autobiography." In P. A. Schilpp (ed.), *The Philosophy of Rudolf Carnap.* LaSalle, IL: Open Court, 3–84, 1963.

IPoS — *An Introduction to the Philosophy of Science.* New York: Basic Books, 1966.

IS — *Introduction to Semantics.* Cambridge, MA: Harvard University Press, 1942.

LFP — *Logical Foundations of Probability.* Chicago: University of Chicago Press, 1950.

LFP2	*Logical Foundations of Probability*. 2nd ed. Chicago: University of Chicago Press, 1962.
LSL	*Logical Syntax of Language*. London: Routledge & Kegan Paul, 1937.
LSS	*Logische Syntax der Sprache*. Vienna: Springer, 1934.
M&N	*Meaning and Necessity*. Chicago: University of Chicago Press, 1947; 2nd ed., 1956.
Raum	*Der Raum: Ein Beitrag zur Wissenschaftslehre / Space: A Contribution to the Theory of Science*. In *CW1*, 21–171.
RSE	"Replies and Systematic Expositions." In P. A. Schilpp (ed.), *The Philosophy of Rudolf Carnap*. LaSalle, IL: Open Court, 1963, 859–1013.
T&M	"Testability and Meaning." *Philosophy of Science* 3 (4): 419–471; 4 (1) (1936): 1–40.

Introduction
Carnap's Transformation of the Canon
Alan Richardson and Adam Tamas Tuboly

Rudolf Carnap (1891–1970) is praised as one of the leading figures of analytic philosophy. Although the received narratives about his role and place in the historical canon and contemporary philosophy have undergone many changes, Carnap continues to be a frequently cited source in new research programs, which frequently frame him as the archenemy par excellence of the nonanalytic traditions. While his influence on the practice of Anglophone philosophy in the mid-twentieth century is unquestionable, its exact nature and extent are still under discussion by historians and philosophers.

As is often noted, after his death in 1970, Carnap's philosophy was largely seen as flawed, outdated, and too simplistic for philosophers. But one person's flaws are another's strengths, and "outdated" is thus never a final judgment – every generation considers the previous one to be obsolete, and today's scholars are rejecting those who judged Carnap to be outdated in the first place. Furthermore, oversimplification on the surface, especially in secondhand reconstructions, often turns out to be a simplification on the part of the interpreters. Historically informed research has revealed that Carnap was intellectually integrated into a colorful scholarly landscape during the first few decades of the twentieth century and that he indeed mastered his field and made good use of it in his early texts. His alleged shallowness was thus rather a new form of philosophical practice on purpose.

How and when exactly the philosophical community started to reinterpret and advance our understanding of Carnap is discussed in several chapters of this volume. Many of them also examine the factors and sources that fostered Carnap's rehabilitation: these relate to the troves of archive materials that have been unearthed in the last few decades – and due to digitalization and the existence of edited publications, it is now easier to search for the required items among the vast volumes of data at hand. Furthermore, it is also important to note that even though many of these things have been around for decades, *our interests* and *perspectives* have changed, and we thus highlight radically different things about Carnap today. We always knew that Carnap took certain sociopolitical moves outside academia as a citizen, but scholars considered this to be no more than interesting but philosophically unimportant biographical information. As Audrey Yap shows in Chapter 4, however, there are important parallels between Carnap's social engagement and his collectivist philosophical agenda.

Assessing an author's place in the history of philosophy, from a philosophical point of view, goes hand in hand with listing and contextualizing his or her additions to the philosophical canon. Such a list could feature sharp and characteristic *theses*, a well-defined and table-turning *argumentation*, or a specific *role* that the philosopher in question played in reviving a certain topic or concept. Carnap, in fact, did all of that. He is known for his confirmed, enduring, and extreme anti-metaphysical ideas that differentiated him even from other traditional empiricists; he put the modalities back on the table and showed how one could argue for a well-defined differentiation of extensions and intensions within philosophy and linguistics; finally, he was one of those figures who revived the notions of probability and induction in the mid-twentieth century.

As the literature on Carnap is vast and deep, including many more accessible pieces for a general audience, one might think that discerning Carnap's legacy and place in history is now a straightforward business. Nonetheless, because of the painstaking efforts of many scholars, even the latest, refined, and revised discussions are mixed up and somewhat blurry. By scratching the surface again and again, we find ourselves in a somewhat inconvenient, complex, and puzzling situation about who Carnap was, and what he claimed and achieved, after all. In demystifying old and new narratives, there is always hope – a hope that all our challenges, archival diggings, and conscious changes of the received norms of interpretation will contribute to an even more refined, or an entirely novel, picture and understanding of Carnap's actual place and role in the history of philosophy.

An example of such puzzlement that later produced new knowledge and interpretations is Carnap's early work, which resulted in the much celebrated and criticized *Der logische Aufbau der Welt*: it can thus be shown that Carnap's *sociological* and *institutional* embeddedness, or lack thereof, fueled his novel philosophical project. Carnap enrolled at the University of Jena in 1910 and studied mathematics, physics, and philosophy, the customary triplet before the outbreak of the First World War in 1914.

Meanwhile, in 1911 and 1912, he also spent several semesters in Freiburg, where he studied philosophy under such important neo-Kantian philosophers as Jonas Cohn, Georg Mehlis, and, above all, Heinrich Rickert. In Jena, however, the most influential impact on his thinking came from the logician Gottlob Frege, the neo-Kantian Bruno Bauch, and from Herman Nohl, who lectured on Lebensphilosophie, education, psychology, and even Hegel's philosophy of law (*IA*, 4).

Although Carnap returned to his studies after his service in the German Army during World War One, he rather "followed [his] interest without thinking about . . . a professional career" (*IA*, 3), thus deciding to become a secondary school teacher of physics and mathematics. But after passing the teaching exams in 1920, he began to consider an academic career in pure science and prepared for the submission of a doctoral dissertation on the borderline of physics and philosophy. It wasn't an easy task, however. Carnap went first to the physics department with a project concerning space and time. As the head of the institute, Max Wien, rejected it as being too philosophical, Carnap took it to the philosophy department, where Bruno Bauch considered it too physical. "In the end we came to an agreement", recalled Carnap (*IA*, 11), "that I would choose another project in philosophy, namely the philosophical foundations of geometry." This was a transformative experience for him that shaped his entire career: Carnap often worked in gray zones, and only at a very late point in his career did he witness the rise of all those institutional frameworks and programs that we now call analytic philosophy of science or "logic and methodology of science."

During those years of envisioning, writing, submitting, and defending his dissertation, Carnap was living close to Freiburg and made great use of this proximity. He not only attended Edmund Husserl's seminars and discussion group on several occasions (Carus 2016) but organized his own groups and small workshops with his closest friends and similarly minded distant colleagues (Dahms 2016). In the years that followed, he became friends with scientific philosophers like Hans Reichenbach and psychologists like Kurt Lewin and Wolfgang Köhler and discussed methodology with Paul Hertz, aesthetics and politics with Hans Freyer, and the arts with Franz Roh and László Moholy-Nagy.

For years, Carnap was on the intellectual move without letting any cognitive strictures restrict his journey. In fact, he did not have a proper institutional position until 1926 and was financially independent: he came from and had married into a wealthy family. At the time, scientific philosophy was a hobby for him, a joyful interest that he pursued out of intellectual curiosity and for that reason alone. Around 1923, however, given some friction in the family and the deteriorating economic situation in Germany, Carnap reconsidered his career plans and started to look for an established academic position, which, after some years, he found in Vienna.

During the early 1920s, Carnap published a few articles with strong conventionalist and neo-Kantian leanings, but they did not have a significant impact on the community of scientific philosophers (all of them have been recently translated, edited, commented, and published in Carnap 2019). More important were Carnap's dissertation and his first major book, *Der logische Aufbau der Welt*. Though the specific Viennese atmosphere left a mark on the final, published version of the book, it can still be seen as the result of Carnap's free-floating thinking during the early 1920s. And in fact, this is what makes it significant for many scholars today (see the essays in Damböck 2016).

It is a rather demanding and pointless task to attempt to summarize, within a few sentences, the aims and goals of the *Aufbau* – it was a complex, grand endeavor, purporting to answer and settle many, if not all, philosophical questions. There is an interpretational problem due to the variety of sources that Carnap used without further ado. The sense-data–certainty–Russellian–reformed-empiricism reading of the book (propagated for many years by W. V. O. Quine and to some extent by Carnap himself) has been challenged historically and conceptually for decades. Today, it is appreciated that certainty was not Carnap's goal and that sense-data considerations only come into play at a rather late point in the book. And while empiricism is certainly there, it is not at all the only player in town. Alternative interpretations have been offered in abundance: neo-Kantianism's strive for objectivity and scientific pursuits, a refinement of empiricism on German grounds, or a reexamination of scientific philosophy through the lens of the Enlightenment. Specific, restricted, but still influential sources have been identified in the persons of Wilhelm Ostwald, Henri Poincaré, and Hugo Dingler, the tradition of Geisteswissenschaften, and value theories.

This is a substantial list that could quite possibly be continued further, as certain archived sources are being even more broadly circulated concerning Carnap's readings, diaries, and correspondence (Damböck 2022a, 2022b). Furthermore, his early work is a clear synthesis of all of Carnap's readings, influences, and discussions between 1910 and 1927. The same goes for disciplinary issues beyond personal influences, which ranged from Lebensphilosophie, philosophy of science, logic, and mathematics, to physics, value theory, color theory, psychology, and the social sciences. But seen through the lens of our present, systematically and institutionally shaped self-understanding as analytic philosophers, this list is inconsistent, puzzling, and dangerous. The *Aufbau* is often read or noted as a foundational text of our canon; something that has shaped our problems, methods, views, and the sources we deem respectable for further consideration in analytic puzzle-solving. If the *Aufbau* comes close to anything like that (which one might doubt, given the very late English translation dating to 1967 and the fact that the *Aufbau* had little resonance among Anglophone scholars besides Quine and Nelson Goodman during the mid-twentieth century), then institutionally, it might indeed seem dangerous for a foundational text to combine substantial engagement with outsider figures and themes such as Husserlian phenomenology, neo-Kantian value theory and concept formation, Nietzsche's Lebensphilosophie, Dilthey's Geisteswissenschaften, and Hans Freyer, with discussion of such leading fathers of the movement as Mach, Comte, Russell, Frege, and even a little bit of Wittgenstein.

We do not have to resolve this issue, of course, as others have already pointed toward the possibility of stratified readings (most importantly, Carus 2007 and Damböck 2016) and certain tensions within the book. What is to be noted here, however, is that Carnap's significance, especially with regard to the *Aufbau* (though one might also include his doctoral dissertation, *Der Raum*), lies in the fact that he was able to speak to many *nonoverlapping philosophical circles*. Almost everyone could find something significant and relevant in it, and the book offered explicit meeting points for all these traditions and movements. As a result, many European scholars could read and connect to Carnap's project, and Quine was able to forge a narrative that would get the attention of their American colleagues. Even if it is true that the content of the *Aufbau* is not at all exhausted by Russellian philosophy and a concern for sense data and phenomenalism, these aspects are partially there in the book and provide an expedient base for constructing a restricted narrative – just as Quine did.

Due to this richness of materials, sources, concepts, viewpoints, and often implicit minuscule steps toward alternative traditions and discourses with the past, Carnap's early work earned a remarkable place in the history of twentieth-century philosophy. While many have previously read it as a single-minded, hard-boiled, and – consequently – failed logical attempt at achieving the unachievable, we are now in a better position to engage with and interpret the relevant early texts from radically different and more sophisticated perspectives. One might even say that while Frege's works created the problem horizon for analytic philosophers in the philosophy of mathematics, and Russell's for a general epistemological program, Carnap's texts show us how to deal with philosophy in a more traditional manner, by reaching out to all cognitive enterprises that might contain the germs of solutions for the chosen problems within a grand scheme. Carnap wrote the book when the analytic-continental rupture was either less visible or less significant for philosophers, which surely contributed to his freedom to take the "other camp" more seriously. But for years, Carnap was not committed to any institutions, philosophical movements, schools, or for that matter, any personalities (like Wittgenstein). He was a freelancer, a seeker of solutions and cognitive challenges, and due to his widespread readings, countless personal contacts, and first-order experiences in various reading groups, the mixture he created in the 1920s was unique.

One final point of importance: through Carnap's diverging interests and readings, our attention has also been redirected to lesser known, already forgotten, never really recognized, or even rejected figures, such as Hans Freyer, Theodor Ziehen, or Richard Gätschenberger, that have not caught the attention of historians and philosophers in their own right. One might even say that, unintentionally, Carnap did important service to the history of philosophy by keeping up the interest of analytic philosophers in, and making available useful backdoors and transitory points to, continental philosophy (to Husserl, Dilthey, Rickert, Driesch, and Vaihinger), for example.

Working in Vienna and later in Prague, subsuming himself to the more traditional strictures of academic life and institutional barriers, significantly changed Carnap's thinking and perspective, which neither needs to be emphasized nor examined here. What should be noted, however, is his idea that the critical-interpretational business is an open-ended challenge that involves overthrowing the hard-gained simplicity of previous interpretations – and that by engaging with the empirically founded complexities of history, we are always reminded of how we arrived at our current predilections by means of past determinations and how our picture of the past is drawn by current expectations and dominant strains of thought.

Some further information about the motivation and reasoning behind this volume's place and standing in a field where scholarship is continuously growing may be required. *The Cambridge Companion to Carnap* was published in 2007 (Friedman and Creath 2007). While it has facilitated a more nuanced and contextually grounded picture of Carnap's life, this has not yet been put to broader use. On the other hand, *all* the available monographs on Carnap focus on *particular* aspects of his thinking and influence. Michael Friedman's (1999) groundbreaking collection, *Reconsidering Logical Positivism*, brought new dimensions to the study of Carnap's early philosophy of science and logic, mainly within the context of logical positivism. Meanwhile, Alan Richardson's *Carnap's Construction of the World* (1998) offered a critical reevaluation of Carnap's *Aufbau* against the broader historical background, including its relevance to the changes of the early 1930s. Finally, A. W. Carus' *Carnap and Twentieth-Century Thought* (2007) is perhaps the most comprehensive treatment of Carnap's philosophy, while also featuring a substantial overview of his life. Nonetheless, Carus' book is a detailed exploration of one major idea (namely, the method and process of explication) in the life and work of Carnap.

Consequently, *Interpreting Carnap* aims to deliver a more comprehensive account of Carnap from various *new* and hitherto *unexplored* or *underrated* perspectives. The volume looks anew at a range of interesting and important things that Carnap did from a variety of historical and philosophical perspectives. It is an invitation to be curious – and by highlighting the contemporary relevance of Carnap's philosophical thinking, the chapters it contains will also help to reassess his long-standing influence. The interpretative filters of novel historical, argumentative, and more systematic standpoints not only make it possible to discuss Carnap's better-known works from lesser-known viewpoints but also to apply the received and existing perspectives to his minor and lesser-known writings, with the aim of reevaluating their place in his overall philosophical oeuvre.

The essays in Part I set the tone of the volume by taking a general look at Carnap scholarship, while Part II deals with Carnap's views on naturalism, explication, and the analytic–synthetic distinction. The third part focuses on philosophy of logic and language. Finally, Part IV is concerned with traditional topics of and within the philosophy of science from new perspectives, delineating the contours of possible roads ahead in Carnap scholarship.

In particular, Christian Damböck (Chapter 1) highlights the importance of archival and less well-known primary sources for our understanding of Carnap's philosophy by investigating several examples of concrete, and often overlooked, influences on his thinking that include a broad range of heterogeneous movements. Damböck draws important and challenging lessons about Carnap's place in the history of philosophy, mainly through the guiding idea of noncognitivism.

In Chapter 2, Vera Flocke starts from the received view that Carnap is a great opponent of metaphysics. But closer scrutiny reveals the simplicity of this perspective, and by asking what exactly Carnap rejects when he repudiates metaphysics, Flocke provides a novel critical interpretation of Carnap's business by distinguishing phases of Carnap and showing that Carnap rejects a particular methodology that he regards as conflicting with empiricism; and thus, Flocke argues, much of contemporary metaphysics is, from Carnap's late perspective, in good standing.

Christopher Pincock's contribution (Chapter 3), despite its title, focuses on Carnap's work in a more general setting. As most philosophical texts generate interpretive controversy, he argues that some of those controversies arise from a reasonable pluralism of interpretations. Pincock illustrates this reasonable pluralism through recourse to six of the most important interpretations of Carnap's *Logical Structure of the World* or *Aufbau*.

The first part of the volume is closed by Audrey Yap's essay (Chapter 4), which discusses Carnap's engagement with various social issues through the lens of his scientific world view, connecting it to the idea that Carnap intended his philosophy to be political in the broadest sense of the term. From this new perspective, Yap also considers the extent to which certain social activities, by reflecting Carnap's concern for the intellectual community as a whole, can be seen as continuous with his commitment to philosophy as a collective enterprise and how these ideas might improve the practice of philosophy generally.

Part II begins with André W. Carus's comparison of Carnap's and Quine's naturalism (Chapter 5). Carus starts from Dreben's slogan of 'working from within' to characterize what Quine calls his 'provincial' — in contrast to Carnap's 'cosmopolitan' — naturalism. Quine's vacillations (e.g. about analyticity) make this tricky, but Carus argues that the abyss between Carnap and Quine can in principle be bridged.

Joseph Bentley and Thomas Uebel (Chapter 6) approaches W. V. O. Quine's criticism of the distinction between analytic and synthetic sentences. They argue that Quine's epistemological objection against the distinction is misdirected. According to Carnap's semiotic approach to philosophy, analyticity is a strictly semantic concept differentiating meaning relations of sentences within constructed formal language systems. Epistemological questions fall outside semantics and belong to pragmatics where they are to be answered by empirical means. Insofar as epistemological objections are applicable to the pragmatic counterparts of semantic concepts, they are shown to be very much answerable by naturalistic standards.

Introduction 9

In Chapter 7, Erich H. Reck discusses Carnap's now famous process of explication. To gain a more critical *and* interpretative perspective, he raises several historical questions. Answering all the possible challenges one by one, Reck examines the origins of, subsequent tendencies and shifts in, as well as the resulting gains and losses associated with explication. Finally, he examines the conception of philosophy that would make explication one's main, or even only, philosophical method.

In Part III, Pierre Wagner (Chapter 8) considers Carnap's views on syntax and semantics and renews the importance of Carnap's semantical turn that is sometimes underestimated. Wagner's chapter discusses Tarski's influence on Carnap and the impact of semantics on several topics such as formal languages, logical truth, and the principle of tolerance.

Georg Schiemer (Chapter 9) approaches a specific feature of logic and mathematics. A general line of continuity in Carnap's philosophical work is the conviction that mathematics and logic are formal or nonfactual in nature. Given the centrality of this idea, a natural question is how precisely Carnap understood the formality thesis concerning mathematical knowledge. According to Schiemer, there were several significant shifts in Carnap's understanding, corresponding to changes in his conceptual framework.

Sandy Zabell (Chapter 10) looks at the field of probability, where, although he arrived somewhat late, Carnap's groundbreaking work immediately established him as a central figure. This surprising midlife shift in Carnap's career raises some natural questions and Zabell aims to tackle these in novel ways. One of the chapter's central themes is that although reference is often made today to Carnap's views on probability and inductive inference, these views underwent a significant evolution over time: to genuinely understand Carnap on probability and inductive inference one has to recognize that there is actually a $Carnap_1$ and a $Carnap_2$.

Finally, Başak Aray (Chapter 11) discusses how Carnap's philosophy of language affects his position on language planning issues. Carnap was an Esperantist from an early age, and he kept his interest for international auxiliary languages active throughout his life. Aray argues that the antimetaphysical rejection of the romanticist view of language, sustained by Vienna Circle, led to a more liberal and flexible attitude toward language planning issues.

By taking a new stand in old debates, in Part IV, Lydia Patton (Chapter 12) goes back to Carnap's ideas about empirical significance and theory construction. Carnap's account of the relationship between theoretical frameworks and methods of observation has come in for plentiful criticism in the twentieth century. Patton presents evidence that Carnap's approach to the distinction between theoretical and observation languages is more flexible than it is usually depicted to be and is motivated by his philosophy of science.

Bianca Crewe and Alan Richardson (Chapter 13) attempt to rise above the details of various formulations of the unity-of-science doctrine in Carnap's work to investigate instead the philosophical significance of his commitment to the unity of science. They approach this problem by reflecting on the "dangerous disunities" in knowledge, action, and society that Carnap hopes to overcome through the unity of science.

In Chapter 14, Richard Creath turns his attention to an overlooked problem, that is, free will and its relation to determinism, which has exercised the minds of metaphysicians and ethicists for thousands of years. By his own account, Carnap engaged in neither metaphysics nor ethics, nonetheless, in his major text on the philosophy of science, he devotes an entire chapter to this problem. By illustrating the historical situation and the problem nexus in which Carnap worked, Creath argues that Carnap's chapter should be seen as a reaction against and rejection of Hans Reichenbach's conclusions about the same issues, including free will, laws of nature, and causation. Creath examines and assesses Carnap's arguments and asks whether they amount to a deviation from his anti-metaphysical stance.

Individually, but especially when taken together, these chapters provide much food for thought for historians and systematic thinkers alike. As the contours of new possible research agendas and expectations relating to historical figures are continuously emerging, we hope to make a useful and illuminating contribution to both current and future research.

PART I

Philosophy in New Dress

CHAPTER I

Carnap's Noncognitivism
Paths and Influences
Christian Damböck

1.1 Introduction

With a view to highlighting the importance of archival and less well-known primary sources for our understanding of Rudolf Carnap's philosophy,[1] this chapter investigates several examples of concrete influences on his thinking. These influences, which enable us to better understand Carnap's philosophical views, include a broad range of heterogeneous movements: nineteenth-century Herbartianism and empiriocriticism, the German Youth Movement, Bauhaus modernism and the revolution from the right, as well as the Vienna Circle and post–World War II (WWII) analytic philosophy.

While Carnap is best known for his work on logic and the philosophies of science and language – that is, as a theoretical philosopher – it is fair to say that his philosophy had always been shaped by practical motives as well (Richardson 2007). This becomes evident not only in Carnap's involvement in a variety of political activities (see the contribution by Audrey Yap to this volume [Chapter 4]) but also in his development of a philosophical stance that is directed at the reality of life and integrates cognitive as well as noncognitive elements – as such, this stance is as theoretical as it is practical/political.

At the heart of Carnap's philosophy lies his noncognitivism. The origin of this philosophical agenda is the Vienna Circle's so-called criterion of meaning (*Sinnkriterium*), which argues that statements being neither

---

[1] The main portions of the *Nachlass* are located at the University of Pittsburgh, Archives of Scientific Philosophy, Rudolf Carnap Collection (call numbers starting with RC), as well as the University of California at Los Angeles, Young Research Library, Special Collections Department, Manuscript Collection No. 1029, Rudolf Carnap Papers (call numbers starting with UCLA). Electronic versions of large parts of these materials have been incorporated into the database VALEP (Virtual Archive of Logical Empiricism), see https://valep.vc.univie.ac.at. In October 2021, the Carnap materials available in VALEP comprised about 70,000 scans. The entire *Nachlass* contains approximately 90,000 pages. For Carnap's diaries, see Carnap (2022a, 2022b).

completely verifiable/falsifiable nor logically true/false are meaningless.² Put in the more careful language that Carnap adopted in his later years, such statements can be "interpreted neither as factual nor as analytic (or contradictory)[; they are] devoid of cognitive meaning, and therefore the distinction between truth and falsity is not applicable to [them]" (*RSE*, 999). Noncognitive statements represent attitudes rather than epistemically justifiable claims. They comprise a very broad spectrum of statements: moral, political, and aesthetic *value statements* (*RSE*, 999–1013), as well as all kinds of *scientific attitudes*. The latter include both theoretical statements (Carnap 1962) and "linguistic frameworks" (*ESO*).

There are important differences between value statements and scientific attitudes. Even though a scientific attitude, not unlike a value statement, can neither be absolutely true nor false, scientists can still epistemically justify it. If the attitude is a scientific theory, then its empirical predictions can be tested; if the attitude is a linguistic framework, then the experts are able to identify it as more or less "expedient" or "fruitful" (*ESO*, 31). The application of tests (theories) and practical trials (frameworks) is crucial for every scientific attitude and the reasons for scientific attitudes being either accepted or rejected by the scientific community tend to be clear and consistent. However, even protocol statements and proven mathematical theorems are never absolutely cognitive,³ seeing as our senses and reasoning abilities might fail. Yet there does exist a strong *cognitive backup*: A statement, theory, or framework becomes justified via confrontation with the available facts.

In the case of values, we cannot match the cognitive backup that justifies scientific claims and attitudes, for where values are concerned, our final word tends to be a matter of sentiment rather than cognitive evidence. Cognitive backups nonetheless do play a crucial role here, as there are various factors that *might* influence people's personal values. For instance, do you still stick to a certain attitude once you understand the consequences it will bring about, once you know about its logical relationships (the statements it logically implies and the statements from which it can be logically derived), or once you recognize its links to the values of other individuals in your social group? We may certainly criticize people

---

² That Carnap's noncognitivism was first formulated in Carnap (1932/2004), in direct connection with the Vienna Circle's criterion of meaning, was correctly highlighted in Menger (1994, 179) and in Siegetsleitner (2014, 142).

³ See (Carnap in preparation, entry on September 2, 1940): "I am more and more inclined to put all concepts of the language of science into the 'floating net', not just the abstract notions of theoretical physics. Then no 'solid rock' remains, and there are no unshakable protocol sentences."

Table 1.1 *The epistemic spectrum of values*

Protocols and proven mathematical theorems	Scientific attitudes:		Value statements
	Scientific theories	Linguistic frameworks	
… are almost entirely cognitive due to reproducing empirical facts and logical truths.	… enable predictions, procedures of testing, and corroboration.	… can be identified as more or less expedient or fruitful.	… are a matter of noncognitive choice of a lay person, although there are cognitive factors involved.
… are considered true by the relevant experts on the basis of observation or proof.	… are considered corroborated by the relevant experts on the basis of their inductive intuition and empirical evidence.	… are considered expedient or fruitful by the relevant experts based on their scientific experience.	… are adopted by a lay person or a group of lay persons after carrying out a cognitive backup that may include expert knowledge.

who seem immune to scientific and rational advice of that kind as being illogical and anti-scientific (see Section 1.3); at the same time, we have to acknowledge the importance of sentiment when it comes to values. A value statement cannot reasonably be called "true," "corroborated," or "fruitful" – we can only say that we adopt it in a most reasonable and rational way: After considering all relevant cognitive information we identify this value statement as "our pure optative" (*RSE*, 999–1013). Expert knowledge is indispensable to ensure value statements being reasonable. However, a value statement is in itself neither knowledge nor a matter for experts at all. Every moral question is relevant for everybody and therefore everybody is a lay person when moral rather than scientific questions are due. Values are positioned within an epistemic spectrum that gradually moves from the almost entirely cognitive toward the almost entirely noncognitive (Table 1.1).

Carnap and other logical empiricists discussed two caveats to this relativist view on value statements. First, one might think that there is a third form of epistemic justification, in addition to empirical and logical justification; namely, synthetic a priori truth: Though failing to be empirically or logically justifiable, value statements are justified at the level of synthetic a priori reasoning and therefore can be seen as cognitive. As antimetaphysical thinkers, all logical empiricists reject this idea. Second, one might conceive a situation where value statements are perceived as objective once they – for reasons such as cultural development or divine mercy – are shared by everybody (or every reasonable person at least). This quasi-realism is nothing but a fallible empirical claim: "There are value statements that every reasonable person actually shares." As an empirical claim, this idea is an option for the logical empiricist. Indeed, in his later years Carnap sympathized with the "optimistic opinion" of his friend Wilhelm Flitner who claimed "that through the development of culture first in smaller groups, then in nations etc., and finally in the whole of humanity a shared system of values emerges" (Carnap in preparation, entry on September 7, 1964).

This is exactly the point where noncognitivism and naturalism overlap. Moral objectivity becomes an empirical claim stating that all reasonable individuals tend to share certain value statements. If we accept this to be empirical (rather than logical or metaphysical), then the following philosophers appear to be noncognitivists who disagree with Carnap only insofar as they put a different weight on the option of universal consensus: theologians in the Herbart tradition such as Carnap's grandfather Friedrich Wilhelm Dörpfeld (see Section 1.2); naturalist theologians à la Henry Nelson Wieman, who enthusiastically subscribed to Carnap's noncognitivism;[4] noncognitivists in the style of Franz Brentano and Oskar Kraus, who thought that all reasonable individuals must share the very same attitudes (Damböck 2022a, section 2.1); Gibbard-style quasi-realists (Gibbard 1990); and pragmatists such as Dewey (1939). Dörpfeld, Wieman, Brentano, Kraus, Gibbard, Dewey, and Carnap share the idea that consensus among all reasonable individuals as regards certain fundamental value statements is an empirical fact rather than a consequence of certain synthetic a priori judgments or logical truths.

Carnap's noncognitivism is a philosophical theory about the relationship between science and values. This theory is *political* in a specific and far-reaching (as well as timely) manner, in that it proposes the following

---

[4] See (Wieman 1937, 323–324): "[Value statements] are neither true nor false. They are not cognitive. They do not designate anything that exists ... We who work in the field of religion should take this criticism to ourselves. It is certainly right and good to use language to share sentiments and incite to worthy action. No doubt much of religion should be devoted to that. But great evil ensues when we fail to distinguish between words used to do this and words used to state what is present in reality as actuality and possibility ... Carnap's criticism will help to correct that chronic error in all those interests of man where deep sentiments and high passions are involved."

value as being relevant to absolutely everybody: You must adopt all possible strategies to maximize rationality, rather than act illogically (see Sections 1.4 and 1.5). Though scientifically sound, this is no longer mere internal scientific advice but rather a value whose adoption the "scientific humanist" (*IA*, 83) recommends to both the scientist and the lay person. As John Dewey put it and as it was later echoed by Carnap:

> [The] science that is put to distinctively human use is that in which warranted ideas about the nonhuman world are integrated with emotion as human traits. In this integration not only is science itself *a* value (since it is the expression and the fulfilment of a special human desire and interest) but it is the supreme means of the valid determination of all valuations in all aspects of human and social life. (Dewey 1971, 446, original emphasis)

Happiness, moral responsibility, and aesthetic pleasure are purely noncognitive matters insofar as everybody must evaluate these matters for themselves. A scientist is no more competent here than a layperson. However, to study the cognitive aspects of values before we accept or reject them is something we can very well learn from science. And exactly for that reason is science (or "scientific humanism") both a value in its own right and a political enterprise that is relevant for the whole of society.

To think that there exists an aporia between noncognitivism and political engagement/moral responsibility was a trivial though widespread misunderstanding among those who erroneously assumed that noncognitivism implies the abstinence from taking a stance (cf. Hegselmann 1979, 59–66). Being free to take a stance does not mean, however, that scientists in their role as experts are asked to take a stance always and everywhere. In their role as experts, scientists are certainly wise to only propagate those scientific attitudes that directly belong to their field of competence. The scientist's genuine moral sentiments may exclusively refer to science:

> We too, have "emotional needs" in philosophy [and science], but they are filled by clarity of concepts, precision of methods, responsible theses, achievement through cooperation in which each individual plays his [*sic*] part. (*Aufbau*, xvii)[5]

Once scientists go beyond recommending well-established scientific findings of their field, they stop acting as scientists and become laypersons. Scientists who fail to reveal this difference were criticized for good reason (see Weber 1919). Carnap reformulated Max Weber in an anti-

---

[5] See Uebel (2020, 43ff.) for an alternative interpretation of this passage.

metaphysical fashion: People who sell their layperson opinions in scientific disguise are not to be labeled as great philosophers but rather as bad scientists and philosophical charlatans who produce "meaningless metaphysics" (Carnap 1932/2004) and "opium for the educated";[6] the only reasonable moral sentiment that is genuinely scientific is science itself. The "scientific world-conception" is the ridge walk of the politically engaged scientist who seeks to negotiate their position in between the abyss of philosophical charlatanry and apolitical technocracy.

1.2 Friedrich Wilhelm Dörpfeld: Herbartian Roots of Noncognitivism

Carnap's intellectual development started surprisingly slowly. Before World War I (WWI), he was more interested in the social activities of the German Youth Movement than intellectual classroom activities (Werner 2003, 231–307). Since the war later interrupted his growing intellectual ambitions, he only arrived at the decision to aim for a career in science in 1920 at the age of twenty-nine (Carnap 2022a, Einleitung). Nevertheless, during his studies in Jena and Freiburg before and immediately after WWI, he not only gained a solid education in experimental physics and took classes in philosophy (with Herman Nohl, Bruno Bauch, Heinrich Rickert, and Jonas Cohn) and logic (with Gottlob Frege) but also studied some of the works of leading philosophers and scientist such as Ernst Haeckel, Ernst Mach, Wilhelm Ostwald, Gustav Theodor Fechner, Henri Poincaré, Wilhelm Wundt, Moritz Schlick, and Paul Natorp (Carnap 2022a, Leselisten). Some key influences on Carnap's early intellectual development also came from his own family. In the extended version of his autobiography, he mentions two relatives of his mother's family whom he "regarded from childhood as models of men."[7] These were his uncle Wilhelm Dörpfeld, the famous archaeologist, and his grandfather Friedrich Wilhelm Dörpfeld (Siegetsleitner 2014, 92; Damböck 2022c; Heidelberger 2024), a pedagogue firmly rooted in the Herbartian tradition, who was quite famous in his time as well. Grandfather Dörpfeld accumulated a remarkable corpus of philosophical and pedagogical writings that were collected in an eleven-volume edition at the prestigious publishing house of C. Bertelsmann. Carnap's mother Anna Carnap wrote a biography of her father when Carnap was a child

---

[6] See "Philosophie – Opium für die Gebildeten. 26.3.34." RC 110-08-17. Cf. Carnap (1934, 260).
[7] UCLA CM3 M-A5, A7.

(A. Carnap 1897) and taught him and his sister Agnes at home. This she did in the spirit of her father,

> [who] had always strongly emphasized that in the education of a child's character, the moral principles should be based only on the child's own conscience and not on God's will. He criticized the church severely for making ethics dependent upon theology because once young people would begin to doubt the dogmas, they would also be in danger of losing their moral ground. (UCLA CM3 M-A5, A8–A9)

Anna Carnap read to her children from her father's main philosophical work *On Ethics* (Dörpfeld 1895), a book that Carnap himself also read several times as an adult, in 1920 and 1964.[8] The key idea of Dörpfeld's book is that it is impossible to arrive at moral judgments at an epistemic level, either by way of induction and deduction or through metaphysics. Rather, moral judgments are based on "a certain feeling" that the "purely objective observer," whose view "may not be clouded and affected by any personal interest, partisan sympathy, or antipathy etc." (Dörpfeld 1895, 14), develops. We ought to trust these feelings alone. Objectivity is not meant here in the semantic sense of "correspondence with an external objective reality" but in the sense of an "objective" attitude of impartiality or disinterestedness. In referring to his mother, Carnap said: "What convictions, including religious beliefs, anybody had, was for her a morally neutral matter, as long as he would seriously search for the truth and in the forming of his convictions follow his best insights."[9]

Although Dörpfeld embedded his ideas in a deeply religious world view, he clearly was a noncognitivist, pretty much in the same way that Carnap later adopted himself. Two crucial theses of Carnap's later noncognitivism can already be found in Dörpfeld. His first thesis was:

(NCOG) Moral statements are not based on any cognitive insight, they are neither (1) empirically nor (2) logically nor even (3) metaphysically justifiable; because there is no objective reality to which they correspond, they are not truth-apt.

Option (3) – that is, the metaphysical insights – falls away for Carnap and Dörpfeld, because they both adopt an anti-metaphysical stance and reject

---

[8] See Rudolf to Anna Carnap, February 20, 1920 (RC 025-85-32), Carnap (in preparation, entry on August 28, 1964).
[9] UCLA CM3 M-A5, A9.

the idea that there could be any cognitive knowledge based on either logical or empirical insights. Options (1) and (2), in turn, form what he describes as cognitive statements, namely, statements that are either factual or logical (*RSE*, 999). Both Carnap and Dörpfeld understand moral statements as being noncognitive, as they can be justified on neither factual nor logical grounds.

Carnap's second thesis was:

(IMPART)   We should trust only impartial and genuine attitudes.

"[V]alue statement[s] express more than merely a momentary feeling of desire, liking, being satisfied or the like" (*RSE*, 1009), as he points out with reference to John Dewey; rather, value statements ought to express "satisfaction in the long run" (*RSE*, 1009). In matters of moral discourse, we may only trust our own feelings, which is why we should ensure that what we feel now is a reflection of our genuine attitude. As such, we are not in danger of entirely changing our views tomorrow, after today's feelings have turned out to be nothing more than momentary emotions or even something that was imposed upon us by others (Damböck 2022a, section 3.1). Whether impartiality in this sense also means that everybody who only trusts their impartial feelings also shares all feelings with every other impartial individual is ultimately an empirical question. People like Dörpfeld, Brentano, Kraus, and Gibbard seem to think that the answer to this question is yes; Carnap and Flitner are more careful, even though they tend to sympathize with such a view. (Cf. the remarks at the end of the Introduction as well as at the end of Section 1.5).

While sharing the above-mentioned two aspects of Dörpfeld's noncognitivism, Carnap's metaethics diverges from Dörpfeld in that Carnap rejects the idea that people who act impartially and in accordance with their very own feelings are *necessarily* bound to arrive at the same moral judgments. If we all arrive at similar moral judgments then this is just a matter of empirical coincidence and not a matter of divine mercy or logical or transcendental reasoning. For Dörpfeld, the matter was different: if we manage to follow our own authentic feelings and attitudes, this means nothing less than following the voice of God, which must be the same for every individual. In Dörpfeld's view, therefore, moral noncognitivism is inevitably linked with a religious world view and moral objectivism that follows from the unequivocalness of God's voice (Damböck 2022c, section 2). Carnap, by contrast, defines as central to his view the understanding that (even if there is an empirical convergence of some kind that unites the humanists in some widely shared moral ideals) we must at least consider the logical possibility that even those who share the very same knowledge may adopt diverging moral views:

> It is logically possible that two persons A and B at a certain time agree in all beliefs, that their reasoning is in perfect accord with deductive and inductive standards, and that they nevertheless differ in an optative attitude component. (*RSE*, 1008)

In contrast to Dörpfeld, Carnap claims:

(DISAG) It is logically possible that two persons that agree on all matters of rational belief might still diverge in questions of moral attitude.

There are numerous other currents of thought that might have influenced Carnap's noncognitivism (Carus 2021, 2022). Yet Carnap himself highlights the importance of Dörpfeld's views in his autobiography. He read Dörpfeld again in 1920 and referred back to him in 1964. It is therefore very likely that the three cornerstones of his moral noncognitivism as highlighted above directly stem from Dörpfeld: (NCOG) and (IMPART) appear as results of Dörpfeld's positive influence, while (DISAG) presents as a statement that Carnap formulated in negation of the religious views of his grandfather.

1.3 Hans Freyer versus Bauhaus: Revolution from the Right Negated

The influence of Hans Freyer – who was a friend of Carnap in the early 1920s – on the views in the *Aufbau* on mental objects is already well investigated (Dahms 2016, 172–179; Tuboly 2022). In this section, I will therefore focus on another aspect of the philosophy of Freyer – the well-known sociologist and major representative of late-1920s revolution from the right (Muller 1987, ch. 4) – namely, on his metaethical stance (Damböck 2022b).[10] Like Carnap, Freyer was a noncognitivist who shared (NCOG) and (DISAG). At the same time, Freyer's views were also connected to a strong anti-rational world view, here combining noncognitivism with fascism. This, in turn, allows us to highlight the importance

---

[10] The story here and in Section 1.4 is closely connected to Carnap's (and also Reichenbach's) relationship with the German Youth Movement, a topic that is investigated in Damböck, Sandner, and Werner (2022).

and nontrivial nature of the fact that the rational attitude is so crucial for Carnap's noncognitivism. Freyer can be seen as the typical defender of a view that Carnap rejects.[11]

Freyer's views that combine moral noncognitivism with a fascist and *völkisch* ideology are outlined in (1926, 108–120; 1930). On the one hand, Freyer (1930, 112) sees the "moral subject" as "the ultimate authority, a solitary judge, an organ that perceives the demands of the world within itself." This is basically a rephrasing of (NCOG): there is no other reason for or against a moral statement than our feelings, our "inner voice." Freyer (1930, 112) also adopts (DISAG) while instrumentalizing it in a way that is not intended by Carnap: "The political powers are put into the world to historically realize a closed value gestalt that is contained within a people." There must be a strong dictator or "Führer" (Freyer 1926) who follows his instincts and puts into practice a new closed value gestalt for his state. Other individuals may also have their inner voices, but Freyer claims that the people/nation – that is, the mass of ordinary non-*Führer* individuals – must be brought into line with the *Führer* by way of strong propaganda institutions. "The plain secret of all *Führung* is this: to take the others as they ought to be and to commit this noble fraud in such a way that they actually become it." "The people is the *Führer*'s ever-growing, always renewed work." (Freyer 1926, 110, 114) In reality, it is only the *Führer* who follows his inner voice, creating new values that shape his people. For that purpose, a propaganda machinery is needed that manipulates the inner voice of each member of the people in a *Führer*-conducive way.

The crucial feature of this aspect of fascist noncognitivism is not the emotional side of propaganda. It is not the framing of an announcement with bombastic music, strong words, nice colors, and props. To propagate one's views and to try "to influence other people by a suitable choice of emotive language" (Ayer 1946, 22) is not necessarily a bad thing. Not only fascist ministries of propaganda use music, words, colors, props, and other emotive sources to make their views appear favorable – everybody has the right to do so, and everybody becomes emotional as soon as there arises a disagreement on questions of utmost moral importance. What makes Freyer's idea of fascist propaganda special is that it recommends to

---

[11] It is also very likely that it was Freyer personally who, among others, inspired Carnap to sharpen the rational profile of his noncognitivism. Unlike other more well-known representatives of the anti-rational turn in German philosophy in the 1920s, Freyer was a person with whom Carnap had been in close contact for several years and also shared several philosophical views. Unfortunately, there is hardly any concrete evidence to confirm this because the correspondence between Carnap and Freyer is lost. Cf. Dahms (2016, 172).

systematically hide the truth and produce misinformation in order to influence people. The key idea of fascist propaganda, in the sense of Freyer, is the "noble fraud" of making people share our values although we know perfectly well that they only accept them because we manage to hide the consequences of what we propagate. Thus, Freyer's main principle of noncognitivism as a means of fascist propaganda is this:

(OBSC) You ought to obscure facts, spread misinformation, and make people act irrationally whenever it becomes necessary to make them share the closed value gestalt of their *Führer* state.

What Carnap could learn from fascist noncognitivists like Freyer was that the key principle for them, while clearly rejecting (IMPART), was (OBSC): to make people act irrationally, without them being aware of the causal consequences of an action. Therefore, as Carnap realized, the entire way of describing the noncognitivist stance had to change fundamentally. It was no longer sufficient to highlight (NCOG) – value statements are neither factual nor logical – but it needed to be highlighted that, for a scientifically minded person, noncognitive values must relate to cognitive facts. This led to a new way of framing noncognitivism that was entirely different from older varieties, such as those found in the German Youth Movement before WWI, when Gustav Wyneken, Hans Reichenbach, and Carnap all exclusively focused on (NCOG), varieties of (IMPART), and (DISAG) without any explicit appeal to rationality (see Damböck 2022b, sections 2–4).

It was only in 1929 that the picture changed, when Carnap provided the first account of his mature noncognitivism in the context of a lecture entitled "Science and Life" that he delivered at the Bauhaus in Dessau (Dahms 2004, 368–369). Though values still are considered noncognitive in the sense of (NCOG) – "the direction of our acts" is determined by "irrational instincts" (RC 110-07-49, 4) – the main objective of value philosophy now is to highlight the various ways in which science and rationality are important for value statements – not as a "leader [*Führer*]" (who imposes his intentions upon us) but rather a "signpost [*Wegweiser*]" (that allows us to identify and follow our own inner voices and aims; RC 110-07-49, 4).

"The valuation itself cannot be found via theoretical knowledge, because it is not the grasping of a fact, but a *personal attitude*."[12] Science still plays a role for our determination of "the direction of the will, of practical action" (RC 110-07-49, 2), namely, in a twofold way: "Through reasoning,

---

[12] RC 110-07-49, 2.

theory, knowledge, [and] science can and must be examined (1) what are *the inner consequences* of a valuative attitude ... (2) what are the means that we have to achieve an intended aim."[13] Whereas a fascist will hardly reject point (2) – seeing as technical-scientific progress is not something that fascism typically wants to avoid – point (1) is entirely ruled out by fascist ideologues like Freyer. Therefore, (1) becomes one of the most crucial features of Carnap's and other logical empiricists' branch of noncognitivism. Science becomes a normative demand:

(CAUS)   One ought to investigate the causal and logical consequences of a possible aim and accept that aim only if one is also willing to accept its consequences.

Is my value system consistent (logical consequence)? Am I willing to embrace/accept every probable outcome in a world that fits my value system (causal consequence)? All varieties of Carnap's practical philosophy – as exemplified in the 1929 lecture, (Carnap 1934), as well as (*RSE*, 999) – are centered around this fundamental moral commitment: one's practical decisions must take into account all relevant logical and empirical questions rather than hide them. This message was clearly directed against those who, like Freyer, wanted to set up a system of noncognitivism that explicitly negates rationality. The core of Carnap's noncognitivism, in other words, is the normative claim that for all practical purposes we ought to maximize rationality and minimize irrationality. This is also the key point of his Bauhaus lecture:

> It is wrong to grant *the irrational an influence* beyond its territory, namely, *in the rational*: If we do not want to commit fraud ourselves, we must be extra careful in our judgments whenever feelings and our will attempt to seduce us. (RC 110-07-29, 4)

Looking at Freyer's take on noncognitivism is an important lesson for a noncognitivist. For, without facing the reality that there exists an understanding of noncognitivism that forcefully and systematically rejects rationality, it may not be possible to fully understand the normative (and fundamentally moral) nature of Carnap's defense of rationality in connection with moral questions. Carnap's noncognitivism was clearly developed as an antidote to irrational and fascist modes of reasoning.[14]

---

[13] RC 110-07-29, 2–3.
[14] Cf. Carnap (1937, 118) where logic is described as a tool that allows us to diagnose the "disease" of "illogical reasoning" that is typical of fascist societies. However, Carnap also adds that logic

1.4 The Neurath Circle: Toward a Political Philosophy of Science

In 1929, Carnap delivered the Bauhaus lecture. The Verein Ernst Mach also published the famous Vienna Circle Manifesto (Carnap, Hahn, and Neurah 1929/2012), a text that was mainly written by Carnap and Otto Neurath (Uebel 2012b). This manifesto is very important for the practical and political aspects of the Vienna Circle's scientific world-conception. Its key passage connects the scientific world-conception with socialism, stating that "in many countries the masses" tend to see a convergence between "their socialist attitudes" and "a down-to-earth empiricist view" (Carnap, Hahn, and Neurah 1929/2012, 90). This development, as the authors of the manifesto suggest, may lead to an entirely new foundation for Marxism:

> In the past, *materialism* was the expression of this view; meanwhile, however, modern empiricism has left behind a number of inadequate forms in its development and has found a defensible form in the *scientific world-conception*. (Carnap, Hahn, and Neurah 1929/2012, 90)

This statement was formulated against the backdrop of Lenin (1927), who intended to remove all empiricist interpretations from Marxism and replace them with "dialectic materialism." Though Lenin was quite successful in his attempt – after 1918, the official communist ideology had nothing left in common with empiricism – his approach was criticized by Austrian social democrats such as Otto Bauer, Friedrich Adler, Max Adler, Rudolf Goldscheid, Otto Neurath, and other unorthodox Marxists (such as Karl Korsch) who were affiliated with the logical empiricist movement.[15] Though Carnap hardly engaged with Lenin's discussion, the principal challenge was clear: Carnap, Neurath, and the Austro-Marxists were convinced that (a) dialectic materialism is ultimately meaningless metaphysics and unsuited as a proper basis for rational politics; therefore,

---

"whenever it finds symptoms of this disease" can only "pronounce the unwelcome diagnosis," while "the logician himself [sic] has no remedy to offer, and must turn to the psychologists and social scientists for help."

[15] The background of this constellation is currently being investigated by Bastian Stoppelkamp in his forthcoming dissertation "Wiener Naturalismus: Die Philosophie der österreichischen Sozialreform und die Entstehung der wissenschaftlichen Weltauffassung des Wiener Kreises." Cf. also Stadler (1997, 157–160). The first Russian edition of Lenin's book appeared in 1908 and was written in exile in Geneva. Lenin's polemic was directed against Alexander Bogdanov and his "empiriomonism," which Bogdanov had developed at the beginning of the twentieth century as a forceful alternative to "materialist dialectical" Marxism. As a consequence of Lenin's polemic, this empiriomonist tradition was suppressed in the Soviet Union. However, in Austrian social democracy the empiriocriticist standpoint remained strong and the "materialist dialectic" of doctrinarian communism was widely rejected.

(b) the only possible road for the scientific world-conception is a strictly empiricist one, arguing along the lines of those currents of thought that Lenin rejects; hence, the new scientific world-conception has to offer a nonmetaphysical approach, which, at the same time, can form the basis for a Marxist (or social democratic) world-conception.

The immediate result of the manifesto's vision was the founding of a new discussion group, the so-called Neurath Circle, which met on Mondays and stayed active for several months in the first half of the year 1930 (Damböck 2022a, section 2). Neurath and Carnap utilized the Neurath Circle to start rephrasing their anti-metaphysical and noncognitivist views, now calling "Marxist" everything that they had previously called "scientific." This meant that this new version of Marxism was indeed foundationless insofar as it was based on noncognitivism, which "only restricts the way in which the Marxist individual may justify their actions in a Marxist manner."[16] Marxism is reduced to a fallible empirical prediction: if the working class is given access to higher education and freedom of opinion, then it will choose in free elections those parties that propose socialist values. In dialectical materialism, by contrast, the socialist values become identified as absolute truths being justified by synthetic a priori judgments. Ideology thus becomes deflated: "Marxist reasoning makes it impossible to derive demands from reasoning and to create a 'Marxist ethics' in this way."[17]

The great question that is now left to ask is in what sense this deflationary form of Marxism – which is only seen as the empirical prediction of success of a value system, no epistemic justification of this system is available at all – is still Marxist and, indeed, in what sense it is political at all. My interpretation is similar to the one articulated by Romizi (2012) and Uebel (2012a). I share with Uebel and Romizi the rejection of S. Richardson (2009a), who attributes the following view to the "Left Vienna Circle":

(NEUT) A politically neutral philosophy of science (PNPS) is defended. (PNPS) is compatible with both the political program and practical rationality (PCAUS) propagating (CAUS) being embraced by Carnap and Neurath. However, (PNPS) would also be compatible with a political agenda (POBSC) propagating (OBSC) and negating (PCAUS), as well as with an entirely apolitical world view.

---

[16] The protocols from the Neurath Circle are located at Teilnachlass Otto Neurath, Österreichisches Staatsarchiv, AdN 1433, 1–11, "Wiener Kreis Protokolle," and AdN 1433, 17–21, "Weltanschauung der Tat, Weltanschauung." Cf. Damböck (2022a, section 2.3).
[17] "Wiener Kreis Protokolle."

(NEUT) states that the theoretical views of the (left wing of the) Vienna Circle are political only insofar as they do not explicitly rule out (PCAUS). Defenders of (PNPS) *can* also be defenders of (PCAUS), but – as noncognitivists – they could very well also adopt an entirely apolitical stance or even defend a different political agenda (POBSC) that is totally at odds with (PCAUS).

The picture I draw here and Section 1.3 suggests a different view. The approach Carnap (together with Neurath) recommends is political not despite but rather *because* of the specific form of noncognitivism it promotes. Carnap's theoretical and political doctrine is twofold: (a) one must take into account all available scientific knowledge and base one's decisions on it; (b) one must reject every pseudo-justification that cannot be carried out on mere scientific grounds. The political implications of this doctrine are massive, because (a) and (b) force us to reject the cornerstones of totalitarian politics that I outlined in Section 1.3. In other words, there is a political agenda (PCAUS), which is *logically implied* by the Vienna Circle's non-neutral philosophy of science (PNNPS). The result is an alternative to (NEUT) that now ascribes to the Vienna Circle a political agenda in a much more specific sense:

(NNEUT) A politically non-neutral philosophy of science (PNNPS) is defended, which forces us to accept the political agenda (PCAUS) and reject (totalitarian) alternatives (POBSC) even when the defender of (PNNPS) remains passive in the political arena (in the sense of refraining from openly propagating measures in the field of [PCAUS]).

When Carnap states in his autobiography that his political convictions are independent from his philosophical views – and that it was a key stance of the Vienna Circle to keep these things separate (*IA*, 23, 82–83; cf. Uebel 2012a, 133) – he certainly means this in the way I just specified. An advocate of (NNEUT) does not necessarily have to be a social democrat and an atheist like Carnap – there are other options. But an advocate of (NNEUT) cannot defend any political view that is incompatible with (PCAUS).[18]

---

[18] Recently, one of the general editors of the Moritz Schlick edition, Prof. Hans-Jürgen Wendel, committed himself to the right-wing extremist and anti-rational AfD. From the perspective of (NEUT), one would have to contest that despite being at odds with (PCAUS), this decision is still compatible with the politically neutral foundational doctrine (PNPS). A defender of (NNEUT), however, must diagnose that Prof. Wendel's decision is not just negating (PCAUS) but also contradicting the theoretical doctrine (PNNPS).

Those instances of (CAUS) that have a more publicly oriented nature are here labeled (PCAUS), which includes any practical attempt to spread the scientific world-conception throughout society and culture. Whereas Neurath was quite active at the level of (PCAUS) throughout his life, Carnap hardly ever engaged at this level. Nonetheless, Carnap was certainly more prolific at the level of (PNNPS) than Neurath: Carnap's agenda was the development of the theoretical foundations of a politically non-neutral philosophy of science, without much engagement at the public level of (PCAUS).

1.5 The Capstone of Carnap's Philosophy

How did Carnap proceed? As it became obvious already at the end of the 1920s, the question of confirmation or, as Carnap then called it, "constitution of the non-given"[19] is crucial for both theoretical and practical matters. This is the case because most of the statements we are making in real-world conditions are neither purely logical nor purely empirical. Therefore, the following question arises: to which degree might any such statement h be supported or confirmed by our present empirical knowledge e? Carnap spent several decades of his philosophical career investigating this question, specifying functions of the type $c(h, e)$ that express the degree of confirmation or "logical probability" of h, when faced with evidence e (Sznajder 2018).

There is a crucial aspect of Carnap's theory that I can only touch in passing, namely, the question of what exactly is empirical and how we constitute the set of empirical knowledge e of a person or group. In short: The Vienna Circle's protocol-sentence debate led Carnap to overcome his initial prioritization of the autopsychological and to finally arrive at a thing language empiricism that no longer provided room for traditional *Erkenntnistheorie* (Uebel 2021). The goal of this process of overcoming *Erkenntnistheorie* was to develop a language that enables us to get a grasp of the empirical, in an intersubjectively determinable way. The *Aufbau* failed to serve that purpose because of its autopsychological basis. Only the subsequent choice of a heteropsychological basis allowed for a consistently practicable empiricist strategy; and it is precisely here where Carnap's philosophy finally converges with empiriocriticism. That this is the case was also acknowledged by Carnap in his autobiography (*IA*, 16, 18, 20, 45, 50); and, most importantly, in the preface to the second edition of the

---

[19] See "Konstitution des Nichtgegebenen" (UCLA 04 – CM13).

Aufbau, where he indicated that he would no longer use elementary experiences as basic elements "but something similar to Mach's elements, e.g. concrete sense data, as, for example 'a red of a certain type at a certain visual field place at a given time.'" (*Aufbau*, vii) The key aspect of this shift is certainly the transition from the autopsychological to the heteropsychological. In 1967, "sense-data" no longer refers to empirically unfounded "phenomena" but rather to the empirically detectable elements of a heteropsychological thing language in the spirit of Avenarius and Mach.[20]

In Carnap (2017), a sketch from 1958 that was only recently published by A. W. Carus, we are shown how the framework for human decision-making that Carnap developed in the final four decades of his life is directly related to the initial metaphilosophical proposal from the Bauhaus lecture and Carnap (1934). Carnap addresses the notion of a "possible history of the world" W, here represented as a set of atomic propositions of the thing language that specify a causally possible world history (2017, 191). If W_T is "the true history," that is, everything that empirically characterizes our world up to the present day, then we intuitively obtain a bundle of possible histories of the world that characterize different possibilities of how W_T might develop in the future.[21] Carnap evaluates these possibilities by means of the function $\mathfrak{c}(W, e)$ where W is a possible history of the world, e is the present empirical knowledge of an agent, and $\mathfrak{c}(W, e)$ is the probability that the agent ascribes to W on the basis of the empirical evidence e. This function allows us to evaluate all causal possibilities in light of our present knowledge.

The second building block of Carnap's proposal is what he calls a "value function" V. This function assigns to each possible history of the world a value $V(W)$: if W is more favorable to an agent than W' then it must hold that $V(W) > V(W')$ for the agent's value function. What distinguishes value functions representing moral attitudes from any other value or utility function is this: "A person X at a given time has not just a *single*

---

[20] There also seems to be a connection between the Marxist period of 1929/30 as described in Section 1.4 and the development of heteropsychologically founded physicalism. However, the details of this connection have not yet been investigated. In 1929, Carnap read Otto Bauer and reread several writings of Mach Carnap (2022b). For the time being, we can only speculate that these empiriocriticist sources influenced his physicalist attitude, together with the works by Avenarius that were presented to him by Neurath (Baccarat 2024). Future research will have to corroborate this assumption.

[21] Carnap (2017, 191–192) develops a promising proposal on how to identify this bundle of possible histories of the world by means of a rudimentary possible world semantics that cannot be discussed here. For a discussion of this proposal see Damböck (forthcoming).

value function, but a great many of them," all representing local preferences regarding matters of politics, health, economics, and the like. At the same time, Carnap thinks that there is one "comprehensive value function of X that comprises all aspects, and in which the relative weight of each aspect in any possible overall situation finds expression." It is this comprehensive value function – where all conflicting moral matters must be resolved and weighted – that Carnap (2017, 192) recommends to use as a basis for "moral value judgments." Comprehensiveness is crucial here, because only a function that weights all conflicting interests and value systems is a proper basis for practical decisions that reflect the personality of an actor. Which relative weight do I, personally, put on issues such as dietary measures, health, economic growth, environmental sustainability, employment, individual pleasure, and social life? It is everyone's very own moral duty (as it is the moral duty of politics and society as a whole) to arrive at decisions here, in every single case. Only comprehensive value functions will serve that purpose.

Besides comprehensiveness, there are some additional features of moral value functions that Carnap (2017, 193) finds desirable, namely, (1) that value functions are "derivable from general principles" – there must be certain main values from which others are logically derived – and (2) that they are "expressible by mathematical functions ... that are continuous and relatively smooth, rather than jumping up and down." The latter feature seems to somewhat converge with (IMPART) – since only impartial and genuine attitudes are pure and long-term – but Carnap's proposal remains quite sketchy here.

What makes the 1958 manuscript so special is that it demonstrates something that other writings by Carnap on the topic of human decision-making hardly touch: namely, that he had intended the famous function for calculating the preference $\mathfrak{P}$ for an action a as a framework for human decision-making. It is a framework that brings together the moral/non-cognitive and the rational/cognitive side of preference formation. We calculate

$$\mathfrak{P}(a) = \sum V(W)\mathfrak{c}(W, a \cdot e)$$

for each possible action and then choose the action a that receives a maximum value for $\mathfrak{P}(a)$.[22] Here, $a \cdot e$ is the evidence that results from e when the action a is adopted. An action is "perfectly rational" if it results

---

[22] This formula is described by Carnap just informally, in Lemma (ζ) of his text (p. 192) which, in turn, refers to (*RSE*, 968–971). Cf. Damböck (forthcoming).

from a calculation like this that uses the best possible normative standards at all levels: regarding inductive logic, deductive logic, and value functions (Carnap 2017, 192–194).

What we learn here is that in his later years, Carnap identifies the two main philosophical problems that remain important to him as inductive logic and the analysis of value functions (Carnap and Hochkeppel 1993, 143–147). We also learn that these two realms are combined in a framework of decision theory that covers the entire spectrum of cognitive theoretical questions and noncognitive practical decisions.

For the purpose of this chapter, I will define the crucial point of Carnap's considerations on value functions as follows: value functions show that and how the political stance of any individual is both (a) an essentially private matter and (b) affected by the scientific world-conception. That value functions need to be comprehensive and "smooth" is required by the scientific world-conception, in the same way that we always need to take seriously the available evidence and strive to act rationally instead of anti-rationally. This directly follows from the scientific doctrines of (PNNPS). Yet even while accepting all of these rules, we are still free to choose a value function that meets the criteria of (PNNPS): we obtain (DISAG) as the noncognitive limes of a scientific world-conception.

This also allows us to rethink the seemingly neutral and meager considerations on "scientific humanism" that Carnap formulated at the end of his autobiography (*IA*, 83). His attitude can be rephrased as the claim that everybody should always try to make their decisions in a maximally rational way. True, there remains the possibility of diverging value functions (DISAG). On the other hand, how likely is it that people knowingly adopt value functions that are entirely misguided from the standpoint of democracy and human rights? The real fascists arrive at catastrophic decisions not because they knowingly adopt catastrophic value functions but because they unknowingly act illogically and irrationally (Carnap 1937). It seems very likely that the only thing that we need to do to change the world for the better is to make people act in accordance with "scientific humanism." The pragmatist and naturalist optimism of noncognitivist reasoning implies that only a demographically irrelevant minority (which can be kept under control in a democratic society where everybody is willing and able to carry out cognitive backups) would still mess things up by using anti-humanist value functions. Scientific humanism is all we need to insist on, because the real threat to political progress is not the existence of deviant moral systems but people's unwillingness or inability to act rationally.

CHAPTER 2

Carnap Is Not against Metaphysics
Vera Flocke[*]

2.1 Introduction

Rudolf Carnap is commonly considered a great opponent of metaphysics. For example, according to Thomas Hofweber (2016, 20), Carnap thinks that "the whole project of ontology is confused." Stephen McLeod (2019, section 1.1) says that Carnap regards "all metaphysical discourse [as] meaningless." Huw Price (2009) says that Carnap "left" metaphysics "dead." And Fraser MacBride (2021, 1) says that "it's Carnap who has perhaps the strongest and the best-known claim to being the great antimetaphysician of analytic philosophy." Carnap's influence on contemporary philosophy has also been staunchly anti-metaphysical, as his work has inspired two influential views that are critical of ontology. For one, according to Eli Hirsch's (2011) "quantifier variance" view, ontologists of seemingly different viewpoints merely speak different languages and do not truly contradict each other. Second, according to Amie Thomasson's (2015) "easy ontology" view, all meaningful existence questions can be answered "easily," by using only our ordinary conceptual skills, perhaps together with some empirical investigations or pragmatic decisions. Both Hirsch's and Thomasson's views are inspired by Carnap.

The reception of Carnap as a great anti-metaphysician can claim seemingly solid textual support, as he made numerous derogatory remarks about metaphysics and metaphysicians throughout his philosophical career. For example, Carnap calls metaphysical questions "pseudo-problems" (1929/2004) and "non-cognitive" [*ESO*, 26]), says that "all metaphysics is without sense"(1932/2004 98), calls metaphysical debates "wearisome" (*LSL*, xv), suggests replacing metaphysics with a logical analysis of language (1932/2004), and, in a particularly delicious passage,

---

[*] I would like to thank Daniel Nolan, Alan Richardson, Adam Tamas Tuboly, an anonymous referee, and audiences at New York University, at the University of Oxford, and at a memorial workshop for Katherine Hawley for helpful comments and discussions.

compares metaphysicians to "musicians without musical talent" (1932/2004, 107). It is natural to think that the author of "the Elimination of Metaphysics through the Logical Analysis of Language" (1932/2004) is, well, proposing the elimination of metaphysics.

But there also is countervailing evidence, pointing in a different direction. At places, Carnap is careful to distinguish between different kinds of meaning and emphasizes that metaphysics is not *entirely* without meaning. He says that metaphysics lacks "theoretical meaning" but still has a sort of "expressive meaning" (1932/2004, 108). This makes it seem as though Carnap does not outright reject metaphysics but is rather trying to find its proper place. Furthermore, at places, Carnap appears to be *defending* metaphysical theses. For example, in "Empiricism, Semantics, and Ontology" (*ESO*), Carnap defends the seemingly metaphysical thesis that numbers exist against empiricist objections. How could this be compatible with rejecting all of metaphysics as meaningless?[1]

In this chapter, I argue that Carnap does not outright reject metaphysics but is best understood as the proponent of a distinctive metaphysical methodology. My argument is based on a distinction between two interpretations of what Carnap rejects when he rejects "metaphysics." According to The Subject Matter Interpretation, Carnap rejects a certain set of questions and views, whose subject matter he regards as defective. But according to The Methodological Interpretation, Carnap merely rejects a certain methodology that the metaphysicians of his time often employed.

A key difference between the two interpretations concerns whether, on Carnap's view, metaphysics is fixable. If, as The Subject Matter Interpretation claims, by rejecting metaphysics, Carnap rejects a certain set of views, not much can be done to fix it. Metaphysics is beyond repair. But according to The Methodological Interpretation, nothing is in-principle wrong with metaphysical questions and views. Carnap merely thinks that metaphysicians approach their research questions in the wrong way, leading to defective research projects and misguided debates. But we can, in principle, save at least some of metaphysics by changing the methodology.

I will grant that The Subject Matter Interpretation may be correct about the views of Early Carnap, up until August 1930, when Gödel discovered

---

[1] To give a second example, MacBride (2021) argues that, in the *Aufbau*, Carnap adopts a view that, by his own lights, would count as problematic metaphysics, by considering "recollection of similarity" a "founded" relation, gainsaying his otherwise purely extensional account of relations.

the incompleteness theorems.[2] Gödel's discovery had a profound impact on Carnap's views, which subsequently changed significantly. But regarding the views of Late Carnap, after 1934, I will argue for The Methodological Interpretation over The Subject Matter Interpretation. I will thereby focus on *Meaning and Necessity* (*M&N*) and "Empiricism, Semantics and Ontology" (*ESO*).[3]

If my argument succeeds, then our view of Carnap as a great anti-metaphysician must be revised. At least Late Carnap is not simply "against metaphysics." He rather defends a distinctive metaphysical methodology. From Carnap's viewpoint, metaphysics is defective where it conflicts with this methodology. But this is compatible with large parts of metaphysics being in-principle fixable. Indeed, I contend, much of contemporary metaphysics is, from Late Carnap's perspective, in good standing.

My discussion will proceed as follows. In Section 2.2, I explain Early Carnap's views on metaphysics. In Section 2.3, I introduce Late Carnap's views on metaphysics and explain the difference between The Methodological and The Subject Matter Interpretation. In Section 2.4, I argue against The Subject Matter Interpretation. In Section 2.5, I explain Late Carnap's metaphysical methodology, according to The Methodological Interpretation. In Section 2.6, I go on to argue that much of contemporary metaphysics is compatible with Late Carnap's metaphysical methodology. In Section 2.7, I conclude with a summary.

2.2 Early Carnap's Anti-metaphysics

By "Early Carnap," I mean Carnap and his writing up until 1930. This includes his dissertation *Der Raum*, as well as his first major work *The Logical Structure of the World* (*Aufbau*), and most of the explicitly anti-metaphysical writings I cited in the introduction. Carnap produced these works as a doctoral student in Jena (until 1921) and later as a lecturer in Vienna (from 1926 until 1931). In Vienna, Carnap attended meetings by the Vienna Circle, a group of "logical positivists," who thought that all knowledge is either logical or empirical (more on that below).

---

[2] Some of these writings were published a few years after 1930, since there is often a time lag between the writing and the publication of an article. I will count articles published up until 1932 as belonging to Early Carnap.

[3] The distinction between Early and Late Carnap is rough, and more fine-grained distinctions in the historical development of Carnap's thinking could be drawn. But they won't matter for my argument.

The main publication to emerge from Carnap's philosophical work in the 1920s is the *Aufbau*, and the *Aufbau*'s basic ambition is to definitionally reduce all concepts to a small basis of only logical and empirical concepts. Carnap constructed a chain of explicit definitions, according to which all concepts are ultimately defined in terms of only logical and empirical concepts. More precisely, Carnap thought of an individual's sensory experience as a "stream" of elementary experiences (see section 68). The basic concept in Carnap's hierarchy of concepts is "recollection of similarity," which applies to pairs of elementary experiences in an individual's stream of experience if and only if they are similar. The *Aufbau* is often regarded as one of the finest works of logical positivism. Carnap did not merely speculate that all knowledge can be reduced to logical and empirical knowledge but instead tried to demonstrate rigorously how such a reduction can be achieved.

Carnap motivates the *Aufbau* project by a demand for "clarity" and saying that every thesis requires "compelling justification." This, he says, entails that all "speculative" and "poetic" work should be eliminated from philosophy (see *Aufbau*, xiv–xv). His basic idea seems to be that, if all concepts can be reduced to a logico-empirical basis, then we can specify the logical and/or empirical conditions under which any given thesis is true, which allows us to distinguish theses that possess a compelling justification from theses that do not. Aiding clarity may not be the only goal of the *Aufbau*, but it is one of Carnap's central ambitions, which he continued to pursue through later stages of his career.

Early Carnap, at least at times,[4] embraced verificationism: the view that every meaningful scientific sentence can be verified or falsified on logical and/or empirical grounds. He expresses this view as follows:

> Every scientific sentence must prove to be meaningful when analyzed logically. Either it will be found that it is a tautology or a contradiction (negation of a tautology); in which case the sentence belongs to the domain of logic including mathematics. Or [it will be found that] the sentence is a statement with content, i.e., it is neither tautological nor contradictory; in which case it is an empirical sentence. It is reducible to the given and is, hence, in principle decidable as either true or false. (Carnap 1930/2004, 79; my translation)

---

[4] In *Physikalische Begriffsbildung* (1926/2019, 353), Carnap seems to explicitly deny verificationism as defined in the passage quoted below. He argues that all physical concepts can be defined from a basis of dispositional concepts, with the effect that many physical statements can ultimately not be verified or falsified but merely possess certain probabilities.

In this passage, Carnap articulates special requirements on scientific sentences: they are meaningful only if they are either a tautology, contradiction, or empirical. Furthermore, Carnap says that only mathematical and logical sentences can be tautologies or contradictions. More precisely, he thought that logical truths are tautologies and that mathematics can be reduced to logic (see, for instance, Carnap 1931/1983, 41–42). Carnap also distinguishes between *meaningful* sentences and sentences *with content*. Tautologies, contradictions, and empirical sentences are all meaningful, but only empirical sentences have content. Finally, Carnap implies that the truth-value of every meaningful scientific sentence is in principle decidable, on either logical or empirical grounds.

Given Early Carnap's verificationism, he attributed a specific role to philosophy. He thought that the job of philosophers is to clarify scientific concepts and sentences by logically analyzing them (in the manner modeled in the *Aufbau*). He regarded metaphysical sentences, which possess neither logical nor empirical verification conditions, as having no scientific meaning. To give an example, Carnap (1932/2004, 87–88) discusses sentences of the form "x is a principle for y." He does not specify which views or philosophers he has in mind, but he plausibly means metaphysical views about the underlying nature of observable phenomena or hidden principles explaining them. For instance, Thales thought that everything is water; Plato thought that all observable phenomena are explained by underlying Forms; Berkeley thought that everything is an idea; and so on. Carnap (1932/2004, 87–88) complains about these views that the truth-conditions for sentences of the form "x is a principle for y" are unclear. He points out that these sentences do not have empirical truth-conditions and that metaphysicians typically do not specify any alternative, nonempirical truth-conditions. They therefore have no theoretical meaning.

However, for all Carnap says, metaphysical sentences may possess nonscientific meaning even if they are neither tautologies, nor contradictions, nor empirical.[5] In his intellectual autobiography, he clarifies:

> Unfortunately, following Wittgenstein, we formulated our view in the Vienna Circle in the oversimplified version of saying that certain metaphysical theses are 'meaningless'. This formulation caused much unnecessary opposition, even among some of those philosophers who basically agreed with us. Only later did we see that it is important to distinguish the various meaning components, and therefore said in a more precise way that such

---

[5] See also Carnap's distinction between theoretical and expressive meaning, e.g., in (1932/2004, 108).

theses lack cognitive or theoretical meaning. They often have other meaning components, e.g., emotive or motivative ones, which, although not cognitive, may have strong psychological effects. (*IA*, 45)

Carnap never fully explained what this kind of noncognitive meaning could be, but Flocke (2020) proposes an interpretation.

Given this exposition of Early Carnap's views, The Subject Matter Interpretation may offer an accurate account of at least some strands of Early Carnap's early views on metaphysics. Early Carnap thought that metaphysical sentences do not have scientific meaning. That means that the subject matter of metaphysics is at least in one important dimension defective. It does not follow that The Methodological Interpretation is incorrect. Early Carnap's views are compatible with thinking that metaphysics has some sort of nonscientific, perhaps poetic or musical meaning. But Early Carnap also thought that metaphysicians are not particularly good at expressing this kind of poetic meaning, which is why he compared them to "musicians without musical talent" (1932/2004, 107). From Early Carnap's perspective, metaphysicians choose the wrong methodology, by trying to express the sort of expressive meaning metaphysical sentences may have by the wrong means: seemingly theoretical sentences, rather than music instruments or poetry.

Carnap abandoned his early view and for good reasons. One reason had to do with more general developments in metamathematics. The incompleteness theorems, discovered by Gödel in 1930, showed that there are true sentences that cannot be derived from the axioms of classical mathematics.[6] Gödel's discovery showed verificationism to be false: not every meaningful scientific sentence is decidable on either logical or empirical grounds.[7]

In Section 2.3, I discuss the views of Late Carnap and argue that The Methodological Interpretation offers the better interpretation of Late Carnap's views, after he gave up verificationism.[8]

---

[6] An interesting historical fact is that Gödel's very first public statement of the first incompleteness theorem, at the famous congress in Kӧnigsberg in September 1930 specifically addressed Carnap's work, and Carnap was one of the first people to learn about the theorems, through a private conversation with Gödel months before the congress .

[7] Furthermore, Carnap had pursued a major research project on the foundations of mathematics in the late 1920s, in which he tried to develop a view that combines aspects of logicism with aspects of formalism (see Carnap 2000). The incompleteness theorems showed Carnap's project to be fundamentally flawed, which is why he never published it. For further discussions of this point, see Awodey and Carus (2001) and Flocke (2019).

[8] Carnap did not seem to think that giving up verificationism altered his metaphysical views much, see, e.g., Carnap (*IA*, 45). This suggests that The Methodological Interpretation may provide the

2.3 Late Carnap's Views on Metaphysics

After 1930, Carnap's life and his views changed significantly. In 1931, he moved from Vienna to Prague where he became professor of natural philosophy; and in 1935 he moved on to the United States (first as a guest professor at Harvard, with later appointments at the University of Chicago, Princeton, and UCLA). Around that time, the notion of a *form of language* (*LSL*) or *framework* (*ESO*) began to play a central role in his thinking and in his views on metaphysics. Late Carnap thought that metaphysicians (or philosophers more generally) typically discuss questions which are "external" to a "framework," and he argued that external questions are "non-cognitive" (*ESO*, 26). So, to understand Late Carnap's views on metaphysics, we need to understand what "frameworks" and what "external questions" are.

The internal/external distinction is a distinction between two interpretations of a given question. For example, Carnap says that, when somebody asks, "Do numbers exist?," we can think about what he or she is asking in two different ways.[9] First, it can be understood as internal to the "framework" of mathematics. When understood in this way, its answer is "yes," and this answer can moreover be trivially read off the "rules of the framework" and is therefore analytic. Alternatively, it can be understood in an "external" sense, where what is at stake is the existence of numbers in a framework-independent sense. Carnap argues that this external question would be "non-cognitive" (*ESO*, 26).[10]

The Methodological and The Subject Matter Interpretation correspond to two different ways of interpreting the internal/external distinction. Let's first look at The Methodological Interpretation. Carnap says that metaphysical statements have an "external" character, and proponents of The Methodological Interpretation think that when Carnap rejects "metaphysics," he rejects a certain methodology. Putting these two claims together yields that frameworks must encode a kind of *method*. This basic view can

---

better account of even Early Carnap's view. But my argument here is more limited. My main point is that, whether or not The Methodological Interpretation is right about Early Carnap, it is right about Late Carnap.

[9] Carnap individuates questions on the level of utterances (rather than on a sentential or propositional level). So, one and the same sentence can be used to ask different questions, even in contexts where the sentence has the same propositional content.

[10] Related to the distinction between internal and external *questions* is a distinction between internal and external *statements*. I will assume that "statements" are utterances of sentences and that internal statements are answers to internal questions, while external statements are answers to external questions.

be spelled out in various ways. Here is one way (due to Flocke [2020]): Carnapian "frameworks" are collections of rules for the assessment of propositions. For example, the framework of mathematics provides a collection of rules for assessing whether numbers exist.[11] On this view, when philosophers ask, "Do numbers exist?," they ask a question that is in a sense meaningful; they are asking whether numbers exist. But philosophers typically do not intend this question to be assessed using a specific set of rules. For that reason, philosophers typically debate "external" questions. Carnap thought that debates regarding such external questions are problematic because it is unclear how we ought to decide between competing answers. Because of this unclarity, there's often little progress in these debates.

Proponents of The Subject Matter Interpretation will not agree with this account of what frameworks are. Again, Carnap says that metaphysical statements have an "external" character, and proponents of The Subject Matter Interpretation think that when Carnap rejects "metaphysics," he rejects a certain class of views or questions as not properly meaningful. Putting these two claims together yields that external statements are not properly meaningful. That suggests that "frameworks" are interpreted languages or systems that confer meaning onto otherwise meaningless strings of symbols.

The idea that external statements are distinguished by their lack of meaning has been well explored in the literature. Yablo (1998, 234) assimilates Carnap's internal/external distinction to the use/mention distinction.[12] According to this interpretation, "internal" statements *use* certain key terms ("number" and "exist") with its ordinary meaning, while "external" statements merely *mention* these terms and therefore are not properly meaningful. Thomasson (2015) uses this idea to further develop a deflationary view on ontology. She argues that "numbers exist" when understood in its ordinary sense is trivially true, since 5 is obviously a number and trivially entails that something is a number. But metaphysicians try to make a nonstandard use of the sentence "numbers exist" and therefore end up making utterances that are not properly meaningful.

Having explained how the Methodological and the Subject Matter Interpretation differ regarding Carnap's internal/external distinction, I will in Section 2.4 go on to argue for the Methodological over the Subject Matter Interpretation.

---

[11] It also provides rules for assessing whether numbers of particular kinds exist, such as a prime number greater than 7.
[12] Price (2009, 324) and Thomasson (2015, 36) also endorse this interpretation.

2.4 Against The Subject Matter Interpretation

The main argument for The Methodological over The Subject Matter Interpretation has to do with Carnap's broader goals in the article "Empiricism, Semantics and Ontology." Carnap wanted to reconcile *empiricism* with the acceptance of *abstract entities*. He says:

> The nature and implications of the acceptance of a language referring to abstract entities will first be discussed in general ... It is hoped that the clarification of the issue will be useful to those who would like to accept abstract entities in their work in mathematics, physics, semantics or any other field; it may help them to overcome nominalistic scruples. (*ESO*, 21)

Carnap here says that he wants to defend the acceptance of numbers against empiricist concerns. By the "acceptance of abstract entities," he means the use of quantifiers that bind variables that range over abstract entities, such as numbers, propositions, properties, and the like (see *M&N*, 42). Empiricism is, roughly, the view that all knowledge ultimately is empirical knowledge. We do not experience abstract entities, and empiricists therefore typically think that we do not know they exist. If quantifying over abstract objects is permissible only if we know they exist, then empiricism conflicts with the acceptance of abstract entities. But Carnap argues that there is no conflict. He thinks that using quantifiers that bind variables that range over abstract objects is permissible even if we do not have empirical evidence of their existence.

Prima facie, it is hard to understand why Carnap would want to reconcile empiricism with the acceptance of abstract entities if he thought that metaphysical sentences are meaningless (or have an otherwise defective subject matter), as The Subject Matter Interpretation claims. The thesis that numbers exist appears to be a metaphysical thesis. If Carnap thought that something is wrong with the subject matter of metaphysical sentences, why would he defend a metaphysical claim against epistemological concerns?

Furthermore, I will argue that proponents of The Subject Matter Interpretation do not have a good account of *how* Carnap wanted to reconcile empiricism with the acceptance of abstract entities.[13] In more detail, Carnap suggests that "$\exists x Nx$" formalizes the English sentence "numbers exist." He argues that the sentence "$\exists x Nx$" *when understood in its internal sense*, does not conflict with empiricism. The reason is that,

---

[13] The argument in this section is due to Flocke (2020). Here I merely try to explain some of the key junctures more clearly and draw out consequences in subsequent sections.

when "$\exists x Nx$" is understood in its internal sense, it is *analytic*. I will argue that proponents of The Subject Matter Interpretation have no good explanation of why "$\exists x Nx$," understood in its internal sense, should be *analytic*. To begin with, I want to highlight two aspects of Carnap's notion of analyticity.

First, a sentence is analytic, on Carnap's view, when it is entailed by the rules of a given framework. In *Meaning and Necessity*, he "explicates" analyticity by means of the concept of an L-truths, where: "a sentence S_1 is *L-true* in a semantical system S if and only if S_1 is true in S in such a way that its truth can be established on the basis of the semantical rules of the system S alone, without any reference to (extra-linguistic) facts."[14] Second, the relevant notion of analyticity derives from the notion of a tautology that he used earlier in his career. Analytic sentences, on Carnap's view, lack descriptive content. They do not distinguish between ways the world might be. He thought that analytic statements therefore do not require empirical justification.[15] So, if "numbers exist" is understood in its internal sense, it is analytic and therefore does not require empirical justification and does not conflict with empiricism.

Now, The Subject Matter Interpretation entails a particular account of what "framework rules" are. On this view, "internal" statements are uses of meaningful sentences of a given language, while "external" statements are not properly meaningful. So, "framework rules" are semantic rules that assign meanings to sentences.[16] But I will argue – against The Subject Matter Interpretation – that "framework rules" do not merely map otherwise meaningless strings of symbols to meanings.

---

[14] When we "explicate" a concept, we replace it by a formally precise concept. The explication makes certain features of the original concept explicit and precise but may also differ from the original concept. On this, see further Erich Reck's chapter in this volume (Chapter 7).

[15] The idea that analytic sentences do not need to be confirmed empirically goes back to Wittgenstein's *Tractatus* (1922, 4.46), according to which tautologies (and contradictions) are not genuine propositions, since they are true under any (or no) distribution of truth-values over atomic propositions. Carnap (*IA*, 47) comments on this theory as follows: "What was important in [Wittgenstein's] conception from our point of view was the fact that it becomes possible for the first time to combine the basic tenet of empiricism with a satisfactory explanation of the nature of logic and mathematics." The key idea is that, since tautologies are not genuine propositions, they do not stand in need of empirical justification. Carnap (*IA*, 64) therefore feels warranted "in asserting the thesis of empiricism only for factual truths." Late Carnap speaks of "analytic sentences" in place of tautologies.

[16] This view may seem to be well supported by the textual evidence, since Carnap *says* that a sentence is analytic when it is entailed by the "'semantical rules" of a framework. However, it is important to keep in mind that, by writing *Meaning and Necessity*, Carnap *invented* what is today known as possible worlds semantics. What he meant when he talked of "semantical rules" may not match what today's readers have in mind when they think of "semantic rules."

Why is that? A crucial point of Carnap's view is that the rules of the framework of mathematics entail the sentence "$\exists x Nx$," where the existential quantifier that appears in "$\exists x Nx$" binds a variable that ranges over numbers. He wants to argue that using such a quantifier requires no empirical justification, given that "$\exists x Nx$" is analytic in the framework for mathematics. The problem for The Subject Matter Interpretation is that semantic rules do not entail the existence of anything and, in particular, do not entail that there are any numbers that could function as values for the variable x. But if there are no numbers, then "$\exists x Nx$" is false, no matter our semantic rules. So, if "framework rules" merely are semantic rules, it is unclear how the sentence "$\exists x Nx$" could be analytic.

A potential way out of this problem is to argue that the rules of the number framework map the sentence "numbers exist" to a tautologous proposition, such as the proposition that either 2 is or is not a number. In that case, the rules of the number framework in a sense entail the sentence "numbers exist," since this sentence is trivially true on the given interpretation. But notice that this view hardly solves the problem that Carnap tried to solve. He was concerned with reconciling empiricism with the existence of numbers; he was not concerned with reconciling empiricism with the sentence "numbers exist." (Indeed, it is hard to see what it could mean to reconcile empiricism with a sentence.)

How does The Methodological Interpretation avoid the problems of The Subject Matter Interpretation? Proponents of The Methodological Interpretation can give a different account of what framework rules are and hence can give a different account for why "$\exists x Nx$" is analytic in the framework of mathematics. According to the specific version of The Methodological Interpretation developed in Section 2.3, "framework rules" are rules for the assessment of propositions. For example, consider the sentence "numbers exist." This sentence says that numbers exist. The framework of mathematics formalizes this sentence as "$\exists x Nx$" and provides rules for the assessment of this formal sentence. Furthermore, the rules of the framework of mathematics entail that the sentence "$\exists x Nx$" is to be evaluated as true. That's why the rules of this framework entail the sentence "$\exists x Nx$" and hence (in a derivative sense) entail that numbers exist.

Let's look in more detail at why the rules of the framework of mathematics entail that the sentence "$\exists x Nx$" is to be evaluated as true.[17] The

---

[17] Carnap gave us several examples of "frameworks." For example, the formal system S1 that he discusses in *Meaning and Necessity* (*M&N*) is an example of a framework. Section 10 of *Meaning and Necessity*, on variables, is a clear precursor to "Empiricism, Semantics and Ontology" (*ESO*).

number framework contains the rules of designation "'five' designates five" (interpreting the numeral "five") and "five is a number" (partially interpreting the predicate "is a number"). It also contains the rule of existential generalization. The rules of the number framework hence allow us to reason as follows: "'five' designates five"; five is a number; so, something is a number.[18]

One might object that it cannot be analytic that numbers exist. For, if numbers do not exist, then the rule "'five' designates five" is false, and the argument concluding that something is a number is unsound. However, it is crucial for Carnap's view that framework rules are analytic in the framework to which they belong. A sentence is analytic in a framework if it is entailed by the rules of the framework, and a framework entails all of its rules. So, the rules of a framework always are analytic in that framework. Put differently, "'five' designates five," understood as a framework rule, is not a piece of *descriptive* semantics. It does not describe what the numeral "five" designates. It rather is a piece of what Carnap calls *pure semantics*. The rule of designation stipulates a rule for assessing sentences in the framework of the framework. As a piece of pure semantics, it is analytic and therefore lacks descriptive content and requires no empirical justification.[19]

On the interpretation that I have developed, external statements do have a meaning; they say something. However, it is unclear how *what they say* ought to be evaluated. That is a methodological defect. We can, however, construct frameworks for assessing these statements and thus turn them into methodologically unproblematic internal statements. In Section 2.5, I will work out the consequences of this interpretation for Late Carnap's approach to metaphysics.

2.5 Late Carnap's Metaphysical Methodology

I want to point out three differences between Early Carnap's views (before 1930) and Late Carnap's view (after 1930).[20] Late (but not Early) Carnap distinguishes between framework principles and other sentences. Framework principles are analytic, which means that they lack descriptive content. Other sentences are either analytic (if they are entailed by the

---

[18] For more details on this point, see Ebbs (2017) and Flocke (2020, sections 4–5).
[19] More precisely, Carnap (*LSL*, 6–7) distinguishes between descriptive and pure *syntax*. But what Carnap (*LSL*) called "syntax" contains many elements that would today be regarded as semantics. On this, see further Pierre Wagner's chapter in this volume (Chapter 8).
[20] I am counting *The Logical Syntax of Language* (*LSL*) as a work of "Late Carnap."

framework rules), contradictory (if their negation is entailed), or empirical (if neither they nor their negation is entailed). Framework principles can include seemingly descriptive sentences, such as "Fido is a physical object" (see Ebbs, 2017, §2.3) or "five is a number."

Second, on the view of Late Carnap, analyticity is a framework-dependent concept. Early Carnap thought that *logic* is analytic, and mathematics can be shown to be analytic by reducing it to logic. But according to Late Carnap, a given sentence can be analytic in one framework and nevertheless be empirical in another. Since different speakers may accept different frameworks, a sentence can be analytic for one and descriptive for another speaker. Applied to mathematics, that means that we can show a specific mathematical sentence S to be analytic (in a framework) by constructing a mathematical framework whose rules entail the sentence S. A definitional reduction to logic is not needed.

The third big difference concerns meaningful and meaningless sentences. Early Carnap, at least at times, embraced verificationism and thought that sentences are meaningless if they cannot be verified or falsified by either logic or experience. The view of Late Carnap is very different. Late Carnap distinguishes between *internal* and *external* statements, where internal statements are meant to be assessed using the rules of a given framework, and external statements are not meant to be assessed using the rules of a given framework. Internal statements are either analytic or empirical and hence meaningful; external statements are ("cognitively") meaningless. So, according to Late Carnap, whether a sentence is meaningful depends on how speakers intend to assess it. A sentence is meaningful for a speaker if he or she intends to assess it using the rules of a framework that yield a clear assessment. Otherwise, it is cognitively meaningless for that speaker.

There's an important caveat to what I just said. Carnap thought that ordinary English sentences, phrased in natural language, are in a sense meaningful. To see why, notice that the metalanguage used for defining framework rules is English (e.g., "'five' designates five"). For the definition of these rules to be successful, English must be in at least some sense meaningful, even before any frameworks have been defined.

Late Carnap's view therefore implies a distinction between *meaningless* strings of symbols, *cognitively meaningful* sentences, and sentences with *noncognitive* meaning. Sentences are cognitively meaningful if they are associated with clear rules for their assessment. Sentences are cognitively meaningless if they are not associated with clear rules for their assessment. But cognitively meaningless strings of symbols do not have to be meaningless altogether. Cognitively meaningless sentences can still have a "non-cognitive" meaning, as exemplified by many ordinary English sentences.[21]

For present purposes, the important upshot of this discussion is that, on Late Carnap's view, there is no in-principle problem with metaphysical sentences. Let's look again at "x is a principle of y." Carnap's earlier complaint was that there are no clear conditions for the verification of sentences of this form. "Principles," I assume, are meant to include hidden, underlying causes or natures of things. He therefore thought that claims about the underlying causes or natures of things are meaningless. However, given Late Carnap's view, there is no in-principle problem with sentences of the from "x is a principle of y." We can construct a framework that specifies rules for assessing when y counts as a principle of x. In this framework, "everything is water" (for instance) will either count as analytically true, analytically false, or empirical. Either way, it is cognitively meaningful in the framework. Late Carnap should therefore not be understood as outright rejecting metaphysics. He should rather be understood to be proposing a distinctive metaphysical methodology.[22] On Late Carnap's view, metaphysics has two main parts. First, we construct frameworks, which encode rules for the assessment of propositions. Next, we explore the consequences of given frameworks and what's true or false in a given framework. Carnap thinks that framework rules have no descriptive content. Speakers who accept (or reject) a given framework therefore are not making a factual mistake. But given a specific framework, there are facts about what it does (or does not) entail. So, claims about what follows from a given framework can go wrong.

Metaphysical arguments then fall into two groups. First, there are arguments about which framework we ought to accept. Since frameworks themselves have no descriptive content, and accepting a framework never involves a factual mistake, Carnap thinks that these arguments ultimately must appeal to speaker's preferences, which he regards as noncognitive. For example, one may argue for one framework over another on the

---

[21] Flocke (2020) argues that this noncognitive meaning is a noncognitive disposition to assess propositions by following particular kinds of rules and can be compared to the kind of attitude that, according to norm-expressivists (such as Gibbard 2003), utterances of normative sentences express.

[22] Carnap describes the development of frameworks as "semantics" and not as "metaphysics." The reason perhaps is because framework principles are analytic and therefore do not have descriptive content. Accepting one metaphysical theory over another therefore does not turn on factual questions but turns on making a noncognitive decision between alternative frameworks.

grounds that it is simpler. Someone who values simplicity may be moved by such an argument. But, according to Carnap, someone who does not value simplicity, or values other theoretical virtues overs simplicity, would not be making a factual mistake (and would not be moved by this argument). Second, there are arguments about what follows from a given framework. Arguments of the second kind can thereby feed back into arguments of the first kind. For example, pointing out an undesirable consequence of a framework may be a reason for not adopting it.

Given this metaphysical methodology, there are two main ways in which metaphysical debates can go wrong. First, some metaphysicians do not distinguish clearly enough between frameworks and their consequences or, more generally, between claims they accept and the grounds on which accept them. Failure to draw this distinction leads to confusing debates, since it is unclear which claims are taken to be basic and what is supposed to follow from what. Second, some metaphysicians may misunderstand what they are doing and think that they are offering evidence for the factual correctness of a given framework when all they are doing is expressing their preference for one framework over another.

However, even so, there does not *have to* be anything wrong with metaphysical debates. Many metaphysicians are admirably clear about the difference between the claims they are making and the grounds on which they are advocating for these claims. Furthermore, not every metaphysician is committed to a specific view on what they are doing when they are arguing for a metaphysical framework. Finally, in some cases where metaphysicians think they are arguing for the factual truth of a thesis where all they are doing is expressing a preference, this mistaken self-conception may not affect the first-order metaphysical debate much at all. In Section 2.6, I will go on to discuss a few examples of contemporary metaphysical debates that, from Late Carnap's perspective, are in good standing.

2.6 Consequences for Contemporary Metaphysics

To begin with, views that have recently been discussed under the heading "conceptual engineering" often conform with Late Carnap's metaphysical methodology. For example, Haslanger (2000, 42) proposes to engineer the concept of a woman so that "S is a woman iff S is ... observed or imagined to have ... bodily features presumed to be evidence of a female's biological role in reproduction ... and ... the fact that S satisfies [this condition] plays a role in S's systematic subordination." Haslanger here effectively proposes a framework for assessing claims about who is a woman. Her main argument for accepting this framework is *not* that it captures the true essence of womanhood but rather that this framework helps in women's struggle for equality and liberation. This kind of metaphysics is entirely compatible with the views of Late Carnap.

As a second and perhaps more surprising example, consider the debate between necessitists and contingentists, initiated by Williamson (2013). Necessitism is the thesis that, necessarily, everything is necessarily something. Contingentism is the denial of necessitism. Williamson bases his argument for necessitism on certain methodological considerations. Williamson describes this methodology as follows:

> Very general theories are formulated in a formal notation that facilitates complex rigorous deductions of their consequences. The theories are judged partly on their strength, simplicity, and elegance, partly on the fit between their consequences and what is independently known. The fit has at least two dimensions. Theories should not entail anything we are in a position to falsify, since then they are false. Equally, the more they entail of what we are in a position to verify independently, the better. 'Entail' here means by the standards of the theory in question, rather than by the correct standards, since we are trying to find out what the latter are: logic here is no mere background framework but the very thing at issue. (Williamson 2013, 423–424)

A few aspects of the methodology that Williamson suggests are very Carnapian. He says that we should develop general, formal theories that entail answers to metaphysical questions (e.g., whether necessarily, everything is necessarily something). We should then answer these questions by deciding between these theories based on virtues like elegance, simplicity, and strength. Late Carnap is in full agreement.[23]

But some other aspects of the methodology that Williamson suggests are not Carnapian. First, Williamson speaks of things that can be known "independently" from the theory under consideration. He thinks that, when judging a given theory, we need to compare its consequences with what is known independently. Carnap would agree, but he thinks that nothing can be known *completely* independently. When we compare the consequences of a theory with what is known "independently," we

---

[23] What's more, Williamson suggests to replace the debate between actualists and possibilists with the debate between contingentists and necessitists, since he regards the former debate as unclear (see section 1.6). This is a very Carnapian move, given that Carnap was often frustrated with confusing debates where it is unclear how progress can be made.

effectively compare the consequences of the theory with the consequences of some background theory that we accept. There is no such thing as completely framework-independent knowledge. Second, Williamson says that, when we compare the consequences of a theory with what is known independently, we are trying to figure out whether the theory is *true*. But Carnap thinks that frameworks are not absolutely speaking true or false.

However, looking into the details of Williamson's argument reveals that the differences between Late Carnap's and Williamson's views on methodology do not really matter. Williamson's core argument for necessitism is that the view is based on the simpler quantified modal logic:

> An unrestricted modal comprehension principle combines naturally with necessitism. Its combination with contingentism is much less natural, since it automatically generates the higher-order analogues of necessitism and thus creates an awkward logical asymmetry between the first and higher orders; for example, contingent objects have non-contingent haecceities. Attempts to make the asymmetry look metaphysically natural are unconvincing, while leaving it un- explained leaves contingentism vulnerable to the greater simplicity and strength of necessitism. (Abstract to ch. 6 of Williamson 2013)

Williamson here argues that contingentism leads to an unpleasant asymmetry between first- and higher-order quantified modal logic, which ultimately shows that necessitism is simpler and stronger. From Carnap's perspective, this is a good argument for the acceptance of one framework over another. Of course, Williamson considers simplicity and strength as a guide to the truth of a theory, and Carnap disagrees with that. But you can fruitfully engage with his arguments without taking a stance on this metaphilosophical issue.

As a final example, consider recent debates concerning *grounding*. A fact A grounds a fact B if B is true in virtue of A's being true.[24] Philosophers have used the grounding relation to clarify what is really at stake in different philosophical debates and have occasionally given arguments for or against specific views by arguing that they conflict with formal properties of the grounding relation. For example, Rosen (2010) and Schwartzkopff (2011) propose a version of Hume's principle, according to which facts involving cardinal numbers are *grounded in* facts about one-one mappings between collections of objects; and Donaldson (2017)

---

[24] Some philosophers prefer to think of grounding as non-truth functional sentential connectives, to avoid a commitment to the existence of facts. I'll remain neutral on this issue here. My points could easily be made about grounding as a sentential connective.

argues against this proposal on the grounds that it is insufficiently general and leads to an objectionable regress. Grounding thus offers a rigorous framework for expressing and assessing claims about the hierarchical structure of reality.

2.7 Conclusion

I have distinguished between two phases in Carnap's thinking and two interpretations of his views. The two phases are Early Carnap (until 1930) and Late Carnap (after 1930). The two interpretations are The Methodological and The Subject Matter Interpretation. I have argued that, even though The Subject Matter Interpretation may perhaps be correct about the views of Early Carnap, The Methodological Interpretation is correct about the views of Late Carnap. The reason is that The Subject Matter Interpretation cannot explain how Late Carnap tried to reconcile empiricism with the acceptance of abstract entities without trivializing his views. A consequence of this argument is that Late Carnap is not simply against metaphysics but rather proposes a distinctive metaphysical methodology. But if metaphysicians merely use the wrong methodology, we can in principle save some of metaphysics by fixing the methodology. Focusing on the recent debate between necessitists and contingentists, I have argued that much of contemporary metaphysics is, from Late Carnap's perspective, indeed in good standing.

CHAPTER 3

Interpreting Carnap's Construction of the World

Christopher Pincock

3.1 Introduction

Most philosophical texts generate interpretive controversy. In this chapter, I argue that some interpretive controversies arise from a reasonable pluralism of interpretations. This pluralism can be traced to two factors. First, an interpretation of a philosophical text is sensitive to both normative and descriptive elements. Second, there is a reasonable pluralism with respect to the normative elements of an interpretation, especially the philosophical aim that an interpreter attributes to the author of the text. I illustrate this reasonable pluralism of interpretations using six of the most important interpretations of Carnap's *Logical Structure of the World* or *Aufbau*. To make this survey tractable, I focus my discussion on one central interpretive puzzle raised by this text.

What is the relationship between "construction theory" and the specific "construction system" that Carnap sketches in the *Aufbau*? The contrast is present in the very first section of the book. Carnap begins by saying that "the present investigations aim to establish a 'constructional system', that is, an epistemic-logical system of objects or concepts" (*Aufbau*, section 1).[1] But Carnap ends the second paragraph by invoking "construction theory" with its own theses: "It is the main thesis of construction theory that all concepts can in this way be derived from a few fundamental concepts, and it is in this respect that it differs from most other ontologies" (section 1). The basic contrast that Carnap has in mind becomes clear enough in the following pages: construction theory is occupied with characterizing a variety of construction systems. Once these systems have been presented, the construction theorist is in a position to establish a number of claims or theses. One such claim is the "main thesis" just given. It is supported through the sketch of what Carnap calls the "autopsychological" system,

---

[1] All section references are to the *Aufbau*.

which is the focus of part IV of the book. Parts I, II, and III of the book discuss how construction systems could be developed, and there a number of other systems are mentioned as viable. Finally, part IV of the book offers "clarification of some philosophical problems on the basis of construction theory." Our interpretive puzzle is thus how to connect the claims offered by Carnap as a construction theorist to the features of the autopsychological system that Carnap sketches. Are the "theses" of construction theory simply an extrapolation for this system or do they have some independent justification (see esp. sections 4, 10, 16, 125)?

In Section 3.2, I will argue that any resolution to this kind of interpretive puzzle must draw on a combination of descriptive and normative claims advanced by the interpreter. Beaney has argued for a similar conclusion, but I contrast my take on this question with his. Then I deploy this historiographical approach to consider six of the most important interpretations of the *Aufbau*. In Section 3.3, I consider the broadly empiricist interpretations offered by Grelling, Goodman, and Quine. Section 3.4 discusses the more recent work by Friedman, Richardson, and Carus. In each case, we can see how descriptive and normative claims are central to each interpretation.

3.2 Descriptive and Normative Aspects of Philosophical Interpretation

In a number of papers, Beaney (2013, 2016, 2020) has persuasively argued that the history of philosophy must combine descriptive and normative elements. He reaches this conclusion based on a critical consideration of "analytic historiography," that is, how analytic philosophers have characterized their historical work. Beaney rightly singles out Russell's Leibniz book as an influential exemplar of one historiographical position. Russell there contrasts "a purely philosophical attitude towards previous philosophers" with a concern with "what process of development he came to this opinion" (Beaney 2020, 602). Beaney rejects this contrast as too simplistic. One objection draws on Kant's notion of the "quid juris" to show how the evaluation of the truth of a claim made by Leibniz will involve both normative and descriptive elements. For example, Russell supposes that Leibniz's philosophy is a system whose commitments can be reduced to a small number of basic assumptions. Russell argues that these fundamental commitments include that "every proposition has a subject and a predicate" (Beaney 2020, 604), which requires Leibniz to reject the reality of relations. The normative frame of a system leads Russell to a sparse "rational reconstruction" of Leibniz's philosophical commitments and arguments. As Beaney emphasizes, Russell's reconstruction is motivated by Russell's own conviction that relations are real.

Beaney is rightly suspicious of Russell's assumptions about systems and their ahistorical rational reconstruction. As he puts it, "We are not doing history of *philosophy* if we are not continually asking and trying to answer philosophical questions, and we are not doing *history* of philosophy if we are not seeking to understand what a past philosopher or text actually said" (Beaney 2020, 610). So for Beaney it is inevitable that we provide some kind of rational reconstruction of a past philosopher's work, but this evaluation should be based on descriptive, contextual investigations that establish what a claim in a text actually meant. Beaney is clear that an initial rational reconstruction may need to be refined once it is tested through descriptive investigations. So a kind of hermeneutic spiral results where normative and descriptive elements are both eventually taken account of.

While I am in broad agreement with Beaney's arguments, I am reluctant to endorse all of what he says in his historiographical papers. My hesitation can perhaps be appreciated by noting Beaney's claim that doing philosophy requires "continually asking and trying to answer philosophical questions" (Beaney 2020, 610). This is one of the conceptions of philosophy that is intimately associated with analytic philosophy, although it also predates analytic philosophy. An alternative conception of philosophy is the systematic one. And yet a third conception is that philosophy is an activity of clarification, not problem-solving or system-building. Given this diversity, we cannot suppose that one conception of philosophy is the right one to inform our history of philosophy. This seems to be a feature of the history of philosophy that we must learn to live with. Beaney may ultimately agree with this point that various conceptions of philosophy are available and that we cannot tell in advance which conceptions are legitimate.

Beaney also offers a puzzling account of how we might justify the basic normative assumptions that drive our historical work. He rightly criticizes Russell's appeal to "intuition" to justify Russell's own assumptions in, for example, *The Principles of Mathematics*. However, Beaney then goes on to seemingly endorse a version of Windelband's even more problematic alternative: "rational reconstructions can be teleologically validated by recognizing the role that they play both in the reconstructor's own philosophical project (as I have illustrated in the case of Russell) and in expanding the hermeneutic space of interpretive possibilities" (Beaney

2020, 611). A teleological validation of some assumption consists in showing that this assumption is necessary to achieve some end. While Windelband supposed a kind of "transcendental" deduction of such teleological necessities, Beaney at times suggests something much more flexible. Russell's own philosophical project is animated by the conviction that *not* all propositions are of subject-predicate form, so this makes it appropriate for his rational reconstruction of Leibniz to make central the assumption that all propositions *are* of subject-predicate form. Other approaches to Leibniz might legitimately deploy other assumptions that are justified by their use in other kinds of rational reconstructions, for example, Cassirer's preoccupation with Leibniz's account of substance and its relations to Cassirer's own functional approach (Beaney 2020, 610). So it seems that for Beaney a normative assumption may be legitimately used to shape a philosophical interpretation as long as it produces a new way of interpreting that text. This is presumably what "expanding the hermeneutic space of interpretive possibilities" involves.

Beaney's methodological reflections inform a striking philosophical conclusion: "Such a defense [of rational reconstruction], however, requires giving up the idea that one of the main aims of philosophy is to find fundamental premises or principles that are unconditionally true or valid – as opposed to simply what govern a particular way of seeing or thinking" (Beaney 2020, 611). Beaney's argument seems to be that the difficulties in establishing the truth of some philosophical claim should lead one to conclude that it should not be an aim of philosophy to establish the truth of such claims. All we should say, on this model, is that the object of our historical investigations was governed in their thinking by the principles that we offer.

This aspect of Beaney's discussion is not convincing, and it may not represent his considered view on the matter. One could say that in the short term it is valuable for the historian to expand the range of interpretive options for a given text, and the best means to do this is to put forward debatable claims about the aims or goals of the author of the text. Ultimately, though, the historian of philosophy could aspire to the very same aims as any other philosopher. These aims will include the goal of practicing philosophy in a legitimate way. This legitimacy involves paying attention to the relations between one's normative and descriptive commitments. In Sections 3.3 and 3.4, I will follow Beaney in supposing that an essential element of an interpretation of a philosophical text is a rational reconstruction of the text, where that reconstruction is decisively informed by a normative account of what the author of that text is aiming to accomplish. At the same time, for this interpretation to be plausibly tied to that text and that author, the interpretation must draw on an appropriate range of descriptions of the text and its influences. This conception of how philosophical interpretations work is consistent with supposing that only some philosophical aims are legitimate. It is just very difficult for us to know which aims are legitimate. Ongoing work in philosophy may help to resolve this issue, but in the meantime, we should accept a reasonable pluralism of philosophical aims. As far as we know, there are many legitimate aims for philosophical work, and some of these aims may conflict. So we should expect and allow a reasonable pluralism of interpretations of a philosophical text, even when those interpretations conflict. I will return to the significance of this reasonable pluralism in Section 3.5.

3.3 Early Interpretations of the *Aufbau*

3.3.1 Grelling

Grelling published one of the first extended discussions of the *Aufbau* in 1929. He starts by saying that "one may doubtless say that it [the *Aufbau*] is conceived throughout in the spirit of Russell" (Grelling 1929, 501). Still, despite being united by their common methods and aims, Grelling concedes that Russell and Carnap reach different results, especially on the viability of realism. The methods are the constructional methods that apply mathematical logic to some empirical subject matter. Their common aim is both epistemic and reductionist: "Both alike pursue an *epistemological aim*. They seek, so far as possible, to carry human knowledge back to, and to base it on, the immediately given (data). From this it follows that, so far as possible, the basic entities upon which the entire constructional system is erected must be such as are immediately experienced" (Grelling 1929, 505). Grelling notes, though, that Russell and Carnap disagree on the fundamental elements that they start from, partly due to the differences in the relations these elements stand in. Russell begins with events that stand in causal relations. Only some of these events are experienced, and these events are called percepts. Russell assumes percepts from different persons and also supplements his basis with events that are not percepts. Russell is thus a realist about events and their causal relations: their existence and character is largely mind-independent. This metaphysical position is contrasted with Carnap's "methodological solipsism." The autopsychological construction system that Carnap sketches in part IV of the book takes for granted only the momentary total experiences of one person and only one relation between them: "recollection by similarity" (Grelling 1929, 508).

A more significant divergence becomes clear in the last part of the *Aufbau*. There Carnap explicitly rejects Russell's metaphysical realism (Grelling 1929, 510). This conclusion arises by considering what a range of construction systems can provide. For the traditional debate to be scientific, there must be a concept of reality that can make sense of the disagreement between the realist and the idealist. However, no such concept is constructable in an "epistemic [erkenntnismässige] constructional system." So no such debate is scientific. The crucial passage from Carnap is:

> It must be noted that this holds, not only of a constructional system which has the system form represented in our outline, but for any epistemic constructional system, even for a system which does not proceed from an autopsychological basis, but from the experiences of all subjects or from the physical. The (second) concept of reality cannot be constructed in an epistemic constructional system; this characterizes it as a nonrational, metaphysical concept (section 176).[2]

On Grelling's reading, to be legitimate from "the standpoint of science," a concept must be constructible in some epistemic construction system. As section 54 makes clear, an epistemic constructional system respects an order of "epistemic primacy." This is not a psychological point about the actual process of cognition but instead a rational reconstruction of how knowledge of these various kinds of objects may be achieved. In section 176, Carnap appears to be saying that, no matter what choice is made for the basis, if the ensuing constructions respect an order of epistemic primacy, they will not find a place for the concept of reality at issue in the debate between the realist and idealist. In this sense, the concept is unavailable for scientific consideration and is thus "metaphysical."

The disagreement between Russell and Carnap on realism thus comes down to the scientific credentials of Russell's treatment of events that are not percepts. Should we treat these events as metaphysically real, or is Carnap right to insist that such a treatment would transcend the bounds of scientific knowledge? Grelling argues that Russell's arguments about the role of events that are not percepts in science can at best support what

---

[2] I have here corrected George's translation of "erkenntnismässige" to be "epistemic" instead of "experiential," in line with earlier uses of this German word in the book, esp. section 54's "epistemic primacy." I believe this translation error was first noted by Friedman (1999, 110 n. 32).

Carnap would call the empirical reality of these events. But this does nothing to establish the metaphysical reality of these events. Grelling thus concludes that "we must give Carnap credit for the greater consistency" (Grelling 1929, 520).

Grelling's praise for Carnap extends to Carnap's pamphlet *Pseudoproblems in Philosophy*, which Grelling characterizes as an extension or advance on the *Aufbau*. Here Carnap adds a verificationist account of meaning to the arguments against metaphysics from the *Aufbau*. The result is that such concepts are not only unscientific but illegitimate for any purpose. Grelling seems convinced by this account of meaning, at least if "this demarcation may at all be made without arbitrariness" (Grelling 1929, 516). He thus concludes that we "arrive at the conclusion that the controversy between these doctrines may not at all be settled on the plane of science; perhaps we are even compelled to say that the whole question is meaningless" (Grelling 1929, 517). Here, then, we see an aim for philosophy that Grelling attributes to Carnap and that Grelling endorses himself. Philosophy should aim at eliminating pseudo-questions, where these are either nonscientific or simply meaningless. This preserves the project of rationally reconstructing our scientific knowledge in empiricist terms.

3.3.2 Goodman

Goodman arrived at a quite different interpretation of the *Aufbau* based on his alternative conception of the aims of philosophy. This difference is clear even in Goodman's 1940 paper "The Calculus of Individuals and Its Uses," coauthored with Leonard. This paper was initially presented in 1936 and reflects some of Goodman's earliest reactions to Carnap's *Aufbau*.[3] Leonard and Goodman begin their paper by noting that "one task of applied logic is to determine which entities are to be construed as individuals and which as classes when the purpose is the development of a comprehensive systematic discourse" (Leonard and Goodman 1940, 45). Whitehead and Russell's *Principia Mathematica* took for granted a domain of individuals, but the character of these individuals remained somewhat obscure. Leonard and Goodman argue that "applied logic" should supplement the classes of *Principia* with an additional mereological primitive. The resulting system is called a "calculus of individuals" (Leonard and Goodman 1940, 46). After sketching this calculus, Leonard and Goodman claim that "the calculus of concepts of lowest type equips us to exhibit and

---

[3] My understanding of Goodman is indebted to Cohnitz and Rossberg (2006).

deal with certain relational properties which are often ignored or misunderstood, sometimes to the detriment of constructional undertakings like Carnap's *Logischer Aufbau der Welt*" (Leonard and Goodman 1940, 50). They single out in particular sections 67–93 of the *Aufbau*. These are the sections where Carnap develops the lowest levels of his autopsychological construction system. Starting with the momentary elementary experiences of a person, Carnap considers the relation of recollected similarity on these experiences. This relation allows experiences to be grouped into classes, classes of classes, etc. Carnap claims that for all the required sensory qualities, a class can be arrived at through what Carnap calls "quasi-analysis" that will involve all and only the experiences that exhibit that quality. For example, for a color like a shade of blue, there will be a quality class that involves only experiences that exhibit that shade of blue somewhere in the individual's visual field.

Leonard and Goodman argue that problems arise for such procedures when the relation at issue is "multigrade" in the sense that it has varying numbers of relata across its applications. They start with the example of "met with" but also mention the "is at" relation (Leonard and Goodman 1940, 50). To appreciate the worry, we can consider the more specific example they provide in the paper: three columns a, b, c of colors with a top, middle, and bottom. Suppose that any two of these columns share a color in a place but that there is no color at a place shared by all three columns. We might then define classes using a relation S that obtains between columns just in case the columns agree on their color in some one band (top, middle, or bottom). So we have aSb, bSc, and cSa. If this is sufficient to group the columns together in a "quality class," then we will have a, b, and c together in a class even though they have no common quality.

To see what problems this poses for Carnap's quasi-analysis, we can imagine that Carnap's experiences have something like the color and location structure of these columns. Suppose further that Carnap is trying to construct the quality classes such that for each quality class, its members are all and only those columns with the same color at the same band. This is not possible if we proceed using a two-place relation like S. As we have just seen, each pair of columns bear the relation S to one another, but they have no such quality in common. This is what Goodman later referred to as the problem of "imperfect community" (Goodman 1977, 119).

Leonard and Goodman go on to illustrate how the problem can be avoided once a mereological primitive is added to the means of construction. For example, if "y+z" refers to the sum of y and z, then xSy+z obtains just in case there is some level for which x is "identically colored" to both y and z (Leonard and Goodman 1940, 52). A class of columns that are each identically colored in this sense can then be specified using this condition. It will easily extend to relations of any grade as the variables now range over all the mereological sums of the basic columns.

After sketching this solution, Leonard and Goodman add a brief remark about how this problem impacts Carnap's *Aufbau*: "the defects in the construction [of quality classes in the *Aufbau*] consist in, or result from, mistakenly supposing that a class of things each member of which is similar to each other is a class of things which are all similar" (Leonard and Goodman 1940, 53). The upshot is that Carnap should include some mereological primitive in his construction system. But once this is done, a further issue arises: one can no longer suppose that the individuals of lowest type are things as opposed to qualities. A nominalist about qualities treats things as basic and constructs qualities, while a realist about qualities treats qualities as basic and constructs things. Once mereology is added to *Principia*, either option seems viable: "The dispute between nominalist and realist as to what actual entities are individuals and what are classes is recognized as devolving upon matters of interpretative convenience rather than upon metaphysical necessity" (Leonard and Goodman 1940, 55).

The 1940 paper leaves open how these constructive options are to be resolved. But in his 1940 dissertation *A Study of Qualities*, Goodman uses the problem of imperfect community and an additional problem to motivate a construction of things on the basis of qualities (Goodman 1990). This "realism" is supported through a detailed engagement with Carnap's nominalism, especially his quasi-analysis. Cohnitz and Rossberg note that Carnap could address the problem of imperfect community using the mereological tools that Goodman deploys in his system (2006, 135). So the objection to Carnap's nominalism turns almost entirely on the second problem, which Goodman calls the companionship problem. The companionship problem was explicitly discussed by Carnap in the *Aufbau*, especially in sections 70 and 81. It arises whenever all the elementary experiences that exhibit one quality (e.g., "red") also exhibit another quality (e.g., "blue") as a "companion." A two-place relation of color similarity will fail to produce a similarity class that involves just the cases of red. So if such an "unfavorable case" (section 70) arises, then there will be fewer quality classes than the genuine qualities would mandate. Carnap notes this issue and says a few things to address it. First, if we suppose that there are "no systematic connections between the distributions of the different colors," then the problem is unlikely to arise for a collection of many elements where each element only has a few of the many available colors (section 70). Second, the companion problem "can occur only if circumstances are present under which the real process of cognition, namely, the intuitive quasi analysis which is carried out in real life, would also not lead to normal results" (section 81).

After giving this second response, Goodman clarifies why he takes it to be inadequate: "the simple and obvious fact that the proposition to be demonstrated is untrue" (Goodman 1990, 150). Goodman describes a case where an individual's experiences of red in the top of the visual field are always accompanied by green in the bottom of the visual field but not vice versa. These red experiences would then be grouped with these green ones through quasi-analysis, and so one quality class would be missed. Goodman takes for granted that in such a situation it would be possible for the individual to discriminate these two sensory qualities. So the "real process of cognition" that Carnap imagines is not accurately tracked by the procedure of quasi-analysis.

As noted above, Leonard and Goodman begin their paper by setting the aim of achieving a "comprehensive systematic discourse" (1940, 45). This involves some awareness of different kinds of entities, such as the experiences and qualities that drive Goodman's discussion. It is assumed that this pre-systematic material is to be recovered within the logical system. So this pre-systematic material is available as a yardstick to measure how well a proposed system achieves this goal. Goodman seems to take a flexible, holistic attitude toward how well an element that is built up in the system must match its pre-systematic character. But the divergences that arise through imperfect community and companionship are too severe to discount. Here there are new pseudo-qualities generated as artifacts of the construction procedure (imperfect community) or entire qualities that we can know of that are absent from the system (companionship). Goodman measures his own system by the same aim and yardstick, and it is for this reason that he favors his own mereological, realist system.

3.3.3 Quine

Quine engages with the *Aufbau* for the purpose of identifying a viable form of empiricist epistemology. In "Two Dogmas of Empiricism" Quine supposes that Carnap aims at "radical reductionism": "Every meaningful statement is held to be translatable into a statement (true or false) about immediate experience" (2004, 47). However, Carnap's "treatment of physical objects fell short of reduction not merely through sketchiness, but in principle" (2004, 48). Quine focuses in particular on the way that sensory qualities are assigned to the space-time points of the perceptual world. Carnap makes this assignment using various canons that include minimizing the "rate of change" of colors at space-time points along a world line (desideratum 10, section 126). But Quine objects that this assignment procedure "provides no indication, not even the sketchiest, of how a statement of the form 'Quality q is at x;y;z;t' could ever be translated into Carnap's initial language of sense data and logic" (2004, 48). The crucial relation "is at" is thus not appropriately integrated into Carnap's reductionist system. In "Two Dogmas," this criticism is used to motivate a rejection of one sort of empiricism. This form of empiricism considers a statement in isolation and aims to assess its content and justification in empirical, sensory terms. Quine supposes that such an empiricist must endorse radical reductionism, at least in principle. Carnap's failure thus indicates that a statement-by-statement version of empiricism is untenable. An "empiricism without the dogmas" would then evaluate our theories or even "total science" (Quine 2004, 50) in holistic terms rather than through considering individual statements.

The same basic argument is repeated in the later paper "Epistemology Naturalized." Now, though, Quine is more careful to distinguish what he calls the doctrinal from the conceptual. An empiricist epistemologist focused on doctrine will try to justify all our statements by tracing them back to evidence that is sensory or experiential. Quine takes this doctrinal project to be hopeless and does not attribute it to Carnap. However, there is still the potential to clarify our scientific concepts in experiential terms. This is the project that Quine attributes to the *Aufbau*, again following Russell: "To account for the external world as a logical construct of sense data – such, in Russell's terms, was the program. It was Carnap, in his *Der logische Aufbau der Welt* of 1928, who came nearest to executing it" (2004, 263). This project requires a "translational reduction" (Quine 2004, 264) of each scientific statement. This would have at least two advantages. First, it would "clarify the sensory evidence for science." Second, such a reduction could "make all cognitive discourse as clear as observation terms and logic and, I must regretfully add, set theory" (Quine 2004, 263).

Quine emphasizes that a rational reconstruction of all scientific concepts in these terms would establish the legitimacy of these concepts in an especially forceful way. The success of this sort of project requires that we can use the reconstruction to effect, at least in principle, a translational reduction of each scientific statement. This reconstruction may thus depart from our actual process of cognition to show what is in principle possible.

Interpreting Carnap's Construction of the World   61

And to be of any value with respect to legitimacy, the reconstruction should not assume the correctness of any of our accepted scientific statements. This would block us from establishing "the essential innocence of physical concepts, by showing them to be theoretically indispensable" (Quine 2004, 264).

However, as in "Two Dogmas," Quine claims that Carnap failed to achieve a translational reduction of these statements. Carnap's plan with respect to the assignment of "sense qualities to positions in physical space and time ... does not offer any key to translating the sentences of science into terms of observation, logic, and set theory" (Quine 2004, 264). The diagnosis of this failure is the same as in "Two Dogmas": "the typical statement about bodies has no fund of experiential implications it can call its own" (Quine 2004, 266).[4] This undermines the value of the sort of rational reconstruction that Carnap aimed at. Now there is no point in departing from the actual process of cognition that led us from our sensory inputs to our scientific account of the world. Our presentation of this process should be informed by our best scientific theories of such processes. Quine, then, argues for a naturalistic empiricism and conceives of the aim of philosophy in these terms. He uses the sort of empiricism that he finds in Carnap's *Aufbau* and its purported failures to support his own kind of naturalistic empiricism.

3.4   Later Interpretations of the *Aufbau*

3.4.1   *Friedman*

Friedman's two papers "Carnap's *Aufbau* Reconsidered" (1987) and "Epistemology in the *Aufbau*" (1992) generated a new and highly fruitful round of interpretive controversy about the *Aufbau*.[5] Friedman argues that a number of features of the text and Carnap's earlier work undermine any empiricist reading. He emphasizes the connections between construction theory and construction systems that we discussed in Section 3.1. While empiricist readings focus on the autopsychological construction system, Friedman considers the aims of construction theory itself. According to Friedman, the *Aufbau*'s aim "is to use recent advances in the science of

---

[4] This qualification to a "typical" statement leaves open the possibility of "observation statements" that can be more closely tied to sensory stimulation. See Quine (2004, 271–273).

[5] I draw on Friedman (1999), which reprints these papers along with an introduction, new footnotes, and a postscript.

logic ... together with advances in the empirical sciences (Gestalt psychology in particular) to fashion a scientifically respectable *replacement* for traditional epistemology" (1999, 5). This replacement targets not only traditional empiricism but also various versions of neo-Kantianism. The promise of the logically refashioned epistemology that Carnap aimed for was that it could provide a metaphysically neutral basis for ongoing collaborative work.

At the heart of the replacement to epistemology that Friedman attributes to Carnap is a structural conception of objectivity that is summarized in section 16. On this reading, the point of logically constructing all concepts from a sparse basis is to exhibit the logical structural relations between concepts and thereby establish their objective character. This general approach is developed out of a similar preoccupation with objectivity in neo-Kantianism: both have "a concern for depicting how the cognitive process transforms inherently private and subjective sensations into fully objective experience capable of validity and truth" (Friedman 1999, 141). But unlike the neo-Kantians, who often deployed some kind of "transcendental" logic for this purpose, Carnap tries to get by with the formal logic of *Principia Mathematica*. This promises the kind of neutrality that Carnap would need to truly detach his epistemology from metaphysical presuppositions.

The emphasis on the structural notion of objectivity and the aims of philosophical neutrality led Friedman to diagnose the failures of the *Aufbau* in novel terms. Friedman initially emphasized the problems associated with Carnap's attempt to eliminate his basic relation of recollected similarity using a supposedly logical notion of a "founded" relation (sections 153–155). This is required: "since all other concepts have been reduced to Rs, all we have really shown so far is that they are objective if it is" (Friedman 1999, 101), and the only way to show that Rs is objective is to provide a structural characterization of it. In his 1999 discussion of these issues, Friedman no longer takes this problem to be as serious. For Carnap, "all stages in the epistemological construction of knowledge take place *within* a single 'constitutional system,' which is equally formal-logical (and therefore equally 'objective') at every level" (Friedman 1999, 43).

Friedman instead locates the problems with the *Aufbau* in the philosophy of logic itself. For, in the book, Carnap provides no real account of the standpoint from which construction theory is to be developed or how that standpoint achieves the required kind of neutrality. A symptom of this lack of standpoint is the "serious technical problems" (Friedman 1999, 160) that Carnap encounters in his assignment of sensory qualities to space-time points. As we have seen, Quine targeted this very stage in the *Aufbau* and complained that it showed that Carnap had not achieved the translational reduction that he aimed for. This in turn supported Quine's conclusion that individual statements lack determinate empirical content. Friedman sees the problem quite differently. For the objectivity of a given concept to be established, that concept must be assigned a definite position or rank in the overall logical structure that Carnap develops. The open-ended character of the assignments of qualities stops the concepts at issue at this stage from being given a definite rank. For Friedman, this fatally undermines Carnap's response to a Marburg neo-Kantian like Cassirer. Cassirer claimed that objects of scientific knowledge are never fully completed and that there is a residual need for synthetic a priori principles to guide further constructions. So if some of Carnap's concepts are never fully constructed and assigned a definite rank in Carnap's logical structure, then Carnap cannot rule out the role of such synthetic a priori principles. As Friedman puts it, "The status of these methodological principles thus remains fundamentally unclear, and Carnap ends up with no objection, in particular, to the synthetic a priori" (Friedman 1999, 162).

According to Friedman, Carnap aimed to address the limitations of the *Aufbau* in his successor project, which culminated in the *Logical Syntax of Language*. Here Carnap tries to articulate a neutral standpoint through his more sustained investigations into the philosophy of logic. This metalogical project is also said to fail, essentially due to reasons tied to Gödel's incompleteness theorems. Still, Friedman is quite clear that the project he attributes to Carnap is the right kind of project for philosophers to work on. If "there is no privileged vantage point from which philosophy can pass epistemic judgment on the special sciences," then "from what perspective does it [philosophy] then respond to and rationally reconstruct the results of the special sciences?" (Friedman 1999, 10). Friedman explicitly sets aside the Quinean naturalistic response to this puzzle that we canvassed in Section 3.3.3. He thus identifies his own aims with the broad aims he finds in Carnap. Unlike Carnap, Friedman does not try to develop this perspective in purely logical terms. Instead, Friedman (2001, 2010) draws on the resources offered by the history of science to clarify his notion of a relativized a priori and its role in rational scientific change.

3.4.2 Richardson

Richardson acknowledges the importance of Friedman for his own interpretation of the *Aufbau* but departs from Friedman in a number of important respects. The most significant change is that Richardson takes Carnap to be working with two distinct notions of objectivity in the *Aufbau*. The first notion of objectivity is deployed in section 16 when Carnap mandates that all scientific concepts be given a purely structural definite description (PSDD). This is what Richardson calls "the project of achieving objectivity via PSDDs" (1998, 50). This project requires that all genuinely scientific concepts find a place in such a structurally specified structure. Richardson supposes that this project leads Carnap to suppose that "there is no external perspective against which to check the constructions for correctness" (1998, 64). Goodman's concerns about Carnap's constructions are thus based on a misunderstanding of Carnap's aims.

However, Richardson argues that Carnap is forced to introduce a second notion of objectivity in order to fully develop a construction system that includes all genuine concepts. This notion of objectivity relies on "the extra, superadded formal structure of mathematically expressed physical concepts and laws" (Richardson 1998, 89). This structure goes beyond the logical structures that are built using the basic Rs relation. Carnap deploys this mathematical structure when he embeds sensory qualities in the perceptual world. So, as with Quine and Friedman, Richardson focuses attention on this stage of Carnap's construction. But Richardson emphasizes a third aspect of this stage. For Richardson, this stage is "crucial for the intersubjectivity of knowledge" (1998, 89). For Richardson, the physical world and its law-governed regularities are needed to construct what Carnap calls the intersubjective world. This construction occupies sections 146–149. The basic plan is to create an intersubjectively available analogue for each of the concepts from earlier stages so that there are versions of these concepts available for intersubjective scientific investigation. For example, Carnap first singles out a human body in the perceptual world that is identified with the body of the person whose experiences form the basis of the autopsychological construction system (section 129). But this concept is distinct from how another person M takes that body to be. Fortunately, the world of that other person M can be developed within the autopsychological construction system so that M's take on that body will largely agree with what the construction system originally ascribes to it. This sets up an "intersubjective correspondence" (section 146) between distinct concepts that allows for the autopsychological construction to make sense of their intersubjectively available properties.

Crucially, Carnap adds: "The intersubjective world (in the sense of the above-given construction) forms the actual object domain of science" (§149). For Richardson, this signals the importance of this sort of objectivity for Carnap's project. For here we see Carnap trying to distinguish between the subjective and the objective from within the autopsychological construction system. Ultimately, though, Richardson argues that Carnap fails in this ambitious aim. The crucial difference between objective and subjective is "not a distinction within the empirical sciences, since they deal only with the objective. Epistemology must comprehend both halves of a distinction in order to demarcate science from subjective experience, on the one hand, and metaphysics, on the other" (Richardson 1998, 189). This objection takes seriously the Kantian origins of Carnap's project, which Richardson traces in great detail in his book. A naturalized epistemology like Quine's gives up trying the settle the preconditions for the possibility of objective experience. On Richardson's reading, Carnap is trying to clarify these preconditions through his constitution system and an associated structural conception of objectivity (Richardson 1998, 203). But this attempt fails when we consider how an epistemic notion like objectivity itself gets its objective content. Either the construction system includes an inadequate version of epistemic concepts or these epistemic concepts receive no clarification in the *Aufbau* (Richardson 1998, 197).

Carnap's further development involves avoiding this dilemma by shifting from epistemology to "the logic of science," especially as it is clarified in *Logical Syntax*. Like Friedman, Richardson takes Carnap's importance to be tied to the viability of an alternative to Quine's naturalized epistemology. He thus devotes much of the last chapter of his book to considering why Quine's criticisms of Carnap misfire (Richardson 1998, 223). This leaves the Carnapian option as an important alternative to Quinean naturalism. Although Richardson does not here endorse Carnap's approach, he suggests that keeping it in mind could help with the "methodological confusion" Richardson (1998, 228) found in contemporary philosophy of science.[6]

3.4.3 Carus

Carus' 2007 book develops another interpretation of the *Aufbau* and its place in Carnap's intellectual development. Carus embeds his account of the *Aufbau* in a broader take on the Enlightenment and its varieties. One

---

[6] See also Richardson's later remark that "a detailed philosophical history of analytic philosophy provides a much richer set of resources upon which to draw in thinking about how properly to do philosophy here and now and to explain why one has the philosophical projects one does have" (2010, 281).

Enlightenment project is what Carus calls "rational reconstruction." This is "an iterative, step-by-step (though not always tidy or unidirectional) process of replacing intuitive, initially rather vague concepts by more precise ones" (Carus 2007, 15). This reconstruction of our knowledge serves a number of theoretical and practical goals. On the theoretical side, placing these reformed concepts into a system helps to clarify our knowledge and what it amounts to. On the practical side a rational reconstruction serves to "rid humanity of the ghosts holding us in thrall to the ancient superstitions of traditional society as well as the unreflective conformities of modern societies" (Carus 2007, 16). The language of rational reconstruction is of course prominent in the *Aufbau*, as when Carnap says, "The constructional system is a rational reconstruction of the entire formation of reality, which, in cognition, is carried out for the most part intuitively" (section 100, see also section 54). Carnap also at times emphasizes the practical reasons for this reconstruction, as when he writes in the preface of the "inner kinship" between the attitude motivating the *Aufbau* and "movements which strive for meaningful forms of personal and collective life, of education, and of external organization in general" (xviii). Carus traces the development of this reconstruction project throughout Carnap's earlier writings and discusses how a preoccupation with a structural notion of objectivity served the goals of this reconstruction. At the same time, Carus denies Richardson's diagnosis of the tensions within Carnap's *Aufbau* project, arguing that the construction of the intersubjective world within the autopsychological system is sufficient for Carnap's purposes (see esp. 2007, 172 n. 10).

Carus argues that a more telling problem for the *Aufbau* project is tied to a difficulty with integrating the theoretical and practical that has its roots in the Enlightenment. A resolute rational reconstruction threatens to ignore our standing commitments and values due to its one-sided emphasis on precision and structural integration. The alternative to this sort of reconstruction is what Carus calls "explication": "Unlike rational reconstruction, explication no longer envisaged one-way replacement of the ordinary, intuitive world view by a scientific view, but a dialectical interchange between the two kinds of systems" (Carus 2007, xi). Carnap arrived at this more flexible explication project in his later work, most explicitly in the 1950 book *Logical Foundations of Probability*. For Carus, the explication project aims to improve our existing concepts but in a way that is continually sensitive to the practical implications of these changes. Explication finds a place for our values, while reconstruction threatens to eliminate these values as unscientific.

For the purposes of this essay, it is interesting to note that Carus characterizes his interpretation of Carnap as "unashamedly teleological" (2007, 40): "The ideal of explication, the standpoint toward which this earlier development is to be seen as progressing – and from which particular steps in that development are thus to be judged – was never fully enunciated by Carnap" (2007, 38). One motivation for taking Carnap's thinking to have this goal or direction is the ongoing philosophical significance of the ideal of explication as Carus clarifies it. In a helpful footnote, Carus argues that this sort of teleological approach is needed for good history of philosophy. If we aim to assess what "is of permanent value" in Carnap, then we "must be guided by two not always fully compatible standards." First, there is "accuracy, or faithfulness to the textual evidence." Second, there is "attractiveness as a philosophical position in the present context" (Carus 2007, 40 n. 64). Carus, then, would agree with the main historiographical claim of this essay, namely, that both descriptive and normative elements are essential for philosophical interpretation. For Carus, there is a "danger" in balancing these two standards, but "one hopes that awareness of the danger may help to mitigate it."[7]

3.5 Conclusion

Our motivating interpretive puzzle was to determine how the construction system sketched in the *Aufbau* related to the construction theory and its theses that Carnap also emphasizes in the *Aufbau*. The first three interpretations of Grelling, Goodman, and Quine focused on the apparent goals and limitations of the autopsychological construction system. The other three interpretations of Friedman, Richardson, and Carus considered instead the status of construction theory. In each case, there is a delicate interplay of descriptions of Carnap's text and its context as well as normative judgments about the proper aims of philosophy. Grelling claims that Carnap aims to eliminate metaphysics, Goodman sees Carnap trying to provide a comprehensive systematic discourse, and Quine takes Carnap to aspire to a translational reduction of our scientific statements. More recently, Friedman argues that Carnap is trying to replace traditional epistemology, while Richardson interprets Carnap to be addressing the

---

[7] Unsurprisingly, I would endorse this attitude toward my own more naturalistic and Quinean interpretation of the *Aufbau*'s project of rational reconstruction in Pincock (2005). From this vantage point, the major difference with Carus is that I do not see much hope for the explication project that he discerns in the later Carnap. This informs a more pessimistic assessment of the "permanent value" of the *Aufbau* for contemporary philosophy.

possibility of objective knowledge. Finally, Carus supposes that Carnap is trying to rationally reconstruct our concepts. In each case, except Grelling, the aim ascribed by an interpreter is used to diagnose where the *Aufbau* failed to realize its aims. For all six interpretations, it should be clear that the interpreter takes the aim ascribed to Carnap to be legitimate or to be closely related to a proper aim for philosophical investigations into science.

Juxtaposing these six interpretations helps to clarify Beaney's point that an interpretation may serve to expand "the hermeneutic space of interpretive possibilities" for a text like the *Aufbau*. In Section 3.2, it remained unclear what we are to do with this expanded space once it has been articulated. As both historians of philosophy and philosophers, it is almost inevitable that we will go on to criticize some of the possibilities as somehow defective or at least less promising than others. This is especially tempting for the classic interpretations of Grelling, Goodman, and Quine. While there are no obvious descriptive errors in their interpretations, the aims that they each endorse may strike us as illegitimate. For example, Grelling says that Carnap aims to eliminate metaphysics. But many philosophers would now say that there is no way to eliminate metaphysics, and so this aspect of Carnap's *Aufbau* is not especially important. Conversely, the more recent interpretations of Friedman, Richardson, and Carus seem to identify aims that are more viable and urgent to address.

Perhaps it is not too surprising that the aims of interpreters in our time will tend to seem more coherent and viable than the aims of interpreters of the past. There is another respect in which we might also find new interpretations to be better or more compelling. It does seem that, in their own ways, Friedman, Richardson, and Carus are more methodologically aware of the problems with doing history of philosophy than Grelling, Goodman, and Quine. As we have seen, Carus says explicitly that he interprets Carnap with an eye to "attractiveness as a philosophical position in the present context." Friedman has also developed a sophisticated understanding of what philosophical activity is aimed at and how current philosophy can relate to the history of philosophy and science. I also noted how Richardson pursues his two notions of objectivity so that we can develop the resources for a non-Quinean epistemology. Friedman, Richardson, and Carus are thus likely to agree with Beaney and myself on two methodological points. First, the history of philosophy is important to philosophy and, second, the importance turns largely on figuring out how to integrate the normative and descriptive elements found in philosophy and its history.

The upshot of reflecting on these interpretations of the *Aufbau* is, however, far from clear. On the one hand, in the short term we must live with a reasonable pluralism of interpretations of the *Aufbau*. For any interpretation will involve normative claims about the aims of philosophy, and we are not in a position to settle which of these normative claims are viable. In my judgment, all six of the interpretations surveyed here should be included on a list of reasonable interpretations. This is because they fit well with aspects of the *Aufbau* and what we know of Carnap's various aims in this period.[8] On the other hand, one's own judgments about how philosophy should be done will incline one to rank some available interpretations as superior to others. This ranking can proceed from at least two sources. First, if some aims just seem misguided, then the interpretations that involve those aims will be uninteresting or mistaken. Second, if some interpretations are more methodologically aware, then this might seem to be some evidence that they are on the right track. So, from within a broad list of reasonable interpretations of the *Aufbau*, some can be argued to be more reasonable than others. And, unsurprisingly, the most reasonable interpretation of a text like the *Aufbau* will turn out to be an interpretation that draws on aims that one endorses for oneself.

---

[8] For recent scholarship on Carnap, see esp. Damböck (2016); Damböck and Wolters (2021); and *CW1*. One could argue that this scholarship eliminates some interpretations as viable, but I do not think any such argument is very persuasive.

CHAPTER 4

Philosophy in a Collective Spirit as "Politics in Its Broadest Sense"

Audrey Yap

4.1 Society and the Scientific World-Conception

In his intellectual autobiography, Carnap claimed that although many members of the Vienna Circle were politically active, they nevertheless preferred to keep their philosophical work separate from their political aims (*IA*, 22). While Carnap was not engaged in politics in the ways that, say, Otto Neurath was, Thomas Uebel (2012a) has argued that Carnap's work was nevertheless intended to be "political in its broadest sense." In Uebel's view, Carnap was always cognizant of the potential for philosophy (particularly scientific philosophy) to contribute to the improvement of human life. And in that sense, we can see Carnap as holding a kind of "activist understanding" of his philosophy (Uebel 2012a, 134). Donata Romizi (2012) has also made similar arguments, though applying to the Vienna Circle more generally, in favor of viewing their philosophy of science as politically engaged, in particular by focusing on their *activities* as opposed to focusing primarily on their theoretical writing.

This is admittedly not a universally accepted view of Carnap or even of Neurath. Uebel's (2005) characterization of the Vienna Circle as including a "left wing" has been challenged by Sarah Richardson (2009a), who argues that its members adopted a more politically neutralist stance. Since Uebel (2010) has defended his own characterization at length, and Romizi's article also addresses this question, I will not spend the time here to go over those arguments in detail. But I do take Uebel's idea of "politics in its broadest sense" to be aiming at something different than the idea of political engagement that Richardson's article targets. Following Uebel, the argument that Carnap's philosophy is in fact political does not mean that I take him to have been a political philosopher or to have put forward views with explicit political content, such as views that entail supporting a particular party or candidate. Instead, I aim to draw out some social implications of Carnap's views about how philosophy ought to be done.[1]

This chapter, then, is intended to complement Uebel's and Romizi's arguments with a focus on Carnap in particular. I will make the case that Carnap was genuinely committed to a politically engaged philosophy (in general) by focusing on his ideas about philosophical practice and the ways in which he chose to engage in philosophy. More specifically, I argue that Carnap exemplified a commitment to philosophical work done in a collective spirit, and that this view about how philosophy ought to be arranged should also count as a political stance in this broad sense. I think that Carnap's overall (broadly socialist) views about how society ought to be arranged have implications for how he thought of philosophy as something in which we engage as a collective endeavor.

One initial puzzle in thinking about this issue is how best to understand the connection between the scientific world-conception endorsed by Carnap and the Vienna Circle more generally and the attitudes toward questions of life to which that world-conception is supposedly linked. After all, though Carnap and Neurath were well known to have had socialist political orientations, the same cannot be said of Moritz Schlick, to whom the circle's unofficial manifesto (Carnap, Hahn, and Neurath 1929/2012) was dedicated. Schlick may even have been uneasy with the deeply collectivist and activist spirit of the manifesto itself (Edmonds 2020, 92–93). Uebel (2020), in raising this very problem, notes that both the Preface to Carnap's *Aufbau* and the Circle's *Wissenschaftliche Weltauffassung* celebrate an "inner link" between the scientific world-conception they explicitly endorse and more normative ideas about forms of personal and public life that do not appear in any of their official writings (Uebel 2020, 43).

Given the disparate philosophical orientations of the various members of the Vienna circle, we cannot (as Uebel also admits) view the scientific world-conception as leading us directly to any *particular* political position or social arrangement (Uebel 2012a, 140). Yet not long after the initial publication of the *Aufbau*, Carnap visited the Bauhaus in Dessau, to give a lecture. In that lecture, Carnap told the audience that while he worked in science and they worked in visible forms, the two were only "different sides of a single life" (Galison 1990, 710). So while it is clear that Carnap took there to be a close connection between the scientific world-conception of the Vienna Circle and questions about the organization of society as a

---

[1] Thanks to an anonymous reviewer for pushing me to clarify this point.

whole, what is less clear at this point is how that connection is to be made. This is not only due to Carnap's own claims about his political and philosophical work being separate endeavors but also due to the fact that several of those, like Schlick, who endorsed his philosophical views, did not seem to share his socialist views about the organization of public life in general.

Peter Galison, starting from Carnap's address in Dessau, draws out the connection between the progressive elements of the Vienna Circle and the Bauhaus in a range of ways. Both groups had similar political opponents: religious conservatives, nationalists, and Nazis, in part due to their shared rejection of the metaphysical and nationalist and embrace of internationalism and collective work (Galison 1990, 710, 736, 749–750).[2] This emphasis on the need for wide and accessible collaboration complements Uebel's analysis, given in terms of the idea of intersubjective accountability, namely, that our claims must be made available to others for critical scrutiny (2020, 45). This leaves us with a collective practice that must be fundamentally anti-authoritarian and committed to transparent argumentative practices.

I agree with Uebel that the emphasis on collectivity and intersubjectivity is crucial to understanding the connection between Carnap's theoretical and practical commitments. After all, philosophy is a social practice, embedded in a particular world and a particular social/political climate. The extent to which various philosophers are affected by that climate may vary, but it is quite clear that many members of the Vienna Circle were very aware of the political climate in which they were working, and the extent to which it enabled or prevented them from doing their research. With this embeddedness of philosophical practice in mind, we can see how this commitment to collectivity is embedded in Uebel's description of the norm of accountability.

It requires of participants in factual rational discourse that they only make claims that can be justified to an interlocutor – at the very minimum that they are open to their claims or proposals being interrogated in this fashion. Justifying a claim is a matter of making intelligible the state of affairs that is alleged to hold both on the object level (why should this be the case?) and reflexively concerning the claimant (what puts her in the position reasonably to make this claim?). In this fashion, the norm of

---

[2] Though I agree with this aspect of Galison's analysis of the connections between the Bauhaus and the Vienna Circle, see Potochnik and Yap (2006) for some concerns about other aspects of his analysis.

intersubjective accountability justifies and secures consensus about arguments (Uebel 2020, 46–47).

One important aspect of this description is the role of the claimant and their own epistemic position with respect to the claim. While we might choose to view epistemic position in a very narrow sense, perhaps only concerned with formal expertise, we might also view this more broadly as connected to a claimant's social location more generally. But if we attend to the social locations of different epistemic agents, a range of other questions emerge about who our interlocutors are in the first place.

Though ISOTYPE (International System of Typographic Picture Education) was Neurath's project, it was carried out in a socialist spirit that Carnap also shared (though Carnap himself was not involved with it). The motivation behind the development of this system of picture statistics was the concern that many people did not have the education that would allow them to understand complicated statistical information, even when that information could be key to their understanding of economic and social processes that might significantly impact their lives (Jansen 1996, 144).[3] This is important if we think that intersubjectivity also requires us not to engage in exclusionary practices. After all, we might be able to arrive at intersubjective agreement on our claims among a small and homogenous audience of specialists. On a narrow view of the norm of intersubjective accountability, this might be acceptable. But I think we have good reason to believe that Carnap would not have endorsed this narrow norm and was in fact generally in favor of expanding our intellectual communities and the breadth of our intellectual engagements.

I think this will further strengthen the connection Uebel makes between the scientific world-conception and social arrangements, as well as help to solve some of the puzzles brought up earlier about how this shared conception could lead to such different political views. After all, while different members of the Vienna Circle might share a commitment to a certain kind of scientific practice, they do not necessarily need to agree on what we want the scientific community to look like in the first place. That way, a commitment to intersubjective accountability might look different for different people, depending on the people to whom we think we are accountable. Those who have more inclusive ideals would be much more likely to favor social practices that allow a greater range of people to

---

[3] For example, see Olúfẹ́mi Táíwò's (2021) brief account of Marie Neurath, during her time as director of the Isotype Institute, being hired by the Western Regional Government of Nigeria to help pictorially convey the content and rationale behind some of their programs.

contribute to knowledge production in the first place. Also, by looking at the ways in which Carnap *engaged* in philosophical practice itself, I think we can also see that he did have an inclusive vision, like Neurath, for intellectual communities. For instance, Carnap and Schlick differed in their attitudes toward the openness of Vienna Circle meetings, where (for example) the latter reportedly thought Karl Popper was "far too rude to receive an invitation" (Edmonds 2020, 22). This line of investigation is further supported by a suggestion from Romizi, who, in looking at the question of whether the (Left) Vienna Circle's philosophy of science counts as political, suggests viewing philosophy of science "as being also a form of practice, as the expression of an attitude, as a way of acting in the world" (Romizi 2012, 208). As such, the next sections will attempt to draw out some of Carnap's views about intellectual life by looking at some of the ways in which he was engaged in it.

4.2 Carnap's Philosophical Practice

This section does not attempt to be an exhaustive catalog of ways in which Carnap seemed to endorse an inclusive vision of intellectual life. But I will draw out several occasions on which he displayed a clear commitment to the role of broad intellectual community and encouraged wide participation by others. And we can see this trend in Carnap relatively early in his intellectual development, after the completion of his military service in the First World War, during which many of his friends and acquaintances were killed and in which he himself was wounded.[4]

In 1918, having recently joined the Independent Social Democratic Party in Germany, Carnap wrote an essay considering the reasons behind Germany's wartime defeat (Carus 2007, 59). Among the people he singled out as responsible for the war itself were academics and intellectuals, who, in his opinion, had displayed too great an indifference toward political life. Those who had chosen the life of the mind, in Carnap's view, had failed to find an appropriate balance between contemplation and action (Carus 2007, 61–62). Intellectuals ought to be involved in politics but politics "in the broadest sense":

> For everything belongs to politics, in our view, that has some connection with the public social life of people, not only the spirit that animates the society but also its structure ... So all vocations – education and

---

[4] Further biographical considerations about Carnap's socio-ethical involvement can be found in Christian Damböck's chapter in this volume (Chapter 1).

maintenance of bodies and minds, research into the interconnections of nature, mind, and world events, shaping of things or human relations according to inner conviction, production and distribution of the objects that body and mind require for life – are specialised functions according to their kind, but by their effects they are contributions to the same project. (Quoted in Carus 2007, 62–63)

When we consider this interpretation of politics, as anything having to do with the ways in which public social life is shaped, it becomes much clearer that the scientific world-conception will have to be political, insofar as certain arrangements of public life are more conducive to science than others. We can see clear examples of this from relatively recent political life; for instance, many Canadian scientists protested what they saw as the muzzling of climate science research by the Conservative Harper government ("It's Official – the Harper Government Muzzled Scientists. Some Say It's Still Happening" 2018). And scientific research on issues related to climate change has a great many political implications for how our lives, social institutions, and economies must change in order to mitigate potentially disastrous effects (UN News 2021). In these kinds of cases, the value we place on science seems immediately to lead to political implications.[5] But even in the cases that Carnap himself was considering, his idea of political involvement required arriving at a "'form of community' [*Gemeinschaftgestalt*] that could serve to coordinate [human activities]" (Carus 2007, 63). In such a way, this kind of engineering attitude would help us improve society and allow us to operate with "goal-oriented reason." This attitude is continuous with Carnap's view of scientific philosophy generally, as an activity aimed at providing tools for science (Richardson 2007, 303–306).

The cultivation of scientific and philosophical community seems to have been a concern of Carnap's since his early days in the German Youth Movement. During a visit to the United States in the mid 1920s, Carnap met with many American mathematicians and others interested in scientific philosophy. He and Hans Reichenbach had already been

---

[5] Moreover, many feminist philosophers of science would argue that science is inevitably entangled with politics since it just *is* part of our social life (for instance, Fox Keller 1982; Longino 1983, 1990; Harding 1991). It's not so clear, though, that Carnap would have agreed with them entirely on the connection between social values and scientific practice (Yap 2010). Carnap's view is probably much more similar to someone like W. E. B. Du Bois, whose arguments in favor of value-free ideals in science are grounded in a similar kind of view about the role that science can play in social life (Bright 2018, 2230–2235). For Du Bois, and likely for Carnap as well, one reason to keep at least party politics out of science would be to maintain public trust in science as an institution.

discussing plans to create a journal for scientific philosophy, and his visit to the United States prompted him to reconceive his journal plans and develop something international. This would be a way to unite what he saw as "isolated but like-minded communities of scientific philosophers" (Verhaegh 2020, 4). And although this initial attempt was not successful, Carnap and Reichenbach were later able to found *Erkenntnis* in 1930.

These attempts to develop means through which scientists and scientifically minded philosophers would be able to share work with one another also seem at the heart of Neurath's *International Encyclopedia of Unified Science*, of which Carnap was an associate editor for some time. Carnap's interest in the possibility of communication across national boundaries was also closely connected to his study of Esperanto, a constructed language.[6] He wrote in his "Intellectual Autobiography" of discovering Esperanto as a teenager and remarked on both its practical value and the ease with which he was able to use it to communicate with many others that he met. While it would be easy to see his interest in these constructed languages as just the academic interests of a professional logician, he was very clear that one of the driving motivations behind his long-standing interests in them was the "humanitarian ideal of improving the understanding between nations" (*IA*, 68).

In general, many of Carnap's friends and colleagues have written about his community-minded way of engaging in philosophy. After his death in 1970, there was a memorial session at the Philosophy of Science Association's Boston meeting. While his colleagues certainly spoke highly of his intellectual abilities, many of them also went out of their way to note that he was not merely engaged with abstract theoretical concerns. Rather, he seemed clearly to have retained the attitude that he wrote about in 1918, that even those who devote themselves to abstract intellectual pursuits should not allow themselves to ignore people themselves and social life. This sentiment is expressed in very moving terms by Hempel:

> To observers who did not know him closely, Carnap may well have appeared as intellect and rationality incarnate, as a powerful thinker moving in a theoretical realm far distant from the domain of human passions and hopes and fears; but this picture does not do him justice. Carnap formed very strong human bonds; he was a warm-hearted and loyal friend, a most interested and sympathetic listener, and a broad-minded observer of the human scene who sought earnestly and with imagination to

---

[6] Carnap's involvement in international auxiliary movements is discussed by Basak Aray in this volume (Chapter 11).

understand – sometimes in psychoanalytic terms – personalities of a case quite different from his own. (Feigl et al. 1970, XVIII)

Though Hans Reichenbach predeceased Carnap by over twenty years, his wife Maria befriended Carnap and his wife Ina after they came to UCLA in 1954. Her remembrances of Carnap mention his efforts (with her husband) to help mutual friends leave Europe during Hitler's time. She also recalls his methodological advice to her husband with respect to negative criticism:

> Even though their mutual critiques were very frank, he advised Hans not to publish too many replies to negative criticisms of his books and articles by others, but rather to correct eventual misunderstandings within the framework of other positive contributions. And I know that on the whole Hans took this advice to heart. Another time Carnap wrote "I had indeed misunderstood your position. If one has a different opinion from another, then he easily misunderstands the explanations of the other man. I see that in your letter you also misinterpret my position …" (Feigl et al. 1970, LI)

We also find others who had met him as students, or as very junior academics, remarking on his intellectual generosity and his willingness to take their ideas seriously. W. V. O. Quine spent several weeks with Carnap in Prague at a time when he was, in his own words "an inconsequential foreigner," yet he was nevertheless welcomed by both Carnap and his wife. Quine writes, "It was extraordinary of anyone, and characteristic of Carnap, to have been so generous of his time and energy. It was a handsome gift" (Feigl et al. 1970, XXIV) Though Carnap was certainly interested in what Quine could teach him about the United States, as he hoped to move there (Verhaegh 2020, 10–11), the engagement was also clearly genuine.

David Kaplan's remembrance of Carnap is centered on a meeting with him in UCLA in 1958, as a graduate student who had just written a report critical of Carnap's paper, "The Methodological Character of Theoretical Concepts." Carnap evidently read and accepted the results of the report, reflected enthusiastically that he had been wrong about the related issues for the last thirty years, and insisted that Kaplan communicate his results immediately to Carnap's critics. This was not the expected response from such a noteworthy figure in philosophy, particularly to someone so junior. Indeed, Kaplan is very clear about the emotional impact that this had on him as a second-year graduate student. To have had Carnap respond to his criticisms with such selfless enthusiasm was apparently immensely transformative. Yet it also revealed a particularly striking attitude toward the practice of philosophy itself:

> It took me some time to understand Carnap's response. After reading my report, Carnap had improved his understanding of a subject which he had studied for many years. It was an advance in Philosophy, and whether it was initiated by a student's criticism of Carnap or by Carnap's own work made as little difference to Carnap as it did to Philosophy. His enthusiasm for the subject and his drive to understand the phenomena he studied, completely submerged any concern with his own role in the process. (Feigl et al. 1970, XLVII)

In other words, the insight itself was the important thing – the source of the insight was secondary. Even though Kaplan's report might have meant the end of a long-standing project in which Carnap was personally invested, it was nevertheless a valuable contribution to the development of philosophy overall. This kind of attitude, where Carnap placed a higher priority on making progress on philosophical questions than on the credit he got for his contributions, is arguably a good one for making philosophical progress. This might lead us to consider (in a Carnapian spirit) how the discipline might be better organized to enable and encourage such attitudes. More concrete Carnapian disciplinary proposals will be the focus of the concluding section of this chapter, but it's at least worth noting at this point that the Vienna Circle's unofficial manifesto was authored by several people and that even Carnap's single-authored work was extensively discussed with others, just as he was often in conversation with other authors about their own manuscripts.[7] The manifesto itself, in articulating the goal of unified science, clearly emphasizes, to that end, the need for collective effort and a focus on what can be intersubjectively grasped (Carnap, Hahn, and Neurath 1929/2012, 81). Gereon Wolters, for one, takes that to provide us with an outline of a collective and objective way that philosophy ought to be done, writing of Carnap in particular that collectivity and objectivity are "the invariants of Carnap's philosophical work at every stage of its development" (Wolters 2004, 33). Then even if the content of our philosophical work changes, perhaps in response to criticism, our way of engaging in philosophy, in this collective spirit, might nevertheless remain more or less the same.

4.3 Philosophy and Academic Freedom

While up to this point, we have primarily been discussing the political implications of Carnap's philosophical practice, we will now look at some

---

[7] Though for a more radical contemporary proposal related to authorship, see Habgood-Coote (2021)

of the ways in which Carnap reacted to the political climate of his time. Though it was previously mentioned that the Left Vienna Circle shared common political enemies with the Bauhaus – nationalists and fascists in particular – the political climate in the United States also posed its share of challenges for him. Carnap and others who were involved in the Unity of Science movement, such as Neurath and Philipp Frank, fell under suspicion, as the movement was viewed as "communistic." George Reisch, who documents extensive FBI investigations of philosophers of science during the Cold War, suggests that one thing that might have helped to protect Carnap's professional life during this decline was his ability to separate philosophy and politics and his turn to more formal matters (Reisch 2005, 382). This does not contradict the observation from Uebel with which we began, however. Reisch does not argue that Carnap saw philosophy of science as entirely disconnected from social life but rather that the two should be seen as different activities. Carnap's postwar work on semantics and probability (seen as much less suspicious by the FBI) was then not a rejection of his politics, but, Reisch argues, the reflection of his personal choice about how best to allocate his labor (2005, 383).

Despite his theoretical focus on formal philosophy, Carnap did remain politically engaged. As did many other academics, he declared himself in favor of clemency for Julius and Ethel Rosenberg, who were, despite such statements, convicted and executed for espionage. He also joined the ranks of others who called on the US government for peace and an end to the arms race. Though the FBI interviewed informants and gathered data for several years in an attempt to find any evidence of subversive activity on Carnap's part, they did not find any eventual reason to interview him or place him on the list of dangerous individuals (Reisch 2005, 271–276). In 1951, Carnap also quite notably turned down a visiting position at UCLA and declined to give the Howison Memorial Lecture at Berkeley because of a controversial loyalty oath then required by the University of California system. This oath required all UC employees to swear that they were not members of the Communist Party; several faculty who resisted signing were dismissed.[8] Carnap's letter declining both offers contains the following remarks clearly outlining his commitment to academic freedom:

> I wish both refusals to be regarded as expressions of solidarity with the dismissed colleagues, and of protest against the violation of the principle that scholarship, teaching ability, and integrity of character should be the

---

[8] A detailed timeline of the loyalty oath controversy can be found here: www.lib.berkeley.edu/uchistory/archives_exhibits/loyaltyoath/symposium/timeline/short.html.

only criteria for judging a man's fitness for an academic position. I am in deepest sympathy with all efforts to restore full academic freedom at the University of California, and thereby to help the University to regain its old honored place among our universities (published in the "Interim Report of the Committee on Academic Freedom to the Academic Senate, Northern Section, of the University of California" 1951, 40).

A similar concern for academic freedom also seems to have motivated his cowritten letter to the *New York Times* outlining concern for imprisoned Mexican professors Nicolas Molina Flores and Eli de Gortari. In it, they express strong protest against "abuses committed by the Government in Mexico City against students and professors who were merely exercising their constitutional rights," naming Molina and de Gortari specifically. They write that there is no evidence of either man having encouraged rebellion among students and call for their immediate release. The short letter concludes with the following remarks:

> The fact that the Mexican Government, which is a product of [a revolution that was condemned by conservative forces], should try to silence the voices of its youth, who represent the hope for the future, is not only ironic but deserving of condemnation. This repressive attitude can only have tragic consequences for Mexican well-being and for the reform spirit that since the time of the revolution has done so much to improve the democratic and intellectual life of Mexico. (Ayer et al. 1968)

Though he did not know de Gortari personally at the time, Carnap and the other signatories had received a letter from him, written from the jail. He was, however, acquainted with Molina as well as other Mexican philosophers, having met them at the International Congress of Philosophy in 1963. In early 1970, one of these friends, Rafael Ruiz Harrell, was able to put Carnap in contact with the imprisoned philosophers, when Carnap was in Mexico City, and Carnap was able to visit them in jail. Together, they discussed their work in progress as well as future plans, and Carnap promised to send them his book on the foundations of physics in Spanish translation (which of course he did). Upon leaving, Carnap was able to write some words of encouragement for them on blank cards, arranged by de Gortari's wife.

> So I wrote for each of them some words of admiration for their fortitude, tenacity, and stoic equanimity with which they bear their hard fate, devoting their time to positive, fruitful work; and I also expressed the hope that the day of liberation would not be too much delayed. (Carnap 1970, 1029)

Carnap's report on his visit to Mexico was completed only a few weeks before his death and posthumously published. But the visit as well as its surrounding circumstances seem to exemplify the fact that, for him, philosophical work depends deeply on both intellectual community and the overall social/political climate in which it is to take place. So while Carnap did in many ways see his philosophy as officially "neutral" with respect to politics, such neutrality comes up against its limits when politics threatens academic freedom and the freedom to conduct research. This means that Carnap likely took himself to be more politically neutral than his commitment to collectivity and collaboration would genuinely have allowed. Again, as many feminist philosophers and historians of science have pointed out, science takes place within a society shaped by politics; any methodological stance in favor of scientific practice for human good cannot possibly be *entirely* politically neutral, since it would then need to be divorced from human affairs. The next and final section of the paper will look further at some of the ways that thinking about academic freedom requires engaging with at least some social issues.

4.4 Academic Freedom and the Philosophical Community

This final section of the chapter will consider what philosophy in a Carnapian, collectivist spirit might look like today. It is obvious that imprisonment and government investigation are threats to scholars' academic freedom, and ought to be opposed, as Carnap was well aware. The same goes for attempts to dictate curricula, sanction scholars for their choice of research topics, or provide heavy-handed directives for how that research ought to be undertaken. Under some descriptions of academic freedom, it seems to support a collectivist vision of academic practice like the kind Carnap endorsed. In distinguishing freedom of speech from academic freedom, Shannon Dea writes

> while freedom of expression is regarded as supporting both social and individual goods, academic freedom is intended to support only social goods, not individual ones. It is for this reason that academic freedom is adventitious and alienable. A person is entitled to academic freedom only inasmuch as in their professional capacity they play a certain part in the university's important social role. Professors have academic freedom so that they can play this part. (Dea 2021, 212)

What this means is that academic freedom should not be narrowly focused on the individual rights of academics; for that, we have freedom of expression. Rather, when we think of academic freedom, we should think of the overall well-being of our intellectual communities. And when we justify the need for academic freedom, we ought not do it in terms of people's individual rights to freedom of expression but rather in terms of the ways in which the university community as a whole might serve the social good. This might help us sort through some issues that seem potentially thorny if viewed as clashes of individual rights.

After all, while all professional scholars might be able formally to lay claim to the protections of academic freedom, it might not be so evenly distributed in practice. For instance, Dea (2021, 214–215) cites Anishnaabe scholar Sheila Cote-Meek (2014), pointing out that ongoing racism and colonial attitudes can negatively impact the participation of Indigenous scholars in the university setting, which we might well see as a violation of their academic freedom. But of course, the environment of racism and colonialism is itself shored up by many of their own colleagues' research, which is itself protected by academic freedom. A collectivist approach then allows us to see that we cannot expect one-size-fits-all solutions or stances that treat scholars' academic freedom to which we can take an absolutist stance. After all, Cote-Meek's argument implies that some academics will be doing research that undermines the academic freedom of others; though we might want them to be doing so responsibly and in ways that minimize potential harm, it is at least clear that attending to social inequality makes questions of academic freedom much more difficult and that in a heterogenous environment some infringements are inevitable.

There were also limits to Carnap's own views about philosophical inclusiveness.[9] After all, the Vienna Circle was well known for its antimetaphysical stance, and Carnap certainly did not think that all philosophical methodologies were equally good or worth protecting. Yet his rejection of traditional metaphysics (particularly as exemplified by German philosophers like Heidegger) in favor of scientific philosophy was not a matter of stylistic prejudice. Part of Carnap's opposition to metaphysics is based in his assessment of its inability to resolve philosophical problems (*IA*, 43–44). Also, Michael Friedman (2000, 18–21) argues that Carnap, opposed to Heidegger both politically and philosophically, saw his attack on Heidegger as part of a larger sociopolitical struggle in Germany. This is not too far removed from the point above that some people might exercise

---

[9] Thanks to Adam Tamas Tuboly for raising this point.

their academic freedom in ways that undermine the community as a whole.

Now, while Carnap was politically active before emigrating to the United States, we have less evidence about his engagement with social inequalities in North America more generally. Notably, though, Abner Shimony remarks on Carnap's concern for the oppressed as being among his praiseworthy moral characteristics (Feigl et al. 1970, XXVII). And despite some indications that Carnap might have thought of racial terms as biological categories, he seems consistently to reject racially based explanations of human difference (Bright 2017, 12–13). There are also some indications that he had involvement with civil rights groups. Wolfgang Stegmüller writes that Carnap

> was in long term association with and supported a peaceful [Black] organization in Los Angeles, which sought to help achieve better education and better life conditions for its members. The last photograph we have of Carnap shows him in the office of this organization, in conversation with various members. He was the only white in the discussion group. (Feigl et al. 1970, LXVI)

The photograph in question is in the Pittsburgh archives, with "ca. 1966, Watts, Operation Bootstrap" written on the back.[10] Watts, a Los Angeles neighborhood with a significant Black population, was the site of several violent confrontations between civilians and police officers in August 1965. The spark for these confrontations, in which 34 people died and over 1,000 were injured, was the arrest of a Black man named Marquette Frye that involved a violent exchange between police and the crowd of onlookers; but arguably the segregation and poverty experienced by Watts residents contributed greatly to ongoing tensions and set the stage for the six-day riot. Operation Bootstrap was an organization launched by Lou Smith and Robert Hall in order to combat the poor social conditions in the neighborhood. Its goal was to provide opportunities for education and economic empowerment among residents. The organization was even able to start businesses like the groundbreaking Shindana Toys (Nittle 2019). In many ways, Operation Bootstrap was well aligned with Carnap's values and approach to social improvement. They had a strong focus on providing educational opportunities to residents, and in one clip, we can hear Lou Smith talking about how he saw it

---

[10] Christoph Limbeck-Lilienau offers a reproduction of this photo here: https://twitter.com/lilimbeck/status/1065174987319988225.

as their job to open people up to "the technological world that they haven't been involved in." The group's slogan, counteracting the Watts uprising slogan of "Burn, baby, burn", was "Learn, baby, learn" (PBS SoCal "Lost LA: Operation Bootstrap" n.d.). Though Operation Bootstrap did have volunteer teachers from a variety of backgrounds, including UCLA, we don't have evidence that Carnap was involved in such a capacity. The group was very open to others, including having "sensitivity sessions" that included white residents as well, to involve them in and educate them about community issues (Nittle 2019).

When we put all of this together in practice, we find an approach to intellectual life that is conscious of the fact that scholarship is not an isolated practice, and an approach focused on individual credit might hamper progress by stifling criticism from more marginal members of the community. But academic rank is not the only way that community members might be marginalized. Carnap, living in a deeply segregated and racially divided Los Angeles,[11] would certainly have been aware, through his acquaintance with Operation Bootstrap, of some of the effects of systemic racism on Black people's life outcomes. Following these threads ought to lead us to a view of academic freedom that takes such background factors into account. Providing an environment in which scholars are able to exercise their academic freedom in order to have a positive impact on society means more than just non-interference in their work. It also needs to mean ensuring that their environments are free from racism, misogyny, homophobia, transphobia, ableism, and other kinds of factors that prevent them from contributing to scholarship.[12] This, as suggested above, might well mean making difficult decisions about whose scholarship to prioritize, when some scholars' research makes the academy more hostile for others. It will also mean ensuring that the language we use is adequate for communication across difference. Though that might not be as straightforward as adopting one of the international languages that Carnap favored, it ought at least to motivate us to be attentive to things like conceptual gaps that disadvantage some groups of people.[13]

---

[11] See, for instance, Comandon and Ong (2020) on the long-standing effects of racial segregation in South LA and how this might have related to the Watts uprising.

[12] This is not to say that Carnap himself was (or indeed that any of us really are) immune to such prejudices. While Carnap does seem to have been conscious of issues of human rights, broadly speaking, there is also evidence that he was not as considerate with respect to the feelings of his sexual partners, including his first wife Elisabeth, to whom he was frequently unfaithful (Edmonds 2020, 20). Thanks to an anonymous reviewer for pointing out this issue.

[13] Though arguing for this is beyond the scope of this chapter, I think that one way of putting this would be to say that we have a Carnapian reason to pay attention to hermeneutical injustice in Fricker's (2007) sense.

This might also help us make sense of the fact that academic freedom needs to be bound up with academic responsibility. More specifically, part of the understanding ought to be that those who have greater freedom must not abuse that privilege. For example, while academics should be free to teach and research on topics of their choice, they might also be rightly criticized if they do not do their due diligence familiarizing themselves with existing literature on the topic before weighing in (Dea 2019). But rather than viewing this as a curtailment of a freedom that they have, personally, if we view academic freedom as something a *community* has, a single member should not do things that violate the community's freedom, like engaging in irresponsible research or related activities that prevent others in their community from contributing to scholarship.

To conclude, I think that this consideration of what a Carnapian stance on academic freedom might look like helps to complete Uebel's picture of intersubjective accountability as politics in its broadest sense. In particular, it shows how the issue of intersubjectivity has as background the question of who the community is to which we are accountable in the first place. People who do not generally share Carnap's left-wing sensibilities might be content with a narrower and less inclusive view of community. But if we want to take Carnap's collectivist vision seriously, it is hard to see what good reason we might have to do so. A Carnapian philosophical community is still one in which we might have to make some politically vexed choices; perhaps individual brilliance does not look so valuable after all if the brilliant person bars others from the intellectual community – perhaps through their encouragement of discriminatory views or actions or their own treatment of people with less status. And while we certainly don't *have* to adopt this kind of model of philosophy, in which we prioritize possibilities for community advancement over individual achievement, we might also take Maria Reichenbach's advice: "He was a good model and when I have a problem I still catch myself thinking: I must ask Carnap" (Feigl et al. 1970, LII).

PART II

Naturalism and Method

CHAPTER 5

Shades of Naturalism
Carnap and Quine
André W. Carus

5.1 Introduction

In the course of his reply to Evert Beth, Carnap makes the following remark:

> Since the metalanguage ML serves as a means of communication between author and reader or among the participants in a discussion, I always presupposed, both in syntax and in semantics, that a fixed interpretation of ML, which is shared by all participants, is given. This interpretation is usually not formulated explicitly; but since ML uses English words, it is assumed that these words are understood in their ordinary senses. The necessity of this presupposition of a common interpreted metalanguage seems to me obvious. (*RSE*, 929, quoted by Ricketts 2004, 194)

Is this or is this not to be understood as essentially equivalent to Quine's well-known termination of the regress of background languages "by acquiescing in the mother tongue and taking its words at face value" (Quine 1969a, 49)? Ricketts (2004, 199) maintains that it is. But since this retreat to the mother tongue as the metalanguage of last resort exemplifies Quine's insistence on "working from within," situated *in mediis rebus* (Dreben 1994) rather than at some imagined Archimedean vantage point in outer space, Ricketts would thereby appear to think that Carnap and Quine agree about this. This "working from within" program has been seen as the core of Quine's "naturalism" (Hylton 2014, Verhaegh 2018; George 2011 and Weir 2014 dissent), but if Ricketts is right, then Carnap was there first – Quine's naturalism is just a rhetorically warmed-over version of Carnap's, as some have maintained (e.g., Isaacson 1992).

Most interpreters, though (including Ricketts himself), are not willing to go that far and detect distinct *shades* of naturalism in Carnap and Quine. There is little agreement, however, about how to characterize those shades and about what underlying differences they reflect. This chapter suggests that we proceed directly from Dreben's suggestive but vague talk of "working from within" and try to see what sense can be made of it. On the surface, Carnap appears to reject this idea, at least in the radical form Dreben attributes to Quine, and allows for at least a limited external perspective on our cognitive struggles. Though Carnap takes a fixed interpretation of ordinary English for granted in his makeshift, ad hoc metalanguage for the discussion of syntax and semantics, that is never his final or ultimate retreat; even in the reply to Beth from which Ricketts quotes, Carnap made clear that he didn't think we need to "acquiesce" in a mother tongue. He thought, rather, that we could step back from our ordinary-language commitments, examine them critically, and repair our shared metalanguage from a perspective he classified as belonging to "pragmatics" – the study of language in use and of the practical usefulness of different linguistic options (Carus 2017). And of course it was precisely the availability of such a practical perspective – the possibility of judging language forms to be more or less suitable for some purpose – that Quine denied. In *Quiddities*, his philosophical dictionary, he made fun of pragmatics (in the entry on "Trinity"):

> A predilection for threes has invested song and story. We have the Three Fates, the Three Graces, the Three Magi, the Three Musketeers, the Three Bears ...
>
> Charles Morris, [another] admirer of the number three ... divided the domain of semiotic into *syntax*, *semantics*, and *pragmatics*. This trichotomy, taken up by Carnap, has been faithfully cited and adhered to for forty years, despite the fact, as I see it, that the separation between semantics and pragmatics is a pernicious error. I suspect that the durability of this trichotomy is due to its trinity. (Quine 1987, 210–211)

Along the same lines, a little less frivolously, he rejects what he calls the "cosmopolitan" perspective of appraising the conceptual scheme we happen to be situated in by comparison with others:

> When we compare theories, doctrines, points of view, and cultures, on the score of what sorts of objects there are said to be, we are comparing them in a respect which itself makes sense only provincially. It makes sense only as far afield as our efforts to translate our domestic idioms of identity and quantification bring encouragement in the way of simple and natural-looking correspondences ... There is a notion that our provincial ways of positing objects and conceiving nature may be best appreciated for what they are by standing off and seeing them against a cosmopolitan background of alien cultures; but the notion comes to nothing, for there is no ποῦ στῶ. (Quine 1958, 6)

This is of course exactly the point on which Quine differs from Carnap. So following Quine's own terminology, let us call his viewpoint here one of "provincialism," which we compare to Carnap's "cosmopolitanism."

But again, what is actually the issue between these standpoints? It ultimately seems to amount to a difference of perspective on the relationship between our native, intuitively most immediate language and the special-purpose language systems we have constructed over the centuries to understand our world. To get a perspective on this, let us regard "provincialism" and "cosmopolitanism" about this relationship not as two fixed points but as a matter of degree. Carnap's cosmopolitanism may, provisionally, be regarded as one extreme on this scale, but Quine doesn't represent a pure form of provincialism – he's not at the other extreme. He's somewhere in the middle; that's part of what makes this so confusing. So to characterize provincialism more precisely, we need to start with purer forms of it, such as those of the later Wittgenstein or the Oxford ordinary-language philosophers of the mid-twentieth century. This chapter focuses on Strawson, not because he was particularly extreme but for convenience, since Strawson actually engaged in debates with both Carnap and Quine. We will then try to locate Quine on the provincialism scale between Carnap and Strawson, but as we will see, this is not at all straightforward – Quine is not easy to pin down. Partly this is because his intermediate position isn't entirely stable; he is pulled in both directions in different contexts and doesn't always manage to square them with each other consistently.[1] A paradigmatic illustration of this is his vacillation regarding analyticity, which we briefly focus on (Section 5.4). In conclusion, the fundamental difference between the provincial and cosmopolitan stances is diagnosed – in agreement with Carnap himself, at a colloquium with Quine in 1950 (Stein 1992) – as a "non-cognitive" one about which neither side could be right or wrong.

5.2 Pure Provincialism

The hallmark of provincialism, in the sense just introduced, is the idea that it is impossible for us to step outside the linguistic framework or conceptual scheme we operate in (as humans, say, or as a particular cultural subgroup of humans). If there were such a thing as a completely alien conceptual scheme, we could only interpret it in the terms of our own

---

[1] Weir (2014) discusses an analogous (and perhaps related) inconsistency in Quine's conception of reduction and reductionism.

framework. But this idea can be understood in different ways and from different perspectives, so before going any further, we had better sort those out.

Strawson regarded logic and mathematics (scientific language more generally) as a tiny, artificially restricted subdomain of the ordinary language we all speak – whose logic, he thought, had been largely neglected in favor of the tiny subdomain that had hogged a disproportionate amount of philosophical attention. Unlike, for example, Wittgenstein, he thought a logic of ordinary language could certainly be delineated and systematized and devoted a significant proportion of his career to this effort:

> There is a massive central core of human thinking which has no history – or none recorded in histories of human thought; there are categories and concepts which, in their most fundamental character, change not at all. Obviously these are not the specialities of the most refined thinking. They are the commonplaces of the least refined thinking; and yet are the indispensable core of the conceptual equipment of the most sophisticated human beings. (Strawson 1959, 10)

Thus, even the most theoretically sophisticated and mathematically formulated scientific discourse was ultimately parasitic, for its basic conceptual structure, on this "massive central core of human thinking," is embedded in ordinary language. And Strawson set out to delineate this structure in his books *Individuals* and *The Bounds of Sense*. He continued to believe that this conceptual system, common to all human discourse, was also the basis of all scientific discourse, as he reiterated in his contribution to the Quine volume in the *Library of Living Philosophers*:

> The language of science is simply this or that natural language, enriched, sometimes, by the symbolism of mathematics; differing from the language of law reports or Parliamentary debates only in descriptive vocabulary, not in grammatical structure. (Strawson 1986, 531)

It is from this point of view, then, that Strawson regarded ordinary usage as more immediate and thus as the more basic raw material we must rely on for our conception of reality, than anything sense perception or theoretical science could tell us. As he says in the concluding paragraph of his critique of Carnap,

> the actual use of linguistic expressions remains [the philosopher's] sole and essential point of contact with reality; for this is the only point from which the actual mode of operation of concepts can be observed. (Strawson 1963, 518)

This is the idea that we can provisionally regard as a "pure" form of provincialism. There are of course other versions. From a certain perspective, Wittgenstein's conception can seem "purer," since he – as Strawson (1954/1974) complained – rejected the idea that one could explicitly articulate the structure of the "massive central core of human thinking" that Strawson set out to delineate in his books. Wittgenstein did not think ordinary language could be viewed as a single system, an "indispensable core" of the more sophisticated conceptual systems. He thought of our language rather as a "motley" in which various language games peacefully (if somewhat chaotically) coexist, like a city (to use one of his own metaphors) with an old center of irregular streets and crooked lanes and modern suburbs in which everything is regular and predictable.

One of Strawson's American contemporaries, Wilfrid Sellars, seems to have had an idea closer to Strawson's "massive central core of human thinking" in his conception of the human "manifest image" of the world, the system of folk categories in which we negotiate everyday life. However, unlike Strawson, Sellars did not see this manifest image as supplying the basic structure for the "scientific image" in which the world is law-bound, distanced, and depersonalized. On the contrary, he saw the two as prima facie incommensurable and thought the task of philosophy was to reconcile them. Some cognitive scientists, notably Daniel Dennett, think that such a "manifest image" is part of our genetic equipment, presumably hard-wired into the basic, reptilian parts of our brains and that it can be delineated and mapped out just as Strawson or Sellars thought, though by lab experiments and neurophysiology rather than the investigation of ordinary language.

In any case, these considerations point to an aspect of this notion of a "manifest image" or "massive central core of human thinking" that seems quite distinct from Strawson's version of a pure provincialism – the idea that a single basic structure underlies all the different apparently heterogeneous human languages and cultures. The best-known instance of *this* idea is probably Chomsky's conception of universal grammar, a generative mechanism, representable in recursion theory, that is genetically hardwired in every human being and that underlies all human languages, however apparently divergent on the surface. This idea was fundamental to the rise of cognitive science as a new paradigm for the study of the mind in the 1980s, though it no longer dominates the field as it did during those early years.

So we need to distinguish between these two aspects of a thoroughgoing provincialism such as Strawson's: (a) the idea that "ordinary language is our only contact with reality" – the epistemological aspect, if you like – and (b) the universalist Cartesian aspect that Chomsky makes explicit, of "innate ideas" that shape the structure of all language and thought. While both aspects seem entwined in Strawson's own work, Wittgenstein illustrates that the two aspects are separable (he embraces the first and rejects the second). For Strawson, the connection between these aspects is inherent in his emphasis on the *immediacy* of ordinary language as "our only contact with reality" and thus as subordinating scientific discourse to, classifying it as parasitic on, ordinary language.

5.3 Quine's Provincialism

Quine's conception of ordinary language is more elusive than any of these rather clear-cut cases (Strawson, Wittgenstein, Sellars). His reliance on an idea of immediacy is evident in his heavy use of the idea that certain things are "obvious," which may seem to have a bearing on this, but what he means by it isn't always clear. In his painstakingly detailed study of Quine's use of "obvious" and its cognates, Rick Creath (2003) finds Quine to be very cagey, never quite endorsing or rejecting the "obviousness" of elementary logic, for instance, and never entirely explicit about what he means by it. After an exhaustive survey of the possibilities, Creath concludes that Quine must have meant by "obvious" something like "deeply entrenched" (2003, 246). But, Creath objects, "That some theory is deeply entrenched *among ourselves* is no reason at all to think that people in other communities or at other times could not possibly disagree with us." He concludes that Quine's use of obviousness (especially in "Carnap and logical truth") either fails to engage with Carnap's actual view or lacks any argumentative force against it.

A different perspective on Quine's use of "obvious" and his conception of ordinary language was promoted by Burton Dreben, most forcefully in his paper "*In mediis rebus*" (Dreben 1994), where he paints a broad picture of Quine's metaphilosophy as characterized above all by the perspective of the knowing subject as the starting point of any inquiry, with all its embeddedness in random and chaotic surroundings, all its temporal and spatial *Geworfenheit*.[2] This characterization has been spelled out in more detail by Alexander George, who sees Quine's principal legacy as "the great lesson that we must work from within, that we are always in the thick of it" (George 2011, 304).

---

[2] Dreben did not of course use that word – but he might reluctantly, with a wry smile, have agreed that it is appropriate in this context.

What is "obvious" in this context is our own choice of reference frame. Though there is no fact of the matter about which reference frame to attribute to someone else, and the reference of her words remains indeterminate, each of us individually has made a choice (possibly by default), and so the reference is obvious to us; we are "at home in our language, with all its predicates and auxiliary devices" (Quine 1969a, 48), George continues, and "there, in terms of these [predicates and auxiliary devices], [each individual] finds himself with something obvious to say about the references of his words: for instance, 'rabbit' refers to rabbits." Acquiescing in the mother tongue and taking its words at face value is "part of what it is for that language to be one's mother tongue" (George 2014, 45).

Note that this does not actually conflict with Creath's diagnosis that what Quine means by "obvious" is "deeply entrenched." It adds only that there is no alternative to working from within our deeply entrenched habits; Creath's (and presumably Carnap's) imagined alternative of a more objective, universal, trans-personal – that is, cosmopolitan – perspective it deprecates as an Archimedean fantasy. But this seems fundamentally at odds with the role assigned to progress in scientific precision and "regimentation" in the developmental progression sketched in *Word and Object* (and elaborated in *The Roots of Reference*), an advance from a fully provincial starting point in infancy to an ultimately more objective perspective – one that is less dependent on an individual subjectivity, that is, more cosmopolitan.

Indeed, it would appear that Quine never resolved the tension between these two poles of attraction, and this lack of resolution is nowhere more vividly illustrated than in this very narrative of cognitive advance from infantile subjectivity to the more objective perspective attained by science. The parochial starting point of Quine's "mother tongue" doesn't *remain* parochial beyond the initial steps, at least for the individual person "at home in" or "working from within" it. As she begins to learn science, and learns to regiment her mother tongue of origin, the regimented version *becomes* her new mother tongue. In the process of this cognitive advance, certain portions of the original mother tongue go by the board – the portions that no longer fit into the regimented versions (such as the prescientific, magical, or naively metaphysical usages revealed by regimentation and science to have no reference):[3] "Putting our house in

---

[3] "As we become clearer and more explicit in ontological matters we come to appreciate the urgency of individuation principles, which are weak or wanting in the case of intensions ... The result can be that we find the intensional entities to be less help than hindrance, less simplificatory than complicatory, and out they go" (Quine 1974, 135).

ontological order is not a matter of making an already implicit ontology explicit by sorting and dusting up ordinary language. It is a matter of devising and imposing" (Quine 1974, 88). This is the cost of the broader perspective attained by regimentation in the service of science. But what has happened now to the original mother tongue, as a home base to fall back on or "acquiesce" in? It was only there as the starting point, strictly speaking, and didn't stick around once it was overcome. In Quine's sparse ontology, there is no room for social entities, and hence not really for languages, except as fortuitous collections of conditioned responses (Quine 1960, 9–13). These behavioral dispositions to respond in certain ways to specific stimuli do not add up to a Chomskian *competence* – an idea specifically rejected by Quine.[4] So Quine is actually being a bit sloppy when he holds out "*the* mother tongue" as a refuge that will still be there to receive us when we need a metalanguage of last resort. He means the *current* mother tongue, wherever in the developmental trajectory its speaker happens to be; the term "mother tongue" requires both a personal index and, within the personal trajectory, a temporal index.

This makes it hard to see how the differing developmental stages of many individual speakers could be aggregated into anything one would ordinarily conceive of as a language (it is hardly surprising that Davidson later seized on this void and made it more explicit). For Quine it remains a bit unclear, in the end, *what* exactly is to be "acquiesced in" and taken "at face value." He certainly leaves no doubt that in many specifically philosophical cases, the deliverances of the mother tongue can no longer be taken at anything like face value once scientific sophistication has been achieved:

> As we go on modifying theory to accommodate observation, the consideration of simplicity of theory may indeed so far outweigh conservatism that we give up our old belief in witchcraft; perhaps also religion; perhaps modal logic; but there are limits. (Quine 1974, 137)

---

[4] For reasons spelled out by George (1986) better than by Quine himself. George essentially shows why Quine was led to reject what in cognitive science, following the terminology of Marr (1982), is often called the "computational theory" of a computational system (which specifies its task or purpose and its inputs and outputs) but neither the specific computational steps or algorithms that turn the inputs into the outputs (Marr's level of "representations and algorithms") nor the physical implementation of the system. Marr's now-standard terminology probably goes back to Herbert Simon's (1969) general notion of an "artificial system," which has a function or purpose (Marr's "computational theory") in addition to an internal structure (i.e., "representations and algorithms") and an environment (which constrains the physical implementation).

Shades of Naturalism

And he also makes clear that he has little or no investment in anything like Strawson's epistemological immediacy of ordinary language in a highly revealing passage where he discusses Strawson's own *Introduction to Logical Theory*:

> Actually the formal logician's job is very different [from what Strawson suggests], and may be schematized as follows. To begin with let us picture formal logic as one phase of the activity of a hypothetical individual who is also physicist, mathematician, *et al*. Now this overdrawn individual is interested in ordinary language, let us suppose, only as a means of getting on with physics, mathematics, and the rest of science; and he is happy to depart from ordinary language whenever he finds a device of extraordinary language which is equally adequate to his need of the moment in formulating and developing his physics, mathematics, or the like. He drops "if-then" in favor of "⊃" without ever entertaining the mistaken idea that they are synonymous; he makes the change only because he finds that the purposes for which he had been *needing* 'if-then', in connection with his particular scientific work, happen to be satisfactorily manageable also by a somewhat different use of "⊃" and other devices. He makes this and other shifts with a view to streamlining his scientific work, maximizing his algorithmic facility, and maximizing his understanding of what he is doing. He does not care how inadequate his logical notation is as a reflexion of the vernacular, as long as it can be made to serve all the particular needs for which he, in his scientific program, would have otherwise to depend on that part of the vernacular. He does not even need to paraphrase the vernacular into his logical notation, for he has learned to think directly in his logical notation, or even (which is the beauty of the thing) to let it think for him. (Quine 1953/1976, 149–150)

Quine's tergiversations about "acquiescence in the mother tongue" are vividly illustrated in what immediately follows: "Not that this logical language is independent of ordinary language," he lets us know; "it has its roots in ordinary language, and these roots are not to be severed." (1953/1976, 149–150.) But what could he mean by this? Is the "not to be severed" meant as a claim or as an exhortation? What "roots" remain presently operative in the scientist-logician who, as Quine just said, "has learned to think directly in his logical notation" – bypassing those historical roots entirely? Here the mother tongue is not even given a temporal index anymore; here it is well and truly left behind, and Quine has joined the cosmopolitan Carnap, not far from the other end of the provincial-cosmopolitan spectrum. On some occasions, at least, the supposed provincialism was mostly window-dressing (Isaacson 1992).

It seems clear, then, that Quine was strongly attracted *both* to this Carnapian cosmopolitanism *and* to Strawsonian provincialism and sought somehow to fuse or combine them. But on the evidence we've just reviewed, we have to concede that this aspiration remained unfulfilled. The cosmopolitan and provincialist agendas in Quine's mind remain unreconciled, side by side, in open conflict, rather than arriving at the hoped-for synthesis.

5.4 Analyticity

However Quine may have vacillated between provincialism and cosmopolitanism, surely – one might think – at least his best-known philosophical move, the attack on analyticity, stems from the provincial end of this itinerary? Even here, though, there is manifest vacillation, since at first, in "Two Dogmas," Quine maintained there was nothing to explain. In Carnapian terms, there was no ordinary-language "explicandum" for the intensional synonymity stipulated by meaning postulates (resulting in analytic statements) to "explicate." The two best-known responses to "Two Dogmas", that of Strawson and Grice (1956) and that of Carnap (1955a), dismissed this denial with some incredulity as absurd and sought in different ways to show that analyticity has roots in ordinary discourse and intuition. Quine eventually came around to this view himself, bit by bit; in *Word and Object* (1960) he adopts Davidson's notion of "stimulus analyticity" for statements that (almost) everyone would assent to, including observational "occasion sentences" but also the more standard examples such as "all bachelors are unmarried." In *The Roots of Reference* (1974) he went further, and in view of the fact that whenever we learn to assent to "dog" we learn also to assent to "animal,"

> it would seem reasonable, invoking the controversial notion of analyticity, to say that by this account the sentence "A dog is an animal" is analytic; for to learn even to understand it is to learn that it is true. Where the rub comes, however, is in numbers: the number of different universal categorical sentences and the number of persons learning them. My hypothesis is that each of us learns his first few universal categorical sentences in the described way, but that different persons will begin with different sentences ... If the samples first acquired qualify as analytic, still they gain thereby no distinctive status with respect to the language or the community; for each of us will have derived his universal categorical powers from different first samples. Language is social, and analyticity, being truth that is grounded in language, should be social as well. Here then we may at last have a line on a concept of analyticity: a sentence is analytic if *everybody* learns that it is true by learning its words. Analyticity, like observationality, hinges on social uniformity. (Quine 1974, 79)

So in response to the critiques, Quine "socialized" analyticity, after a fashion, something he'd omitted to do (as we saw in Section 5.3) in the case of the "mother tongue." He allowed for the divergence of individual learning paths but conjectured that their analytic sentences (in his sense) largely overlap in certain categories of sentences (at least among the adult population). Other sentences, about which there is less unanimous agreement, for example, excluded middle, he therefore diagnosed as synthetic (1974, 80). However, Quine's belated recognition of an ordinary-language explicandum does not, as Carnap (1955a) had assumed, lead Quine to consider an explication of analyticity (Hylton 2019). And even his explicandum is not at all in Carnap's spirit. Carnap (1955a) had proposed an empirical procedure to determine an intension for a particular speaker, in the service of making the explicandum clear (scientifically respectable) enough to serve as the basis for an explication: "The existence of scientifically sound pragmatical concepts of this kind provides a practical motivation and justification for the introduction of corresponding concepts in pure semantics with respect to constructed language systems." (1955a, 46). For Quine, it did not; in him, the engineering impulse was constrained by and subordinated to philosophical priorities.

Carnap took the need for such an explication so completely for granted, unfortunately, that he provided only perfunctory examples of what he had in mind; he thought it sufficient to cite Einstein's famous lecture *Geometry and Experience* (Einstein 1921), where the distinction between (analytic) mathematical and (synthetic) physical geometry is held up as indispensable to his discovery of general relativity. This was a real missed opportunity, as it would have been easy for Carnap to adduce endless further examples from just about any branch of science. As a recent example, consider the results reported in 2021 from the muon g-minus-2 experiments at Fermilab (Abi et al. 2021; Castelvecchi 2021; Overbye 2021), which replicated to a much higher degree of precision the 2006 Brookhaven muon-experiment results that had raised eyebrows back then because they supposedly contradicted the standard model, thereby raising the possibility of a fundamental reconstruction of physical theory. But on the same day as the new Fermilab results were announced in 2021, an article was published in *Nature* (Borsanyi et al. 2021) that claimed that the 2006 Brookhaven results had, in fact, all along been largely consistent with the standard model, on the basis of new calculations taking a different mathematical approach from the one previously assumed in the predictions from which the Brookhaven (and now Fermilab) experimental findings had departed. It seems we are faced here with a clear-cut case of language choice, in which the experimental results, on the one hand, are clearly distinct from the mathematical models, on the other hand. The ubiquity of such choices seems obvious, and if Carnap had cited a few more of them from different sciences, he might have persuaded Quine to take the task of explicating "analytic" more seriously.

Quine might still have balked, though, since his 1974 majority-vote conception of analyticity portrays it as merely an artifact of human language acquisition, and this approach could conceivably be extended even into the higher reaches of particle physics – who knows, a Quinean might ask, whether a clear majority of physicists would, in the Fermilab case, regard either the new or the old mathematical predictions from the standard model as actually consistent with (i.e., analytic consequences of) the standard model? And even if a survey were to show that they did, that may be only in this single case, the Quinean might object, or at this particular point in time. So the stand-off could go on and on. Is there any way to resolve it?

One way of getting things unstuck might be to provide evidence that the explicandum is more deeply and pervasively rooted in human practices than merely the Quinean synonymy or class inclusion that results from the order in which we happen to pick up natural language concepts. So far we have considered only ordinary language (presumably in some "pure" form) at the one extreme and mathematical physics at the other extreme. But in his reply to Strawson, Carnap takes issue with Strawson's dismissal of constructed languages as being of any conceivable philosophical interest by, first of all, denying that "scientific" and "non-scientific" languages (as Strawson calls them) can actually be opposed to each other so diametrically. There is, rather, a scale or continuum of precision, Carnap argues, from the vaguest and most rudimentary natural languages to the most precise parts of algebra or logic (*RSE*, 934). And there is no cutoff anywhere along this continuum, where one could say that everything to the left is ordinary language and everything to the right is an artificial or a constructed language. It is a matter of degree, as in Carnap's larger project of explication, whose goal is to provide a *more* precise "explicatum" to replace a *less* precise "explicandum," that is, to replace vaguer concepts with more precise ones, regardless of where they are on some imagined absolute scale of precision. This is not just a progression from vague concepts to more precise ones, but – for Carnap – a progression from concepts whose use *evolves* socioculturally to concepts that are consciously and explicitly *defined* – that are *engineered* to suit our purposes, whatever those be. From the viewpoint of Strawson's thoroughgoing provincialism, this distinction –

so critical for Carnap – is *not* a distinction at all, as we have seen; scientific language, however technical and however self-consciously at odds with natural-language intuitions, is parasitic on natural language. And Quine, as we saw, wavered on this question.

From Strawson's point of view, then – and perhaps Quine's (who knows where he would have come down in this case?) – it hardly matters that we can distinguish these gradations of precision; they are all collapsed into natural language. From a Carnapian viewpoint, the most important difference lost in this collapse is not so much the degree of precision as the degree of purposeful engineering, which begins soon after the simplest ordinary language; in any case, it begins long before we get to particle physics. Strawson's neglect of these gradations led him to overlook crucial differences in the degree to which different kinds of language are purposefully devised and shaped. As we have seen, he often took the language of the law as an unproblematic instance of ordinary language. But legal discourse has a long history of self-conscious devising; this is considered so obvious in the vernacular as to be proverbial – "the wheels of the law grind slowly, but they grind exceeding fine." The language of the law is by no means as vague as ordinary natural language, as Strawson was surely aware, despite his careless assimilation. Explicit definition plays a central role in the law, in contrast to everyday life. Just about every contract starts with a series of definitions, for instance, stipulated synonymies (or "legislative definitions" of the sort Quine was skeptical about). It would never occur to anyone, in a court proceeding or a dispute, to challenge these definitions (though of course they may later be found to be ambiguous in ways not foreseen when drafted). They are essentially meaning postulates – analytic, in other words (unless they turn out to be contradictory through some sloppiness or drafting error). These definitions are not regarded as provisions of the contract, they're just part of its language – and this language as a rule has a fixed interpretation in the larger framework of the law, which specifies a fundamental distinction (in just about every legal system on earth) between questions of law and questions of fact. (It might seem redundant to point out that the law relies on what Quine called "legislative" stipulation.) So the legal profession, too, like Einstein and present-day particle physics, takes a robust analytic-synthetic distinction completely for granted and couldn't operate without it. Strawson would presumably have agreed – but he would have been wrong to think that these legal distinctions are already to be found in some purer and more innocent form of ordinary language. The law, outside of certain rare tribal contexts, is a highly artificial product of millenia of engineering. Even something as basic as the distinction between questions of law and questions of fact remains highly counterintuitive to many people and always has to be explained carefully to juries.

Law is deeply embedded as a framework for nearly all sectors of modern life. Nearly as universal, though perhaps less visible to the majority, is the practice of accounting, structured by its embedded language of accounting. And in accounting, even more than law, the language itself is constantly under scrutiny. A lot of time in corporate board meetings, for instance, where management presents the last quarter's numbers to the directors, is spent discussing or arguing about whether some result is an artifact of the accounting system or actually reflects some real change in the business. (This new product, for instance, looks like it's doing worse than the old one because we had to expense more of the development cost – because a lot of the work on it was done, for example, by freelance programmers, which our accounting rules say have to be expensed rather than capitalized – but if you look at the product-specific cash flow statements for the past few months you'll see it's actually doing better than the old one.) This goes beyond the obvious instances of analytic statements in the case of the law (in accounting, statements such as "total assets of a company equal total claims on the assets [liabilities plus equity]" or "for every credit there must be an equal debit in some balance sheet account"); in the accounting case, we also have the people who run companies devoting significant time and attention to the question of whether some observed outcome in the numbers is an artifact of the system itself or represents actual change in the behavior of the company or its environment. Once again this is, of course, a particular practical manifestation of the distinction between analytic and synthetic. There could hardly be a clearer illustration that this distinction is of fundamental importance to practical life.

One could easily imagine working out these examples in more detail and sharpening them up. One would also need to talk about comparisons among different countries' legal and accounting systems, for instance, as illustrations of cosmopolitanism in practice and of the poverty of provincialism in real life. One would need to grapple with Quine's indeterminacy arguments (Uebel ms.) in such specific practical contexts. And one would need to generalize to a wider-angle sketch of the pragmatics of intensional language, beyond just analyticity, in these contexts.

5.5 Distinct Shades or Pale Grey?

So how to characterize the Quinean and Carnapian shades of naturalism? Is the "lore of our fathers," to pursue the metaphor in the closing paragraph of "Carnap and logical truth," all "pale grey," as Quine avers, "black with fact and white with convention"? Not content with portraying our entire cultural and intellectual inheritance, in all its riotous, cacophonous, heterogeneous variety and internecine tension as a uniform pale grey, Quine goes even further, to claim that even among the particular components of this pale grey, the particular threads of the linguistic fabric constituting this lore, none are entirely white or entirely black. This drab metaphor suits its provincial provenance. A corresponding cosmopolitan metaphor would acknowledge colored threads and accuse the provincialist of reducing all the colors to shades of grey by ruling out any but black-and-white photographic representations of an actually much richer and more complex fabric than the black-and-white (or any single-color) reduction can reveal. And once it is recognized that it is only our representation of the fabric, not the fabric itself, that reduces or permutes it to black and white, any thread in the fabric can, by suitable color permutations analogous to black-and-white photos (or their negatives), be represented as white when viewed in isolation. In this cosmopolitan subversion of Quine's metaphor,[5] then, we are not stuck with a single, drab representation of the fabric but can decide which threads to regard as conventional on any particular occasion or for any particular purpose.

Seen this way, the Quinean, provincial shade of naturalism amounts to a kind of self-denying ordinance, a resolve to swear off temptations lurking beyond the confines of the fabric we grew up with. It shares this ascetic impulse with intuitionism, the impulse not only *not* to indulge certain intellectual temptations (alien conceptual systems, Cantor's paradise) but to exclude them puritanically from consideration altogether, as wrong or mistaken. The idea that we could step back from the conceptual scheme we grew up in and reconsider its framework(s) from a practical perspective (i.e., that we could step back from semantics to a workspace of pragmatics), Quine regards as a "pernicious error," as we saw. The Carnapian, cosmopolitan shade of naturalism sees this moralistic exclusion of wider perspectives and roomier workspaces as unmotivated and, as the above examples from legal and accounting practices suggest, completely at odds with certain essential features of modern social organization, with practical requirements that are deeply embedded in our social and economic life.

---

[5] Apologies to Huw Price, whose own (similarly cosmopolitan) subversion of this same metaphor (Price 2007) makes a different (though related) point; in a subsequent exposition, Price (2013) compares what he calls "object naturalism" unfavorably to "subject naturalism," which map quite well onto the Quinean and Carnapian shades of naturalism, respectively, discussed here.

In terms of the perennial question – often associated with Kant and Poincaré – whether our knowledge is imposed on nature by us or on us by nature, Quine's naturalism tends more to the former, Carnap's to the latter (Friedman 2006). It is less this difference that ultimately distinguishes Carnap from Quine, though, than another, more fundamental one that has been hovering in the background throughout this exposition but is hard to pin down explicitly: Carnap's attitude that our linguistic systems are tools, at our disposal, to be used or abandoned according to our convenience and our values and according to the purposes we have in mind for them. This primacy of the engineering impulse is perhaps most vividly manifested in what has been called his "voluntarism":

> [Carnap's] persistent, central idea was: "It's high time we took charge of our own mental lives" – time to engineer our own conceptual scheme (language, theories) as best we can to serve our own purposes; time to take it back from tradition, time to dismiss Descartes's God as a distracting myth, time to accept the fact that there's nobody out there but us, to choose our purposes and concepts to serve those purposes. (Jeffrey 1994, 847)

Carnap's ideals, in short, says Jeffrey, "were those of the Enlightenment." This aligns well with his open-minded, tolerant attitude toward proposals of all kinds – "in logic there are no morals" – a constructive, engineering attitude rather than a search for "the" right answer that excludes other possible answers as mistaken or wrong. Quine's provincial naturalism, in contrast, represents "just as much of an externally motivated, purely philosophical intrusion into the ongoing progress of empirical science and the logic of science as Quine's earlier defense of nominalism" (Friedman 2006, 52), from a Carnapian perspective. And with reference to Carnap's restatement of the principle of tolerance in the final paragraph of "Empiricism, Semantics, and Ontology" (*ESO*), Friedman continues:

> Here Carnap has specifically in mind Quine's empiricist doubts about the use of abstract entities (properties, modalities, intensions, and the like) in semantic theory, but the moral is much more general. Quine's rejection of the analytic/synthetic distinction ... rests, from Carnap's point of view, on nothing more nor less than a fundamentally "irrational" *philosophical* "prejudice." (Friedman 2006, 52)

Quine's requirement that proposals pass certain philosophical qualifications before being admitted for consideration, in this view, "cuts the logic of science off at its root" (Friedman 2006, 53) and deprives us of the best tools we possess for understanding science in broader contexts and for confronting it with our values. In Carnap's presence, Quine could be reminded, apparently, that – as Carnap put it – the differences between them did not concern "any matter of fact, nor any question with cognitive content" (Stein 1992, 279). But he soon forgot and reverted (along with many followers) to his default – provincial – mode of insisting that he was right, and that Carnap was wrong.

CHAPTER 6

On Quine's Epistemological Objection to Carnap's Analyticity

Joseph Bentley and Thomas Uebel[*]

6.1 Introduction

Few disputes in the analytic tradition have been as protracted and problematic as that between Rudolf Carnap and W.V.O. Quine over the tenability of the analytic/synthetic (a/s) distinction. Over time, Quine's criticism of its utility, early on even its intelligibility, has widely come to be viewed as defining the methodology of epistemological naturalism in contradistinction to traditionalist aprioricism. We believe this to be a mistake.

Very broadly speaking, there are two strands to Quine's criticism of the a/s distinction. One focusses in varied ways on the concept of analyticity itself and the problems of comprehending it within an extensionalist framework. The other focusses on the difficulties of attaining the goals of the epistemological program that the a/s distinction is said to subserve. The purpose of this chapter is to explore a partially new way of responding to the latter type of criticism in order to highlight the compatibility of Carnap's a/s distinction with naturalism as far as empirical science is concerned. It is argued that the epistemological objection is misdirected, as it relies on a misapprehension of Carnap's intentions and consequently makes demands of the distinction that Carnap has no intention or need to meet.

6.2 The Significance of the Epistemological Objection

Note, to begin with, that once Carnap's nonstandard logicist agenda for arithmetic is set to one side, it is not immediately obvious what the epistemological aims are supposed to be that his formulation of the a/s

---

[*] Thanks are due to our colleagues Chris Daly and Fraser MacBride for instructive conversations and constructive criticisms and to our editors for further suggestions. The typical disclaimers apply.

distinction furthers. The suggestion that upholding it contravenes fallibilism – encouraged by the earlier Quine (1951a, section 6) and lingering still in (1963, section 1) but disposed of by Carnap himself (*LSL*, 318; *RSE*, 921; 1990, 432) – can be discounted. It makes sense therefore to begin by locating the epistemological task of the a/s distinction in marking the difference between (i) ways of determining the truth of sentences and (ii) ways of justifying changes in their truth values. Carnap is widely understood to have endorsed both (i) and (ii). The later Quine came to accept a behavioural variant of (i): a sentence is 'analytic for a native speaker' if he learned its truth 'by learning the use of one or more of its words' (1991/2008, 395f., cf. 1974, section 21) – but he upheld his rejection of (ii).

In their comprehensive survey of Quine's philosophy, Peter Hylton and Gary Kemp ascribe to him (and themselves endorse) the view that Carnap's Principle of Tolerance (PoT)[1] – which underlies (ii) – 'puts analytic sentences on an entirely different epistemological footing from synthetic sentences. Synthetic sentences are answerable to evidence; analytic sentences are a matter of the choice of language, which does not require theoretical justification'. Accordingly, the a/s distinction marks an epistemologically significant difference in receptivity to empirical evidence and the relevance of theoretical considerations to statement revision. Like Quine, Hylton and Kemp question the significance of the difference. They agree that changing the truth value of an analytical sentence can be considered a change of language, but they hold that 'we might have reasons to make such a change, reasons that are *of the same sort* that lead us to make revisions to synthetic sentences' (2019, section 3.1, emphasis added; cf. Hylton 2007, 68–74).

Quine extended analyticity, behaviourally understood, further still to include first-order logical truths and their logical consequences, but no agreement with Carnap obtained. Quine stated: 'I recognize the notion of analyticity in its obvious and useful but *epistemologically insignificant* applications' (1991/2008, 397, emphasis added). Hylton and Kemp summarise:

> Quine's rejection of the Principle of Tolerance is the deepest aspect of his disagreement with Carnap. Quine sees all our cognitive endeavours, whether they involve formulating a new language or making a small-scale

---

[1] PoT was given its canonical form in Carnap (*LSL*, §17) and it is discussed in Section 6.9. A later formulation reads: '*Let us be cautious in making assertions and critical in examining them, but tolerant in permitting linguistic forms.*' (*ESO*, 40, original emphasis)

theoretical change, as having the same very general aim of enabling us to deal with the world better; all such endeavours have the same very general kind of justification, namely, as contributing to that end. In this picture, there is no basis for Carnap's insistence that philosophy is in principle different from science. Philosophy, as Quine sees it, has no special vantage point, no special method, no special access to truth. (2019, §3.3)

With the a/s distinction as drawn by Quine, it is claimed, it no longer serves the purposes for which Carnap invoked it – and not only because arithmetic now remains out of bounds. Carnap's a/s distinction is disqualified on account of a perceived allegiance to a very traditional conception of philosophy. According to the Quinean reading, the purpose of the a/s distinction is to draw a principled line delineating two epistemologically distinct forms of enquiry.

To be sure, Carnap no longer stands accused of hankering after eternal truths of reason but only of reserving for philosophy a residue of specialness in its 'vantage point', its 'method' and its 'access to truth'. To quite a few of Carnap's recent readers, however, this charge no longer rings true. Yet dismantling it is no easy matter. Does PoT not take pride of place in accounts that stress Carnap's deflationist approach to philosophical subject matters overall, seeking to replace substantive pronouncements on the nature of the often controversial phenomena under investigation with proposals for how to speak and think of them more fruitfully? It does. But this does not mean that PoT plays the role that Hylton and Kemp and, according to them, Quine have assigned to it.

Many observers of the debate have been puzzled by the fact that Quine disregarded Carnap's prominent reminder (*RSE*, 918; cf. 1990, 427–428) that the a/s distinction as he understood it only applies to formal languages. (Hylton and Kemp follow Quine in this.) This disconnect indicates a significant difference between their philosophical programs and suggests that a solution adequate to both will be hard to find. But it also points to a resource that so far has not been fully exploited for a Carnapian response to Quine's epistemological objection: the distinctions Carnap carefully drew between different semiotic disciplines so as to locate investigations employing notions like analyticity correctly. Accordingly, it must be asked whether epistemological concerns are germane to the home discipline of analyticity, where and how the epistemological distinction that PoT does draw properly applies and, finally, whether Quine's criticism holds there.

We begin by asking how it might make sense to relieve Carnap's a/s distinction of epistemological duties. This line of defence confronts

Hylton and Kemp's Quinean charge directly by broadening the interpretation of Carnap's philosophically deflationist attitude. On its own it does not look very promising as it contradicts all too squarely what is known about the project Carnap pursued with his logic of science. Progress requires the recognition of two distinct questions. Speaking loosely, we must distinguish the different ways in which the truth of sentences of a language are determined from the different ways in which speakers of that language determine whether to hold true sentences of their language. With analyticity properly located and the epistemological office reassigned amidst the semiotic disciplines, we will return to Hylton and Kemp's Quinean challenge to PoT and applications of Carnap's a/s distinction.

6.3 Analyticity, Semantics and Epistemology

Let defenders of Carnap's a/s distinction agree that choices of language are informed by theoretical considerations, like acceptances of synthetic sentences, just as theory choice is subject to pragmatic considerations, like the acceptance of (a system of) analytic sentences. Let these defenders claim instead that this parallel does not undermine Carnap's a/s distinction. What the critical argument to the contrary presupposes, namely, that the distinction has an epistemological office to fulfil, is open to objections. Defenders of Carnap's a/s distinction can question the nature of this presupposition. They can press the charge that while many versions of the distinction may have an epistemological office assigned to it, Carnap's has not.

Defenders of Carnap's distinction may point to two widely recognised facts: first, that ontological and epistemological issues stand in a relation of mutual dependency, second, that abstention from ontological claims is a hallmark of Carnap's philosophy. Would it not make sense, they ask, to grant him relief as well from the epistemological demands? With no epistemological ambition on Carnap's part, the Quine-Hylton-Kemp objection would pass his project by.

While it aims in the right direction, this move is too crude. Carnap's philosophy, when not given to explication, is best understood as an exploration of just how far our knowledge claims may reach, given our evidence. It is ontology as answering to external questions of existence, as answering them independently of any logico-linguistic framework, that Carnap rejected. Internal questions of existence are unaffected and so are attempts to justify their answers. It is only the epistemology of framework-independent truths that is precluded. But this provides no help against the charge that the theoretical nature of the considerations involved in language change undermines the a/s distinction.

How then to account for Carnap's unperturbed use of the a/s distinction alongside his pursuit of 'non-metaphysical' epistemology? Carnap's defenders must begin by determining the a/s distinction like he did, as a strictly semantic distinction. For Carnap, 'analytic' was a 'traditional term' for 'the concept of logical truth, truth for logical reasons in contradistinction to empirical, factual reasons'. This term requires the formal explication in semantical analyses as 'L-truth' in order to be fully serviceable for the 'logical analysis of science' (*IS*, 60–61). Speaking of Carnap's concept of analyticity thus means speaking of the semantical concept of L-truth: this must be understood when the terms 'analytic' and 'analyticity' continue to be used in discussing Carnap's conception (as he did himself). Insisting on this point is no mere foible: only awareness of relevant distinctions drawn by Carnap in circumscribing this formal inquiry allows us to see his concept of analyticity in the correct light.

Note then, first, that Carnap carefully distinguished semantics and pragmatics:

> If in an investigation explicit reference is made to the speaker, or, to put it in more general terms, to the user of the language, then we assign it to the field of *pragmatics* ... If we abstract from the user of the language and analyse only the expressions and their designate, we are in the field of *semantics*. (*IS*, 9, original emphasis)

Note, second, what falls under pragmatics in Carnap's understanding:

> Examples of *pragmatical* investigations are: a physiological analysis of the processes in the speaking organs and in the nervous system connected with speaking activities; a psychological analysis of the relations between speaking behaviour and other behaviour; a psychological study of the different connotations of one and the same word for different individuals; ethnological and sociological studies of the speaking habits and their differences in different tribes, different age groups, social strata; a study of the procedures applied by scientists in recording the results of experiments, etc. (*IS*, 10, original emphasis)

Pragmatics, for Carnap, encompasses all enquiries pertaining to the use of language. Note then, third, that this has implications for how to think of (legitimate, i.e. non-metaphysical) philosophical activities:

> [T]he task of philosophy is *semiotical analysis*; the problems of philosophy concern – not the ultimate nature of being but – the semiotical structure of

the language of science, including the theoretical part of everyday language. We may distinguish between those problems which deal with the activities of gaining and communicating knowledge and the problem of logical analysis. Those of the first kind belong to pragmatics, those of the second kind to semantics or syntax – to semantics if designata ('meaning') are taken into consideration; to syntax, if the analysis is purely formal. (*IS*, 250, original emphasis; cf. *IS*, 245)

Carnap's division-of-labour distinction between pragmatics and semantics is highly consequential for the question of whether and how his concept of analyticity – to be precise: L-truth – can be saved from Quine's criticisms. Note then that epistemological questions (as far as permitted) fall under pragmatics.[2]

The semantics/pragmatics distinction as outlined helps address the criticism that no epistemological difference marks the distinction between analytic and synthetic sentences when their revision is contemplated. It allows defenders of Carnap's analyticity to undercut a presupposition this criticism makes. As a semantic concept, L-truth was not meant to address epistemological questions. As can be seen from his differentiation of semantics from pragmatics, Carnap removed semantics from the reach of epistemology. In consequence, it cannot count as a failure of Carnap's account of the a/s distinction that it failed to make good on the promise to provide a principled epistemological distinction between analytic and synthetic sentences that would illuminate how their revision is dealt with (what considerations are relevant). Carnap's account never gave such a promise.

6.4 Semantic Concepts and their Pragmatic Counterparts

The claim that the epistemological criticism of analyticity does not apply because it misses the point of Carnap's understanding faces a strong objection. It will be noted that Carnap typically associated analyticity with 'truth in virtue of meaning' or 'truth based on meanings' and the like (1952, 65; *RSE*, 916; 1990, 432) and once even stated that in such cases it is 'sufficient to understand the statement in order to establish its truth'

---

[2] Carnap's use of 'pragmatics' in both the 'wide' methodological version appealed to here and in a more 'narrow' linguistic version is chronicled in Uebel (2013a) where it is argued that despite a terminological shift in later years (he preferred 'practical' to the wide sense of 'pragmatical') he retained his allegiance to the schema outlined here. Howard Stein also employs this wide sense of 'pragmatic' to spell out the views of the later Carnap in (1992), as do André Carus in (2007) and, independently, Alan Richardson (2007).

(1952, 65). Does the latter phrase not show that Carnap himself assigned an epistemological office to analyticity?[3]

The counter that these remarks for Carnap were 'informal characterization[s] of logical truth' (*RSE*, 916) and that a proper explication can only be given in a formal semantical system (1952, 65–66; 1990, 427) is likely to face scepticism. Carnap may indeed seem vulnerable. He proposed the following 'convention' concerning L-truth:

> Convention. A sentence S_i is true in a semantical system S if and only if S_i is true in S in such a way that its truth can be established on the basis of the semantical rules of the system S alone, without any reference to (extra-linguistic) facts.

And he continued:

> This is not yet a definition of L-truth. It is an informal formulation of a condition which any proposed definition of L-truth must fulfil in order to be adequate as an explication for our explicandum. Thus this convention has merely an explanatory and heuristic function. (*M&N*, 10)

For Carnap it was a material adequacy condition for any explication of 'analytic' that it picked out sharply enough the class of statements the understanding of which is sufficient to establish their truth. Undeniably, it is an epistemological condition that is here elevated to the status of material adequacy condition of semantical analyses: does this not tie semantics all too closely to linguistic practice and so what's dealt with in pragmatics?

To see that this worry is without justification, let's begin by taking Carnap at his word that both his 'truth based on meanings'–talk and his 'statement the understanding of which establish its truth'–talk was informal preparatory talk. As it was therefore not intended as a characterisation of the *explicatum*, it aimed at the *explicandum*. Such a preparatory delineation of scope is always the first step of the explicationist method, which Carnap calls the 'informal *clarification of the explicandum*' (*RSE*, 933, original emphasis). Fittingly, as expressing a material adequacy condition the 'establishes truth'–talk covers the territory of pragmatics: it specifies a subject's cognitive ability. Likewise, 'based-on-meanings'–talk pertains to pragmatics by addressing the question of what makes such abilities

---

[3] Carnap's 'informal characterization of logical truth' as 'truth based on meanings' in (*RSE*, 916), being couched in epistemological not truth-making terms, could, for instance, be read as endorsing the 'epistemological' variant of analyticity that Paul Boghossian (1996) distinguished from the 'metaphysical' variant.

possible. It also was not intended as a characterisation of the *explicatum* but aimed at the *explicandum*.

Locating Carnap's elucidations thus does not, however, leave the *explicatum* without any connection to the *explicandum* as critics may fear. Retaining this connection is precisely what the material adequacy condition ensures. Recall also that semantics 'abstracts' from many of the features that characterise language in the wild, in particular from those features related to being used by speakers. It follows what Carnap duly acknowledged, namely, that there are pragmatic counterparts for semantic concepts that play a role in psychological, sociological and other broadly historical accounts of language use (1955a, 1955b).[4] By contrast, the concept of L-truth is a suitably purified, formal version of the informal notion of analyticity employed in accounts of actual or potential language use.

When Carnap distinguished semantics from pragmatics, he rejected both the metaphysical and the epistemological versions of analyticity and any role for L-truth in the search for or appeal to truth-makers and foundation-givers. To his semantics such pursuits are entirely alien. It is this deflationism that enabled Carnap to park ontological questions (insofar as they made sense) with the empirical sciences and to find space in pragmatics to explore the epistemological concerns surrounding language use that remain – all the while retaining the formal purity for semantics.

6.5 Semantics as an Auxiliary Science

It will of course be asked about Carnap's semantics: what is the point of clarifying a term by means of formal explication if in so doing we sidestep the problems the *explicandum* is customarily if sloppily applied to? Carnap has an excellent answer: we gain a powerful tool for the analysis and construction of logically perspicuous languages. Exploring these he regarded as aiding 'the development of logic' generally, but it also has concrete applications through the use of 'corresponding pragmatical concepts' (1955a, 35). (That semantical analysis may thereby help dispel epistemological worries does not turn it into epistemology.)

For instance, semantics can help in clarifying existing languages of science and aiding 'mutual understanding and effective communication'

---

[4] However, Carnap still denied 'that it is necessary in general to provide a pragmatical concept in order to justify the introduction of a concept of pure semantics', underlining the independence of the latter from descriptive semantics (*RSE*, 919).

by reducing their 'intensional vagueness' in the application of expressions to non-actual cases (1955a, 39). Moreover, intensional semantic analyses can illuminate the structure of extant scientific theories (we'll see an example in Section 6.7). In general, within semantic systems it is possible to develop variations of already existing concepts or entirely new ones and investigate the consequences for the rest of the language under investigation. With their consistency provisionally established, such newly explicated concepts can then be further considered in pragmatics for potential applications and resolution of the problems the old *explicandum* posed.

Formal explication can also help settle claims concerning contested individual concepts. Carnap's first example of explication in action was the distinction of two concepts of probability: of probability$_1$, the concept of degree of confirmation of a hypothesis, from probability$_2$, the concept of the relative frequency of a type of event. Carnap showed that (in their metric versions) the former is a semantical concept that attributes a numerical value determined by the logical relation between sentences representing hypotheses and the evidence for them, while the latter is an empirical concept attributing a numerical value that is determined by the observation of relevant facts. Accordingly, simple statements of probability$_1$ are either L-true or L-false, whereas simple statements of probability$_2$ are factual (1945a, §4). Here semantical analysis played a central role in disambiguating a concept at the centre of a long and seemingly intractable debate between proponents of each version of probability.[5]

But that is not all. Recognition of the domain of semantics sustains philosophical reflexivity, awareness of the distinctive office of what Carnap called 'the logic of science'. In a response to Quine, he once remarked:

> Usually, a philosophical insight does not say anything about the world, but is merely a clearer recognition of meanings or of meaning relations. If an insight of this kind is expressed by a sentence, then this sentence is, although meaningful ... not factual but rather analytic. Thus I would interpret, e.g., the principle of verifiability (or of confirmability), or the empiricist principle that there is no synthetic a priori, as consisting of proposals for certain explications (often not stated explicitly) and of certain assertions which, on the basis of these explications, are analytic. (*RSE*, 917; cf. *RSE*, 1003)

Note especially how Carnap here conceived of 'philosophical insight': not as a description of facts in a third realm, as Quine once interpreted him

---

[5] For discussion of Carnap's views on explication and probability, respectively, see also the chapters by Erich Reck (Chapter 7) and Sandy Zabell (Chapter 10) in this volume.

(1948), but as 'proposals for explications'. Thus, Carnap added, distinguishing his view further from Quine's: 'Such philosophical principles or doctrines are sometimes called theories; however, it might be better not to use the term 'theory' in this context, in order to avoid the misunderstanding that such doctrines are similar to scientific, empirical theories.'[6]

If the primary task of semantics is clarification and explication of meaning relations, then what about Carnap's non-standard logicism? Even though this program of Carnap's is not discussed here, it should be evident by now that its constructional aspects were meant to be covered by semantics. But what about the epistemological dimension of logicism, the task of explaining in broadest terms knowledge of arithmetic in terms of knowledge of logic? There can be no denying that what seem to be semantic terms are often invoked in epistemological discussions. When what is at issue are practical applications of Carnap's notion of analyticity, however, it is important to bear in mind once again his careful distinction between the semantic and its 'corresponding pragmatical concept'. In Carnap's 'semiotical' conception of philosophy (see Section 6.3) he later dropped the name but not the idea – epistemology falls under pragmatics, which deals with what people do with languages and symbol systems. The epistemological dimension of logicism too would be a matter for pragmatics (if its constructive ambitions were successful).

6.6 Explaining Language Change

Carnap's separation of semantics from pragmatics also supports the counter-charge that it is a misunderstanding of the office of the a/s distinction to demand that it offer explanations of changes in the meaning of concepts by specifying reasons for making the changes at issue. Changes of definitions happen for all sorts of reasons and often cannot be fully explained without reference to the factual matters to which they are applied. Explaining language change is a matter for pragmatics. All semantics can do in this regard is specify the logico-linguistic changes and offer comparisons of language systems.

One worry to consider about this strategy of response is this. When scientists revise their concepts, according to Carnap, this is a shift from one

---

[6] That Carnap's stress on the distinctive office of the logic of science is compatible with his recognition of a complementary 'pragmatics of science' (Philipp Frank's term), both jointly comprising what nowadays is called 'philosophy of science', is argued elsewhere; see Uebel (2015, 2022) and especially Bentley (2023).

language to another language with different semantical rules. As noted, this is guided by theoretical knowledge. But in what language is that theoretical knowledge expressed? It cannot be the earlier language because its semantical rules preclude the new theory. But the semantical rules of the later language preclude the earlier theory. Is there not a metalanguage required to facilitate the shift between languages – and does this not involve us in semantics again?

At issue is the rationality, broadly conceived, of the theory/language change: how can the theoretical knowledge that is said to inform the change be brought to bear on it? There are two issues here: in which discipline we are to account for theory/language change and how to do it wherever we do it. Kuhnian Gestalt-switches between paradigms name a similar problem, less focussed on language, leaving it unexplained. With Carnap's focus on language come new resources that need to be deployed appropriately. The change in question concerns overcoming perceived limitations on expressive power and so relates to language use, which is dealt with in pragmatics, not semantics.

The process of change takes its start from problems with the application of the original language. In response, alternative ways of expressing the issues at hand are explored and one is ultimately accepted. Once that point is reached, it can be explained retrospectively in the new language what led to and justified the change. (It can be stated what the old language was incapable of expressing.) So when we are speaking of the theoretical knowledge that prompts or informs the change, we are either referring to the growing awareness of speakers of the old language that it has become unsatisfactory or we are referring to knowledge that speakers can express once in possession of the new language. The former kind of knowledge spells out the pressure for change, while the latter explains it retrospectively and vindicates it in the new language. To be sure, the two languages can be compared by means of a separate formal metalanguage, but it does not follow that we must attribute such fully explicatory metalinguistic reasoning to the users.

6.7 A Problem from Putnam: P-Rules and Extended Frameworks

There is yet another problem in the vicinity that it would be cavalier to ignore. Quine's epistemological objection can also be put so as to turn on Putnam's example of law-cluster terms that are defined not by a simple criterion but their inferential role in scientific theories (see Putnam 1962). As definitions, we may consider characterisations like 'force equals mass times acceleration' (Hylton and Kemp's example) to be part of the logico-linguistic framework of the theory under investigation; this would seem to place them with analytic statements. Yet they are integral to scientific theories and express facts like synthetic statements. So the semantic status of law-cluster definitions appears to be ambiguous. Yet to reject their legitimacy in reconstructions of scientific theories on this account would entail the inapplicability of Carnap's methodology of explication to science altogether. How then is the argument to be resisted that the acceptance of law-cluster concepts is incompatible with the application of the a/s distinction to the languages of science?

The answer begins once again with the non-standard nature of Carnap's conception of analyticity, its non-apodictic framework-relativity and austere explicationism, but now we must also note that Carnap was prepared to supplement his apparatus of semantic analysis to expand its reach. What needs attention is how he managed to avoid compromising his basic concepts and distinctions by this supplementation.

These matters were discussed by Carnap when he noted that nothing prevents us from constructing languages with 'extra-logical rules of transformation' (*LSL*, §51). Such languages may include among their primitive sentences so-called laws of nature, the universal sentences of a scientific discipline, as 'P-rules'. P-rules are transformation rules distinct from the more common type, the logico-mathematical 'L-rules'. They are formally distinguished from L-rules by the fact that consistent substitution of their nonlogical terms 'by expressions of the same genus' does not preserve relations of logical consequence. This difference notwithstanding, P-rules can be part of the logico-linguistic framework and play significant roles in the analysis of scientific theories. Note that here, as with law-cluster definitions, specifications of an empirical, synthetic character appear to be infiltrating what is typically held to be a domain of a priori thought, so the worries engendered are highly similar.

A striking example of the use of P-rules is provided by Carnap's demonstration of a radical discontinuity between the theories of special and general relativity. According to *Logical Syntax*, logical symbols are such that sentences built solely from them are determinate (their truth values are fixed for all occasions). Counting the laws of special relativity theory as P-rules, we find that the sentences giving the values of the fundamental tensor are determinate, whereas counting the laws of general relativity as P-rules, we find that the sentences giving the values of the fundamental tensor are indeterminate. It follows that the fundamental tensor is a logical term in special relativity and a descriptive term in general relativity

(*LSL*, §50). The significance of this semantic difference between the two theories becomes apparent when we switch our attention to the pragmatics of their languages. Then we can see that in special relativity the homogeneity of physical space is assumed (its curvature is determined by mathematical laws alone), whereas no such assumption is made in general relativity (where empirical data are required to calculate the curvature of space). So formal semantic distinctions (here that of an expression being either a logical or a descriptive symbol) can mirror further distinctions, but the import of these further distinctions and their applicability cannot be explained by semantics itself. The epistemological distinction mirrored here is to be explained in pragmatics.

Granting this to be an interesting result, the task is to defend the methodology used. Since logico-linguistic frameworks are established conventionally, nothing stops language constructors from adopting not only logical truths but also empirical generalisations as transformation rules and law-cluster definitions besides arbitrary definitions. Including P-rules and law-cluster definitions only requires awareness of the terminological complexities that come with such a move. Extending Carnap's original model in this way does not bring any epistemological commitments not previously incurred; in fact, such extended frameworks for semantical analysis continue to focus on logical structure. (Epistemological concerns can be addressed with their help but, again, this is done in pragmatics.)

One consequence is that in such an extended framework we cannot equate the truths of all framework principles and derived theorems with logical truths or truths following from logical rules and purely conventional definitions. Such extended frameworks present us with a mix of analytic and non-analytic sentences and allow the derivation of either. As long as the distinction between logical and non-logical truths is upheld, as Carnap claimed (*LSL*, §51), no confusion ensues. Instead it ensures that Carnap's defence of analyticity as L-truth yields a workable apparatus for semantical analysis that is applicable, when suitably supplemented, to the analysis of scientific theories. P-rules and law-cluster definitions can be treated as framework principles, but this does not make them 'analytic' in Carnap's sense. Carnap did not spell this out, but his final position on analyticity in the theoretical languages of science is consistent with this.[7]

---

[7] Note that what for Carnap was the analytic component of a scientific theory was only its so-called Carnap sentence, which may be understood as a meaning postulate and its logical consequences. Roughly, the Carnap sentence says that if a theory's Ramsey sentence is true, then so are the theory's pre-Ramseyfied sentences which name the theoretical entities the Ramsey sentence had replaced with second-order variables (see *IPoS*, 270–272).

6.8 An Important Aside

Readers will have noted that the story so far omitted comment on the fact that the logical/descriptive distinction, the differentiation on which the P-rules depended, was not correctly made.[8] One reason for neglecting this notable fact has been the intention not to disturb the flow of argumentation. Even more importantly, the mistake is not fatal. The damage is repairable, as Steve Awodey (2007) showed, by a move that in effect was Carnapian even though it was not he but his associate John Kemeny who made it (1948, 1956). This move involved treating logical validity as truth in all models – truth in all possible interpretations of the non-logical symbols over all possible domains of quantification, as in modern model-theoretic semantics – a move that by the mid-1940s was not yet available to Carnap but that he was happy to presuppose in the 1950s.[9] Along with this, logical operations can be characterised as those that remain invariant under all permutations of the domain of variables. In other words, plugging the modern conception of logical truth in the place Carnap held for it will do nicely.[10]

6.9 The Principle of Tolerance Defended

So far, we have argued that, contrary to widespread presumption, Carnap's a/s distinction is a semantic distinction unburdened by an epistemological office. Its inability to discharge epistemological tasks cannot therefore be counted a failure. It is only the pragmatical counterparts of semantic concepts – the 'corresponding pragmatical concepts' – that figure in epistemological discussions. The conceivable objection that this amounts

---

[8] Logical terms cannot be distinguished as terms that are such that propositions composed purely of them possess a determinate truth value, independent of empirical input, because it is not possible to determine a unique maximal class of symbols (a class that is not extendable) that meets this semantic condition. Nor can, for obvious reasons, the intersection of possible system of symbols yield the maximal set of terms that were to count as logical. See Awodey (2007, 237–240).

[9] Carnap can be read to be doing so at, e.g., (*RSE*, 916) and he explicitly remarked on Kemeny's definition of the 'generalized concept of a model, which is applicable to logical systems of very different forms' (*RSE*, 979). Part 1 of Kemeny (1956) is listed also in the bibliography of *M&N*.

[10] There would be costs, Awodey notes, if the issue of the metalinguistic relativity is resolved as it could be by category theory. This issue – that the logical validity of sentences of object languages depends on that of those we choose to hold true in the metalanguage – was what prompted Carnap to adopt PoT in the first place. Notably, his discussion in (*ESO*) indicates that he did not see this metalinguistic relativity as problematical and we may follow him in this (see Leitgeb and Carus 2020, Appendix B).

to nothing more than inconsequential moving of terminological furniture must now be considered.

Consider Hylton's restatement of Quine's rejection of PoT ('the deepest aspect of his disagreement with Carnap'). 'Carnap holds that analyticity is significant because he holds that the [a/s] distinction corresponds to a distinction between two kinds of justification' and that since Quine 'does not accept the latter distinction' (2021, 458), he also denies that the former distinction is significant. This rendition of Quine's criticism focuses on PoT as the engine behind the a/s distinction, as legitimating the differentiation of the justification available for sentences of each type. Whether the issue is a change of truth value for sentences within an accepted language or an outright change of language, for Quine, 'justification is the same in both cases – equally theoretical and equally pragmatic' (2021, 458). Quine concluded (1951b) that a difference central to Carnap's model of epistemology becomes untenable: the difference between internal and external questions.[11]

Placed squarely in pragmatics, Quine's argumentation criticises PoT's legitimation of the difference in justification accorded to answers to internal and external questions. This diagnosis can be fleshed out further. As we saw, Hylton and Kemp point to the difference that matters by stressing that choices of language do 'not require theoretical justification'. Thus, Quine objected to the (perceived) difference in justification because he rejected what he thought it presupposed: a deficit model of practical reasoning according to which language choice lacked in or did not require some unspecified aspects of theoretical reasoning. For Quine, language choice was no less theoretical than theory choice.

In response, we must question whether Carnap would agree with Quine's reading of PoT as presented here. Where Quine appears to have focussed on how much justification is provided in theoretical and practical reasoning, Carnap focussed on one aspect of the justification involved. Carnap did not think language choice to be less demanding theoretically. So we must ask whether Quine had good reasons to dismiss the significance of the distinction Carnap drew. To find out, let's consider how Carnap could respond to the three charges that can be discerned in

---

[11] In (*ESO*) Carnap distinguished between existence questions internal to a given logico-linguistic framework and existence questions external to such frameworks, and he argued that questions like 'Are there real numbers?' make good sense as internal questions (say within the framework of standard arithmetic) but not externally, as when it is asked outside of any framework whether there really are real numbers. External questions only make sense as questions about whether a framework that allows for them to be spoken about realistically should be adopted.

Quine's criticism: that PoT engaged in unjustifiable justificatory activities, that Carnap held to a deficit model of practical reasoning and that the distinction between theoretical and practical justification was somehow pernicious.

Consider Carnap's PoT. It spelt out the freedom enjoyed by language constructors: '*It is not our business to set up prohibitions, but to arrive at conventions.*' After an intervening paragraph discussing how only utilitarian and context- or purpose-bound reasons can ever be given for issuing proposals for language construction, Carnap continued: '*In logic, there are no morals.* Everyone is at liberty to build up his own logic, i.e. his own form of language, as he wishes. All that is required of him is that, if he wishes to discuss it, he must state his methods clearly, and give syntactical rules instead of philosophical arguments.' (*LSL*, 51–52, original emphases)

As is evident, PoT did not discuss, even less justify differences in justification. To be sure, tolerance in language construction presupposes the abandonment of the view shared still by Frege, Russell and early Wittgenstein that there was a true form of logic. Carnap simply drew out one consequence of this move and left others implicit. But to imply that language construction does not aspire to truth but utility does not amount to denying that language construction proceeds without theoretical justification. Instead it justifies adopting a tolerant attitude to language construction, no more.

To dispel the idea that Carnap held practical reasoning to a lower standard than theoretical reasoning, consider briefly how much rational thought goes into the former on Carnap's own account. He stated apropos a particular language choice: 'The decision of accepting the thing language, although itself not of a cognitive nature, will nevertheless be influenced by theoretical knowledge, just like any other deliberate decision concerning the acceptance of linguistic or other rules.' (*ESO*, 23). Evidently, language choices are open to theoretical considerations. What may be stressed, moreover, is how cognition and conation are intertwined and how that which is 'itself not of a cognitive nature' – here the decision to speak one way or other – is cognitively embedded while retaining executive autonomy. It is only the exercise of will in fixing a goal and embarking upon conscious action that is non-cognitive (and could not be otherwise). This exercise of will can be informed by theoretical knowledge but it is not determined by it. The theoretical knowledge that becomes relevant here can be of all sorts, but this relevance is not arbitrary, as Carnap stressed: 'The purpose for which the language is intended to be used, for instance, the purpose of communicating factual knowledge, will determine which factors are relevant for the decision' (*ESO*, 23). Note that it is a two-step process that Carnap envisaged here: it is not the purpose alone that fixes what candidate language best serves it. Rather, the nature of the purpose indicates what the factors are in the light of which a ranking of candidates is possible. Far from not requiring theoretical justification, making pragmatic choices tends to be a highly theoretically informed affair.

But what about the distinction introduced by Carnap's non-cognitivism (*RSE*, 1003–1005) between truth-valuable and non-truth-valuable sentences? That the pure value statements that are fundamental for normative discourse are not truth-valuable indicated for Carnap merely the semantic difference between normative and descriptive, fact-stating discourses. It is a distinction without ontological import. In epistemological terms, choice of language is not worse off in principle than theory choice: agreement about intersubjectively accessible data concerning which logico-linguistic forms are useful for what purposes guides the choice of languages, just as agreement about intersubjectively accessible data of experimental fact guides theory choice.[12] In short, it need not be denied that there are differences between theoretical and practical considerations; but despite the difference in target (truth vs. utility), the epistemic labour going into both types of investigation is fully comparable. (That Carnap implicitly accepted purposes other than communicating factual knowledge as legitimate options for determining the criteria to evaluate candidate languages also suggests that wide applicability of his model, not a ranking of rationalities involved, was his concern.)

There remains the charge that PoT wrongly distinguishes two types of justification. It is undeniable that according to PoT theoretical and practical reasonings answer to different criteria, truth and utility respectively. They differ in that determining utility presupposes that a goal has been set and the determination of this, unless itself instrumental, is not truth-evaluable. Carnap appears to have taken this difference to be a basic fact of cognitive life and awareness of it to mark a reflective cognitive life; it is not something he argued for when he first announced PoT or later adverted to it. Only once did he discuss how he understood the descriptive/normative distinction. Strikingly, he then specified his non-cognitivism also as a linguistic proposal (*RSE*, 1003). Clearly, PoT is not a free-standing doctrine but is an integral part of how Carnap thinks of philosophy as explication.

---

[12] As Quine himself once put it: 'The normative here, as elsewhere in engineering, becomes descriptive when the terminal parameter is expressed' (1986, 665).

But is this distinction of theoretical justification centring on truth and practical justification centring on utility mistaken? We can ask whether Quine would wish to revert to the idea of there being one true logic and whether he would wish to oppose the distinction between theoretical and practical reason and the non-cognitivist denial of truth valuability to unconditional norms. The answer is negative. Quine's extensionalism is legendary, of course. However, 'limit[ing] the term "logic" to the logic of truth functions, quantification and identity, drawing the line at the reification of classes' (2001/2008, 504) leaves a lot of leeway still and certainly does not appeal to there being one true logic. As regards the distinction between types of justification, Quine endorsed 'the bipartite nature of motivation: belief and valuation intertwined ... the deep old duality of thought and feeling' and with it the idea that 'ultimate ends' remain 'unreduced and so unjustified' (1978/1981, 55 and 64). When he concluded: 'Natural science owes its objectivity to its intersubjective checkpoints in observation sentences, but there is no such rock bottom for moral judgments' (1986, 664), Quine was no less non-cognitivist than Carnap.

We conclude therefore that with PoT not engaging in justificatory activities, with Carnap not holding to a deficit model of practical reasoning and with the distinction between theoretical and practical reason rendered innocuous – indeed shown to be shared by Quine himself – the epistemological criticism of the a/s distinction and of PoT fails.

6.10 Pragmatics and Naturalised Epistemology

We may add that unless other arguments are forthcoming, it also follows that Carnap's a/s distinction and epistemological naturalism vis-à-vis empirical science are not incompatible. Concerning the pursuit of epistemological questions in pragmatics, several points bear mentioning to stress the naturalistic perspective that Carnap took on these matters.

First, there is the nature or status of PoT itself. We saw that it comes with a significant number of descriptive presuppositions about what is involved in theory change and in change of language, but they do not detract from the normative message demanding tolerance of logicolinguistic variety provided the rules involved are made transparent. In this respect, PoT is a regulative principle of scientific metatheory. That tolerance is instrumentally justifiable makes the norm it represents acceptable for use in naturalistic accounts of science.

Another important consequence of Carnap having designated pragmatics to be the proper arena of epistemological contention is that it indicates clearly that such questions are to be answered in a naturalistic setting (informed by psychology, sociology and other empirical studies of the processes of reasoning and decision-making) and not in an a priori fashion from a logician's armchair. However tentative Carnap's understanding of model theory may have been initially, he did not mistake it for epistemology. Justification of theory choice in science was no less holistic or pragmatic for Carnap than for Quine and the same holds for choices of language (see his *LSL*, 317–318). This seeming banality needs stating in view of claims to the contrary encouraged by Quine's occasional rhetoric (1969b) and should dispose of one source of disquiet felt about Carnap's use of the a/s distinction.

To be sure, pragmatical counterparts of the semantic concepts are far from wholly conventionally chosen: not any old explication of a confused meaning will fit the bill of the explanatory project now pursued. The pragmatic concept of analyticity is a theoretical concept pertaining to linguistics, psychology and sociology that has to prove its worth in the causal explanation of behaviour.[13] In that context, the a/s distinction – to be precise: the pragmatical counterpart of the semantic a/s distinction – may also perform some epistemological duties, like Quine's version in language learning. But it may also do still more, thanks to the resources that Carnap's version can call upon. Once an explication of a concept has been identified that is more or less true to the usage of speakers (demanding more would be unrealistic), insights from semantics (which abstracts from the business of justifying knowledge claims) can be called upon to establish logico-linguistic facts of given languages – call them 'framework dependencies' – that no individual knowledge claim can contest. By laying bare presuppositions and exploring variations of the meaning relations that pragmatics indicates to obtain in particular historical situations, semantics can add the information required to establish within pragmatics a 'space of reasons' amidst the push and pull of the interests of different researchers.

Consider therefore the point made by Hannes Leitgeb and André Carus that Carnap's notion of analyticity 'always seems to have more or less the same functional role to play – to keep track of those statements in a linguistic framework that 'come with' the framework, that express the

---

[13] How the (inevitably less precise) pragmatic counterparts of analyticity are fallibly to be identified in behavioural terms as theoretical terms of empirical science is shown in Carnap (1955a). How Carnap could have responded to what is widely held to be Quine's response (e.g., Harman 1996, 397) – the indeterminacy of translation (1960, ch. 2) – must be discussed on another occasion.

framework's own resources, that are presupposed in the framework, and which do not have any empirical content on their own'. Following Friedman (2001) Leitgeb and Carus suggest that 'the Carnapian conception of analyticity in a framework may serve to explicate' what elsewhere was called 'relative or constitutive apriority: the relational property of sentences being presupposed by, and enabling, the formulation, truth-conditionality and empirical justification of scientific hypotheses belonging to a joint scientific paradigm' (2020, Supplement B, emphases dropped). This suggestion is readily implemented in our understanding: while the logical presuppositions of the formulation and truth-conditionality of hypotheses are dealt with by semantics, their bearing on issues concerning empirical justification is dealt with by pragmatics. (In this fashion, the conception of relative apriority may be considered to have been naturalised.) Again, the semantic a/s distinction facilitates but remains distinct from epistemology.

In short, far from representing superannuated philosophical ideas that ought to be retired, Carnapian analyticity provides means for gaining insights into scientific theories – epistemological insights no less, once semantic distinctions are applied via their pragmatical counterparts – that are highly significant for understanding the history of science. Was it a coincidence that, in his reply to Quine, Carnap remarked about a change of scientific language (as opposed to changes in truth values of synthetic sentences within it) that it 'constitutes a radical alteration, sometimes a revolution, and it occurs only at certain historically decisive points in the development of science' (*RSE*, 921)?[14]

6.11 Conclusion

Carnap's distinctions between analytical and synthetic truths and logical and descriptive terms are formal distinctions drawn for specific purposes. They are tools for the semantical analysis of sets of sentences generally and the theories of science in particular, allowing the determination of certain formal properties and meaning relations, but they do not describe a reality beyond them. Constituting themselves as linguistic proposals, Carnap's distinctions make no ontological or epistemological claims. They are

---

[14] Carnap's reply was written in the mid-1950s, well before Kuhn (1962) for which Carnap was one of the series editors who happily accepted the manuscript for publication (see Reisch 1991). For Carnap's earlier comment about incommensurable language change in science see his (1936/1949, 126).

fundamental and indispensable for Carnap's project but not foundational, neither in the former nor the latter sense. Beyond descriptive analyses, they are intended for purposes of formal language construction and of what Carnap called 'explication', the clarification of contested concepts (1945a; *ESO*).

Carnap's distinctions are not meant to mirror language use in the wild. As a semantic concept, analyticity is not obliged to respond to the epistemological concerns that are rightly placed on its unexplicated colloquial version. In order to bear on languages actually used, of course, explications must meet the conditions of material adequacy that are set out in pragmatics. Then their pragmatical counterparts can be employed for criticism or support of knowledge claims in the context of a naturalistic epistemology. Investigations of language change likewise must be pursued in pragmatics. Puzzlement incurred by the inclusion in extended semantical frameworks of determinations of distinctly empirical provenance is resolved by guarding against misleading attributions of analyticity. More generally, the Quinean objection to PoT has been shown to be inapplicable in pragmatics. In sum, by explicitly drawing the distinction between applications of analyticity in semantics and pragmatics it is possible not only to defend Carnap's a/s distinction against Quine but also to retain important insights into the structure of scientific theories.

To conclude, let us first note that Quineans like Hylton and Kemp are fully justified in foregrounding the epistemological objection to analyticity and tolerance in their account of Quine's conception of philosophy: undoubtedly, it plays a constitutive role there. If the argument that we have developed here holds, however, this objection fails against Carnap's understanding of tolerance and analyticity. That the latter faces still other challenges goes without saying.[15] But progress can be made when the philosophically deflationist agenda driving Carnap's explicationism is recognised.

---

[15] For a new defence in the context of the so-called bipartite metatheory conception of science, see Bentley (2023).

CHAPTER 7

Carnapian Explication
Origins and Shifting Goals
Erich H. Reck[*]

7.1 Introduction

One of Rudolf Carnap's enduring contributions to philosophy consists of his explicit articulation, in writings from the late 1940s and early '50s, of the method of "explication."[1] Very roughly, an explication involves the replacement of a vague and relatively informal concept by a similar, simpler, more exact, and more fruitful substitute. As a philosophical method, Carnapian explication is a descendant of "logical analysis," "logical construction," and "rational reconstruction"; but it is also modeled on the use of definitions in mathematics and the natural sciences. There is a strand within analytic philosophy where methods of this kind have been applied continuously, from Frege and Russell in early analytic philosophy, through Carnap, Quine, Goodman, and others in the middle of the twentieth century, all the way to twenty-first-century "formal" or "mathematical philosophy."[2] Current approaches called "conceptual

---

[*] Earlier versions of this chapter were presented as talks in the *Logik Café*, University of Vienna, November 22, 2021, and at *HOPOS 2022*, UC Irvine, June 21, 2022. I am indebted to audience members at both events for comments, especially Anton Alexandrov, Gergely Ambrus, Christian Damböck, Gary Ebbs, Martin Kusch, Sean Morris, and Georg Schiemer. I am also grateful to Georg Brun, André Carus, Mirja Hartimo, Sean Morris, and Georg Schiemer for valuable feedback on a written draft. Finally, I would like to thank Alan Richardson and Adam Tamas Tuboly, the editors of this volume, for inviting me to contribute to it and for their helpful suggestions. The responsibility for all remaining problems remains with me, as usual, especially since I did not follow all the advice I received.

[1] See Carnap (*M&N*, *LFP*), the two texts on which I will focus, as well as Carnap (1945a, *IA*, *RSE*). Instead of calling explication a "method," one could talk about a "program" or "ideal"; cf. the last chapter of Carus (2007).

[2] Often this strand in analytic philosophy is misleadingly called "ideal language philosophy." For recent discussion of "formal" or "mathematical philosophy," see Leitgeb (2013); Hanson and Hendricks (2018); and the references in them.

engineering" and "ameliorative analysis" are also related, in more or less direct ways.[3]

A significant number of analytic philosophers have thus used explication or methods close to it but typically without addressing methodological aspects much. Such philosophers want to give explications rather than talk about the method they embody.[4] In fact, until recently Carnap was one of very few thinkers who elaborated on methodological aspects; hence the value of his corresponding remarks. At the same time, Carnap's elaborations remained sketchy and incomplete too. Apart from that, he highlighted a distinctive pragmatist and pluralist side of explication that deserves more attention. Basically, for Carnap an explication is not meant to be correct in any veridical sense; instead, it is meant to be pragmatically useful or more useful than its alternatives. This invites a crucial question: Useful with respect to what goal or goals? The present essay considers possible answers to that question and their consequences.

The essay proceeds as follows: I will start with a brief summary of Carnap's valuable but incomplete elaboration of explication. Then I will approach my topic again from a different angle, by raising several historical questions: What were the models, prototypes, or paradigms for Carnap when he articulated this method? Which specific goals, and which broader agendas, were involved in them? How are those related to Carnap's own goals and agendas? And can we draw any conclusions, also systematically, about the strengths and weaknesses of explication from such considerations? Put differently, I will examine the origins, subsequent tendencies and shifts, as well as resulting gains and losses associated with explication. Another main goal will be to examine the conception of philosophy that corresponds to making explication one's main, or even one's only, philosophical method.[5]

---

[3] For current discussions of conceptual engineering, see Cappelen (2018) and Burgess, Cappelen, and Plunckett (2020); for its relationship to ameliorative analysis, see Dutilh Novaes (2018) and the references in it.

[4] There are notable exceptions, e.g., Greimann (2007, 2012); Brun (2016, 2020); and Feldbacher-Escamilla (2021). Concerning Carnap, see also Carus (2007); Reck (2012); and Dutilh Novaes and Reck (2017).

[5] In examining explication critically, my own method will be "philosophical history," i.e., the contextually sensitive examination of historical figures and developments with the goal of contributing to current philosophy. My focus on origins and tendencies, on goals and agendas, and on the resulting conception of philosophy is influenced by Ernst Cassirer's critical philosophy. There are also parallels to "genealogy" as used by other philosophers, including Nietzsche, Foucault, Edward Craig, and Bernard Williams; see Dutilh Novaes (2020) and Queloz (2021). Similarly for the study of goals and values in Husserl's mature phenomenology; see Hartimo (2021).

7.2 Carnap's Explicit Discussion of Explication

The first use of the term "explication," in Carnap's technical sense, occurs in his article "Two Conceptions of Probability." A more elaborate discussion of explication, as a philosophical method, occurs in *Meaning and Necessity*. There Carnap characterizes it as follows:

> The task of making more exact a vague or not quite exact concept used in everyday life or in an earlier stage of scientific or logical development, or rather of replacing it by a newly constructed, more exact concept, belongs among the most important tasks of logical analysis and logical construction. We call this the task of explicating, or of giving an *explication* for, the earlier concept. (*M&N*, 7–8, original emphasis)

Similarly but more concisely, he writes in *Logical Foundations of Probability*: "By an *explication* we understand the transformation of an inexact prescientific concept, the *explicandum*, into an exact concept, the *explicatum*" (*LFP*, 1, original emphasis). Later commentators have also used "conceptual engineering" for the method articulated by Carnap, based on the fact that he talks about "language engineering" occasionally.[6]

As its title makes clear, the two core concepts to be explicated in Carnap's 1947 book are "meaning" and "necessity." In this 1950 book, as well as the closely related 1945 article, his focus is on "probability" and "confirmation," two other targets of explication. The longer quote above indicates that Carnap thinks of his approach in the 1940–1950s not as a radical departure from but as the development of earlier approaches, especially "logical analysis" and "logical construction" (Russellian terminology). There is also a direct link to the method of "rational reconstruction" in Carnap's earlier *Der logische Aufbau der Welt* (1928).[7] Among the concepts "analyzed" and "reconstructed" in his earlier works, from the 1920s to the early '40s, are: "space" (in various senses); "completeness" (for axiom systems); and "analytic" or "logical truth" (building on Wittgenstein's notion of "tautology").[8] In the 1950s–1960s, he treats

---

[6] See (*IA*, 66), also Creath (1990a, 412). I owe this point and the references to Georg Brun.
[7] In the preface to the second edition of *Aufbau*, published in 1961, Carnap actually starts to replace the label "logical reconstruction" explicitly by "explication," as Georg Brun pointed out to me. Hence, this early book can be seen as providing Carnapian explications for a wide range of empirical concepts.
[8] Cf. Carnap's *Der Raum*, *Allgemeine Axiomatik* (2000), *Logische Syntax der Sprache* (*LSS*) and *Introduction to Semantics* (*IS*), respectively; see Leitgeb and Carus (2020) for precise references.

concepts from the natural sciences under "explication" as well, for instance, that of "entropy."[9]

When an explication for a concept is proposed, how are we to evaluate that proposal? I already mentioned that for Carnap this does not involve determining whether the *explicatum* is descriptively correct or veridical, in the sense that it gets the *explicandum* right (while perhaps making it more explicit). He emphasizes this point as follows:

> Strictly speaking, the question whether the solution is right or wrong makes no good sense ... The question should rather be whether the proposed solution is satisfactory, whether it is more satisfactory than another one, and the like. (*LFP*, 4)

Why is there no "right or wrong" for an explication? For one thing, Carnap rejects that there are concepts existing "out there," in some realist sense, that might be matched by an explication. For another, he thinks of the meanings of terms for the *explicanda*, as used "in everyday life and in an earlier stage of scientific or logical development," as being too inexact or indeterminate; with respect to them, there would be "no clear-cut answer" whether they have been matched or not (*LFP*, 4). This clarifies how not to think about the success of an explication. By talking about being "satisfactory" (the pragmatist aspect), or "more satisfactory" than alternatives (a form of pluralism), Carnap also points in a more positive direction.[10] But how exactly should "satisfaction" be understood here?

One feature that makes Carnap's discussion of explication in the late 1940s and early'50s valuable is his attempt to answer that question explicitly. He does so by formulating four desiderata that a satisfactory explication is meant to satisfy: "A concept must fulfill the following requirements in order to be an adequate explicatum ... : (1) similarity to the explicandum; (2) exactness; (3) fruitfulness; (4) simplicity" (*LFP*, 5). He then goes on to clarify these four requirements, at least to some degree. Concerning desideratum (i), "similarity," his main clarification is the following:

> The explicatum is to be *similar* to the explicandum in such a way that in most cases in which the explicandum has so far been used, the explicatum

---

[9] Cf. Carnap (1977). For an early discussion of scientific concepts by him (more on which below), see Carnap (1926/2019). I will add to this list of concepts explicated by Carnap later.

[10] As mentioned to me by Christian Damböck, pragmatist and pluralist aspects are already present in Carnap's *Aufbau* and related texts from the early 1920s, although more implicitly. But Carnap becomes more pluralist in the 1930s (e.g., concerning logic); and he is more explicit about both aspects in the 1940s–1950s.

can be used; however, close similarity is not required, and considerable differences are permitted. (*LFP*, 7, my emphasis)

Notice here, for our later discussion, the intended continuity of "uses" of the explicatum with respect to earlier uses of the explicandum, also the fact that "close similarity" is not required. Carnap clarifies "exactness," his desideratum (ii), further thus:

> The characterization of the explicatum, that is, the rules of its use (for instance, in the form of a definition), is to be given in an *exact* form, so as to introduce the explicatum into a well-connected system of scientific concepts. (*LFP*, 7, original emphasis)

In this passage, note the reference to a "well-connected system of scientific concepts" as the proper framework in which to place an explicatum. In Carnap's own cases, "exactness" is often tied to formalization in logic and mathematics. But this is not strictly required by him, as we can see here; and as other passages indicate, "exactness" can come in degrees.

Given his pragmatic and pluralist understanding of explication, Carnap's desideratum (iii), "fruitfulness," is arguably the most central. Concerning it, he tells us: "The explicatum is to be a fruitful concept ... useful for the formulation of many universal statements (empirical laws in the case of a nonlogical concept, logical theorems in the case of a logical concept)" (*LFP*, 7). Noteworthy here, especially for my purposes, is that Carnap mentions only two kinds of "universal statements" in which an explicatum can be used fruitfully: empirical laws and logical theorems. This suggests a tight connection between explication and concept formation in the sciences and in logic, indeed a kind of amalgamation of them. Finally, Carnap is less explicit about his desideratum (iv), "simplicity." Presumably we are to understand it along parallel lines, that is, in terms of how simplicity is judged in the sciences and in logic.

To conclude this section, let me quote one more passage in which Carnap clarifies two of his four desiderata together, "similarity" and "fruitfulness." This passage is also noteworthy because of how it connects Carnapian explication to a simple scientific example, namely, the move from the everyday concept "fish" to that of "piscis" in zoology:

> When we compare the explicandum Fish with the explicatum Piscis, we see that they do not even approximately coincide ... What was [the zoologists'] motive for ... artificially constructing the new concept Piscis far remote from any concept in the prescientific language? The reason was that [they] realized the fact that the concept Piscis promises to be much more fruitful

than any concept more similar to Fish. A scientific concept is the more fruitful the more it can be brought into connection with other concepts on the basis of observed facts; in other words, the more it can be used for the formulation of laws. (*LFP*, 6)

As this quotation confirms, "similarity" is demanded only in a loose sense for Carnap. (Dolphins, wales, etc., included under "fish," can be excluded from "piscis.") In contrast, considerations of "fruitfulness" are crucial. And again, fruitfulness is tied to "the formulation of laws."

One can raise various questions about Carnap's four desiderata for explication.[11] In what follows, I will focus on two: (1) As we just saw, several of them, especially "similarity" and "fruitfulness," are elaborated in terms of relevant "uses." Such uses must involve a goal or goals relative to which the explication is to be judged. This leads to the question: What are the goals at issue here; or more broadly, what kind of agenda is guiding Carnap in this context? (2) As we also saw, in clarifying his four desiderata, Carnap moves seamlessly back and forth between concept formation in philosophy, on the one hand, and in logic and the sciences, on the other hand. That invites the question: What conception of philosophy corresponds to promoting explication along such lines? Answering those questions will be central to what follows.

7.3 Carnap's Paradigms for Explication

In Carnap's discussion of his desiderata for explication in the 1940s–1950s, the two questions just raised are not answered directly and fully, although there are relevant hints. To provide fuller answers, we have to consider more indirect evidence. One source of such evidence is what Carnap writes about earlier prototypes or models for explication. He addresses that topic both in *Meaning and Necessity* and *Logical Foundations of Probability*. In the former, he lists three contributions to logic and the foundations of mathematics as models for his approach, while in the latter he adds several scientific models. Let me consider them in that order.

The first paradigmatic model for Carnapian explication, in the sense of previous work that inspired Carnap methodologically, consists of Gottlob Frege's and Bertrand Russell's analysis of the natural numbers. A widely

---

[11] One can ask, e.g., about tensions between them; see Reck (2012) and Dutilh Novaes and Reck (2017).

known exposition of it, which Carnap follows, is provided in Russell's *Introduction to Mathematical Philosophy* (1919). In Carnap's words, the *explicandum* in this case is "the term 'two' in the not quite exact meaning in which it is used in everyday life and applied mathematics," while the *explicatum*, as provided by Frege and Russell, is "the class of pair-classes" (*M&N*, 8). (Similarly for "zero," "one," "three," etc.) That is to say, Carnap's first paradigm for explication is the "Frege-Russell conception" of natural numbers, as it is often called, in terms of equivalence classes of equinumerous classes.

The second paradigm Carnap highlights occurs again in Frege's and Russell's writings. Here the *explicandum* consists of "phrases of the form 'the so-and-so'" as used ordinarily, in scientific contexts, as well as in philosophy; and Carnap points to "the various interpretations of descriptions by Frege, Russell, and others" as the *explicatum* (*M&N*, 8). In other words, he has in mind Frege's, Russell's, and related analyses of definite descriptions. Frege's approach to this issue centers around his sense-reference distinction, famous from "Über Sinn und Bedeutung" (1892). Russell's alternative consists of his equally famous "theory of descriptions," introduced in "On Denoting" (1905), which postulates a crucial difference between the ordinary grammar and the underlying logical form of sentences as revealed by "logical analysis."

As his third paradigm for explication, Carnap mentions Alfred Tarski's account of truth. In Carnap's words again, the *explicandum* in that case consists of "the concept of truth as used in everyday language ... and in all of traditional and modern logic," while the *explicatum* is "the semantic concept of truth" in Tarski's sense (*M&N*, 8). The latter is introduced by Tarski in the 1930s, then elaborated further, also by Carnap himself, in the 1940s, and turns into the full "model-theoretic notion of truth" in the 1950s (in works by Tarski, Vaught, etc.).[12] Like the first two, this third paradigm grows out of modern logic. More precisely, it is a core product of early meta-logical studies from the 1920s on, by Tarski, Hilbert, Gödel, and others.

In all three models for explication, as just discussed, formalization is crucial. Thus, increasing exactness and fruitfulness, as two central desiderata, is achieved by employing the tools of formal logic. Formal-logical precisifications of informal concepts are typical for Carnap's own works as well (his explications of completeness, analyticity, meaning, necessity,

---

[12] For more on the history, see Schiemer and Reck (2013); see also the essay by Pierre Wagner in this volume (Chapter 8).

etc.). As that makes clear, his elaboration of the method of explication is influenced strongly by work in meta-logic from the 1920s–1940s. In addition, it seems important for Carnap to present himself as standing in the philosophical tradition of Frege, Russell, and Tarski. This indicates his endorsement of the conception of philosophy to which their works leads.

At the same time, several other models are mentioned by Carnap as well, mostly in *Logical Foundations of Probability* (*LFP*, 5–6). Rather than relying on logical formalization, these involve the broader methods of the sciences, especially scientific concept formation. One came up already: the replacement of the concept of "fish" by the zoological concept of "piscis" (truly jawed vertebrate). A second model is the shift from the pre- or proto-scientific concept of "salt" to "sodium chloride" (NaCl) in chemistry. Tied closely to everyday life is a third example: the move from ordinary qualitative comparisons of "warmer" and "colder" to the quantitative concept of temperature (measured in Celsius, Fahrenheit, etc.).[13] A final Carnapian model is more technical again: the transition from informal talk about dimension, in everyday life and earlier mathematics, to Karl Menger's concept and mathematical theory of dimension.[14]

Taking seriously not just Carnap's logical paradigms for explication but also his scientific models is relevant for several reasons. First, and as already noted, it shows that Carnapian explication should not be identified with logical formalization, central as the latter is to his own work. Second, those models illustrate how Carnap wants to tie "exactness" not to formal logic but, more broadly, to "introducing the explicatum into a well-connected system of scientific concepts." Third, they indicate what kind of uses of explication are intended. In the examples mentioned, those uses range from logic and the foundations of mathematics through biology, chemistry, physics, and mathematics, all the way to everyday life. This brings us back to the question of which goals and broader agenda Carnap has in mind for explication.

---

[13] This and similar concepts are discussed extensively, in connection with metrology, in Carnap (1926/2019). I am indebted to Anton Alexandrov and Alan Richardson for making me see their relevance more; see also Richardson (2013). Carnap was influenced by scientists like Mach, Einstein, and Poincaré too; yet he does not include contributions by them in his list of paradigms for explication.

[14] Menger, one of whose main achievements was that theory, interacted with Carnap in the Vienna Circle. It is noteworthy that Menger (1928) includes a discussion of criteria of adequacy for relevant "definitions."

7.4 Frege and Russell on Numbers: Goals and Broader Agendas

It is natural to assume that Carnapian explication, viewed as a method in philosophy, should allow us to address philosophical problems. But does that really fit all the examples Carnap mentions? And where it fits, what kind of philosophical problems are at issue? Concerning these questions, let us return to Carnap's paradigmatic models once more. To start with: Which philosophical problems did Frege and Russell address by introducing the Frege-Russell conception of number? Also, what were their broader agendas in the background? And how does that reflect back on their conceptions of philosophy?

Frege is most explicit about his goals and his broader agenda in *The Foundations of Arithmetic* (Frege 1884/1980). There are two main motivations for his investigation, as he tells us: one mathematical, the other philosophical. On the mathematical side, he thinks it is time to return to a strong demand for rigor, after a period in which important parts of mathematics, such as the Calculus, were pushed ahead without a clear sense of their foundations. In his own words, Frege calls for renewing "Euclidean rigor" (1884/1980, section 1). This includes providing clear definitions of concepts, explicit formulations of basic assumptions, and gapless proofs based on them. More particularly, it is a scandal, Frege urges, how sloppy his contemporaries are with respect to the definition of numbers. This applies even in the simplest case, the natural numbers, as he goes on to document in the first half of *Foundations*. Hence the need to ask: What are numbers? In the rest of *Foundations*, he sketches a more satisfactory answer.

As a second motivation for his inquiry, Frege mentions philosophical questions about arithmetic truths, in particular whether they are empirical or a priori, analytic or synthetic (1884/1980, section 3). In this context, he presents his project as a response to philosophers such as Kant, for whom arithmetic is synthetic a priori, and Mill, who claims that it is empirical. To be able to adjudicate such claims in a definitive way Frege developed his new logic. Based on it, he wants to show that arithmetic can be reduced to logic alone. His definition of numbers, spelled out further in *Basic Laws of Arithmetic* (Frege 1893/1903), is a core part of that project. To pursue it, Frege combines mathematical, philosophical, and logical considerations. Indeed, he urges that a new combination of philosophy and mathematics is needed, with modern logic as the link. But as he soon learns from criticisms of his approach, combining them along such lines is not uncontroversial.

Frege's explicit goals are, again, to provide arithmetic with a more rigorous foundation and to answer certain philosophical questions about it. In pursuing these goals, he starts with a fairly traditional conception of philosophy. But his methods, introduced to enable further progress, are new. Is his logicist reconstruction of arithmetic meant as an explication in Carnap's sense; or is it intended as a stronger form of analysis, one that reveals the "true nature" of numbers? As Frege is often assumed to be a "Platonist," he tends to be interpreted the latter way; yet it is hard to be sure. Sometimes the suggestion seems to be that his approach makes explicit the senses, or at least the references, that arithmetic terms had all along. At other times, he seems to hold that arithmetic was so vague and unsystematic before his work that there are no senses or references to preserve, hence that it is a matter of providing both for the first time.[15]

Like Frege, Russell starts with a fairly traditional, partly Kantian conception of philosophy. The first detailed presentation of his logicist reconstruction of arithmetic occurs in *Principles of Mathematics* (1903). At this early point in his career, Russell's goals are both mathematical and philosophical as well, in the sense of providing mathematics with a more secure foundation and responding to earlier views about its epistemological status. His writings from the early 1900s also display, more clearly than Frege's, adherence to a strong form of analysis, which includes revealing the real but hidden "logical form" of arithmetic and similar truths. In the following decades, Russell's basic assumptions, methods, and goals change, however. This is partly driven by philosophical discoveries, for example, that of his theory of descriptions. As a result, in the 1910s he starts to endorse a form of eliminative reconstruction tied to the use of Occam's Razor.[16]

The eliminativism adopted by Russell is reflected in a remark about the logicist definition of numbers from his *Introduction to Mathematical Philosophy* (1919). As he writes:

> So far we have not suggested anything in the slightest degree paradoxical. But when we come to the actual definitions of numbers we cannot avoid what must at first sight seem a paradox, though this perception will soon

---

[15] Tyler Burge has argued for the former interpretation of Frege's project, i.e., for him aiming at a strong form of analysis, while Joan Weiner has argued for the latter. For references, see Reck (2007a), which connects this debate to Carnapian explication. Frege's relevant views also developed over time; see Reck (2005).

[16] Early on Russell adopts G. E. Moore's form of analysis. The shift to an eliminative approach is implicit in *Principia Mathematica* (1910–1913), e.g., in his remarks on the continuum; see Shieh (2017, 110). In Russell (1914, 1919), it has become explicit. Here I am indebted to Sean Morris and Sanford Shieh.

wear off. We naturally think that the class of couples (for example) is something different from the number 2. But there is no doubt about the class of couples. It is indubitable and not difficult to define, whereas the number 2, in any other sense, is a metaphysical entity about which we can never feel sure that it exists or that we have tracked it down. It is therefore more prudent to content ourselves with the class of couples, which we are sure of, than to hunt for a problematic number 2, which must always remain elusive ... At the expense of a little oddity, this definition secures definiteness and indubitability; and it is not difficult to prove that numbers so defined have all the properties that we expect numbers to have. (Russell 1919, 14)

At this point, capturing the "real nature of numbers," along "metaphysical" lines, is no longer Russell's goal; we can apply Occam's Razor to such ideas. Instead, what suffices is a definition of numbers that provides "definite entities" with the needed mathematical properties.

At the end of the 1910s, Russell has moved a considerable distance beyond strong forms of analysis and towards Carnapian explication. In the early 1920s, he applies the new approach more widely, for example, to the nature of points in space, physical objects, and mental entities. In that context, he formulates a general methodological principle: "Whenever possible, substitute constructions out of known entities for inferences to unknown entities" (Russell 1924/1958, 160). While Russell keeps responding to traditional philosophical problems, his goals have shifted. Compared to Frege, he has also adopted a much more wide-ranging agenda, far beyond the philosophy of mathematics. Finally, by making "logical construction" his core method, Russell advertises a new conception of philosophy: "mathematical philosophy."[17]

7.5 Frege and Russell on Descriptions: Goals and Broader Agendas

The introduction of Russell's theory of descriptions is a core part of the philosophical shift just described. Before discussing it further, let us consider Frege's approach to descriptions briefly. Compared to Russell, Frege's philosophical ambitions remain more constrained, basically to logic and the philosophy of mathematics. Still, he starts to make forays into other areas as well, especially by addressing questions about language and

---

[17] Russell's approach keeps changing. Later in the 1920s, he gives up "logical construction," disappointed by its results, and adopts more naturalistic forms of philosophy. I owe this observation to Gergely Ambrus.

thought. The origin of Frege's interest in such questions is how to understand arithmetic equations. In "On Sense and Reference" (1892) and related writings, this leads to broader discussions. A core problem for Frege, throughout, is the "content" of names and definite descriptions, including "the number two," "the center of the Solar System," and "the Morning Star." To solve that problem, he starts assigning both sense (*Sinn*) and reference (*Bedeutung*) to all of them.

Frege's sense-reference distinction, including his account of definite descriptions, is often seen as the beginning of analytic philosophy of language. Frege does turn increasingly to issues about language; and in doing so, he takes "the linguistic turn," that is, he starts to address philosophical problems by analyzing language. This includes whether numbers should be conceived of as logical objects, as opposed to concepts, mental entities, or mere signs. Did Frege aim at developing a systematic theory of meaning, for example, a truth-conditional account as made prominent by Michael Dummett and Donald Davidson later? This is again a controversial issue in the Frege literature.[18] Without deciding it, I assume it is uncontroversial that he makes suggestions one can try to develop systematically, as Carnap does in *Meaning and Necessity*.

Russell's theory of descriptions grows out of his long-lasting interest in how to analyze propositions. This concerns mathematics but, for example, also his break from British Idealism. Another relevant context is his response to Alexius Meinong's analysis of judgments. While sympathetic to it initially, the theory of descriptions is introduced in "On Denoting" (1905) as a sharp criticism of Meinong (and Frege). It allows Russell to bypass commitments to Meinongian entities, like "unicorns" and "round squares," that "do not exist but subsist." More broadly, his theory is meant to reshape debates in logic, mathematics, epistemology, and the philosophy of mind. Its central thesis – that a proposition's "grammatical form" can differ radically from its deeper "logical form" – is picked up enthusiastically by Russellians like Wittgenstein, Frank Ramsey, and Carnap, as reflected in Ramsey's well-known remark that what Russell provided is a "paradigm for philosophy."

Russell's theory of descriptions allows to avoid problematic metaphysical assumptions seemingly forced on us by philosophical analysis. This applies to Meinong's cases but also to the philosophy of mathematics

---

[18] While many Frege scholars have contributed to this controversy, one might take Michael Dummett and Joan Weiner as main representatives of the "Yes" and "No" sides; see Weiner (2021) also for further references.

where it informs Russell's "no-classes theory of classes." While numbers are still constructed as equivalence classes of classes by him, the seeming reference to classes is now replaced by statements involving "propositional functions" alone. This is what makes Russell's perspective on mathematics eliminative in an even stronger sense. And again, the approach is meant to be used beyond mathematics. In several writings from the 1910s, such as *Our Knowledge of the External World* (1914) and *Introduction to Mathematical Philosophy* (1919), Russell promotes it as the center of a far-reaching, ambitious program, one in which a broad range of metaphysical baggage is "shaved away" by Occam's razor.

7.6 Tarski on Truth: Goals and Broader Agenda

It is well known that Carnap took logic classes with Frege at the University of Jena in the early 1910s, although, as he tells us, he grasped their full significance only after re-reading Frege's works in the early 1920s. During the same period, he also studied Russell's writings. It is plausible, then, that he comes to view the significance of Frege's works through Russellian eyes. Carnap also adopts Russell's logical-constructivist conception of philosophy wholeheartedly. In addition, in 1930 he meets Tarski. He is immediately impressed by Tarski's work on metalogic. Soon thereafter, he becomes one of the first to endorse Tarski's account of truth, as introduced in "The Concept of Truth in Formalized Languages" (1933/1956).[19]

Like the contributions by Frege and Russell discussed so far, Tarski's account of truth is rooted in modern logic. Between 1880 and the 1930s, the main logical systems studied are forms of higher-order logic, although both propositional and first-order logic start to emerge as self-contained sub-systems as well. The reference to "formalized languages" in Tarski's 1935 essay concerns such systems and languages. One purpose of adding a formally precise definition of truth is, then, to develop a more explicit semantics for them, which allows logicians to study the relationship between the syntax and semantics of various logics in novel and fruitful ways. This is clearly Tarski's primary goal; but he mentions a more philosophical goal as well. Namely, his definition is meant to contribute to traditional debates about the nature of truth.

Tarski's broader agenda manifests itself in several ways, including the following two: First, when considering the Liar Paradox in his essay on

---

[19] For Carnap's first meetings with Tarski and its impact on him, see Reck (2007b). For more details about Frege's and Russell's influence on Carnap, see Reck (2004).

truth he notes that natural languages, insofar as they contain an internal and widely applicable truth predicate, are inconsistent. For formal languages we can avoid that problem by situating the truth predicate at the meta-level. We thus get a hierarchy of languages: object language, meta-language, meta-meta-language, etc. Second, Tarski presents his account of truth as the precise working out of a correspondence theory of truth in a general Aristotelian sense. In both respects, the account is meant to be philosophically significant, in addition to its technical value for meta-logic. Implicitly it is also tied to a conception of philosophy, comparable to Russell's, where the tools of formal logic are used to solve, and sometimes to dissolve, traditional philosophical problems.

Yet another relevant feature of Tarski's essay on truth is that it contains an explicit discussion of criteria of adequacy for formalizations. These criteria are specified for the case of truth, but they can be applied more broadly (e.g., to Tarski's treatment of logical consequence). There are two kinds of criteria: conditions of "formal" and of "material adequacy." In the case of truth, the former include consistency, while the latter consists of the well-known T-schema ("Snow is white" is true if and only if snow is white; or more generally: "p" is true if and only if p). The point of material adequacy is that the "conceptual core" of the notion at issue is preserved. This parallels Carnap's "similarity" desideratum for explication. (A formalization is similar enough if it satisfies those criteria.) But Tarski tries to be more explicit and precise than Carnap.[20] Nevertheless, his conditions allow for pluralism too, that is, the possibility of multiple alternatives satisfying them. And with respect to adjudicating between such alternatives, Carnap goes beyond Tarski by adding his other three desiderata.

7.7 From Frege, Russell, and Tarski to Carnap

Tarski's work on truth grew out of the Lvov-Warsaw School, while Carnap's approach took shape in the Vienna Circle. In both, versions of "mathematical" or "scientific philosophy" were cultivated; and projects were often in the service of logico-mathematical goals. But this does not mean that broader agendas were not at play as well, as we saw. Against that background, we can now reconsider Carnap's own goals and broader agenda, implicit as they remained. One may wonder why he was not more

---

[20] This is reflected in the fact that one can try to prove, or disprove, whether all instance of the T-schema follow from Tarski's account of truth. Here I am indebted to Georg Schiemer.

explicit about them. A possible answer is that he did not want to restrict explication unnecessarily. He provided the schematic articulation of a broadly applicable method, in abstraction from specific goals and broader agendas.[21] While plausible, this answer is not fully satisfactory, especially if one wants to evaluate Carnapian explication critically. For that purpose, it matters what kinds of goals and agendas motivated his articulation.

In order to say more about this issue, one option is to consider Carnap's own applications of explication in detail. What is the advantage of looking first at its origins in previous works, as I have done? My answer is: By taking account of those origins one gains a broader perspective, one from which otherwise hidden assumptions and tendencies become visible; and that sheds light on the explications in Carnap's writings in the end. As we saw, Frege's, Russell's, and Tarski's works contained contributions to modern logic, tied closely to the foundations of mathematics. The main goal for them was to make progress in those areas. This includes answering questions about the nature of mathematical objects and the status of mathematical knowledge; it also includes developing logic further, as a tool and as a subject matter in itself. Carnap's conception of philosophy is firmly rooted in such projects.

But again, Frege, Russell, and Tarski had broader agendas as well. This is most explicit in Russell. For him, a main goal became to transform the very nature of philosophy. This means that philosophical problems are often not so much solved as either dissolved or transformed into more tractable ones, that is, made amenable to formal-logical treatment. Thus, questions about the nature of numbers are replaced by the construction of less mysterious substitutes, the Frege-Russell numbers. Similarly, Meinongian worries about the metaphysics needed for analyzing certain kinds of judgments are dissolved by Russell's theory of descriptions. And Tarski's account allows us to leave behind our inconsistent talk of truth in ordinary language and work with a more precise, consistent notion for formal languages instead. With such proposals, we are close to explication. But Carnap pushes the transformation of philosophy further, by aiming to eliminate all of "metaphysics," not just particular metaphysical entities.[22]

In the last few sections, I focused on the origins of Carnapian explication in logic and the foundations of mathematics. But there are two other

---

[21] I am indebted to Gary Ebbs for this way of describing what Carnap meant to provide.
[22] Compare the title of Carnap (1932/2004): "Elimination of Metaphysics through Logical Analysis of Language." To be clear, I am not ascribing a form of ontological eliminativism in the sense of Quine's "desert ontology" to Carnap, but an approach that "shaves off" traditional philosophical questions and problems.

aspects one needs to factor in as well, both of which have come up already. The first stems from the fact that Carnap does not just point to Frege, Russell, and Tarski in terms of paradigms for explication but also to examples from the natural sciences, like replacing "fish" by "piscis" in biology. In cases like these, the intended progress consists not in contributions to logic or philosophy but to the natural sciences. Hence, the main goal seems significantly different. And as Carnap had been interested in such cases for a long time, this should be taken seriously as well.

But maybe it is too strong to say that these cases are so different. In fact, for Carnap there is no sharp line separating philosophy from the natural sciences, just as there is no sharp line between philosophy and modern logic. Or better, one of Carnap's main goals is to erase such dividing lines, so as to create a unified philosophical-logical-scientific perspective. Along such lines, conceptual advances in the natural sciences, like that from "fish" to "piscis," can be seen as models just as much as the logical ones. Conversely, philosophy should contribute to the sciences, as Carnap attempted with his explication of "entropy." Crucial is that the same general tools are used: formalization and mathematization, the formulation of logical and empirical laws, and the precise definition of concepts. The only difference is that philosophers focus more on logico-conceptual issues than scientists. For the mature Carnap, philosophy thus turns into "the logic of science." But there is a further wrinkle that is often neglected: The shared model for philosophy, logic, and science becomes engineering, with Carnapian conceptual engineering as the outcome.

There is a second additional consideration relevant for clarifying the goals and the agenda motivating explication. Remember that Carnap also lists the advance from ordinary comparisons of "warmer" and "colder" to the quantitative notion of temperature as a model. I take this to indicate that Carnapian explications, like basic scientific advances, can and should have practical significance. To make that claim more plausible, note that it is in line with what we know about the Vienna Circle. The Circle's agenda included not just to transform philosophy in the ivory tower but to improve human life and society. In that respect, its members saw themselves as reviving the Enlightenment.[23] A main goal was thus to replace old, fossilized, and oppressive ways of living by new, liberating, and

---

[23] Here I am following Carus (2007). As an illustration, various members of the Vienna Circle participated actively in public education. Moreover, Otto Neurath was deeply engaged in social engineering, and he was in conversation with Carnap about it. Note, in addition, that Carnap has been rediscovered as an ally for social-political engagement and ameliorative analysis recently; see Dutilh Novaes (2018) and the essay by Audrey Yap in this volume (Chapter 4).

invigorating ones. "Metaphysics," and with it most of traditional philosophy, was seen as part of the former, Russellian and Carnapian critiques of it as contributions to the latter. This illustrates another close connection between explication and engineering, now in the form of social engineering.

7.8 Explication and Its Successors: Some Internal Criticisms

In Section 7.7, I identified four goals that motivated and shaped Carnapian explication: (i) to contribute to logic and the foundations of mathematics; (ii) to erase the lines between logic, philosophy, and the sciences; (iii) thereby to transform philosophy into "mathematical" or "scientific philosophy"; but also (iv) to improve human life and society practically. To be sure, these ambitions often remain implicit, including in Carnap's articulation of explication.[24] In most of his own applications, just like in the prototypes for it, the pursuit of goals (iii) and especially (iv) is not readily discernible either, only (i) and partly (ii). Thus it is hard to see the Frege-Russell conception of numbers, Russell's theory of descriptions, and Tarski's account of truth as improving human life practically; similarly for Carnap's explications of completeness, logical truth, meaning, necessity, and probability. On the other hand, his scientific prototypes point in the direction of (ii) and (iii), partly even (iv). And the latter becomes more evident if we remember the enlightenment ambitions of the Vienna Circle.

In terms of goals (i)–(iii), Carnap's approach is strongly science-oriented. This is well known, of course. A common objection is then that the resulting conception of philosophy is scientistic, that is, that it assimilates philosophy to science in a problematic way, including dismissing traditional philosophical problems too quickly. A variant of that objection, less far from Carnap's perspective, would be that his conception of science is inadequate, for example, by underestimating the role of metaphysics within it, thus leading to a conception of philosophy that is too restrictive. Beyond that, philosophy has been turned into a kind of engineering. The implications of that shift should be explored more as well, it seems to me. For example, someone might go along with it at a general level but object to the particular form of engineering envisaged by Carnap because it is too

---

[24] A further explanation for why Carnap left them implicit may be sociological: The practical agenda underlying explication, i.e., goal (iv), was originally tied to Carnap's leftist, socialist leanings. But after moving to the United States, and especially During the Cold War, he largely retreated to "the icy slopes of logic"; see Reisch (2005).

narrow and inflexible.²⁵ Or the shift itself might be resisted, basically because it leads to more losses than gains.

These are very general objections, too sweeping to be adjudicated fully here. In what follows, I want to explore some criticisms that are related but more internal and specific. They also build on the details of our discussion so far. The first concerns the relationship between Carnap's goals (i)–(iv). The basic observation is this: Goal (iv), that is, improving human life in practical ways, seems rather unconnected with (i)–(iii), Carnap's assimilation of philosophy, logic, and science. Put more directly as a criticism: There is a tension, or at least a gap, in Carnap's work that calls for attention, namely, between the very abstract, theoretical nature of the explications provided by him and any practical, socially relevant impact that might be intended. Can Carnap be defended against that criticism? He can, I think, at least to some degree.

Note, first, that in most of the initial applications of explication goal (iv) is not meant to be achieved directly but only by way of (i)–(iii). Thus, to be fair, one shouldn't burden them with misplaced expectations. Second, Carnap's new approach deserves some time to mature. One shouldn't expect many practical, socially relevant effects right away, as long as they emerge eventually. Third, adopting Carnap's scientific conception of philosophy, via (ii)–(iii), can perhaps be seen as liberating in itself, as it was in the Vienna Circle, by freeing us from old and stale metaphysics. Fourth, for some of Carnap's explications, claims about their practical impact are not as indefensible as one might think initially, for example, with respect to his treatment of probability. After all, we encounter probabilistic and statistical claims frequently in modern life, and an improved understanding of them can make a practical difference.²⁶ Fifth, in his late writings, Carnap chooses additional targets for explication, not mentioned so far, for which a practical, social impact is not so farfetched either. This includes the notion of rationality, which points to rational choice theory as used in sociology, economics, etc. Sixth, if we go beyond Carnap's writings, the rise of game theory, say, is another case in

---

[25] It would be interesting to compare Carnap and Wittgenstein here. Wittgenstein started out as an engineering student, as is well known. Their different conceptions of engineering might explain differences between their philosophical methodologies. Another relevant comparison would be with the engineering-inspired philosophy advocated by Mark Wilson recently, for whom Carnap's approach is a main target of criticism; see Wilson (2022).

[26] Carnap argued so himself; see Carnap (1947a), among others.

point, that is, another application of explication with real-life applications via the social and the biological sciences.[27]

These defenses have some force, I believe. But are they fully successful, given the restrictive tendencies in Carnap's approach as tied to his goals (ii)–(iii)? Part of the gap or tension identified above remains, it seems to me. In the rest of this section, I want to justify that negative verdict. This will involve two further challenges to an explication-based conception of philosophy. The first starts with a series of questions, not about Carnap's own approach but about descendants of it today, that is, current forms of "formal" or "mathematical philosophy," "conceptual engineering," and "ameliorative analysis." Starting with "formal/mathematical philosophy," it seems clear that its current proponents share Carnap's ambitions (ii) and (iii), in addition to (i). But what about ambition (iv)? Is there any intended impact by current formal or mathematical philosophy on everyday life; or is there any social agenda behind it? It does not look that way; or at least, I am not aware of any detailed discussion of that aspect in the literature. If none exists, this is telling in itself. It also looks like another gap, one that replicates the one in Carnap's works.

The situation looks different when we turn to "ameliorative analysis," together with much of current "conceptual engineering." For them goal (iv), improving human life and society practically, is at the forefront. A well-known example is the attempt to re-engineer ethically loaded and socially contested concepts. But what about goals (ii)–(iii), not to speak of (i)? The ambition to make philosophy more "mathematical" or "scientific" does not seem to play a significant role here. Similarly for erasing the lines between logic, philosophy, and science or for contributing to logic and the foundations of mathematics. In fact, formal-logical tools are not used much, not even in the form of rational choice theory or game theory. Insofar as that is the case, current "formal" or "mathematical philosophy," on the one hand, and "ameliorative analysis" together with conceptual engineering, on the other, come apart. They build on different, separable sides of Carnap's project. This is another reflection of the gap in Carnap mentioned above.

Now to my second additional challenge. It concerns the tools best used for achieving goals (i)–(iv), as well as other philosophical goals. Undoubtedly, formal explication has been quite effective in logic and the

---

[27] Cf. works like O'Connor (2019), also parts VI–VII of Hanson and Hendricks (2018). For a forerunner of game-theoretic approaches, see Menger (1934/1974); and for the later Carnap, see Carnap (*RSE*, 2017).

foundations of mathematics; similarly, at least to some degree, for the philosophy of science and the philosophy of language. In fact, the tools provided by Frege, Russell, Tarski, and Carnap were tailor-made for those areas; and they led to spectacular successes, such as Gödel's theorems. But should one expect those same tools to be as fruitful with respect to goal (iv), that is, improving human life and society practically? Similarly, should one expect them to be fruitful with respect to other problems in, say, ethics, aesthetics, or social-political philosophy.[28] That seems much more doubtful. And arguably the situation only improves slightly if we also bring in concept formation in the style of the natural sciences.[29]

A committed Carnapian might respond that, insofar as explication is not fruitful when applied to some philosophical problems, the fault lies with the problems, especially traditional metaphysical ones. Those recalcitrant, typically vague problems should either be transformed radically or dropped altogether, in line with Carnap's goals (ii)–(iii). Then again, is this a reasonable response in all areas of philosophy? Is it even reasonable for all problems in the areas where explication has been applied successfully? Or does it show, instead, that Carnap's explication-based conception of philosophy is too rigid and restrictive? Its dominant formal-logical tendencies have certainly been called into question, even within analytic philosophy.[30] Put differently, the conception of philosophy driven by the models of Frege, Russell, and Tarski, on the one hand, and by science, on the other hand, involves a narrowing that calls for scrutiny. At the least, it seems too narrow if used exclusively, that is, if philosophy is reduced to applying formal explication for solving all its problems.

Up to this point, I have focused on a conception of philosophy in which explication is the main, or even the only, method. But perhaps that is unfair to Carnap. In his defense, one might argue as follows: The tools and methods originating in modern logic and in scientific concept formation have proven fruitful in some parts of philosophy; but in other parts they

---

[28] Another relevant case is the history of philosophy. Note that I am not using anything like formal explication in the present essay; it would not be fruitful for my philosophical-historical purposes. However, see Carus (2013) for a different view, including a proposal for how to combine Carnapian explication with historical work.

[29] As an example from ethics, is there any achievement in explication-based philosophy comparable in fruitfulness to Peter Strawson's "Freedom and Resentment"? For an earlier example, compare also Ernst Cassirer's rich, much more inclusive, and fruitful philosophy of symbolic forms, including its influence in art history, anthropology, etc.

[30] This challenge is often associated with Peter Strawson. But one does not have to go to "ordinary language philosophy" for it – Otto Neurath raised similar objections. For him, Carnap's explication-centric logical positivism repeats the mistakes of earlier forms of positivism: narrowness, too much formalism, and scholasticism.

do, indeed, need to be supplemented, for example in large parts of ethics, perhaps also for reaching Carnap's goal (iv). That much has to be, and can be, admitted. In addition, from a Carnapian point of view, one can distinguish a narrower, more formal version of explication from a broader, less formal one. This is in line with the relatively broad formulation of Carnap's four desiderata for explication, as we saw; and it makes explication applicable more widely immediately. With respect to both aspects, my interpretation of Carnap was thus uncharitable; it made him look more rigid and restrictive than he really is. Or so the argument goes.

However, several counterarguments suggest themselves: First, Carnap's articulation of explication does not leave much leeway in this respect. For example, he talks about fruitfulness only in terms of formulating logical and scientific laws. Hence, even a less formal version of Carnapian explication seems narrow and restrictive. Also, formal-logical explication remains the ideal, it appears. Second, if the methodological toolbox is opened up beyond explication, in both its narrower and wider forms, this would seem to create conflicts with other core tenets of Carnap's approach, as reflected in goals (ii)–(iii). More basically, Carnap says very little about what other tools might be acceptable to him, which leaves him open to this challenge.[31] There certainly is no extended, charitable discussion of complementary tools. Third, opening the toolbox further might dilute the position to such a degree that no distinctive, recognizably different conception of philosophy remains.[32] After all, philosophers in other traditions use informal explications of concepts as well, sometimes even formal ones. These counterarguments can be reformulated as three related questions: Suppose we interpret Carnap in a less rigid and restrictive way. How should we conceive of the proper form, goal, and reach of explication then? What will the remaining continuity with (i)–(iv) consist in? And how far can we go until we stop philosophizing in a recognizably "Carnapian" way?[33] Such questions seem pertinent with respect to Carnap's legacy today.

---

[31] A rare exception is when Carnap, in response to Strawson, admits that Strawsonian "connective analysis" might be useful for "clarifying the explicandum"; see Carnap (1963b). But even that is done only very tentatively and half-heartedly by him.

[32] This criticism of Carnap, or of a broadly Carnapian view, was suggested to me by Martin Kusch.

[33] For some Carnapians, it might be crucial to preserve the pragmatist and pluralist aspects of the approach. Several of my arguments in this essay suggest expanding both, i.e., becoming more pragmatist (e.g., in terms of normative aspects) and more pluralist (in terms of methods). For a discussion of Carnap's (limited) relationship to classical pragmatism, see Richardson (2007). For a rich defense of Carnap's conception of philosophy, see Carus (2007).

7.9 Concluding Remarks

Various conceptions of philosophy have been proposed in its history. Why should we choose one over others? A lot depends on the goals and ambitions one has, since the methods associated with a conception may be more or less adequate for them. One of my goals in this essay was to argue that this also applies to the conception of philosophy that has Carnapian explication at its core. Carnap himself was not very forthcoming about that aspect, at least in his explicit discussion of explication. I shed further light on it by reflecting on his paradigmatic models in the works of Frege, Russell, and Tarski, on the one hand, and in scientific concept formation, on the other. If one reflects on those, a number of goals and broader agendas motivating the rise of explication come to the fore. One can also observe relevant shifts, for example, in terms of Russell's new conception of philosophy and Carnap's radicalization of it. And if we follow the trajectory further, significant questions and challenges arise. This does not make explication useless as a tool; but it challenges an overly restrictive conception of philosophy centered around it.

Against that background, it would now be interesting to return to Carnap's own applications of explication. For example, which precise goals and what broader agenda was his treatment of logical probability to serve; and how far did it succeed in them? Similarly for the targets of explication in Carnap's later works, like the notion of rationality.[34] As a next step, we could reconsider appeals to explication by philosophers such as W. V. O. Quine, Nelson Goodman, and Carl Hempel, all of whom adopted it explicitly. We could also explore challenges by its early critics more, including Peter Strawson and Otto Neurath. Doing so would allow us to trace the trajectory in the works of Frege, Russell, Tarski, and Carnap further, including observing how the relationship of an explication-based philosophy not only to science but also to other disciplines developed subsequently (e.g., to art in Goodman).[35]

---

[34] For probability, see Sznajder (2018) and the essay by Sandy Zabell in this volume (Chapter 10). Concerning Carnap's later works, it is noteworthy that he started to address goals and values more, thus normative issues, which he had brushed aside earlier as involving "non-cognitive" aspects; cf. (*RSE*, Carnap 2017). But how far did Carnap actually go in that direction? More generally, how far does a Carnapian approach allow one to go?

[35] For a first take on Hempel, see Reck (2013); for Quine, see Morris (2018). Goodman's work contains a still underappreciated discussion of explication and its ties to reflective equilibrium; see Brun (2020). And besides Goodman's work on aesthetics, Strawson's "Freedom and Resentment" contains relevant references to poetry, as Gary Ebbs pointed out to me. I plan to come back to some of these figures and themes in future work.

After that, we could turn to current approaches related to explication, thus probing both their Carnapian heritage and their divergences from his approach more deeply. There is no space to take these additional steps here; but I hope that what I provided can serve as background and motivation for such investigations.

PART III

The Logical and the Linguistic

CHAPTER 8

Carnap's Approach to Semantics and Syntax
Relations and Tension

Pierre Wagner

8.1 Carnap's Turn to Semantics

In his intellectual autobiography, Carnap recounts the moment when Tarski introduced him to his method for defining a truth predicate in a formalized language (*IA*, 60). The episode took place, in all likelihood, in the autumn of 1934. According to his own account, Carnap did not immediately grasp what Tarski claimed to have achieved because it seemed impossible to him to define "true" by means of a syntactic method if the truth predicate is taken in the general sense that includes factual truth. However, the definition of the truth of an empirical statement that Tarski gave as an example soon cleared up the misunderstanding

"this table is black" is true if, and only if, this table is black.

Unlike the syntactic method introduced in Carnap's 1934 *Logische Syntax der Sprache*, Tarski's approach allowed, in the metalanguage, not only the use of mathematical means such as sets, numbers, and quantification but also that of a semantical vocabulary that includes such terms as "satisfy," "designate," and "true" and that of empirical words such as "black" and "table" in the definition of these terms. Carnap very quickly recognized that this broadening of the metalanguage opened up new perspectives and, judging it desirable to make the semantical method developed by Tarski more widely known, he encouraged him to explain its principles at the 1935 Paris Congress on scientific philosophy. Tarski's famous paper (1936/2002) was first presented on this occasion. Tarski (1936/1956) is also included in the proceedings of the congress.

In "Testability and Meaning" (*T&M*), Carnap still strictly adhered to the syntactic method so that this paper may be regarded as a direct extension of *LSS*,[1]

---

[1] *LSS* refers to Carnap's 1934 *Logische Syntax der Sprache* (1934), while *LSL* refers to its 1937 English translation, *Logical Syntax to Language*. Page numbering throughout the text is from *LSL*.

which is prior to the semantical period. In the following years, Carnap adopted a semantical approach to language. Tarski had wanted to show as clearly as possible that the semantical method was in no way incompatible with the requirements of science, despite the reservations that many philosophers of the time expressed about the concepts of meaning and truth. In his 1939 *FLM*, Carnap shows that the syntactic method can be usefully supplemented by both a semantical approach and a pragmatical one. In the 1942 *IS*, which is intended to be largely exploratory in nature, Carnap explains his approach to semantics but also examines, in the spirit of the principle of tolerance, a wide range of possible ways the semantical method may follow. While Carnap discusses the respective advantages and drawbacks of these various ways, he openly acknowledges that the decision to adopt one of them rather than another would require a more thorough investigation than the one he is able to conduct in his book (*IS*, section 16). In *Formalization of Logic* (*FoL*, 1943) Carnap discusses the question of whether it is possible to formalize logic – that is, to characterize logical constants syntactically – in such a way that this formal characterization can receive no other interpretation than the one actually expected. A few years later, he chose one of the semantical methods that had been explained and examined in 1942 and applied it to broader frameworks, which included modal logic (*M&N*) and inductive logic (*LFP*).

The syntactic character of Carnap's method in *LSL* implies that it has restricted means at its disposal. This restriction consists in the fact that the method excludes any recourse to the reference (*Bedeutung*) of the signs or to the meaning (*Sinn*) of the expressions of the object language.[2] Only the category of the signs and the order of their succession in the expressions can be taken into account within the framework of the syntactic method. This method also excludes the use of empirical vocabulary in the definition of logical terms such as "analytic," "L-consequence," "contradictory," etc. That the method is syntactic does not imply, however, that the mathematical means to which it can have recourse are limited. Syntax as Carnap understands it is not a finitary method, in sharp contrast with Hilbert's metamathematics. In spite of the Gödelian incompleteness phenomenon, Carnap was able to show, for the languages he considered in *LSL*, that any

---

[2] Carnap gives definitions of "sense" (*Sinn*), "content" (*Gehalt*, *Inhalt*), and "synonymous" (*synonym*); but in the context of *LSL*, these terms have an extensional meaning based on the syntactic notions of consequence and equipolence (*LSL*, 42, 184). The more usual intensional concepts of meaning and sense are ruled out.

logical-mathematical statement is either analytic or contradictory. This result, which may be considered as some kind of completeness theorem in Carnap's sense, is possible even for languages that include arithmetics because the definitions of "analytic in L" and "contradictory in L" call for infinitary means that go beyond the usual finitary ones that suffice for defining "provable in L" and "refutable in L" for some formalized language L. This infinite character of his syntactic method is made visible in Carnap's characterization of object languages, which includes the definition of a consequence relation by axioms and "transformation rules" and which may be either finitary or infinitary. A typical example of an infinitary rule is the ω-rule (from φ(0), φ(1), φ(2) ... infer $\forall x\varphi(x)$) used for the definition of a consequence relation for Language I in *LSL*.

Commentators have long stressed that the importance of Carnap's "semantical turn" should not be overestimated.[3] On the one hand, this turn does not consist in replacing the method outlined in *LSL* by a method inspired by Tarski's work but in supplementing the syntactic approach by a semantical one. On the other hand, the Tarskian idea of going beyond the finitary concepts of provability and refutability by introducing a relation of consequence based on methods not restricted to finitary syntax had been largely anticipated in Carnap (1935/1937), where we find a definition of logical validity (for language II) that is not based on rules of inference but on a procedure of evaluation that clearly anticipates Tarskian semantics. In Tarski (1936/2002), the author explicitly refers, on several occasions, to Carnap's *LSS* as containing a forerunner of his concept of logical consequence.

The fact that *LSL* largely anticipates Tarskian semantics has been so often and so strongly emphasized by Carnap scholars that there has been a tendency to minimize the importance of Carnap's adoption of a semantical approach in the late thirties. As a consequence, his semantical turn has not always been given the importance it deserves. As a matter of fact, the three main works that embody this turn (*FLM*, *IS*, and *FoL*) have been much less studied than other earlier or later ones, such as Carnap (*Aufbau*, *LSS*, and *M&N*). Once one understands and embraces the idea that the semantical method supplements the syntactic approach without replacing it, and that this method was in some way anticipated in *LSS*, it remains to understand what it means to make the semantical turn and what its

---

[3] Creath (1990b); Ricketts (1996); Carus (1999, 2019). Carnap's semantical turn has been the object of many studies. No detailed account is given here of this literature, for lack of space. For more references than the very few that can be given here, see Awodey (2007) and Tuboly (2017).

consequences are. The present chapter is devoted to a clarification of some aspects of that precise issue.

When dealing with the Carnapian approach to semantics, a prior distinction is required between different periods in his intellectual career. A first set of works regarded as semantical already appeared in the twenties, when Carnap questioned the models and the properties of axiom systems (Carnap 1927, 2000). An abundant literature has been devoted to what is sometimes called Carnap's "early semantics" (see Schiemer 2013). A second period extends from the mid-thirties (at the time Carnap became aware of Tarski's works on semantics) through the forties up to the publication of *LFP*. Finally, in the fifties, a new turning point marks the beginning of a third stage in the development of Carnapian semantics, around the time that Tarski (1954–1955) appeared. This third phase is marked by important interactions with Kemeny and Church, by a renewed use of the concept of model (which was hardly mentioned in the second phase), and by work done in hyperintensional semantics (*RSE*, 900–905, Carnap 1971, 1972). In the present chapter, we focus on the first half of the second phase (essentially Carnap's conceptions in his *FLM, IS, and FoL*) that we compare with Carnap's syntactic approach in the previous period (between 1931 and 1937).

8.2 Was Carnap Following Tarski in Semantics?

For Carnap, adopting a Tarski-inspired semantical method did not mean blindly and slavishly following Tarski. In the preface to *IS*, after acknowledging the considerable debt the book owed to Tarski's work, Carnap underlines points of divergence, the most important of which is certainly Tarski's reservations about the possibility of drawing a clear and nonarbitrary distinction between logical and nonlogical terms in a language (Tarski 1936/2002, 189). For Carnap, making such a distinction is possible but is partly a matter of decision about the choice of a language. *IS* – indeed most of the works published by Carnap in the forties – show that Tarski's goals and his own were quite different (see Wagner 2017). What interested Carnap above all was the possibility of using Tarskian methods and adapting them to the resolution of the questions that had been previously discussed in the Vienna Circle (*IA*, 61). Prominent among these problems is the possibility of a principled distinction between logically valid sentences, considered as a priori, and synthetic ones, which, according to Carnap, have empirical content. Now these questions are obviously not the ones that were of most interest to Tarski, who explicitly expressed his skepticism regarding the possibility of a general characterization of the set of logical constants and of logical-mathematical validity.

The issue of defining a truth predicate is telling of the divergent interests of the two authors. Whereas Tarski takes scrupulous care to elaborate a definition of a truth predicate in which the use of semantical vocabulary is carefully controlled (his definition of a truth predicate is based on a definition of the satisfaction relation that does not presuppose any other semantical term), Carnap makes use of the concept of truth as a mere tool that takes the form of a set of rules (the so-called rules of truth) that are meant to define what he calls a "semantical system." His very peculiar reading of the Tarskian method for defining a truth predicate for a formalized language is that of a set of rules for characterizing a semantical system:

> In his treatise Tarski developed a general method for constructing exact definitions of truth for deductive language systems, that is for stating rules which determine for every sentence of such a system a necessary and sufficient condition of its truth. (*IA*, 60)

Taking for granted Tarski's semantical research on a method for defining a truth predicate, Carnap does not reconsider this question and he takes Tarski's method for defining a truth predicate as a conceptual tool that may be used for other purposes. In the spirit of the principle of tolerance, he lists several possible methods for the definition of a truth predicate but does not elaborate on the general problem of such a definition, whereas this issue was the main focus of Tarski (1933/1956). On the basis of Tarski's work, Carnap admits that the concept of truth as well as other semantical concepts can be defined on the basis of semantical rules and be freely used in the metalanguage, hoping that the semantical approach to language will pave the way for a novel characterization of logical truth as opposed to factual truth.

In view of the goals he was pursuing, was Carnap right to take the semantical turn? The question is debated and some commentators, notably Goldfarb (1997), have forcefully argued that this is actually not the case. Because the adoption of a semantical approach basically consists in the extension of the metalanguage to terms of semantics ("true," "designates," "satisfies," etc.) and to empirical terms ("table," "black," etc.), it becomes more difficult to establish a perfectly well-defined distinction between logical-mathematical sentences and synthetic ones, whose content is empirical, all the more so as no solution is in sight for the problem of a general characterization of the logical terms of a language, as Carnap himself acknowledges (*IS*, 56, 59). Goldfarb has a further reservation about the semantical turn, again in view of Carnap's own goals. He remarks that the concepts and relations defined in a semantical system depend on rules in which the meaning of the empirical terms is supposed to be known. In a rule of designation such as

> predicate P designates the property of being a philosopher,

the meaning of the word "philosopher" is assumed to be known. The interpretation of "P" is not given in a set-theoretic framework, as it is usually done today, but on the basis of the word "philosopher" as used in the metalanguage, and the same remark holds for any empirical term that appears in similar rules. In taking the semantical turn, Carnap thus requires that the meaning of a large number of empirical terms that are used in the semantical rules be known, which was by no means the case in the syntactic method introduced in *LSS*.

8.3 Languages, Formal Systems, and Calculi

Today, commentators carefully distinguish the three following stances that are taken in *LSL*:

- the adoption of a metalinguistic point of view, distinct from that of the object language;
- the adoption of a syntactic method, at work in the metalanguage;
- the adoption of the principle of tolerance, applied to the choice of an object language.

Each of these specific takes date back to a different time, quite precisely traceable in the early thirties, as was shown by Carnap scholarship in the last decades (Awodey and Carus 2009). In all three cases, Carnap takes a decision and makes a proposal that he suggests or urges to follow. Such proposals are neither true nor false. They may be deemed advisable or inadvisable but should not be confused with judgments that may be either correct or incorrect. The motivations for these three decisions are obviously different in nature. It is worth noticing, however, that in *LSL*, the first two points are not as clearly and explicitly separated as we have just indicated. As a matter of fact, Carnap does not talk about the "metalanguage" (this word is absent from the book) but about the "syntax-language" (*Syntaxsprache*), a term that may be retrospectively regarded as conflating two ideas: firstly, the idea of an expository language, distinct from the object language in which knowledge itself is supposed to be formalized and, secondly, the idea of a syntactic method used in the expository language. As for the principle of tolerance, it is presented as applying above all to the choice of an object language. Carnap is well aware that the definition of "analytic in L" is dependent on the choice of a metalanguage and that the concept of analyticity for some specific language L depends on the expressive power of the syntactic language. The principle of tolerance, however, is not explicitly applied to the choice of a metalanguage nor, a fortiori, to the choice of a method. This situation changes radically with the semantical turn. The term "language of syntax" as used in *LSL* then becomes obsolete and inadequate, and a new distinction needs to be made between the adoption of a metalinguistic point of view and the adoption of a particular method in use in the metalanguage. Only then does it clearly appear that several options are open for this method and that a choice needs to be made. The semantical turn thus makes it perfectly clear that the principle of tolerance can in fact apply not only to the choice of some object language but also to the method in use in the metalanguage, by which object languages are characterized and studied.

Because languages as conceived in *LSL* include axioms and transformation rules, they correspond more to what we would now call "interpreted formal systems" than to what we usually understand by "languages." In his *FoL* and in *IS*, Carnap introduces what he calls "semantical systems," defined by rules of formation (which determine a set of formulas) and by rules of designation, of truth, of satisfaction, or of determination, with possible variations on the type of semantical rules used from one system to another. The goal is to use these rules first for the definition of "true," then for the definition of "L-true," "L-false," "L-implicate," "L-equivalent," "L-dependent," "L-exclusive," and of a whole series of "L-terms" related to some specific system S ("L" refers here to "logic," not to "language"). Various ways of obtaining such definitions are explored, of which Carnap is careful to indicate the specificities and limitations.

The syntactic approach is not abandoned; but in *IS*, it becomes the object of a separate treatment, in the last sections of the book, after the sections devoted to semantics. This approach is based on formalisms that Carnap no longer calls "languages" as in *LSL* but "calculi." The "L-concepts," related to semantical systems, are thus clearly distinguished from the "C-concepts," related to calculi ("C" refers here to "calculus"). These two sets of concepts are put in correspondence when a calculus is considered as interpreted by a semantical system or when a semantical system is seen as formalized by a calculus. In order to discuss more easily the possibility and the properties of such a correspondence, Carnap opts for the new terminology of "C-terms" ("C-true," "C-false," "C-implicate," "C-equivalent," etc.), which replaces the more common terminology used in 1934 ("provable," "refutable," "derivable," etc.).

In *LSL*, a fundamental distinction had been made between d-terms (where "d" is an abbreviation for "derivation") and c-terms (where "c" refers to "consequence"). While d-terms ("demonstrable," "refutable," "derivable from," etc.) relied on rules of inference, which are finitary, the definition of c-terms ("analytic," "contradictory," "consequence of," etc.) required infinitary concepts. The definition of the c-terms was of course of major importance in *LSL*. Only they made possible the remarkable anticipation of Tarskian semantics as well as one of the major achievements of the book, that is, the proof, for language I and language II, of a completeness theorem in Carnap sense, to the effect that any logical statement (i.e., any statement formulated in the logical-mathematical vocabulary) is either analytic or contradictory (*LSL*, theorems 14.3 and 34e11). The contrast with *IS* is striking. In *IS*, the distinction between finite and infinite syntactic concepts is still mentioned, but only in passing, at the end of section 25, and it no longer has the central role it had had eight years before. In 1942, there is no longer any discussion, indeed any mention, of the completeness theorem in Carnap's sense, which had been of major importance in *LSL*. The main focus is on a semantical rather than on a syntactic explication of logical truth.

8.4 Truth, L-truth, and L-validity

At the time he was writing *LSS*, Carnap was not aware of Tarski's work on the definition of a truth predicate and on the establishment of scientific semantics. In the languages discussed in this book, what place does he assign to the concept of truth in a broad sense, which includes empirical truth? Although Carnap indicates several elimination procedures that may be applied to a truth predicate (*LSL*, 216–217), he refrains from asserting that the truth predicate can be eliminated from every sentence and that it should be in order for the sentence to become genuinely scientific. Carnap does not adopt any kind of alethic eliminativism. It is worth noticing that while he is careful to remind the reader that the unrestricted use of a truth predicate leads to well-known contradictions, he does not rule out the use of a metalinguistic truth predicate. Indeed, Carnap mentions the possibility of an axiomatic approach to truth in the metalanguage and he even gives a few examples of axioms that might be used for a theory of truth (*LSL*, 216), although such an option is excluded once the framework for a syntactic approach to language is adopted. For this reason, Carnap does not investigate this possibility any further in *LSL*. By contrast, a definition of logical truth, renamed "L-validity," for Language I and Language II, and eventually for any language, is one of the major goals of the book and one of its major achievements. As a synonym for "L-valid," Carnap uses the term "analytic," which therefore does not at all have in *LSL* the meaning it will acquire in the famous later debate on a definition of analyticity, in which analytic truths such as "bachelors are not married" are carefully distinguished from logical truths.

At the time the semantical turn was taken, the terminology used by Carnap evolved. The words "L-valid," "analytic," and "L-contravalid" were dropped and replaced by "L-true" and "L-false." Defining L-truth became one of the main objectives of the semantical method, both for special and for general semantics. As Carnap writes at different places and in different words, the L-concepts "are of the greatest importance for the logical analysis of science" (*IS*, 61). In view of such pronouncement, the reader might expect to find a general definition of L-truth. The truth is that no such final definition is provided anywhere in the book. In the syntactic framework, Carnap had offered a general definition of "L-validity," which was based on a previous general characterization of the logical signs (*LSL*, section 50). This syntactic definition of logicality, however, turned out to be defective, as Mac Lane showed in a review of the book (Mac Lane 1938). Carnap then turned to the semantical approach, hoping it might offer a better way toward a solution of the issue of logicality: "the distinction between logical and descriptive signs ... (has) to be made primarily in semantics, not in syntax" (*IS*, 247). However, no new general characterization of logicality and of L-truth is actually provided: "No complete solution of the problem of defining an adequate concept of L-truth in general semantics is given, but several ways believed to lead to such solution are outlined." (*IS*, 83). What we do find in *IS* are tentative and conditional definitions of L-truth and other L-concepts and explanations about these concepts. Four methods are presented in section 16, each of which presupposes that certain conditions are satisfied in the metalanguage. Two of these methods (1a and 1b) assume that the metalanguage M "contains concepts describing logical deduction in M or in part of M." Two other methods (2a and 2b) assume that the metalanguage already contains the terms "logical" and "descriptive," which means that the issue of a characterization of logicality is supposed to be solved.

This, however, is far from the whole story of what happens in *IS*, which is by no means easy to grasp. The more we get into the details of Carnap's approach, the more we realize how far Carnap was from following Tarski in semantics. Let us first emphasize that Carnap applies a truth predicate both to the *sentences* of some semantical system S and to *propositions*, that sentences of S are meant to designate (in *IS*, Carnap assumes that sentences *designate* propositions). This opens the way (*IS*, 90, notations modified, here and in the following quotations) to such definitions as

proposition p is true $=_{Df} p$

and

sentence A is true in S $=_{Df}$ there is a proposition p such that A designates p in S, and p.

These are quite different from other kinds of truth definitions, given by rules of truth for example in the following way (*IS*, 32):

> A is true in S $=_{Df}$ one of the three following conditions is fullfiled:
> a. if A has the form Pr_i (in_j) and the object designated by in_j has the property designated by Pr_i
> b. A has the form $\neg B$, and B is not true
> c. A has the form (B v C), and at least one of the sentences B and C is true

which presupposes rules of designation such as

in_1 designates Chicago
Pr_1 designates the property of being large.

Because Carnap explores a whole range of semantical methods, he also considers other kinds of truth definitions for sentences. Here is another example (*IS*, 87):

> A is true [in S] $=_{Df}$ the logical attribute determined by A holds for the sequence of the designata of the descriptive signs of A

which is based on a notion of determination for which rules of determination need to be formulated (*IS*, section 11). In this specific case, the truth definition makes possible the following definition for *L-truth* (*IS*, 88):

A is L-true $=_{Df}$ the logical attribute determined by A is universal.

These few examples are meant to illustrate the exploratory character of the book, not to give a detailed account of its content.

8.5 L-states, L-ranges, and State Descriptions

Among the many paths explored by Carnap for the development of a semantical approach are the ones based on the concepts of L-state and of L-range, to which a large part of *IS* is devoted. In sections 18–19, Carnap examines no less than eight different methods for defining the L-range of a sentence or of a set of sentences. Roughly speaking, an L-state is a possible state of affairs with respect to the properties and relations dealt with in some semantical system S, and the range of a sentence A is the range of possibilities that are left over in case A is true. Because the range of A depends on the truth conditions of A, not on its actual truth, it is a logical concept and is therefore called "L-range" in *IS*. It is not immediately clear in sections 18–19 how "L-range" and "L-state" stand with respect to the other previously discussed L-terms. The answer is that there is no uniform answer that would cover all eight methods for defining "L-range." In some cases, L-ranges are defined as classes of propositions (as opposed to classes of sentences), in other cases as classes of state-descriptions, in still other cases as sets of relations, and so on. Because the concepts of L-state and of L-range are meant to be applicable to semantical systems, which are systems of sentences, the focus is on the L-range *of sentences*, or *of sets of sentences*, not on L-ranges per se, although Carnap also considers the case of L-states (with respect to some semantical system S) that are *not* designated by any state description in S (*IS*, 107) and of propositions that are *not* designated by any sentence in S (*IS*, 114–115). In later works such as *M&N* and *LFP*, propositions as designata of sentences are dropped and L-ranges are regarded as sets of states descriptions (as opposed to sets of L-states), that is, as sets of linguistic entities.

In section 20 of *IS*, Carnap explores still another semantical method, in which "L-range in S" (for some specific semantical system S) is based on rules of L-range instead of rules of truth, and in which the concept of the "real L-state" (rs) is taken as primitive.[4] This allows a novel definition of the truth of a sentence (*IS*, 139), to the effect that

sentence A is true in S if, and only if, rs belongs to the L-range of A.

---

[4] In section 20, Carnap writes that in this new approach, the concept of L-range is taken as primitive. This holds for general semantics only. In special semantics, "L-range" is defined by specific rules of range. See also *FoL* (42).

As for L-terms (other than "L-state" and "L-range"), they are defined on the basis of these two terms. For example, the L-truth of a sentence receives the following definition (*IS*, 137):

sentence A is L-true if, and only if, the L-range of A is the class of all L-states.

In later works, semantical systems are defined by rules of formation, of designation, and of truth, whereas the definition of L-terms are based on rules of range (see *M&N*, 5, 9, and *LFP*, sections 17–18).

According to a definition given in *M&N* (10), a sentence A is L-true in S if, and only if, A holds in every state description in S, in such a way that the L-truth of A can be established on the basis of the rules of range, with no reference either to facts or to the concept of truth. It is crucial to note here that Carnap uses the idea of "holding in a state description" and that he *does not* have any notion of "truth in a state description." The definition of L-truth we have just mentioned should not be confused with the idea of truth in every model (or in every interpretations of a language). In Carnap's approach to semantics, truth is defined by rules of designation and rules of truth, not by rules of range, and it does not depend on state descriptions. Truth is truth in the real state, not in anything else. "Holding in every state description of system S" is not to be read as a forerunner of our familiar "being true in all interpretations of language L." This remark is important in order to get a precise idea of Carnapian semantics and its specificities, which are not in the line of what is often called "classical Tarskian semantics" today.

The idea that sentences have a range predates the semantical turn and is already introduced in *LSL*. In *LSS*, the range of sentence A was somewhat vaguely explained as "the domain of possibilities left over by A" (section 56) but also syntactically defined in a precise way. Technically, in *LSL*, the range of A is a class of specific classes of sentences (details are given in section 56). In the original German edition of *LSL*, Carnap explained that in adopting the word "Spielraum," he was following Wittgenstein. This connection was justified by a quote from the *Tractatus* (section 4.463): "The truth-conditions determine the range [*Spielraum*] which is left to the facts by the proposition." In later works, when it comes to the concept of range, the reference to Wittgenstein is repeated again and again (*IS*, 97 and 107; *M&N*, 9 and 10; *LFP*, 83 and 299). Carnap's ambition was to find a precise explication for this general Wittgensteinian idea.

Carnap's reason for using "range" in 1934 was to provide definitions for sentential connectives in the context of general syntax. These definitions were supposed to hold for any language. In two important footnotes dated 1935 and added to the English translation of the book (*LSL*, 200 and 204), Carnap mentioned a remark due to Tarski showing that definitions of connectives based on the syntactical concept of range "are not always in accordance with the usual meanings ... as laid down by the truth-value-table" (*LSL*, 204). Carnap thus admitted that his original syntactic explication of range of 1934 was not adequate for the use he intended to make of it and in the second 1935 footnote, he finally gave Tarskian definitions of sentential connectives that do not make use of range. This move was temporary though. In 1942, he notes that some syntactical definitions for L-concepts "have to be abandoned" (*IS*, 247) and that this holds for "range." He expresses the view that "the concept of range ... is primarily a semantical L-concept" (*IS*, 248). The result is the treatment of L-terms that we find in Carnap (*IS*, *FoL*, *M&N*, and *LFP*), which is primarily based on a new, semantical approach to ranges. Propositional connections receive a semantical definition on the basis of L-ranges in *FoL* (section 11).

It is sometimes argued that in his *M&N* and *LFP*, Carnap finally goes back to a syntactic definition of L-truth, because in these books the range of a sentence is nothing but a set of state descriptions, that is, of linguistic entities. This definition, however, does not amount to a return to the former syntactic approach to languages at all. Carnap by no means gives up semantical systems defined by rules of designation and rules of truth, and he also has a notion of interpretation of sentences, based of rules of designation and rules of range (*M&N*, 9).

Carnap sees several advantages in using rules of range rather than rules of truth for defining L-truth: (i) the concept of range may be taken as a basis for the definition of L-terms, (ii) the concept of range "is also useful in the logical analysis of science in order to characterize sentences and theories with respect to what they say and what they leave undetermined" (*IS*, 96–97), and (iii) it "may be taken as a basis for a theory of probability (Wittgenstein, Waismann) or of degree of confirmation" (*IS*, 97). Obviously, Carnap was inspired by Tarski when writing about truth and semantics (although he was far from just following Tarski on that count) and much more by ideas he found in Wittgenstein (and Waismann) when discussing L-semantics and the definition of L-terms. The second source of inspiration seemed more promising than the first to someone who was looking for a broad logical framework, encompassing nothing less than deductive logic, modal logic, inductive logic, and the logical analysis of science.

8.6 Tolerance

According to the principle of tolerance as formulated in *LSL*, everyone is free to choose the logic and the language system that best suits his or her own purposes, without having to justify this choice by a proof of correctness. No philosophical justification, only the statement of syntactic rules, is required. In *LSL*, the choice is among several object languages, defined in the framework of the syntactic method.

Although tolerance is crucial for a good understanding of Carnap's thought, it has long been ignored or misinterpreted as a thesis based on philosophical arguments. It is better construed as an attitude that consists in deciding pragmatically what rules one wishes to adopt for a logical framework and in giving up the search for allegedly correct ones. This means that the decision to adopt the principle of tolerance calls for a second decision concerning the logico-linguistic system one wants to adopt.

In the foreword to *LSL*, two procedures for constructing a language are compared: the first consists in assigning meaning to mathematico-logical signs and in seeing what sentences and inferences are correct according to that meaning; the second is described in the following way: "let any postulates and any rules of inference be chosen arbitrarily; then this choice whatever it may be, will determine what meaning is to be assigned to the fundamental logical symbols" (*LSL*, xv). Carnap gives two reasons for adopting the second procedure rather than the first: (a) in the first, the assignment of meaning is inexact and ambiguous because it is done with words, while the second method does not have this disadvantage; (b) in the second method, "the conflict between the divergent points of view on the problem of the foundations of mathematics disappears" because "no question of justification arises at all" (*LSL*, xv). For this reason, the second method is clearly more in agreement with the principle of tolerance than the first.

This raises the question of what happens to tolerance after the semantical turn. In a later publication, tolerance is described as "the principle that everyone is free to use the language most suited to his purpose" (*IA*, 18). This principle, Carnap adds, "has remained the same throughout my life" (*IA*, 18). This general formulation, however, does not establish any connection with syntactic rules or with the second method for defining a language, and it clearly differs from the one we find in *LSL*. Should we conclude that the principle of tolerance changed at the time of the semantical turn?

Carnap was well aware that this turn was not without consequence for tolerance:

> The *principle of tolerance* (perhaps better called "principle of conventionality"), as explained in [Syntax] § 17, is still maintained. It states that the construction of a calculus and the choice of its particular features are a matter of convention. On the other hand, the construction of a system of logic, i.e. the definition of the L-concepts, within a given semantical system is not a matter of mere convention; here the choice is essentially limited if the concepts are to be adequate (see above, §16). (*IS*, 247)

A similar point is made in section 36 (*IS*, 219). In his review of *IS*, Church asked for clarification:

> The principle of tolerance is still maintained in its original form, but its effect seems to be greatly modified ... Some statement by Carnap regarding the application of the principle of tolerance ... would seem to be desirable in order to clarify his revised position. (Church 1943, 303–304)

What needs to be clarified is the reason why "logic is not essentially conventional" (*IS*, 219) in the perspective of *IS* while the basic idea of Carnapian tolerance seems to imply the conventionality of logic. In his short discussion of tolerance after the semantical turn (*IS*, 247), Carnap refers to the adequacy requirement, which did not appear in *LSL*. What does it mean for the definition of logical concepts to be "adequate"?

In *IS*, Carnap makes numerous proposals for the definition of "true in S." How do we know that these definitions hit their target, so that the defined concept is precisely truth and not some other concept? In order to solve this problem, Carnap states the following condition: "*to assert that a sentence is true means the same as to assert the sentence itself*" (*IS*, 26). This is not meant as a definition but as a decision concerning the use of the word "true" or as "a standard by which we judge whether a definition for truth is adequate, i.e. in accordance with our intention" (*IS*, 26). This move is clearly inspired by Tarski's famous "convention T," although there are important differences between Carnap's definition of adequacy for truth (*IS*, 26–27) and Tarski's convention-T (Tarski 1933/1956, 187–188, where the term "adequate" is used). Carnap also formulates adequacy conditions for other concepts, the most important of which is certainly the one concerning L-truth. What is the condition for a definition to define an L-truth predicate and not some other predicate? The short answer is that a sentence A is L-true in a semantical system S if, and only if, it is true and its truth follows from the rules of S alone. Again, this is not meant as a definition but as a criterion of adequacy, discussed in Carnap (*IS*, 83–84), where more details and some more precise versions of it are given.

With this criterion in place, it is easier to understand why "logic is not essentially conventional" once logic is interpreted as providing "the rules of a logical deduction expressed in the definitions of the L-concepts" (*IS*, 219). If this interpretation of logic is granted, "the L-concepts cannot be chosen freely if they are to fulfill the requirement of adequacy" (*IS*, 219). It may happen that we want to change the condition of adequacy, for example, if we think that the one Carnap proposes is not in agreement with our use of the term "logical truth" or if we want to introduce a different meaning of that term (we may have good reasons to do so). But we may not drop it entirely on pain of defining a system in which the meaning of "L-truth" is too different from any of the common or proposed uses of the term "logical truth."

Once a semantical system is built (by rules of formation, designation, truth, and range), a calculus K may be constructed (by rules of formation, of inference, or refutation, etc.), but here again, if we want K to be "in accordance with a given semantical system S we are not entirely free. In some essential respects the features of S determine those of K" (*IS*, 218). After the semantical turn, the freedom to build a logical system meets two limitations: first, the rules of a semantical system S, on which the definition of L-truth in S depends, should be such that the L-truth predicate be adequate; second, the rules of a calculus K that is supposed to formalize S should be such that K really be a formalization of S. Are these constraints on the construction of a logical system compatible with the principle of tolerance and was the situation different in the context of *LSL*?

A notable difference between *LSL* and *IS* is that a criterion of adequacy is given for L-truth in *IS* whereas no such criterion for L-validity (analyticity) is provided in *LSL*. How do we know that the definitions Carnap offers in *LSL* actually hit their target? How do we know that the definitions presented as definitions of L-validity do not actually define another concept? Although no definition of adequacy for L-validity is offered, a criterion exists, which sets limits of acceptability. The criterion that Carnap sets takes the form of a theorem that is supposed to guarantee that the concept defined is L-validity and no other concept. This theorem is precisely what we have called "the completeness theorem in Carnap's sense" above, which is proved for Language I, for Language II, and in general syntax. In *LSL*, this theorem has precisely the function of an adequacy criterion. According to Carnap, any alleged definition that would not allow a proof of completeness (in Carnap's sense) should not be received as actually defining L-validity.

This reading of the completeness theorem in Carnap's sense sheds light on a paragraph of *LSL* that is not easy to interpret. In the foreword of *LSL*, Carnap writes that "the mathematico-logical sentences are analytic, with no real content" (*LSL*, xiv). This seems to run against tolerance. Analyticity is relative to a linguistic framework, and the principle of tolerance is supposed to allow any choice of a linguistic system, including one in which mathematical sentences are not analytic (see Goldfarb [1997] for a thorough discussion of that precise point). If this is so, how can Carnap both promote tolerance and assert the analyticity of logico-mathematical sentences? The way out of this quandary is to understand Carnap's assertion about the analyticity of mathematical sentences as expressing his own choice for the adoption of a linguistic system. In the context of tolerance, the seemingly absolutist statement that mathematical sentences are analytic is better construed as a prompt to adopt a logical system in which mathematical sentences are analytic. More precisely: to adopt a logical system in which the mathematical sentences that are recognized as true by the mathematical community can be reconstructed as analytic sentences and in which every logical-mathematical sentence in it is either analytic or contradictory. As a matter of fact, Language I and Language II in *LSL* do satisfy these conditions, and in the fourth part of the book, general syntax is devised so as to satisfy them too. Carnap's statement that mathematical and logical sentences are analytic is not to be read as a thesis about what these sentences really are (that would be an absolutist assertion of the kind Carnap criticizes in *LSL*) but as a proposed criterion of adequacy for L-validity. Although this statement does not have the form of the adequacy criterion for L-truth we find in *IS*, it plays a similar role, for L-validity. Some non-Carnapian philosopher may want to use the syntactic method and build a logical system in which at least some mathematical sentences are reconstructed as synthetic sentences or in which no completeness theorem in Carnap's sense is provable. Although Carnap would not declare such a reconstruction false or incorrect, he would presumably not find it illuminating or simply helpful for the logic of science. At any rate, it would not meet Carnap's criterion of adequacy for L-validity.

The issue of whether logic is a matter of convention is discussed in (*FLM*, section 12), where the distinction between two procedures for building a logical system is taken up again: we can either give the meaning of the logical signs before formal rules of deduction are formulated or establish a calculus C and then give an interpretation by adding a semantical system. In the second case, "we are free in choosing the rules of C" although "the choice is not irrelevant" because "it depends upon C whether the interpretation can yield a rich language or only a poor one" (*FLM*, section 12). Indeed, not any arbitrary choice for the rules of C would produce a satisfactory language system. For example, "we may find that a calculus we have chosen yields a language which is too poor or which in some other respect seems unsuitable for the purpose we have in mind" (*FLM*, section 12). The choice of a set of postulates is usually guided by some ideas about what logic is or about what it should be. In Carnap's case, these ideas include the possibility of proving a completeness theorem.

After the semantical turn, the requirement of adequacy is made completely explicit. As for tolerance, far from being more restricted than in *LSL*, it has a broader application since it is not confined to the choice of syntactic rules anymore. Moreover, it is now applied not only to the choice of an object language but also to the choice of a metalanguage and of a method used in the metalanguage. The reason why tolerance seems to be modified is that the focus is on the semantical approach to logic, with adequacy conditions more clearly explained. This, however, does not imply any restriction of tolerance, only a more general formulation and a broader application of its principle.

Although Carnap's transition from syntax to semantics has already been extensively commented upon, the relations and tensions between these two methods are far from having been fully clarified. In the preceding paragraphs, we have briefly indicated some of the gray areas that still await further investigation. That transition still deserves discussion as can be seen from some recent debates in the literature (see Tuboly 2017).

CHAPTER 9

Carnap on the Formality of Logic and Mathematics
Georg Schiemer[*]

9.1 Introduction

Throughout his intellectual career, Rudolf Carnap developed highly original views on the nature of mathematical knowledge, its relation to logic, and the application of mathematics in the natural sciences. A general line of continuity in his philosophical work on mathematics and logic is the conviction that these disciplines are formal or nonfactual in nature. Let us call this Carnap's formality thesis. The central role of this thesis in his philosophy of mathematics has been emphasized in recent scholarship. Compare, for instance, Friedman (2018, 142), who holds that "Carnap's conception of analyticity was intended, above all, to make clear that both logic and mathematics are empty of factual content." A similar verdict is reached in Koellner (2008, 1): "Throughout most of his philosophical career Carnap upheld and defended ... the thesis that the truths of logic and mathematics are analytic and hence without content and purely formal." As Friedman and Koellner point out, Carnap's formality thesis can be identified in different formulations in his work, connecting his early contributions to the foundations of geometry and to general axiomatics from the 1920s with his later work on the general syntax of mathematical languages in the *Logische Syntax* of 1934.[1]

---

[*] Funded by the European Union (ERC, FORMALISM, 101044114). Views and opinions expressed are, however, those of the author(s) only and do not necessarily reflect those of the European Union or the European Research Council Executive Agency. Neither the European Union nor the granting authority can be held responsible for them. I would like to thank the editors of the present volume, Adam Tamas Tuboly and Alan Richardson, for their helpful comments and suggestions. I am also indebted to Benjamin Marschall, Erich Reck, Christoph Limbeck-Lilienau, and Christian Damböck for valuable feedback on an early draft of the chapter.

[1] See Demopoulos (2013) for a related analysis of "Carnap's thesis" on the "nonfactuality of logic and mathematics." It should be noted that the claim that mathematics is concerned only with the formal features of objects can also be found in Carnap's subsequent semantic work, in particular, in his book *Foundations of Logic and Mathematics* of 1939.

Given the centrality of this idea, a natural question is how precisely Carnap understood the formality thesis concerning mathematical knowledge? Thus, in what sense should mathematics be viewed as formal according to him? Moreover, how was the thesis characterized at different stages in his philosophical work? The central aim in this chapter will be to address these interpretive questions and to retrace the development of Carnap's thinking about the formality of logic and mathematics from the 1920s until the late 1930s. As we will see, in spite of his general adherence to the thesis throughout the period in question, there were several significant shifts in his understanding, corresponding to changes in his conceptual framework in the study of these fields. Specifically, one can identify a transition from an object-theoretic account of formality related to his study of axiomatic theories based on the logical theory of relations to a "syntactic formalism" developed in his *Logical Syntax*. This transition is closely connected to different ways of specifying the notion of "formal" or "structural properties" in Carnap's contributions to the philosophy of mathematics. For instance, in his discussion of a "formal space" in *Der Raum* and in later work from the 1920s, formal properties of a given mathematical system were usually identified with structural or invariant features, studied in abstraction from the intrinsic nature of the objects in question.[2] Starting with his work in the 1930s, this conception changes significantly. Formality is now understood in terms of "linguistic form," to be specified relative to formal systems or languages. In particular, as we will see, *LSS* contains an explicit account of the formality thesis as a purely syntactic claim, that is, as a thesis about the priority of the syntactic features of expressions or theories over questions regarding their semantic interpretation. Moreover, the metatheoretical study of such properties can be developed in a "logical syntax," understood as a "formal theory of linguistic forms."

The present chapter will give a critical discussion of Carnap's different approaches to the formality thesis in the period in question. Specifically, the aim is to further clarify his views, based also on a comparison with recent discussions of notions of formality in logic and mathematics (cf. Sher 2008; Dutilh Novaes 2011). Moreover, it will be shown that despite the conceptual shift from a "semantic" to a "syntactic" account of formality

---

[2] As will be shown, Carnap's relation-theoretic account of formal properties is closely connected to the mathematical structuralism developed in his work on geometry and general axiomatics. See Schiemer (2020) for a more detailed study of Carnap's structuralism.

in his work, there remains a surprising continuity in his specification of the concepts "form," "structure," and "formal properties" in terms of a general notion of isomorphism invariance.

9.2 The Formality Thesis in Carnap's Early Philosophy of Geometry

Carnap's contributions to the philosophy of mathematics from the 1920s can be divided into several research strands. This includes his early work on the philosophy of modern geometry and the nature of space (in particular in *Raum*), his contributions to the foundations of mathematics, specifically a defense of Frege's and Russell's logicism, as well as his work on "general axiomatics" (cf. Carnap 1931/1983, 2000). In what follows, I will briefly survey these lines of work. This will show that, already in the period in question and thus years before his "syntactic turn," the focus on the purely formal nature of mathematics was a central theme in Carnap's work. Moreover, in contrast to his later syntactic phase, the formality of mathematics was understood object-theoretically here, based on the logical theory of relations and closely connected to his early structuralism.

Carnap's monograph *Der Raum. Ein Beitrag zur Wissenschaftslehre* is based on his dissertation completed a year earlier under the supervision of the neo-Kantian Bruno Bauch at the University of Jena. The book offers a novel interpretation of the philosophical problem of the nature of geometrical space. Carnap argues that the long-standing debate, leading back to Kant's theoretical philosophy of geometry, can be dissolved by distinguishing between three concepts of space, namely "formal," "intuitive," and "physical space." The first type of space is characterized as follows:

> *Formal* space is a general order-structure of a certain kind. By "general order-structure" we mean a system of relations – not between certain objects of a sensible or non-sensible domain, but between entirely indeterminate relata about which we only need to know that one kind of link entails a different kind of link in the same domain. So formal space deals not with the figures usually considered spatial, such as triangles or circles, but with meaningless relata whose place may be taken by an enormous variety of things. (*Raum*, 27, original emphasis)

Formal space, viewed as the subject matter of formal geometry, is thus characterized as an "order structure" (*Ordnungsgefüge*), that is, a relational structure that is specified in abstraction from concrete or intuitive interpretations. Intuitive space, in contrast, is understood by Carnap as a "system of relations among 'spatial' figures in the usual sense" (*Raum*, 27). Interestingly, Carnap proposes two methods of how a formal space of a given type can be specified in mathematics. The first approach essentially conforms to the modern axiomatic method as outlined in Hilbert's *Grundlagen der Geometrie* of (1899). Carnap describes this approach to formal axiomatics as opposed to the more traditional descriptive understanding of axiomatic systems (see, e.g., Schlimm 2013). Specifically, in his view, an axiom system abstracts from any intuitive interpretation of its primitive terms and is thus concerned only with its "logical form." The logical form of axioms, in turn, is specified as that "component of meaning" preserved by reformulating a contentual axiom system in terms of purely logical statements in which the constant primitive terms are replaced by universally bound variables. Compare Carnap on this point:

> If we think of all the theorems as put into this more general form, then instead of geometry proper (that of points, lines, and planes) we have a "*pure theory of relations*" or "*theory of orders*", i.e., a theory of indefinite objects and of the equally indefinite relations holding among them ... The object of this discipline is not space, i.e., the system of points, lines, and planes determined by *geometrical* axioms (which we call "intuitive space" to distinguish it), but a "relational or structural system" determined by the *formal* axioms. As this represents the formal design of the spatial system, and turns into the spatial system again when spatial elements are substituted for indeterminate relata, it too will be called "space": "*formal space*." (*Raum*, 31, original emphases)

The general advantage of this approach and the modern understanding of "formal axioms" lies in their general applicability or, in Carnap's own words, in the fact that such theories are subject to a "multiplicity of interpretation."

Carnap outlines a second approach to formal geometry in the 1922 book, based on the genetic construction of spaces in "*formal logic*," that is, the theory of classes and relations first introduced in Russell's *Principles of Mathematics* of 1903. Without going into details here, Carnap's basic idea is to first specify different types of (binary) relations, including the properties of being symmetric, transitive, single-valued, etc. A "series" is then defined as a system consisting of a set of objects (viewed as the extension of a concept) and an asymmetric, transitive relation on the set. The "series of the *real numbers*" is introduced as the order type of all continuous series. Given this setup, and again following Russell (1903), an n-dimensional space is then defined as a continuous series of the n-th level, that is, a set of n-tuples of objects such as numbers.[3] Importantly, as in the axiomatic approach, Carnap emphasizes the formal nature of such a genetically constructed space. This is understood here as the fact that no reference to spatial or intuitive elements or to concrete relations between such elements is presupposed. As Carnap puts it: "For we are here still dealing with merely formal relations, without any assumptions about what sort of objects have these relations to each other. The different R's are therefore also called systems of order-relations (systems of ordinal relations), briefly, order-structures" (*Raum*, 41).

Given Carnap's dual characterization of formal space(s) in 1922, several general remarks are in order here. First, it should be noted that in both approaches, the axiomatic and the genetic one, formal geometry is conceived as an a priori science, freed from its traditional ties to intuitive or physical space, and thus a branch of pure mathematics. Specifically, given the modern axiomatic method of Hilbert and others, the geometrical axioms are viewed as a priori and analytic principles whose validity is independent of empirical or intuitive content. Notice, however, that formality is not yet understood by Carnap in the sense of the syntactic formality of a logical system or calculus. Thus, to say that a geometry is pure or formal in character is not to say that it presents a *disinterpreted* calculus without any meaning or content. In contrary, in Carnap's early view, formal theories do have a specific subject matter, namely, an abstract "*order structure*." Hence, the formality of mathematics is closely connected or explained in terms of his structuralist account of mathematics (see also Schiemer 2020). Geometry, so conceived, becomes part the theory of relations. In other words, formal theories of geometry (such as topology, Euclidean, projective, elliptic, hyperbolic geometry, etc.) turn out to be purely logical in character and thus a branch of formal logic. Carnap, already in 1922, is explicit in this view of a logicized form of geometry: "The theory of formal space is an extension of a special domain of the theory of relations; its propositions, just like those of number theory, are derived from the basic laws of deductive logic and are wholly independent of experience" (*Raum*, 93).[4]

---

[3] See the editorial notes by Michael Friedman in *CW1* for a detailed study of Carnap's genetic approach to formal spaces. Compare also Mormann (2007).

[4] The immediate background for this view is Russell's discussion of geometry in part VI of his *Principles of Mathematics* (1903). Specifically, Russell introduces here his account of geometry as "the science of series of two or more dimensions" and thus a purely logical science. Compare Gandon (2012) for a detailed study of Russell's theory of pure geometry in 1903.

A second point to note is that the notions of "formal relations" or "formal properties" take a center stage in Carnap's understanding of formal geometry. As we will see below, the focus on such relations is a recurring theme in his work on the philosophy of mathematics. In *Der Raum*, it becomes explicit in his discussion of so-called further "specifications (or specializations)" of a genetically constructed formal space of a given dimension. Such a specification of, say, a three-dimensional topological space can be given in either one of two ways. One approach is based on the genetic method and consists in imposing "more restrictive conditions ... on the series-forming relations" of the space in question. The result of such specifications are again formal spaces or, in Carnap's words, other "*order structures*" of a specific type. The second approach is again based on the axiomatic method. Thus, instead of formulating further constraints on the "series-forming relations" of a given order structure, subspaces of the topological space can be specified directly in terms of further axiomatic conditions. Compare Carnap on the differences between the two approaches:

> Now, it has emerged that the resulting order-structures (e.g., R_{3p}), if they are to be investigated on their own (i.e., without reference to R_{3t} or R_{nt}), are simpler to construct if they are presented directly as structures of certain simple relations whose formal properties are given – rather than taking the circuitous route by way of continuous series of the first, and then of the third level subject to certain limiting conditions. (*Raum*, 41–45)

The approach outlined here matches our modern understanding of formal axiomatic theories: geometry, in this view, studies relational systems whose basic structural properties are specified or implicitly defined axiomatically, that is, in terms of a set of axiomatic conditions. For instance, the geometry of finite projective planes is typically viewed as the study of a particular type of finite incidence structure consisting of a set of point, a set of lines, and a binary incidence relation defined between them. The specific type or, in Carnap's words, the "formal properties" of such incidence relations are specified in terms of the relevant incidence axioms in question.

9.3 Pure and Applied Structure Theory

It should be noted that by the time of *Der Raum* in 1922, Carnap did not yet have logically precise notions of "order structure" and "formal property" at hand. This eventually changed in the course of the second half of the 1920s, when Carnap started to employ more systematically the theory of relations and logical type theory in his philosophical work. The ground for this was, in fact, laid just a year after the publication of his 1922 monograph, with Carnap's contributions to the so-called *Erlanger Tagung*. This was a programmatic conference dedicated to scientific philosophy, jointly organized by Carnap and Hans Reichenbach and held at the Philosophical Academy in Erlangen in March 1923. As we know from his *Nachlass*, Carnap first presented two research projects there. The first was an early version of his "constitution theory," that is, the project that would eventually become his *Der Logische Aufbau der Welt* (1928). The second contribution consisted of several talks on "Relation theory and structure theory." Building on a presentation of Russell's theory of relations, Carnap first introduced here a "pure structure theory" ("*reine Strukturlehre*") in which a general definition of the concepts of "structure," "isomorphism," "structural identity," and "structural property" was given in terms of relation theory.[5]

While we lack more information on the specific details of his presentation of a structure theory in 1923, the topic is addressed again in published form in *Abriss der Logistik* of 1929. The first part of Carnap's *Abriss* contains a detailed discussion of the theory of relations and of logical type theory as presented in Russell's and Whitehead's *Principia Mathematica* (1910–1913). Interestingly, the notion of formality is now used in two different senses in Carnap's book. First, motivated mainly by Wittgenstein's account of logical truths in the *Tractatus logico-philosophicus* of 1921, it is used by Carnap to characterize the specific nature of the principles and theorems of propositional logic as "tautological" or "formal" in character. Thus, propositional axioms such as $q \to (p \vee q)$ are described as "formal basic laws" that present the "basis of the theory of deduction" (1929, section 4d). Second, formality is reintroduced in later sections of the book as a concept from relation theory. Specifically, following the introduction of several key concepts of Russell's calculus of relations, including several types of binary relations and operations on them, the book turns to the notion of "relation numbers" or "structures" of relations (1929, section 22). It is here that "formal properties" are mentioned again, now specified as properties of binary relations that are invariant under

---

[5] See RC 091-17-12, Carnap papers, Archive of Scientific Philosophy, University of Pittsburgh. See Limbeck-Lilienau (2022) for further details. Another closely related topic first introduced at the *Erlanger Tagung* is Carnap's "characterization of structures," that is, his attempt to specify a "structure characteristic" or, in modern terms, a complete invariant for relations. Compare also his related remarks in Carnap (1929).

isomorphic transformations (or "isomorphism-correlations" between relations). Following again Russell, Carnap first specifies the notion of "structure" of a given relation as "the class of relations that are isomorphic to it." (1929, section 22c). Thus, a structure of a certain n-ary relation R is simply identified with the isomorphism class of R. Similarly, the structure of ordered sets such as a series or a well-ordered series are identified with the class of systems isomorphic to them. Given this specification, Carnap further holds that relations (or relational systems) that are structurally similar or isomorphic also share the same formal properties. In his own words:

> A relation is fully characterized by its structure as concerns its formal properties, if we understand by the latter those properties that result by taking into account only the identity and difference of the members of the relation, while disregarding the members' other characteristics. The concept of "formal property" that was just elucidated is not precisely delineated. Therefore, in its place we prefer to use the concept of "*structural property*" of a relation P, which has the same objective but is definable precisely. A property is characterized as a structural property in this way: if it holds of any relation R, it also holds of all relations with the same structure, thus of all relations that are isomorphic to R. (1929, section 22d).

Note that a formal property of a relation is specified here, similarly to his informal treatment in (1922), in terms of an abstraction from the intuitive nature of its relata. Moreover, Carnap for the first time explicitly identifies the notions of formal properties and structural properties in this context.[6] The latter concept, in turn, is made precise in terms of the notion of isomorphism invariance. As examples of relational properties that are formal in this sense, Carnap lists the properties of transitivity, reflexivity, of being of a certain arity, functionality, etc.

It should be emphasized here that the pure theory of structures was devised by Carnap with several direct applications in mind, both in mathematics and philosophy. His main and most well-known use of structure theory for philosophical purposes is documented in the *Aufbau* of 1928. A central thesis defended there is that all scientific concepts and statements can be, in principle, transformed into "structure descriptions."[7]

---

[6] A similar informal discussion of formal properties and structure can be found already in Moritz Schlick's (1925/1974) *Allgemeine Erkenntnislehre* of 1918/1925. See Friedman (1999) for a closer study of Schlick's structuralism.

[7] See, in particular, Richardson (1998) and chapters 5 and 6 in Friedman (1999) for detailed analyses of Carnap's constitution theory in the *Aufbau*.

Without going into details, it is worth mentioning that the notion of formal properties again plays a central role in this philosophical endeavor. Specifically, in the first chapter of section II of the book, Carnap holds that in a structure description of the objects of given relational system, "only the structure of the relation is indicated, i.e., the totality of its formal properties." Interestingly, formal properties are not specified in terms of the notion of isomorphism invariance as in the *Abriss* but rather in terms of the notion of definability in a purely logical type-theoretic language. Compare Carnap on this point:

> By formal properties of a relation, we mean those that can be formulated without reference to the meaning of the relation and the type of objects between which it holds. They are the subject of the theory of relations. The formal properties of relations can be defined exclusively with the aid of logistic symbols, i.e., ultimately with the aid of the few fundamental symbols which form the basis of logistics (symbolic logic). (*Aufbau*, section 11)

Thus, formal properties of relations are specified as those properties explicitly definable in a pure language of type theory. Based on this, Carnap goes on to discuss the second central thesis of his structure theory, namely, that structurally similar relations possess the same abstract "form" or, in his words, are "equivalent in all formal properties." Since all scientific statements can, in principle, be translated into statements about the formal properties of a primitive relational system, it follows that scientific knowledge is ultimately knowledge of abstract form or structure.[8]

The second application of Carnap's pure structure theory is discussed in the *Abriss*. The second part of the book, titled "applied logistics," contains a detailed study of the logical formalization of different axiom systems of mathematical theories, including different versions of elementary arithmetic, set theory, projective geometry, as well as of Hausdorff spaces (see Carnap 1929, sections 31–35). The discussion of axiomatic theories is, in fact, similar to his treatment in *Der Raum* from some years earlier. The basic idea repeated in 1929 is that axiom systems function as formal conditions that specify the structural properties of the primitive relations of a theory. The main innovation in 1929 compared to Carnap's earlier account concerns the logical formalization of such theories. According to

---

[8] See chapter 2 of Richardson (1998) and chapter 5 of Friedman (1999) on Carnap's early structuralism. See Leitgeb (2011) for a formal reconstruction of Carnap's constitution theory presented in the *Aufbau*.

his new approach, any formal axiomatic theory in mathematics can be expressed in a purely logical language in the following way: the "primitive signs" of a theory are symbolized by free variables. Axioms and theorems, in turn, express propositional functions. An axiom system, so conceived, can thus be formalized in terms of a complex open formula, formed by the conjunction of the axioms in question.

9.4 General Axiomatics

Carnap's general approach to the formalization of axiom systems is adopted and further developed in his main contribution to "general axiomatics" from the late 1920s, namely, the manuscript *Untersuchungen zur Allgemeinen Axiomatik*. Carnap worked on what he originally devised as a two-volume book on the modern axiomatic method roughly between 1927 and 1929.[9] The general idea in the first, posthumously published volume (Carnap 2000) was to give a logical study of the metatheory of axiomatic theories. More specifically, the *Untersuchungen* manuscript contains an analysis of the logical form of axiomatic theories similar to the account presented in the *Abriss* as well as an explication of several metatheoretical concepts such as the notions of logical consequence, truth in a model, as well as a number of completeness properties of axiomatic theories. Moreover, Carnap introduces several metatheorems, most notably his so-called *Gabelbarkeitssatz*, that attempt to specify the relation between three notions of completeness, namely, "monomorphism," "decidability," and "non-forkability."[10] Interestingly, as we will see below, the relation-theoretic notion of formality again plays a crucial role in this discussion of the logical metatheory of axiom systems. More specifically, formality is reintroduced here as a property of axioms and of theorems meant to capture the idea that these mathematical statements specify only "structural" properties (as opposed to "contentual" properties) of their models.

To see this, let us first outline Carnap's new type-theoretic framework for the study of axiomatic theories. His general approach is characterized as follows: "By 'general axiomatics' ... we understand the theory of the general, logical-formal properties of axiom systems as well as the relations

---

[9] See the editorial introduction in Carnap (2000); Awodey and Carus (2001); and Reck (2007) for detailed studies of Carnap's *Untersuchungen* manuscript and its historical context.
[10] Compare Awodey and Carus (2001) and Schiemer, Zach, and Reck (2017) on Carnap's early metatheoretic results.

between axiom systems" (Carnap 2000, 59). These "logical-formal properties" are spelled out as follows: the logical convention adopted here is to treat both the axioms and theorems as propositional functions that specify the meaning of a number of primitive concepts symbolized by (free) variables of a given arity and type $X_1, \ldots, X_n$. Axioms, axiom systems and theorems are expressed as propositional functions $f(X_1, \ldots, X_n)$, that is, as open formulas in the modern sense. It is interesting to see how models of an axiom system were conceived in this context. Roughly put, according to Carnap in *Untersuchungen*, models should be understood as sequences of predicates or constant relation symbols of a type-theoretic language of the form $M = \langle R_1, \ldots, R_n \rangle$. Given this, the notion of truth or satisfaction in a model was understood substitutionally in the following way: a theory $f(X_1, \ldots, X_n)$ is true in a model M if and only if the sentence $f(R_1, \ldots, R_n)$, resulting from the systematic substitution of the primitive variables by constant expressions forms a true (or valid) sentence of the interpreted background language. Note that Carnap does not further specify the notion of validity in his logical background system in *Untersuchungen*. It is left as a primitive notion, identified in one passage with the informal notion of "tautology" in type-theoretic systems. Given this setup, the notion of formality is then introduced in the context of "general axiomatics" as a way to qualify the type of formulas or propositional functions relevant in the metatheoretic study of axiomatic theories. Carnap again introduces the notion of structural properties as a relation-theoretic concept but now defined for models of axiomatic theories. More precisely, the structural properties of models are those preserved under isomorphism:

> The property fP of relations is called a "structural property" if, in case it applies to a relation P, it also applies to any other relation isomorphic to P ... The structural properties are so to speak the invariants under isomorphic transformation. They are of central importance for axiomatics. (Carnap 2000, 74)

Notice that Carnap's account is directly based on his treatment of structural properties of relations in terms of isomorphism invariance in *Abriss* but generalized now to apply to sequences or tuples of relations of a specified type and order. Similarly, the "structure" of a given model of an axiom system is identified in *Untersuchungen* with its isomorphism class (cf. Carnap 2000, 72). Given this, the notion of formality is then introduced as a property of axioms or axiom systems. More precisely, in a section titled "Formal axioms," Carnap defines an axiom or axiom system (conceived of as a propositional function) to be "formal" if every admissible model that is isomorphic to a model of $f(R)$ is also a model of $f(R)$. In the language of type theory, this can be expressed by

$$For(f) \Leftrightarrow \forall P \forall Q \big((fP \wedge Iso_q(P, Q)) \to fQ \big).$$

The formality thesis for mathematical statements is arguably specified here for first time in Carnap's work in logically precise terms. It can be paraphrased in modern model-theoretic terms as follows: the statements (that is, axioms and theorems) relevant in mathematical work and subject to metatheoretic investigation are formal in character. To say that a statement is formal means that its truth or truth-value is isomorphism invariant. In other words, such a mathematical statement is true in all structures isomorphic to a given model of it.

Summing up, Carnap's general understanding of the formal nature of mathematics in the 1920s can be described as a form of semantic or object-theoretic formality.[11] Thus, mathematical theories are formal in the sense of having invariant forms or relational structures as their subject matter. As we saw, his account of formal mathematics is, in this sense, closely connected to his general structuralism. In particular, the notion of "form" is usually identified with his account of "order structures" or simply with "structure" in his writings. At that same time, his position is also closely related to much more recent systematic discussions of a semantic formalism in logic and mathematics. Compare, for instance, Dutilh Novaes' specification of a version of logical "formality as pertaining to form":

> In fact, variations of the notion of the formal as pertaining to forms are all specific interpretations of a common slogan: "formal corresponds to abstraction from matter." Accordingly, the opposite of all these variations is the notion of "material" ... What is form, and formal, is what remains once matter is removed (abstracted from). (Dutilh Novaes 2011, 306)

This general characterization, even though intended to describe the formal nature of logical reasoning, also applies to Carnap's recurring remarks on the formal nature of mathematics and on formal vs. material properties of relations. Moreover, a semantic notion of formality, as explicitly identified in Carnap's own emphasis of the notion of isomorphism invariance, is developed systematically in work by Sher. Compare an insightful description of this view in Sher (2008):

---

[11] Compare Schiemer (2013) for a more detailed study of Carnap's contributions to an early form of model theory in his work on general axiomatics. See Wagner (2009) for several studies of the various meanings and phases of Carnap's semantics in his philosophical work.

The invariance-under-isomorphism criterion is a criterion of *formality* or *structurality*: isomorphic structures are formally identical; identity-up-to-isomorphism is formal identity. The basic idea is that logic is a theory of reasoning based on the formal (structural) laws governing our thinking on the one hand and reality on the other, and the invariance-under-isomorphism criterion says that to be formal is to treat isomorphic structures as the same structures. (Sher 2008, 307)

This account of semantic formality closely captures Carnap's view on the topic in the period in question.[12] Given this, the question arises how this position evolved in his subsequent work, in particular, with his "syntactic turn" in the 1930s?

9.5 A Syntactic Formalism in *Logical Syntax*

The "general axiomatics" project was eventually abandoned in 1930, mainly as a consequence of Carnap's discussions with Alfred Tarski and Kurt Gödel on their limitative results, that is, the indefinability theorem of truth and the incompleteness theorems (see Awodey and Carus 2001). What these metalogical results showed, among other things, was that a systematic distinction needs to be drawn in logic between object- and metalanguages as well as between the semantic concepts of truth, satisfiability, and validity, on the one side, and purely syntactic concepts of proof and derivability in a formal system, on the other side. Roughly at the same time, Carnap has given up his attempts to generalize a *Tractatus*-style account of the tautological nature of elementary logic in order to apply this also to logical type theory and, a fortiori, to higher mathematics.[13] As a consequence of these shifts in Carnap's thinking about the nature of logic and mathematics, the idea of a logical syntax as a new research program was born. As Carnap recollects in his *Intellectual Autobiography* of 1963, "the whole theory of language structure" and thus the idea of a meta-mathematical approach in the study of logico-mathematical languages came to him during a sleepless night in January 1931. This eventually led to the publication of the monograph *Logische Syntax der Sprache* (*LSS*) in 1934.[14] Compared to his previous work on the philosophy of

---

[12] It should be added here that his approach to formality was not uncommon at the time. A similar approach can be identified in Tarski's early work on the "methodology of deductive sciences." See, in particular, the relevant articles contained in Tarski (1956).
[13] For closer studies of Carnap's engagement with Wittgenstein's account of logic in the *Tractatus*, see Goldfarb and Ricketts (1992); Friedman (1999); and Awodey and Carus (2007).
[14] See, in particular, Awodey and Carus (2007) for a detailed study of the interesting transition period between "Carnap's dream" in January 1931 and the publication of *Logische Syntax* in 1934.

mathematics, the new approach is marked by a number of significant changes. In fact, Carnap develops a new conceptual framework for the study of axiomatic theories and their metatheoretic properties that is based on (i) a clear separation between object- and metalanguages (in his terms, "syntax languages") and (ii) metatheoretical concepts such as analyticity and logical consequence defined for specific object languages, in particular, his languages LI and LII. Most importantly, Carnap's new approach is characterized by a form of logical pluralism, expressed in his famous "principle of tolerance" concerning the choice of such formal languages.[15]

Despite these important innovations, there is also a striking continuity with Carnap's previous work. This is the general formalist outlook for mathematics and logic or, more precisely, the thesis that logic and mathematical theories are formal in nature. How is the thesis characterized in the *Logical Syntax*? In the introduction to the book, Carnap outlines his new approach as follows:

> By the *logical syntax* of a language, we mean the formal theory of the linguistic forms of that language – the systematic statement of the formal rules which govern it together with the development of the consequences which follow from these rules. (*LSL*, 1)

The new framework, namely, the study of logical syntax, is explicitly introduced here as a formal theory concerned with "linguistic forms." Carnap goes on to offer a new specification of the notion of formality:

> A theory, a rule, a definition, or the like is to be called *formal* when no reference is made in it either to the meaning of the symbols (for example, the words) or to the sense of the expressions (e.g. the sentences), but simply and solely to the kinds and order of the symbols from which the expressions are constructed. (*LSL*, 1)

Given this new account of formality, two points of commentary are in order here. First, Carnap's general discussion of "logical syntax" is obviously inspired by Wittgenstein's *Tractatus*. Consider, in particular, Wittgenstein's characterization of logical syntax in his book: "In logical syntax the meaning of a sign should never play a role. It must be possible to establish logical syntax without mentioning the *meaning* of a sign: *only*

---

[15] See the chapters contained in Wagner (2009) for studies of the different innovations in Carnap's *Logical Syntax*.

the description of expressions may be presupposed" (Wittgenstein 1921, 3.33). Moreover, Carnap's discussion of "formal rules" in the passage above closely corresponds to Wittgenstein's notion of "symbolic rules" ("*Zeichenregeln*"), that is, rules that consider only the syntactic form but not the content (or meaning) of signs (see Wittgenstein 1921, 6.126). Thus, it seems well justified to say that Carnap's general account of form in *Logical Syntax*, understood now as "linguistic form" or "syntactic form," comes right out of the *Tractatus*.

Second, it should be noted that the formality of both syntax theory and of object languages is specified by Carnap in terms of a notion of *meaning independence*. Thus, a theory or language is formal according to him if it is not concerned with the meaning or the reference of its expressions but rather with their purely syntactical features.[16] Moreover, following again Wittgenstein's conception of the *Tractatus*, logic is now conceived as part of the syntax of languages and thus also formal since it is only concerned with such syntactical properties. As Carnap puts it, "the logical characteristics of sentences (for instance, whether a sentence is analytic, synthetic, or contradictory; whether it is an existential sentence or not; and so on) and the logical relations between them ... are solely dependent upon the syntactical structure of the sentences." (*LSL*, 1–2).

Given this new setup, the logico-mathematical axioms and theorems expressible in the languages LI and LII are characterized as analytic and thus formal statements whose truth is determined by the "formal structure" of the language in question. As Carnap explains in his foreword: "the mathematical-logical sentences are analytic, with no real content, and are merely formal auxiliaries." (*LSL*, xiv) Moreover, formality, now understood as a kind of meaning independence, is also used explicitly to characterize the metatheoretic properties between statements of these object languages. Next to his definition of analyticity, compare for instance his informal specification of another key notion of his general syntax theory, namely logical consequence:

> But the decisive point is the following: *in order to determine whether or not one sentence is a consequence of another, no reference need be made to the*

---

[16] Carnap's account of formality in terms of meaning independence in *Logical Syntax* is, in fact, comparable to his previous object-theoretic approach developed in *Der Raum* and in *Untersuchungen*. As we saw, formality was understood in these earlier works in terms of a form of abstraction from intuitive content or semantic interpretations as well. It would be worthwhile to give a more detailed study of Carnap's different notions of "(formal) content" and the relation to his evolving views on semantics. On the latter point, see Tuboly (2017).

meaning of the sentences ... It is sufficient that the syntactical design of the sentences be given. (*LSL*, section 71)

Given the ubiquitous talk of "linguistic structures," of the "syntactical design" of formulae, and of syntax as the purely combinatorial study of signs, it seems clear that Carnap defended a new form of syntactic formalism in 1934 that differs strongly from the object-theoretic account of formality present in his preceding work. But how precisely is the formality of linguistic expressions understood in the *Logical Syntax*? More specifically, how does he specify meaning independence in this new context?

To see this, it is important to understand what Carnap meant by logico-mathematical languages. Roughly, his principal idea is that languages should be viewed as "calculi," to be specified in terms to two types of formal rules, namely, formation rules and transformation rules (see *LSL*, section 2). Thus, as other scholars have pointed out, the specific languages investigated in *Logical Syntax* do not match with our modern notion of formal languages but rather with a combination of such languages and formal systems: they do not just include syntactic formation rules but also axioms and rules of deduction as well as the "indefinite" (and essentially semantic) concepts of consequence, analyticity, etc. Given Carnap's emphasis on the rule-based nature of languages, it seems well justified to understand his specific account of formality as a syntactic formalism or as "formality as pertaining to rules" (cf. Dutilh Novaes 2011).[17] This is a natural interpretation not just in light of Carnap's own remarks but given also the immediate intellectual background of the new logical framework introduced in 1934. In particular, next to Gödel and Tarski, Carnap mentions Hilbert and his foundational program from the 1920s as a central influence:[18]

> The point of view of the formal theory of language (known as "syntax" in our terminology) was first developed for mathematics by Hilbert in his "metamathematics," to which the Polish logicians, especially Ajdukiewicz, Lesniewski, Lukasiewicz, and Tarski, have added a "metalogic." (*LSL*, xvi)

---

[17] Compare also Hamami (2018, 681) for a general specification of the syntactic formality of logic.

[18] A second influence on Carnap's account of languages as formal calculi concerns the debate between Ramsey and Wittgenstein on the nature of mathematics, as was discussed also in the Vienna Circle since 1927. The bone of contention in these discussions was whether mathematical expressions (and especially equations) form tautologies as suggested by Ramsey in his "Foundations of Mathematics" or rather purely formal rules as suggested by Wittgenstein. Once the *Tractatus* conception was given up around 1929 and once Carnap rejected Ramsey's view in his paper on logicism presented in Königsberg, the view of mathematics as formal calculi constituted by formal rules gained much attraction. I would like to thank Christoph Limbeck-Lilienau for emphasizing this point to me.

According to Carnap's own version of syntactic formalism, the logical syntax of languages should be concerned with the metatheoretical study of the "formal structure" of languages such as LI and LII or, more precisely, with the "formal properties" of expressions of such languages. But how are these notions cashed out by Carnap in 1934? Interestingly, Carnap's approach is surprisingly similar to his earlier views. In particular, formality, understood as a form of meaning independence or indifference to interpretation, is again specified in terms of the notion of isomorphism invariance. Carnap's view on this matter in *Logical Syntax* is already specified in an insightful passage in the introduction:

> We have already said that syntax is concerned solely with the formal properties of expressions. We shall now make this assertion more explicit. Assume that two languages (*Sprachen*), S_1 and S_2, use different symbols, but in such a way that a one-one correspondence may be established between the symbols of S_1 and those of S_2 so that any syntactical rule about S_1 becomes a syntactical rule about S_2 if, instead of relating it to the symbols of S_1, we relate it to the correlative symbols of S_2; and conversely. Then, although the two languages are not alike, they have the same *formal structure* (we call them isomorphic languages), and syntax is concerned solely with the structure of languages in this sense. (*LSL*, 5–6)

The notion of "formal structure" does not concern properties of relational systems as in Carnap's previous work but rather languages themselves. Nevertheless, the criterion for sameness of form or structural equivalence is again specified in terms of the notion of isomorphism invariance, now understood as the preservation of certain syntactic properties of expressions under isomorphism transformations between languages. Importantly, these formal properties concern not syntactic features in a strict sense of the term (including, for instance, the choice of logical notation) but rather metatheoretic rules or properties such a "being an analytic sentence," "following logically from sentence set X" and so on.

In order to get a better understanding of Carnap's account, it is instructive to look at the details of his new understanding of formality. As the passage above makes clear, invariance is specified now in terms of a syntactic notion of isomorphism, understood as a relation between languages. In part IV of "*General Syntax*," in the section on "*Translation and Interpretation*" (sections 61–62), Carnap first introduces the concept of a "syntactic correlation" between expressions and, based on it, the notion of a "transformance" between all sentence classes (or all sentences) of a language S_1 and the sentence classes (or sentences) of language S_2. Roughly put, a transformance is defined as a mapping between the sentences of the two languages that preserves the consequence relation. The notion of a syntactic isomorphism is then introduced as a transformation of language S_1 into S_2 that is "reversable in respect of symbols."[19] Given this, Carnap investigates several syntactic properties of expressions or sentences of a language that are typically preserved under such isomorphisms and thus turn out as formal. In particular, the concepts of "analytic," "valid," or "descriptive" turn out to be formal properties of sentence classes in this account given that they can be "transferred" by an isomorphism from one language to another one.

Carnap's approach to capture the formality of properties in terms of the notion of isomorphism invariance in *Logical Syntax* is essentially the idea specified already in his contributions to mathematics from the late 1920s. The central discontinuity with his earlier work lies in the fact that isomorphism invariance is now specified as a syntactic concept, that is, as a concept applied to properties of (or relations between) expressions, sentences, or sentence classes of a given language. Moreover, an isomorphism is introduced now as a purely syntactic relation by Carnap. Thus, unlike in the *Abriss* or the *Untersuchungen* manuscript, isomorphisms are not defined as mappings between objects of different domains that preserve the structure of certain relations but rather as mappings between the elementary syntactic units of languages. What are the consequences of this shift from an object-theoretic to a syntactic account of formality *qua* isomorphism invariance?

9.6 General Axiomatics, Reconsidered

To address this question, it is insightful to take into account an interesting section titled "*Relation Theory and Axiomatics*" in the *Logical Syntax*. This section had to be omitted in the original German version of the book for reasons of space but was eventually included in the English version of 1937. Carnap explicitly connects here his new approach to syntactic invariance conditions with his previous work on general axiomatics and relation theory (cf. *LSL*, section 71 a–e). As he makes clear, the new syntactic approach should be viewed as a metalogical reformulation of his original contributions to relation and structure theory. This is true, in particular, of the notion of formal or structural properties:

---

[19] Similarly, given three languages S_1, S_2, and S_3 where S_2 is a sublanguage of S_3, Q_1 is called a "translation" of language S_1 into S_3 if Q_1 is a transformance of S_1 into S_2. See *LSL*, section 61 for further details.

> In the *theory of relations*, the properties of relations are investigated, particularly the structural properties–that is to say those which are retained in isomorphic transformance. A theory of this kind is nothing more than the syntax of many termed predicates. (*LSL*, section 71a)

Thus, according to Carnap, any concept specified in the theory of relations can now be assigned to a corresponding syntactic concept concerning polyadic languages with predicates (of any arity). He goes on to specify how several relation-theoretic properties (such as the properties of symmetry, reflexivity, isomorphism, etc.) expressed in the type-theoretic object language LII can be specified as "syntactical terms" in the "general syntax of the predicates" (*LSL*, section 71, a–b). This indicates that, in Carnap's view, there is a general equivalence between the two approaches to specify the formality of logico-mathematical properties. More precisely, he argues in section 71b that any formal property of relations defined in an object language (e.g., language LII) can be *translated* into a corresponding syntactical property of predicates expressed in a syntax language.

Given this assumption, Carnap then turns again to a discussion of the formal axiomatic method in section 71e. How does his approach, given the new metatheoretic framework of *Logical Syntax*, differ from his previous contributions to axiomatics, from *Der Raum* to his *Untersuchungen* manuscript? His view of axiomatic theories is surprisingly similar to these previous accounts. As before, Carnap stresses the semantic fact that axiom systems provide "implicit definitions" that "determine the meaning" of the primitive terms of a theory. It should be noted that his talk of the "meaning" of primitive terms is not to be conflated with providing a fixed semantic reference or interpretation for them. Rather, the semantic specification of the primitive vocabulary of a theory remains incomplete in the sense that the terms can be interpreted in various systems or models "satisfying" the axioms in question. The main innovation with respect to previous accounts is how the notion of a semantic "interpretation" of the primitive symbols of a theory is understood in 1937. Carnap outlines three ways how to think of such interpretations (of which the first two are relevant in the present context.)

The first method conforms essentially with the one specified in the *Abriss* and, in closer detail, in *Untersuchungen*. According to it, formal axioms systems are sentential functions represented syntactically by open formulas in an object language such as the type-theoretic language LII. The primitive symbols are "primitive variables" of a given type of LII. Models are then specified, as suggested already in his "general axiomatics" project in the late 1920s, as tuples of predicates to be substituted for the primitive variables. Or, as Carnap put it the *Logical Syntax*: "According to this method, a model for the AS is to be understood as a series of k substitution-values $A_1, \ldots, A_k$ for the primitive variables." (*LSL*, section 71e). More precisely, for a given axiom system $\Phi(X_1, \ldots, X_k)$, such a series is called a model if the sentence $\Phi(A_1, \ldots, A_k)$ is "valid" in language S (or LII). The method specified here directly follows his previous work. The only noteworthy difference is that the concept of validity employed here is no longer treated as a primitive notion but rather as a metatheoretical defined concept of his new syntax theory.[20]

The main innovation regarding the early proto-model theory of axiomatic theories in the *Logical Syntax* is related to Carnap's second method of interpretation. Specifically, according to this view, axioms and theorems are expressed as "primitive sentences," the primitive symbols of a theory as constant expressions of a language S_1. Models can therefore *not* be understood as substitution instances but rather in terms of the method of a syntactic translation Q_1 of S_1 into a language S_2. More specifically, a model in this view will usually consist, according to Carnap, of the "Q_1-correlates" of the primitive (nonlogical) symbols of the theory. The truth or satisfaction of an axiom system in a given model is then not specified in terms of the validity of a sentence in language S_1 but rather by the fact that the translation preserves the formal property of validity. Compare again Carnap on this point: "The model is said to be real (or really possible, or logically possible) if the class of the Q_1-correlates of the axioms of the AS is valid ... in S_2." (*LSL*, section 71e). Thus, the semantic concept of the interpretation of a formal axiomatic theory in a model is cashed out here in purely syntactic terms, i.e. in terms of a metatheoretically defined relation of translation between languages. Interestingly, as the main illustration of this approach, Carnap refers to the different ways of specifying formal geometry investigated in his monograph *Der Raum*. Recall that, in 1922, Carnap distinguished between the axiomatic and a genetic, relation-theoretic approach to study formal spaces. Precisely this distinction is now captured formally, in the context of his syntax theory, in terms of an "interpretation" of "axiomatic geometry" in a purely analytic or number-theoretic model. As Carnap points out, "arithmetical geometry (I) constitutes a logical model" in the sense specified above of formal axiomatic geometry.[21]

---

[20] See also Carnap and Bachmann (1936/1981). Compare Schiemer (2013) for a closer discussion of this point.
[21] A similar account of axiomatic calculi and the status of formal geometry is given in Carnap's *FLM*.

9.7 Conclusion

The aim of this chapter was to survey Carnap's evolving philosophical views on the formal nature of logic and mathematics. As was shown, his contributions to the philosophy of these disciplines until the late 1930s are characterized by a general formalist thesis. According to this thesis, mathematical knowledge is, in principle, formal or non-contentual in character. Interestingly, Carnap's formalism can be identified in different versions at various points in his work: in the early specification of formal geometry in *Der Raum* as the study of "order structures" as well as in his work on "general axiomatics" in the *Untersuchungen* manuscript from the late 1920s; the view is also defended in his contributions to the logico-syntactic properties of mathematical languages in *Logical Syntax*. As we saw, the formal character of mathematics was specified differently in these contributions. In particular, we retraced an important shift in Carnap's thinking about formality in the period in question, namely, from an object-theoretic or semantic account to a purely syntactic account in the 1930s. This result is significant for a closer understanding of the development of Carnap's theoretical philosophy. It shows that he had a genuinely semantic or proto-model theoretic account of pure mathematics well before the work on *Logical Syntax* and thus roughly a decade before his "official" adoption of Tarskian semantics in the late 1930s.

In spite of this conceptual shift, one can also identify an interesting continuity in Carnap's thinking on the topic concerning the notion of isomorphism invariance. As we saw, he understood this notion to provide a general criterion for formality or structurality that is applied both in the early relation-theoretic (or type-theoretic) work from the 1920s as well as in his later work on syntax theory. More specifically, the formality of a mathematical statement was originally cashed out in terms of the preservation of its truth conditions under isomorphic transformations of its semantic interpretations. In his *Logical Syntax*, a similar notion is expressed in terms of the preservation of "syntactic concepts" (including the metatheoretic concepts of consequence and analyticity) under isomorphic translations between formal languages. This suggest that there is, in fact, more continuity in the development of Carnap's philosophical views on mathematics than is often assumed. In particular, at least in the period considered, he not only had a stable view on the formal nature of mathematics but also characterized the formalist thesis in a surprisingly similar way.

CHAPTER 10

Carnap on Probability and Induction

Sandy Zabell

10.1 Introduction

Rudolf Carnap received his PhD in 1921 and died in 1970. His research during this fifty-year period underwent a surprising phase transition exactly half-way through: for the first twenty-five years, from 1921 to 1945, he worked almost exclusively on logic, logical empiricism, and the philosophy of science, while during the second half, from 1945 to 1970, he worked almost exclusively on the foundations of probability and inductive inference. Despite being relatively new to the subject, his groundbreaking 1950 book *Logical Foundations of Probability* immediately established him as a central figure in the subject.

This surprising midlife shift in Carnap's career raises three natural questions.

1. Why did Carnap change his focus of research in such an unexpected way?
2. What elements of novelty did this relative novice bring to the field in 1950?
3. Did his views change significantly during the last two decades of his life?

One of our central themes will be that although reference is often made today to Carnap's views on probability and inductive inference, this is often (except among the experts) to either Carnap's 1950 book *LFP* or his 1952 monograph *CIM*, even though these views in fact underwent a significant evolution over time: to genuinely understand Carnap on probability and inductive inference one has to recognize that there is actually a Carnap$_1$ and a Carnap$_2$.

10.2 From Logic to Probability

One important change in Carnap's life in the years leading up to 1945 was where he lived.

Like Richard von Mises, Hans Reichenbach, Carl Hempel, Otto Neurath, Paul Oppenheim, and Kurt Gödel, Carnap left Europe for the stability of the United States in the 1930s. After Hitler's rise to power in 1933, Carnap found the political atmosphere "even in Czechoslovakia" (where he was he was then teaching, at the University of Prague) increasing intolerable, and he left Prague for the US in December 1935. Presciently, even this early on he anticipated the possibility of an "intervention by Hitler" (*IA* 34).

Carnap's move to the United States was easier than that of many other emigrees: after attending the Harvard Centenary Celebration in September 1936, he was invited to teach at the University of Chicago that winter, when he was then promptly offered and immediately accepted a permanent position at Chicago, which he held from 1936 to 1952. (Carnap's familiarity with Charles W. Morris (1901–1979) of Chicago and W. V. Quine (1908–2000) of Harvard, both of whom he knew from their visits to Europe, including Prague, presumably facilitated this relatively painless transition to the New World.) In the United States, Carnap found the philosophical atmosphere to be "very congenial" compared to that in Europe (especially Germany), even in the somewhat idiosyncratic Department of Philosophy at Chicago, which he amusingly describes in his *Intellectual Autobiography* (*IA* 41–43).

During the academic year 1940–1941, Carnap was a visiting professor at Harvard, and this had an important impact on the later direction of his research. Some of his interactions at Harvard were predictable, a natural continuation of his earlier interests: he became part of a group, along with Quine, Nelson Goodman, Tarski, and Russell (the latter two of whom were also visitors that year) devoted to problems of logic. But he also arranged an ongoing colloquium, devoted to the philosophy of science, with the Harvard physicist Philipp Frank (who had been a colleague of his at Prague). He tells us in his *Intellectual Autobiography* (*IA* 36):

> Of special interest to me were lectures on probability by Richard von Mises and by Feigl and the discussions which followed. As a result, I also begin to think about the problems of probability and induction more systematically that I had done up to that time.

This obviously lit a spark, because a year later, when he held a two-year research grant from the Rockefeller Foundation spent near Sante Fe, New Mexico, he was "first occupied with the logic of modalities" but later "turned to the problems of probability and induction." This led to his basic papers "The two concepts of probability" (Carnap 1945a) and

"On inductive logic" (Carnap 1945b). These laid out in broad terms his views on the two subjects, promissory notes that were to be redeemed in a later book.

10.3 The Explication of Probability

> The duality of probability has long been known to philosophers. The present generation may have learnt it from Carnap's weighty tome *Logical Foundations*.
>
> (Hacking 1975, 13)

For Carnap "explication" is the process of replacing an inexact concept (the *explicandum*) by one that is more precise and exact (the *explicatum*) and was introduced by him as part of his attempt to clarify the foundations of probability (Carnap 1945a, *M&N, LFP*; see also Erich Reck's contribution to this volume [Chapter 7] about explication). The process is a common one in mathematics, where intuitive concepts such as continuity, the sum of an infinite series, or the computability of a function receive precise mathematical definitions: the ε, δ definition of continuity, the definition of an infinite series $\sum a_n$ as the limit of its associated sequence of partial sums $s_n = a_1 + \ldots + a_n$, and defining computability in terms of Turing machines have all gained general acceptance.[1]

In terms of human language, explication is the process of taking terms in everyday discourse such as life, planet, or probability and giving them precise definitions. Arguments such as whether viruses are a life form reflect the imprecision in the use of the term rather than some deep underlying philosophical issue: the biology of viruses is well-understood, so if you define exactly what you mean by the term life, the argument evaporates. Similarly, debating whether Pluto is a planet isn't an argument about Pluto but what one means by the term planet.

But as Ian Hacking has noted, such distinctions predate Carnap. Antoine Augustin Cournot (1801–1877) was arguably the first to draw the distinction in terms close to Carnap's, writing of "the double meaning of the word probability, which sometimes refers to a certain measure of our knowledge, and sometimes to a measure of the possibility of things, independently of the knowledge we have of them" (Cournot 1843, iv). Drawing from the language of the "metaphysicians" (i.e., Kant), Cournot

---

[1] Defining computability is a particularly interesting example: several competing definitions were eventually found to coincide with Turing's and no one has ever identified a function that is intuitively computable but not Turing computable.

used the terms subjective and objective "to distinguish radically the two meanings of the term probability" (v).[2]

In the next century, Frank Plumpton Ramsey (1903–1930) made a similar distinction. Probability is important not only in logic but also in statistics; statisticians largely adopt the frequency theory, logicians for the most part reject it; this suggests the two are discussing two different things, the word probability being used by the two schools in two different senses (Ramsey 1931, foreword).

What sets Carnap apart is the detail and complexity in which he explores this. He began by introducing three categories of concept: the *classificatory*, *comparative*, and *quantitative*. In the context of probability, these could be that, given some evidence E, an hypothesis H is respectively likely, more likely than another, or can be assigned some actual numerical measure of how strongly E confirms H (such as its conditional probability $P(H|E)$ or its likelihood $P(E|H)$). His primary interest is in the epistemic side of probability, which he termed the *degree of confirmation* (he later regretted this terminology), and within this, a quantitative measure of confirmation.

10.4 Logical Foundations of Probability

In his 1945 papers, Carnap announced that a book setting out his system was in preparation (Carnap 1945a, 520; 1945b, 74). The goal and centerpiece of the book was to be a foundation for a quantitative inductive logic. This was his *Logical Foundations of Probability*, which appeared in 1950. In his preface (*LFP*, v) Carnap laid out his basic theses:

1. Inductive logic and the logic of probability are one and the same.
2. This logic is a relation between pairs of statements or propositions, one an hypothesis to be confirmed, the other the evidence supporting it.
3. The frequency concept of probability, although important in its own right, is unsuitable as the basis for inductive logic.
4. The principles of inductive logic are analytic, not synthetic, and do not depend on synthetic presuppositions.

---

[2] Cournot's older contemporary Siméon Denis Poisson (1781–1840) viewed the problem somewhat differently: rather than one word having two meanings, in ordinary language two words (*chance* and *probabilité*) were effectively used synonymously. In contrast, in his book Poisson used the two words to distinguish the physical and the epistemic: "an event will, by its nature, have a chance greater or lesser, known or unknown; and its probability will be relative to our knowledge" (Poisson 1837, 31).

Despite its magisterial sweep, it is unclear if initially Carnap fully appreciated the magnitude of the task he had set himself. For what was to be one book was now announced to be only the first volume of a "projected two-volume" work (*LFP*, ix). Having introduced a general class of confirmation functions $c(h,e)$, similar to those of Hosiasson-Lindenbaum (see Zabell 2007), an appendix at the end of *LFP* limited itself to giving a brief summary of a proposed system c^*, it being left to the second volume to present this system in detail, which would give a quantitative explicatum for inductive probability. But even here Carnap hedged his bets, hastening to add that it was "not claimed c^* was necessarily the best explicatum possible" but merely "a concrete example of a quantitative system of inductive logic."

This second volume never appeared. Instead, two years later, in 1952 Carnap published a short monograph, *The Continuum of Inductive Methods*, in which c^* was expanded to a one-parameter family of methods. The quest for a unique explication of inductive inference had been abandoned. (In doing so, Carnap followed almost exactly the same route as a lesser known predecessor, William Ernest Johnson, 1858–1931, a Cambridge logician and economic theorist at King's College; see Zabell 2011, section 5.4) But Carnap had still not given up hope. In the preface to *The Continuum* he wrote "The substance of this monograph is to become part of Volume II of *Probability and Induction*"; but by 1962 he had set aside the project, writing in the preface to the second edition of *LFP*:

> I have abandoned my original plan of writing a companion volume to this book, as announced in the Preface to the first edition. There is now such a rapid development and change in this field that a comprehensive book, trying to describe the present situation, would probably be outdated before its appearance. Therefore we are planning instead the publication of a series of small volumes with the tentative title "Studies in Probability and Inductive Logic," each volume containing several articles, some expository, others in the nature of technical research reports. (*LFP2*, xiii)

This series did indeed appear, one volume the year after Carnap's death (Carnap and Jeffrey, 1971) and a second volume (Jeffrey, 1980) a decade later. They are an invaluable source both of Carnap's evolving view of the subject, as well as containing the contributions of several others, some talented collaborators, and others inspired by Carnap's example but working independently of him.

10.5 Collaborators and Sympathizers

Throughout his life, Carnap was singularly fortunate in his colleagues and collaborators. Two are of particular significance for his work on probability and inductive inference.

10.5.1 John Kemeny

John George Kemeny (1926–1992) was yet another refugee from Europe; he left Hungary in 1940 to join his father in the United States when anti-Jewish legislation was imminent. He started out in logic, receiving both his AB (1947) and PhD (1949) at Princeton under Alonzo Church. (His talent was already apparent at this stage: he was Einstein's mathematical assistant while a graduate student.) After serving as an instructor and then assistant professor of philosophy at Princeton, he left for Dartmouth in 1953, subsequently writing several highly successful books on finite mathematics and Markov chains, as well as inventing, together with his coauthor and close collaborator Thomas G. Kurtz (1928–) the computer language BASIC. He was the president of Dartmouth from 1970 to 1981.

Kemeny overlapped with Carnap during the academic year 1952–1953 while the latter was visiting the Institute for Advanced Study. As a pure mathematician, Kemeny brought an impressive set of skills to bear on the problems of inductive logic and advanced Carnap's program on a number of fronts.[3] His contributions included deriving Carnap's axioms of confirmation based on a Dutch book argument and clarifying the relative roles of coherence and strict coherence (Kemeny 1955, 1963, 719–724), and deriving Carnap's continuum from a core set of its properties (Kemeny 1963, 724–731). His section in the Schillp volume (1963) usefully summarizes his contributions.

10.5.2 Richard Jeffrey

Richard Carl Jeffrey (1926–2002) had a distinguished if somewhat unconventional career. After studying at Boston University for a year as an undergraduate in 1943–1944 (but never receiving a degree), and serving in the Navy 1944–1946, he was a graduate student in philosophy at the

---

[3] Carnap (*IA*, 36) later wrote "Kemeny's fertile mathematical imagination, his ability to anticipate intuitively what types of solution might be mathematically possible, and furthermore his co-operative spirit made this one of my best experiences in active collaboration."

University of Chicago from 1946 to 1952 (MA 1952), where he met Carnap. He then moved between the worlds of philosophy and engineering for the next eleven years: the Digital Computer and Lincoln Labs at MIT, 1952–1955; graduate student in philosophy at Princeton, 1955–1957 (PhD 1957); Fulbright Scholar, Oxford, 1957–1958; assistant professor of electrical engineering, MIT, 1958–1969, and assistant professor of philosophy, Stanford, 1959–1963. After inexplicably failing to receive tenure at Stanford, he then began a second but different kind of oscillation: after moving to the Institute for Advanced Study and Princeton in 1963–1964, he was successively – while always maintaining a residence in Princeton – associate professor at CCNY 1964–1967, professor of philosophy at the University of Pennsylvania 1967–1974, and professor of philosophy at Princeton 1974–1999.

Jeffreys acted as an advocate for Carnap within the context of the subjective probability of Ramsey and de Finetti; perhaps his most lasting technical contribution was his *probability kinematics*, a generalization of Bayesian conditioning. His views are carefully set out in a number of books: Jeffrey (1990, 1992, 2004).

10.5.3 Carnap's Invisible College

In addition to those he directly collaborated with, Carnap's work stimulated many others to explore a wide range of issues arising from his system of inductive logic. A partial list of these include his student Abner Shimony (1928–2015); the Bayesian statistician I. J. (Irving John) Good (1916–2009); the European philosophers Jaakko Hintikka (1929–2015), Ilkka Niiniluoto (1946–), and Theo A. F. Kuipers (1947–), who significantly extended Carnap's initial continuum in a number of ways; the US philosopher Brian Skyrms (1938–); and, in recent in years, Simon Huttegger and Martha Sznajder.

10.6 The Early and the Later Carnap

One of the most important influences of collaborators such as Kemeny and especially Jeffrey had to do with Carnap's technical apparatus and method of presentation. Coming from his background in logic, it was natural for Carnap to present his system in terms of sentences and logical syntax. This was natural and attractive to an important segment of the philosophical community, who paid close attention, but a significant deterrent for many mathematicians and statisticians. But in the decade after the appearance of

The Continuum in 1952, there was a clear shift in how Carnap thought about and presented his system. As Jeffrey later wrote,

> The technical apparatus elaborated in [*LFP*] no longer seemed satisfactory, partly because Carnap's extensive use of mathematical tools like de Finetti's representation theorem, which had not figured in his earlier work, and partly because of a desire to formulate inductive logic in terms that had come to be standard in mathematical probability theory and theoretical statistics, where probabilities are attributed to "events" (or "propositions") which are construed as sets of entities which can handily be taken to be *models*, in the sense in which that term is used in logic. (Carnap and Jeffrey 1971, 1)

One might describe this as part of the shift from $Carnap_1$ to $Carnap_2$. The magnitude of this shift is not always appreciated, since initially it only appeared in a 503-page set of lecture notes distributed in 1965 and was only published in part 1 of his posthumous "Basic System of Inductive Logic" (Carnap 1971, 1980).[4] Nevertheless, it is surprising that even some of his adherents did not appreciate this at the time. For example, shortly before his death Carnap wrote to his student Abner Shimony (1928–2015) on April 29, 1969:

> I was surprised by your statement that my probability functions are only applied to sentences. This is indeed true with respect to my publications. But in my own work I have for a long time accepted the method which seems today more generally used, namely to apply the functions (now C and $\mathcal{M}$) to the subsets of a probability space. I call them "propositions"; most authors use the term "events." This set of propositions is immensely more comprehensive than that of the sentences of a language; it is the σ-field generated by the class of atomic propositions, which correspond to the atomic sentences.[5]

In the following, we will eschew Carnap's original sentential approach and employ the notation and terminology now used in current mathematics and probability, and which Carnap later opted for. In doing so, we will consider a number of the controversies, clarifications, and advances that

---

[4] For a different perspective, which sees greater continuity in Carnap's views, see the very interesting paper of Sznajder (2018).
[5] Abner Shimony Papers, 1947–2009, Archives of Scientific Philosophy, University of Pittsburgh, Identifier 31735033440151. Carnap goes on to note in his letter "this method was first applied" in his "Axiom System for Inductive Logic," a 503-page typescript distributed between September 1960 and May 1965. A later, "final version," revised for publication, subsequently appeared in his posthumous "Basic System of Inductive Logic" (Carnap 1971, 1980); the first half of this had been distributed shortly before Carnap wrote to Shimony.

took place in Carnap's system during the last two decades of his life and beyond.

10.7 Inductive Inference

Although Carnap's distinction between the statistical and the epistemic senses of probability effectively put the two on an equal footing, he was primarily interested in its epistemic side, in large part because it could be used as the basis of a theory of inductive inference. In Carnap's system, one can identify four distinct stages to his theory:

1. The axioms of probability
2. Bayesian conditioning
3. Exchangeability
4. The continuum of inductive methods.

Each of these made presuppositions and, due in part to Carnap's advocacy, generated further developments and critical commentary. The resulting literature was extensive, too extensive to cover in its entirety here. Instead, we will introduce each of the four in the context of a particular topic.

10.8 Coherence

> One guide to an argument's significance is the number and variety of refutations it attracts. By this measure, the Dutch book argument has considerable importance.
> (Armendt 1993, 1)

From a purely mathematical standpoint, a *probability function* is a function P on events E that satisfies three basic properties:
1. It is *nonnegative* ($P(E) \geq 0$).
2. The sure event S has probability one ($P(S) = 1$).
3. P is *additive*: if E and F are mutually exclusive events, then

$$P(E \text{ or } F) = P(E) + P(F).$$

The first two conditions may be viewed as normalizing P (probabilities are never negative, and the probability of the certain event is one), but the third condition has real bite; and if P is to be viewed as a measure of our belief, one might well ask why we should assume it to be additive.

One of the few philosophers to seriously address this question early on was the English logician and mathematician Augustus De Morgan

(1806–1871). His discussion of the issue in his *Formal Logic* of 1847 is instructive: after first arguing that belief is indeed capable of numerical measurement, he introduces additivity as a postulate, spends several pages analyzing why this is far from obvious, and in the end (somewhat lamely) concludes regarding its justification, "I cannot conceive any answer except that it is by an assumption of the postulate" (see Zabell 1991, 232; Zabell 2008, 759–760).

This was hardly a satisfactory state of affairs, but it was only in the twentieth century that the decisive breakthrough was made. In retrospect, the problem is clear: absent a genuine operational definition of exactly what a numerical probability is, one can scarcely derive its properties. The key advance came when both Frank Plumpton Ramsey (1903–1930) and Bruno de Finetti (1906–1985) advanced such operational definitions. In the simplest approach, a probability may be regarded as the statement of a bet, *either* side of which one is willing to accept. For example, a probability of 2/3 for an event means one is willing to offer either a bet of 2 to 1 for it, or 1 to 2 against. (This is somewhat like the classical algorithm for two children to divide a cake: one divides and the other chooses.)

Suppose you assign probabilities to a collection of events in terms of such bets. One says a *Dutch book* can be made against you by a crafty bettor if your opponent can make a (finite) set of bets ensuring you always lose money. For example, in coin-tossing, if you assign probabilities of 2/3 to *both* heads and tails, then the crafty bettor will bet one dollar to two both on heads and on tails, necessarily winning two on one bet and losing one on the other and thereby always ensuring a gain of one. It is an obvious rationality constraint that you never assign probabilities permitting a Dutch book. This condition is termed *coherence*, and Ramsey and de Finetti showed that meant your probabilities had to satisfy the three basic properties of a probability function.[6] As Ramsey noted with satisfaction, his theory "gives us a clear justification for the axioms of the calculus" (Ramsey 1931, 188).

After the appearance of *LFP*, several of Carnap's collaborators, students, and admirers explored and extended this circle of ideas. Carnap's collaborator Kemeny soon showed (1955) coherence was not merely a sufficient condition for the axioms but necessary as well: you are coherent if and only if the axioms are satisfied. (Lehman 1955 independently arrived at this

---

[6] Strictly speaking, the result is that if the numbers $P(E)$ you assign to events E in some collection $\mathcal{E}$ represents a coherent set of bets, then $P(E)$ can be extended to a (finitely additive) probability function on the algebra of events generated by $\mathcal{E}$.

result at the same time.) Abner Shimony, one of Carnap's students, introduced the stronger notion of *strict coherence*. A *weak Dutch book* is one is which loss is possible but gain impossible (so you may break even in some cases but can never profit). A set of bets is strictly coherent if a weak Dutch book is ruled out. This is of course a stronger condition than coherence and holds precisely when every event (other than the impossible event, represented by Ø) has positive probability. This is a meaningful condition when the set of atomic outcomes is finite or countable (for example, 0,1,2, ...), but is impossible in situations such as choosing a point at random from the unit interval, and so its status in the theory is somewhat problematic. Another possible extension of coherence is *sigma coherence*, where a Dutch book is ruled out even if a countably infinite number of bets is permitted. This notion of coherence is equivalent to P being countably additive but has its own set of issues. These different forms of coherence are beautifully set out in Skyrms (1995).[7]

10.9 Total Evidence and the Value of Knowledge

Much learning doth make thee mad.

(*Acts*, 26:24)

On page 211 of the *Logical Foundations*, Carnap stated a requirement of total evidence:

> In the application of inductive logic to a given knowledge situation, the total evidence available must be taken as basis for determining the degree of confirmation.

A. J. Ayer (1957) questioned the justification for this statement.

What is the value of knowledge? Carnap's system tells us how to compute $c(h, e) = r$, but it does not give grounds for preferring evidence e_1 over e_2. In particular, given we currently know e_1, what value is there in adding to this? What is the value of additional information?

I. J. Good gave a neat answer to this in 1967 within the framework of the Savage axioms for utilities. Suppose

---

[7] In *LFP*, the meaning of logical probability was explained informally in several different ways: as evidential support, as an estimate of relative frequency, or as a fair betting quotient (*LFP*, section 41). A decade later, Carnap's views had largely settled on the last of these, writing that probabilities "can best be characterized by explaining their use, in combination with the concept of utility, in the rule for the determination of rational decisions. The explanation of probability as a betting quotient is a simplified special case of this rule" (*LFP2*, xv), another illustration of Carnap$_2$.

Carnap on Probability and Induction

- $H_1, H_2, \ldots, H_r$ is a set of "hypotheses" (states of the world).
- $A_1, A_2, \ldots, A_s$ is a set of "acts" (courses of action open to us).
- $u_{ij} := U(A_j|H_i)$ is the *expected utility* of performing A_j if H_i true.
- $p_i = P(H_i|E)$ is the prior probability of possible state H_i given background information E.
- $\sum_i p_i u_{ij}$ the expected utility of act A_j.

Note the expected utility of an act is computed by averaging the expected utility for a given state using our prior probabilities for each of the states of nature.

The principle of rationality in the Savage framework is to choose that act A_{j*} that maximizes our expected utility; that is,

$$\sum_i p_i u_{ij*} = \max_j \left(\sum_i p_i u_{ij} \right) := B.$$

(B for "before").

Suppose now we are given a "cost-free" observation O impacting the probability of H_i, and that

- $E_1, E_2, \ldots, E_t$ are the possible outcomes of the observation O;
- $p_{ik} := P(E_k|H_i)$ is the probability of observing E_k given the state of nature H_i.

The point is that since the likelihood of seeing E_k depends on what the state of nature H_i is, seeing E_k tells us something about H_i. Thus we can compute

$$q_{ik} := P(H_i | E \text{ and } E_k) = \frac{p_i p_{ik}}{\sum_i p_i p_{ik}},$$

the posterior probability of H_i given E_k is observed). It follows that the expected utility to make the observation and use it is:

$$\sum_k \left(\sum_i p_i p_{ik} \right) \max_j \left(\sum_i q_{ik} u_{ij} \right) = \sum_k \max_j \sum_i p_i p_{ik} u_{ij} := A$$

(A for "after").

Theorem 1 *(no philosophy, just math!).* $A \geq B$, *and equality holds $\Leftrightarrow$ there is an index j (independent of k) that maximizes $U(A_j|E \text{ and } E_k)$.*

This simple result is a complete and satisfying answer to our question; not only is the expected utility at least as large after making the observation as that before, but we have also identified the exact circumstances under which there is no expected benefit in making the observation: this happens precisely when there is an act that has the maximum possible expected utility independent of what we actually observe (which is only to be expected).

But how do we derive this result? It turns out to be an immediate consequence of a standard minimax fact: it is a special case of the simple

Lemma 1. For any (real) function $f(j, k)$,

$$\sum_k \max_j f(j,k) \geq \max_j \sum_k f(j,k)$$

with strict inequality holding unless the array $(f(j,k))$ has a dominating row.

Because this result purports to answer what was once a disputed question in philosophy, it will be useful to review its assumptions and conclusions. It presupposes the following:

- The Savage framework for rational decision making.
- The effect of new information is via Bayesian conditioning.
- There is no cost for making the observation or using its information.

All three of these assumptions can of course be questioned, but there are some natural defenses for each. First, there is the Savage framework for utility and decision-making. The point here is that *some* assumption must be made: in order to argue one is better (or worse) off in making further observations, one has to advance some framework for decision-making. Consider by way of analogy the *Entsheidungsproblem*, the "decision problem," is there an algorithm or decision procedure for determining whether or not a mathematical statement in a given mathematical language has a proof or not. When Alan Turing attacked this problem, he introduced his machinery of "Turing machines" (of course he didn't call them that) in order to precisely formulate what an algorithm was. Until you gave a mathematically precise definition of what an algorithm was, there was no way of giving a mathematical answer to the question. Similarly, in order to answer the question of what is the value of new knowledge, one must propose a precise framework in which this question is to be answered.

Second, there is the question of the mechanism by which information is received. Classically, the answer has been Bayesian: information is acquired by observing an event, say E, and final beliefs arise from earlier, initial ones in the form of posterior probabilities P^* crafted from prior probabilities P by evaluating the conditional probability of other events A given the observation E: $P^*(A) = P(A|E)$. In the last several decades, a number of interesting alternatives to Bayesian conditioning have been proposed, most notably Richard Jeffrey's *probability kinematics* (Jeffrey 1990, 1992, chapters 3, 5–7) and E. T. Jaynes's *maximum entropy* approach (Jaynes

2003, chapters 11–12), the first being not so much an alternative to but a generalization of Bayesian conditioning. These did not, however, pose a problem for Good's approach but led instead to an advance in our understanding: extensions of Good's approach to these more general settings have been advanced, permitting us to see the necessary core underlying structure, that of a *martingale*; see, for example, Skyrms (1990, chapter 4), Huttegger (2017, 119–125 and, for the value of knowledge, sections 6.6–7).

Finally, there is the issue of cost. A little thought will convince one that this is an important element of the problem effectively left out of its initial formulation. It is a commonplace of everyday life that we are constantly making decisions based on cost. One of the attractions of Good's approach is that by formalizing the analysis this point is brought to the forefront. Here is an obvious example: if there is a uniform cost C for making the observation, we are better off precisely when $A - B > C$. (That is, $A - B$ measures our expected gain in making the observation, and obviously this is a bad deal if this is less than the cost of making the observation.)

Note Jack Good was aware of this last issue because of his wartime work at Bletchley Park, computing expected values of the *weight of evidence*

$$\log_{10} \frac{P(E|H_1)}{P(E|H_0)}.$$

More generally, this type of consideration comes into play in the design of experiments.

10.10   The Principle of Positive Instantial Relevance

> It's tough to make predictions, especially about the future.
> (Saying attributed to Yogi Berra)

Next we turn to issues surrounding a very important but special case of inductive inference, namely, enumerative inference. We observe a sequence of successive trials whose outcomes fall into one of two classes (heads or tails, success or failure, life or death, etc.). Let $X_1, X_2, X_3, \ldots$ be indicators recording whether or not something has occurred, say $X_i = H$ if a head, $X_i = T$ if a tail. One important desideratum of any candidate for confirmation is *positive instantial relevance*: if a particular type is observed, it makes it more likely such a type will be observed in the future. In its simplest form, this is the requirement that if $i < j$, then

$$P(X_j = 1 | X_i = 1) > P(X_j = 1).$$

It is easy to see that not all probability assignments, even very natural ones, satisfy the principle of instantial relevance.

Example 1 (Sampling without replacement). Suppose we have an urn with ten balls, five red and five black. If we draw a ball out of the urn at random, then initially it is equally likely to draw a red or a black; in symbols,

$$P(X_1 = R) = P(X_1 = B) = \frac{1}{2}.$$

Suppose our first draw is a red. Now there are four red and five black left, and the (*conditional*) probabilities of red and black on the next, second draw are respectively $4/9 < 1/2$ and $5/9 > 1/2$. In symbols,

$$P(X_2 = R | X_1 = R) = \frac{4}{9}, \quad P(X_2 = B | X_1 = R) = \frac{5}{9} > \frac{1}{2}.$$

There is nothing pathological about this situation – quite the contrary – and yet the principle fails in a very simple way.

10.10.1 Exchangeability

One basic *starting* model for inductive inference is that the outcomes should be *exchangeable* (Johnson 1924, Appendix on Eduction, 183; de Finetti 1937, chapter 3), that is, two sequences of outcomes have the same probability if one sequence is a permuted version of the other. In symbols, if σ is a permutation of the integers $1, 2, \ldots, n$, and $e_1, \ldots, e_n$ represents a specific sequence of outcomes, then

$$P(X_1 = e_1, \ldots, X_n = e_n) = P(X_1 = e_{\sigma(1)}, \ldots, X_n = e_{\sigma(n)});$$

both the original sequence and the permuted sequence have the same probability. This is obviously a natural condition to impose for simple enumerative induction, where the only thing that matters is how many times each type occurs but not the order in which they occur. This assumption was adopted by Carnap in *LFP* (chapter 8, 485–486).

Example 2 (Coin tossing). The probability of getting k heads in n independent tosses of a p-coin (a coin whose probability of heads is p) in a specific order (such as H, H, T, H, T, T, T) is

$$p^k (1-p)^{n-k}.$$

This probability assignment is obviously exchangeable, because (apart from p, the probability of success) it only depends on k (the number of successes) and $n - k$ (the number of failures), and not the order in which they occur.

Example 3 (Sampling from an urn revisited). Suppose an urn has 3 R and 2 B balls, and X_k indicates if a R is drawn. If the sampling is without replacement, then this probability assignment is also exchangeable. For example, letting "RRB" denote the sequence of red, red, black, one has

$$P(RRB) = \frac{3}{5} \cdot \frac{2}{4} \cdot \frac{2}{3} = \frac{1}{5},$$
$$P(RBR) = \frac{3}{5} \cdot \frac{2}{4} \cdot \frac{2}{3} = \frac{1}{5},$$
$$P(BRR) = \frac{2}{5} \cdot \frac{3}{4} \cdot \frac{2}{3} = \frac{1}{5}.$$

Although both of these examples involve exchangeable probabilities, neither satisfies the principle of positive instantial relevance: in coin-tossing, the outcomes are independent (so the conditional and unconditional probabilities coincide), and we have already seen that in sampling without replacement the probabilities change but in the wrong direction. How do we understand this? The answer is facilitated by introducing the *de Finetti representation theorem*.

10.10.1.1 The Finite de Finetti Representation Theorem
In the case of a finite sequence $X_1, \ldots, X_n$, de Finetti's theorem is easy to state: every exchangeable probability assignment on $X_1 = e_1, \ldots, X_n = e_n$ is a mixture of sampling without replacement from urns of different compositions. That is, if $U_{R,N;n}$ is the probability distribution on (ordered) samples of size n drawn without replacement from an urn with R red balls and B black balls, for a total of $N = R + B$ balls, then we pick one of these urns with a probability p_R, and then proceed to draw out n balls from the urn without replacement. That the result is an exchangeable sequence uses the pair of facts

- $U_{R,N;n}$ is exchangeable;
- Any mixture $\sum_{0 \leq R \leq N} p_R U_{R,N;n}$ of these is exchangeable (a mixture of exchangeable sequences is exchangeable).

That *every* exchangeable sequence is of this form is the content of the *finite de Finetti representation theorem*; see Jeffrey (1992, 138–142). (The proof is an easy consequence of the so-called *theorem of total probability*.)

10.10.1.2 Infinitely Exchangeable Sequences
An infinite sequence $X_1, X_2, X_3, \ldots$ is said to be *infinitely exchangeable* if any finite segment $X_1, X_2, \ldots, X_n$ of it is exchangeable. (Such infinite sequences are of course convenient fictions.)

The (infinite) *de Finetti representation theorem* says any infinitely exchangeable sequence can be represented as a mixture of independent tosses of a p-coin. In words, pick a specific probability p with respect to some probability distribution $d\mu$ (for example, pick p uniformly from the unit interval $0 \leq p \leq 1$) and then toss a p-coin n times. In symbols (this will be the only time in this chapter that an integral appears; given what has gone before it should be viewed as a friend, not an enemy, providing a useful notation for representing an infinite limiting case),

$$P(S_n = k) = \int_0^1 \boxed{\binom{n}{k} p^k (n-k)^{n-k}} \, d\mu(p).$$

(Here S_n is the number of heads in n tosses, and $d\mu$ is some probability measure on the unit interval $0 \leq p \leq 1$. The expression in the box represents the case of coin-tossing with known probability of success p.)

In the past, there was a small cottage industry devoted to investigating the precise circumstances under which the principle of positive instantial relevance (PIR) does or does not hold for a sequence of observations. The machinery of exchangeability provides a simple answer to this question: if the observations in question $X_1, \ldots, X_n$ can be imbedded in an infinitely exchangeable sequence, then instantial relevance does indeed hold. After the power of the de Finetti representation theorem was appreciated, very simple proofs of this were discovered (see, e.g., Carnap and Jeffrey 1971, chapters 4 and 5), which considerably improves on and simplifies these proofs. This is part of the power and attraction of the mathematical approach to subjective probability: to strip away the inessentials and reveal the underlying simplicity of the situation. (Which for so intuitive a principle as the PIR is hardly surprising.)

Note In fact there is an even simpler proof of positive instantial relevance, so simple it is worth the brief digression. If $X_1, \ldots, X_n$ is exchangeable, the correlation coefficient $\rho = \rho(X_i, X_j)$ satisfies the simple inequality

$$\rho \geq -\frac{1}{n-1},$$

since if σ^2 is the variance of an X_i, then

$$0 \leq Var[X_1 + \ldots + X_n] = n\sigma^2 + n(n-1)\rho\sigma^2.$$

As a result, if we take $n \to \infty$ (the case of infinite exchangeability), then $\rho \geq 0$. Here $\rho = 0$ corresponds to independence (the future independent of the past); and $\rho > 0$ corresponds to positive instantial relevance.

Exchangeability assumes that our beliefs are symmetric in a very specific way. De Finetti early on recognized that in certain situations other forms of symmetry are natural and termed this *partial exchangeability*; see Jeffrey (1980, chapters 9 and 11; 1992, 144–151). Recognizing that different forms of exchangeability may exist is the subjectivist's answer to Nelson Goodman's grue and the conundrum of *projectability*.

10.11 The Continuum of Inductive Methods

The above result is very satisfying. The standard axioms of probability combined with the assumption of Bayesian conditioning enabled us to give a very simple explanation for the value of new information. By adding the further mild assumption of exchangeability, a natural setting for inductive reasoning, we were able to deduce a further important desideratum of inductive reasoning, positive instantial relevance. But the class of exchangeable probabilities is quite large, Carnap wished to go beyond this and narrow the class of credence functions down to a select few. As we have seen, he had in fact initially hoped to actually single this down to a single function (his c^*), but as he worked on the details of this he came to realize this was not really possible and ultimately advanced instead a one-parameter continuum of inductive methods.

What was this new continuum? Viewed from the perspective of the *later* Carnap (but going back to the *LFP* in terms of its substance), the basic setup is as follows. First, we consider sequences of outcomes $e_1, e_2, \ldots, e_n$, each outcome e_i able to take on one of two *or more* possible values, say $c_1, \ldots, c_t$. (For example, we might be rolling a die, or picking a card, corresponding to $t = 6$ and $t = 52$, respectively.) (Assuming there might be more than just $t = 2$ kinds of possible outcomes was useful, because it could make assumptions of equiprobability more credible. Even if two mutually exclusive outcomes were clearly not equipossible, one could in principle envisage being able to decompose the two into a number of sub-possibilities that were themselves equiprobable. This was an approach endorsed by the great Laplace himself.) Carnap termed the sequences $e_1, e_2, \ldots, e_n$ *state descriptions*. Suppose that in a sample of size n, say $e_1, e_2, \ldots, e_n$, there are n_1 outcomes of type c_1, n_2 outcomes of type c_2, and so on up to n_t outcomes of type c_t, so that

$$n_1 + n_2 + \ldots + n_t = n.$$

The vector of observed frequencies $(n_1, n_2, \ldots, n_t)$ in Carnap's terminology is a *structure description*. The assumption of exchangeability here is easily seen to be equivalent to the property that all state descriptions $e_1, e_2, \ldots, e_n$ giving rise to the same structure description $(n_1, n_2, \ldots, n_t)$ have the same probability. Because the number of state descriptions corresponding to a given structure description is the multinomial coefficient

$$\frac{n!}{n_1! n_2! \ldots n_t!},$$

we can go back and forth between the probabilities of state descriptions and the probabilities of structure descriptions.

Finally, we introduce the one-step predictive probabilities (known classically as *rules of succession*)

$$P(X_{n+1} = e_i | n_1, n_2, \ldots, n_t);$$

the conditional probability at stage n of seeing on the next trial an outcome of type i given one has so far observed the structure description $n_1, n_2, \ldots, n_t$.

Now we are ready to state the celebrated Johnson-Kemeny characterization of P (Johnson 1932; Kemeny 1963). Assume the sequence satisfies the following three conditions:

1. There are at least three types of species; $t \geq 3$.
2. Any state description $e_1, \ldots, e_n$ is a priori possible: $P(e_1, \ldots e_n) > 0$.
3. The "sufficientness postulate" is satisfied:

$$P(X_{n+1} = e_i | n_1, \ldots, n_t) = f_i(n_i, n).$$

In this case there exist constants α_i such that if $\alpha := \alpha_1 + \alpha_2 + \ldots + \alpha_t$, then

$$f_i(n_i, n) = \frac{n_i + \alpha_i}{n + \alpha}.$$

The first assumption (that $t > 2$) is an annoying necessity; without it, the third and final assumption would be vacuous. (If there are only two classes, then knowing n_1, n_2 is equivalent to knowing n_1 and n.) The second assumption is there so that we can compute conditional probabilities with impunity, since by definition $P(A|B) = P(A \text{ and } B)/P(B)$. The real heart of the characterization is the third condition, the "sufficientness postulate" (so termed by I. J. Good): the predictive probability for an outcome of the i-th type on the next trial only depends on how many outcomes of that type have been seen thus far (n_i) and the total sample size (n).

Technical note: The simplest case of the result is when the sequence is infinitely exchangeable, in which case $\alpha_i \geq 0$ (the case $\alpha_i = 0$ corresponding to independent outcomes). The mathematics still goes through in the case of a finitely exchangeable sequence (see Zabell, 1982) but breaks down when the sequence can no longer be extended and the α_i are negative. (Think of sampling without replacement from an urn with R red balls and B black balls, for a total of $N = R + B$ balls. As discussed earlier, the resulting probability on sequences is finitely exchangeable, but the sequences we assign probabilities to cannot be longer than N since at that point the urn is empty!)

Both the de Finetti representation and Carnap's continuum of inductive methods led to a considerable literature extending them to many other settings: for example, Markov and other forms of *partial exchangeability* noted earlier, the confirmation of universal generalizations, initially thought impossible in Carnap's setting (see Zabell 1997b but brilliantly resolved by Hintikka, Niiniluoto, and Kuipers, see Jeffrey 1980, chapters 7 and 8) and the sampling of species setting (see Zabell 2007, 2011). One extension unsuccessfully sought for many years was a truly satisfactory extension of the Carnap approach to analogical inductive inference; in recent years, there has been an impressive breakthrough on this, described below.

10.12 Analogical Predictive Probabilities

> If it be asked why, with several existing helps to the study of the Analogy, I offer another, I frankly reply, because I have found none of them satisfactory, either to the public or to myself.
> (Joseph Butler, *The Analogy of Religion*, Editor's Preface)

The title of this section is a paper written by Simon Huttegger in *Mind* (2019), which for the first time sets out a theory of analogical inductive inference that closely parallels Carnap's continuum of inductive methods. Huttegger assumes that in addition to observing outcomes X one observes their "type" Y and then shows that under four natural assumptions there exist constants β_{jm} and $\varkappa_{ij}$ such that if $\mathbf{X}_N$ records the outcomes observed to date, and $\mathbf{Y}_N$ the types observed to date, then the predictive probabilities can be expressed as

$$P(X_{N+1} = i | \mathbf{X}_N, \mathbf{Y}_N, Y_{N+1} = j) = \frac{n_{ij} + \sum_{m \neq j} \beta_{jm} n_{im} + \varkappa_{ij}}{N_j + \sum_{m \neq j} \beta_{jm} N_m + K_j},$$

with i ranging over outcomes, j over types, n_{ij} the number of times an outcome i of type j occurs, $N_m = \sum_i n_{im}$, and $K_j = \sum_i \varkappa_{ij}$.

This impressive achievement is a fitting point at which to conclude our brief and highly selective review of the impact of Carnap's work after the publication of his 1950 book and 1952 monograph.[8]

10.13 Conclusion

> Nel mezzo del cammin di nostra vita
> mi ritrovai per una selva oscura,
> ché la diritta via era smarrita.
> (Opening lines of Dante's Divine Comedy)

Rudolf Carnap came to inductive inference relatively late in life. He appears to have felt confident at first that by shining the light of modern philosophy on it he could clarify its foundations and perhaps even resolve its controversial aspects. But like both James Bernoulli and the Reverend Thomas Bayes before him, he found the subject did not yield so easily to direct attack. And so his book 1950 book became only the first volume of a projected two, his 1952 monograph became only the initial chapters of that projected second volume, and eventually the entire project was abandoned and transformed instead into a series of research reports incrementally advancing the frontiers of the subject.

The period after 1952 saw a substantial shift in Carnap's view of the subject. Indicative of Carnap's clear shift over time is his statement in his posthumous *Basic System* that he did not think there need be "a controversy between the objectivist point of view and the subjectivist or personalist point of view," that both have "a legitimate place in the context of our work," and that "there is merely a difference in attitude or emphasis between the subjectivist tendency to emphasize the existing freedom of choice, and the objectivist tendency to stress the existence of limitations" (Jeffrey 1980, 119).[9] For my own views on this essential tension between the two tendencies (which closely accords with those of W. E. Johnson), see Zabell (2011, 303).

Nevertheless, Carnap's initial enterprise was not a failure for two distinct reasons. First, he largely shaped the way current philosophy views the

---

[8] For a recent and very interesting discussion of unpublished work by Hosiasson-Lindenbaum on analogical reasoning, and its relation to Carnap's work on analogy by similarity in the 1960s, see Sznajder (2022).

[9] It has been suggested that because Carnap went on to add "I give more attention to the [objectivist tendency], because in my work I am mainly interested in discovering new rationality requirements which lead to narrower boundaries," he clearly places himself in the objectivist camp, but his statement is one of research interests, not ultimate philosophical position.

nature and role of probability, in particular, its widespread acceptance of the Bayesian paradigm. And second, the torch was then taken up by an impressive array of mathematicians and philosophers (including, but not limited to, Richard C. Jeffrey, Jaakko Hintikka, Ilka Niiniluoto, Theo Kuipers, Persi Diaconis, Brian Skyrms, and Simon Huttegger) who continued and continue to generate many interesting results in this field.

CHAPTER 11

Metaphysics, Tolerance, and Language Planning
Carnap on International Auxiliary Languages

Başak Aray

11.1 Introduction

International auxiliary languages (IAL) are languages that were built to serve as a neutral medium of communication between different nations with the aim of enhancing mutual understanding and, ultimately, building world peace. Unlike pidgin languages and creoles (and also dead or living languages used internationally), these languages have been constructed either by a single individual or by an organizing body. With a prehistory dating to seventeenth-century philosophical languages, IAL reappears as an organized and viable practical initiative at the turn of the twentieth century due to the increase in globalization. The reemergence of international languages starts with Johann Schleyer's Volapük, followed by their most emblematic representative Esperanto, first presented to the public in 1897 by Doktoro Esperanto ("the doctor who hopes"), the pseudonym of Ludwik Lejzer Zamenhof. Zamenhof was a Russian-Jewish ophthalmologist from Bialystock (present-day Poland) deeply concerned by the ethnic tensions shaking his homeland and convinced by the positive impact that a neutral common language would have in reconciliating different peoples and preventing wars. The Esperanto movement had a sizeable following that has persisted to this day, but Esperanto was not the only option discussed by the IAL community in the first half of the last century. Reformers supported alternative versions of Esperanto (the most famous one being Ido, created by the French logician Louis Couturat). Other notable IALs include Guiseppe Peano's Latino sine Flexione, Otto Jespersen's Novial, and Alexander Gode's Interlingua.

In his "Intellectual Autobiography," Carnap relates the history of his discovery of Esperanto at the age of fourteen and his experience with the language: how he self-learned it with a book, how he used it in Esperanto congresses, how he enjoyed a staging of Iphigenie in Esperanto (refuting the oft-claimed inability of a constructed language to serve for literary purposes) and how he traveled to the Baltic with a Bulgarian friend, communicating with him exclusively through Esperanto. Carnap was fascinated by this language not only for the humanitarian and pacifist ideal it represented but also for its logical structure, which endowed it with both simplicity and a great expressive power. Throughout his life, Carnap pursued his active interest in IALs and studied many alternative projects (*IA*; Hempel 1973). Despite his participation in the Esperanto community, he did not fall into sectarianism on the subject of IAL and considered Esperanto's competitors seriously, all the while stressing their commonalities over their differences. He took a particular interest in Basic English, a minimalist IAL based on the English language, as attested by his correspondence with Ogden following Neurath's suggestion (McElvenny 2018). Hempel (1973) also mentions a possible correspondence with Lancelot Hogben on the subject of Interglossa, another IAL referred by Carnap as one of the latest in 1944 (Carnap 1944, 303). Neurath, on his side, tried to achieve a universal means of graphic communication through his Isotype method of visual statistics (Burke et al. 2013; McElvenny 2013). He collaborated with Ogden, providing illustrations for *Basic by Isotype* and using Basic English in the Isotype Institute's publications. Initially preferring a systematizing approach based on an ideal language, Carnap was later influenced by Neurath's pragmatic attitude on the question of international language. Neurath convinced him of the viability of Basic English notably because of people's conservative attitude on language that limits the acceptance of constructed languages despite their internal qualities.[1] But Carnap's only admitted contribution to the movement consists in a memorandum addressed to the International Auxiliary Language Association (IALA), founded in New York in 1924.[2] Carnap praised the IALA for its rigorous and detailed comparative studies on European languages as a scientific basis for the interlanguage to come. The association worked with experts such as Edward Sapir, Edward L. Thorndike, and André Martinet. Despite agreeing with their general work, Carnap was skeptical on tailoring an interlanguage by the study of questionnaires without the opportunity of a public discussion. The absence of a platform

---

[1] "We see from the facts – or at least it seems very probable – that the much greater number of men are not ready to make use of a not-natural language system; they have even a disgust at such a one. For this reason a part language of a natural language has much more chance to be taken in use by a great number of men in the near future, on the condition that this language is simple enough (though not so simple as a constructed one). Now, in my opinion, your Basic system is in this condition." (Carnap to Ogden, February 7, 1934, quoted by McElvenny 2018, 140)
[2] See Falk (1999) for a detailed history of the IALA.

to exchange views made the process one-sided and Carnap expressed this view in his correspondence with the IALA.[3]

Carnap (*IA*) points out that a number of logicians and philosophers who attempted a rational reconstruction of concepts and forged symbolic languages to do so were also interested in planning languages for international use. Carnap places himself in this tradition alongside other figures like Leibniz, Couturat, and Peano. Leibniz already dreamed of "universal characteristics," a project that guided Peano in designing Latino sine Flexione. (Indeed, Peano invited Carnap to collaborate with the Academia pro Interlingua).[4] Couturat is another example of this tendency spotted by Carnap, to which he admits to belong as well. Other philosophers supported the idea of an international language for simple communication between people who do not share the same native tongue, such as Russell and Neurath. This chapter examines the connection between Carnap's method of explication in philosophy and the assumptions of various attempts at linguistic interventionism such as IALs and language reforms. The history of Carnap's intellectual trajectory shows us multiple philosophical reasons that explain his interest in the IAL: while his early ideal of a reductive system of concepts lies arguably at the basis of his admiration of IALs as logically consistent structures superior in this sense to natural languages, his later instrumentalism formulated around the central principle of tolerance justified free choice of linguistic forms against the presumed authority of established linguistic structures, often used to dismiss artificial languages. The former aspect of his philosophy will be discussed in Section 11.2, where examples of reductivism in IALs are compared to Carnap's conceptual system in *Aufbau* (1928).

As opposed to ordinary language philosophy, rational reconstruction schemes adopt a proactive attitude toward language and attempt to reform philosophical language by redefining existent concepts and forging new terms with a specific sense differing from their daily use. Section 11.3

---

[3] "In my letters to IALA I urged the necessity of public discussion to be performed in a special periodical and in conferences. My suggestions in this direction were not accepted, however. I thought that the necessary discussions could not be carried on in a fruitful way by the means used by IALA, namely correspondence with individual persons and questionaires, because this method did not leave room for communication between the participants" (Carnap MA5: N24–25).

[4] "Peano recognized the relationship of the two problems of language planning, namely symbolic logic and international language. Therefore after reading my Logistik [1929], he asked me to cooperate in his language project and offered me an honorary membership in his Academia pro Interlingua. But I declined because his language form looked to me too archaic and I thought that it was too difficult to learn for non-Europeans" (Carnap MA5: N21).

discusses the relation between ordinary language and artificial language in Carnap's work and brings up some criticisms addressed against the assumptions of ideal language philosophy. Even though using artificial languages for logical analysis and planning a constructed language for international communication are, as admitted by Carnap, different projects whose practitioners only intersect in the cases of a few logicians such as Leibniz and Couturat, the opposition between the two aforementioned schools of analytic philosophy can be associated with two opposite attitudes concerning the legitimacy of planned innovation in linguistic matters: the romantic view that values spontaneity and tradition versus the instrumentalist view widely adopted by language planners (Section 11.4). This conflict is at the heart of the interaction between Carnap and Wittgenstein on the subject of Esperanto. Wittgenstein's attitude is representative of critics skeptical of language reforms in its organismic conception of language tied with a corresponding organismic conception of Volk, the former assumed to be a product naturally growing from the latter. Such a conception of social wholes was notoriously targeted by the Vienna Circle for its metaphysical assumptions. Formulated earlier by Carnap and Schlick, the empiricist rejection of this abstraction was carried further by Neurath in the name of a physicalist sociology. Wittgenstein's position illustrates the romanticist view of language as an autonomous reality emanating from the historical reality of a Volk, whereas Carnap adopts the instrumentalist viewpoint of language reformers (Section 11.5). The opposition between these two views of language forms the philosophical ground of debates concerning the legitimacy of linguistic interventionism. Finally, Carnap's later adoption of the principle of tolerance is a further step toward the instrumentalist conception of language shared by language constructors (Section 11.6). In the following, we reconstruct the evolution of Carnap's philosophy from the perspective of language engineering, explaining thus the different facets of his support for the IAL. Doing so, we also aim at enlightening some philosophical problems behind language planning.[5]

11.2 System Construction and Universal Languages

An aspect of many universal languages, the early modern ones in particular, that might have attracted logicians and rationalist philosophers is their

---

[5] By language planning we mean planned intervention in language, including reforming a national language and designing a constructed language for international communication. Although our topic is more specifically IAL, many issues about IALs come up in debates around language reforms as well.

attempt to organize the whole of our conceptual apparatus into one coherent logical structure with consistent derivations from a basic subset of primitive concepts. That all-encompassing ideal of a logically perfect structure on the basis of which humans of all nationalities could unite despite the accidental particularisms, irrationalities, and redundancies of their own natural languages was later adopted on a smaller scale by modern logicians like Frege and Russell in the service of a more specific ideal: to ensure the logical foundations of mathematics. The Leibnizian project of universal characteristics examined in detail by Couturat (1901) was a rational reconstruction aimed at overcoming arbitrariness ruling natural languages with the aim of enhancing human knowledge. Artificial languages built in the early seventeenth century were called "philosophical languages" and they had an a priori basis (in the terms of Léau and Couturat) in the sense that they were not based on already existing natural languages, which contributed to their non-practicability and subsequent failure, as many of them remained unachieved projects.[6]

In *Aufbau*, Carnap defines a constructional system as one that "undertakes more than the division of concepts into various kinds and the investigation of the differences and mutual relations between these kinds" (*Aufbau*, section 1). In addition, such a system "attempts a step-by-step derivation" or "construction" of all concepts from certain fundamental concepts, so that a genealogy of concepts results in which each one has its definite place" (*Aufbau*, section 1). The axiomatic-style reconstruction of all concepts into a logically coherent, pyramidal deductive structure is the method used by constructors of early modern philosophical languages. Through these ancestors of IAL, their constructors aimed at building a linguistic structure that truly reflects the world as it is, beyond the imprecision and arbitrariness of natural languages. This method of systematic reconstruction on the basis of primitive concepts, where all complex concepts are reduced to their elementary constituents (which altogether form an "alphabet of thoughts") was used in the early modern times by Leibniz, Wilkins, and Dalgarno. In Leibniz's vein, Carnap's earlier understanding of rational reconstruction supposed a total system of concepts deriving from a primary basis: "By a *constructional system* we mean a step-by-step ordering of objects in such a way that the objects of each level are constructed from those of the lower levels. Because of the transitivity of reducibility, all objects of the constructional system are thus indirectly

---

[6] See Couturat and Léau (1903) for a detailed compilation of the IALs up to the time of publication. The book was followed by a sequel dedicated to the newer projects.

constructed from objects of the first level. These *basic objects* form the *basis of the system*" (*Aufbau*, section 1). In *Aufbau*, Carnap describes several ways to construct a unified conceptual system, grouped by their basic elements and relations into two main categories – physical and psychological. For a physical basis, one can choose either electrons and protons as basic elements and the spatial and temporal relations between them as basic relations of the system or space-time points of the four-dimensional space-time continuum as basic elements and their relative location in the continuum as basic relations. A psychological basis can be constructed in two different ways, depending on whether the basic elements are psychological states of one person only (an autopscychological basis) or of all people (a heteropsychological basis).

In each step of the construction, new elements are defined in terms of predefined ones, starting at the basis (for example, from an autopsychological basis, physical objects will be constructed through individual sense experiences, and other people's sense experiences will be in turn constructed through physical objects). Although Carnap's idea of rational reconstruction evolved toward a pragmatic and pluralistic view of explication in his later years, he nevertheless conserved this inclination to systematize: "I worked on many special problems, always looking for new approaches and improved solutions. But in the background there was always the ultimate aim of the total system of all concepts. I believed that it should be possible, in principle, to give a logical reconstruction of the total system of the world as we know it" (quoted by Carus 2007, 139). He relates that this tendency kept him closer to critical reconstruction than description in the study of language: "I often thought of becoming a linguist. However, I was more inclined toward theoretical construction and systematization than toward description of facts. Therefore I had more interest in those problems of language which involved planning and construction" (*IA*, 67).[7]

Some twentieth-century language constructors, while using an a posteriori method based on commonalities found across natural languages (mostly limited to the European area), nevertheless inherited the ideals of a logical all-encompassing conceptual system as exemplified by philosophical languages and described in the *Aufbau*. For example, Zamenhof compiled the Esperanto grammar into sixteen rules and associated a single word ending for each part of speech, to make the syntactic structure of

---

[7] See Hiz and Swiggers (1990); Tomalin (2009); Goldsmith and Laks (2019) for interrelations between logical positivism and descriptive linguistics.

sentences transparent. In doing so, he was concerned above all by making the international language as simple as possible for the purpose of maximizing its accessibility for everyone. In his reform proposal to Esperanto, Couturat (1910) took this axiomatic tendency further by suggesting a standard and uniform derivation system for building new words. While recognizing that he eventually became convinced of the importance of psychological factors for the adoption of an interlanguage by the masses after his contact with Albert L. Guérard, Carnap remained closer to Couturat's approach to interlinguistics – one based more on logic than historical or psychological facts that have been governing the evolution of natural languages.[8] Both in his criticism of Occidental[9] and Interlingua[10] appears his uneasiness with the naturalistic school of language planning. Yet we should acknowledge that his anti-naturalism is far from being as strict as Couturat's (Aray 2019). The influence of Ogden and Neurath accounts for Carnap's concession to *some* consideration of the extra-logical factors for the success of an interlanguage. This is, for Carnap, rather a necessary evil to ensure the future of the international language, therefore a sacrifice to be tolerated for pragmatic reasons as long as it does not become the main principle guiding its construction. Regularity always comes before familiarity, logic always comes before facts, despite Carnap's efforts to reconcile the two. Similarly, Ogden's Basic English is a minimalist alternative to standard English with a restricted vocabulary.[11] Ogden opted

---

[8] "Only later in America through a conversation with Albert L. Guérard, the great humanist and expert in comparative literature, was I induced to undertake a more thoroughgoing study of the naturalistic movement in language planning and especially, of its main representative de Wahl. The latter's thesis was that for language planning only psychological points of view should be relevant, not logical ones. He certainly has the merit of having called the attention of interlinguists for the first time to the psychological factors in this field. I think he is right in his view that a language which is merely constructed according to maximum regularity is not the easiest one to learn if it is not in accord with the thinking and speaking habits of people. On the other hand I believe that de Wahl underestimated the importance of regularity" (Carnap MA5: N22–23).

[9] "When I first looked at this project [Occidental], I rejected it without detailed study because the sacrifice with respect to logical structure and regularity appeared unacceptable to me" (Carnap MA5: N22).

[10] "This language [Interlingua] has an aesthetically very attractive homogeneity, but in my opinion it is constructed with too much respect for the historical development of natural languages; it sacrifices regularity and rapidity of learning to immediate understandability and closeness to usual language forms" (Carnap MA5: N26).

[11] While leaning toward a language constructed according to the logical need for regularity, Carnap considers Basic English as another viable alternative for international communication. "I have no doubt that in a few decades at the latest there will be an international language of simple structure in general use as the second language of all people on earth who can read and write. But nobody knows today whether it will be a basic language or an artificial one. Therefore, both ways must be tried out" (Carnap 1944, 303), Basic enjoys the psychological advantage of being adapted from a

for such minimalism not only for the ease of learning English as a foreign language but also because he considered "vertical translation" from standard English to Basic English to be an enlightening philosophical exercise that helped one reflect on their concepts (Ogden 1936/1994). Hogben's Interglossa (1943) adopted a similar reductivist strategy in the decomposition of verbs. Himself an Esperantist, Carnap welcomed these concurrent IAL projects in the name of the principle of tolerance, all the while stressing their near-unity as similar forms of a "standard average European."

11.3 Explication and Artificial Languages

In a *Synthese* volume dedicated to Carnap, Hempel spots a connection between Carnap's philosophical method of rational reconstruction by the medium of an artificial language with his sympathy for language planning attempts.[12] In Carnap's philosophical practice, engineered languages have a central function in the conceptual clarification of the imprecise or ambiguous terms of ordinary language. Carnap defines explication in these terms:

> The task of making more exact a vague or not quite exact concept used in everyday life or in an earlier stage of scientific or logical development, or rather of replacing it by a newly constructed, more exact concept, belongs among the most important tasks of logical analysis and logical construction. We call this the task of explicating, or of giving an *explication* for, the earlier concept; this earlier concept, or sometimes the term used for it, is called the *explicandum*; and the new concept, or its term, is called an *explicatum* of the old one. (*M&N*, 7–8)

In other words, "By an explication we understand the transformation of an inexact, prescientific concept, the explicandum, into an exact concept, the explicatum" (*LFP*, 1). For example, explication makes us transition from our intuitive but vague concepts of warmer and colder to the

---

language already familiar to the masses on a global scale while mitigating its logical defects thanks to a reductive process of reconstruction into a minimal core.

[12] "Carnap's predilection for the use of precise model languages in philosophical explication was clearly akin to the keen interest he took in auxiliary international languages, like Esperanto, which in his earlier years he spoke fluently. These international languages, too, were meant to be governed by precisely stated general grammatical and semantic rules without all the usual exceptions, and simple enough to be readily learned and used; and Carnap felt strongly that the wide adoption of such a language would be, among other things, a great help in furthering the international propagation of scientific ideas" (Hempel 1973, 262).

quantitative concept of temperature and from our everyday concept of salt to the chemical concept of sodium chloride (NaCl).

At the heart of the distinction between ordinary language and philosophical reconstruction lies the corresponding distinction between "spontaneous development" and "deliberate formulation." As a transition from unreflected and imprecise concepts to a systematic structure of concepts (differing from the former by their "clarity and exactness"), rational reconstruction defines the task of philosophy for Carnap. It contrasts with descriptivism (especially psychologism) in its superiority in clarity and usability. The purported tendency of the ideal language philosophy to miss the real meanings of philosophical concepts as used in ordinary language was targeted by the Oxford school of analysis. For instance, Strawson says: "typical philosophical problems about the concepts used in non-scientific discourse cannot be solved by laying down the rules of use of exact and fruitful concepts in science. To do this last is not to solve the typical philosophical problem, but to change the subject" (Strawson 1963, 506). He further criticizes rational reconstruction for its inability to connect explicata with explicanda: "the introduction of the scientific concepts may itself produce a further crop of puzzles, arising from an unclarity over the relations between two ways of using language to talk about the physical world, the relations between the quantitative and the sensory vocabularies" (Strawson 1963, 506). Against this objection, Carnap mitigates the distinction between ordinary and reconstructed language and specifies that their difference is not a dichotomy: "I have the impression that Strawson's view is based on the conception of a sharp separation, perhaps even a gap, between everyday concepts and scientific concepts. I see here no sharp boundary line but a continuous transition. The process of the acquisition of knowledge begins with common sense knowledge; gradually the methods become more refined and systematic, and thus more scientific" (*RSE*, 934). Like Neurath, Carnap admits the continuity between everyday language and scientific language linked together by constant interactions. Scientific concepts arise from everyday physicalist concepts of the daily experience and, in their turn, reintegrate everyday language once the technicalities involved in the concept become an ordinary part of practical life (to take Neurath's example, the scientific term hydrogen peroxide is now being used in hair salons, 1936/1983, 148). Spontaneously emerging linguistic material does therefore not stand in a stark opposition with planned scientific terminology. Also, being rooted in the former does not stop the latter from being superior in clarity and efficiency for some purposes. Acknowledging the dynamic interaction between tradition and intervention in language makes room for the latter, in philosophy as well as in language planning.

Quoting Otto Jespersen, linguist and interlanguage constructor, Maxwell and Feigl in their reply to Strawson's critique of Carnap point out that "ordinary language is constantly *being* reformed" (Maxwell and Feigl 1961, 490, original emphasis). In this respect, the activity of rational reconstruction appears to be an extension of the natural evolution of ordinary language, which is subject to continual modification: "quite often we find it necessary to help this evolution along a bit simply because ordinary language provides no univocal guide as to what should properly be said when novel situations arise, whether these arise in actuality or in thought experiments" (Maxwell and Feigl 1961, 490). Like Jespersen who returned criticisms against constructed languages by denying the radical difference between the latter and natural languages, Maxwell and Feigl reject the dichotomy between terms of ordinary language and technical terms as "chimerical both in theoretical science and in philosophy" (Maxwell and Feigl 1961, 493). Speaking of Carnap's philosophical ideal of explication, Carus shows how Carnap dissolves this perceived dichotomy between evolved and constructed languages.[13] He assigns to constructed languages in Carnap's philosophy a progressive political purpose, which makes him a neo-Enlightenment philosopher: "Evolved and constructed languages exist side by side, from the empirical viewpoint, and usually the interactions between them are marginal. From Carnap's ideal viewpoint, however, the liberation of human thought from passive complacency and the shackles of the past depends on the progressive replacement of evolved by constructed languages" (Carus 2007, 276). Explication through artificial languages appears therefore as a potential for improvement in our conceptual structure in the Enlightenment spirit of the *Aufbau*. This ranges Carnap's attitude toward language as a product to improve on next to language planners' instrumentalism that aims at transforming language so that it fulfils its purpose better instead of sticking to a conservatism amalgamating what is with what ought to be. In stating that "what is is not necessarily what should be. We are not bound to the

---

[13] "There is a practical division of labour among those who study the different kinds of systems; as a rule, the study of evolved languages is an empirical discipline (linguistics), while the self-conscious creation of symbolic systems for pure and applied science is regarded as mathematical or formal. But there are many intermediate cases (e.g. music theory, which evolved over hundreds of years in response to musical practice, but has formal elements). So 'evolved' and 'constructed' are useful as comparative or relative concepts, to each other. One language can be more or less constructed than another, but there is no absolute scale of 'constructedness'" (Carus 2007: 275).

language as it is," the Estonian language reformer Valter Tauli (1974, 52) expresses this constructive attitude on language against tendencies to preserve old forms.

11.4 Romanticism versus Instrumentalism about Language

Carnap contrasts two main attitudes toward language: a "descriptive and historical" one versus a "constructive" one. Logicians and language planners share the latter position while linguists consider languages as given historical products and describe them without attempting to bring any changes.[14] Explaining the need for constructed languages in a philosophical discussion of concepts of everyday life that are not as yet sufficiently unambiguous for a scientific treatment, Carnap recourses to an instrumental metaphor central to the discourse of many language reform advocates:

> A natural language is like a crude, primitive pocketknife, very useful for a hundred different purposes. But for certain specific purposes, special tools are more efficient, e.g., chisels, cutting-machines, and finally the microtome. If we find that the pocket knife is too crude for a given purpose and creates defective products, we shall try to discover the cause of the failure, and then either use the knife more skillfully, or replace it for this special purpose by a more suitable tool, or even invent a new one. The naturalist's thesis is like saying that by using a special tool we evade the problem of the correct use of the cruder tool. But would anyone criticize the bacteriologist for using a microtome, and assert that he is evading the problem of correctly using a pocketknife? (*RSE*, 938–939)

The instrumental metaphor of language is commonly used by language reform advocates. To defend language planning, Tauli insists on the instrumental nature of language as a human creation for certain purposes and rejects the dogmatism of the established use and tradition as the proper norm in linguistic issues. Before him, Jespersen was critical of the conception of language as "a self-existent thing or substance" or "as an organism, that lives and dies like a plant or any other organism" (Jespersen

---

[14] In his autobiographical manuscript, Carnap explains his ability to think beyond the traditional and historical forms of language and his openness to logico-linguistic innovation by his family education, especially the liberal attitude of his mother: "Because of this causal attitude of hers [his mother] toward customs, conventions and tradition, I never had the widespread reverence toward the sanctity of tradition, which is such an obstacle in the way of cultural progress. I believe that regarding the forms of customary language as sacrosanct is for some contemporary philosophers a serious impediment in their philosophical thinking, because it leads to a strong inhibition against even considering problems of language" (Carnap MA5: A15).

1925, 4). As opposed to this conservative attitude, which gauges authenticity in language by conformity to past use, he developed an interactive model of language where the speakers have the power to initiate a gradual transformation in their collective language by way of invention when the newly introduced linguistic forms gain adoption through successive imitations. All languages are human creations, after all, and this does not apply to so-called artificial languages only. And from the ineluctably constructed nature of ethnic languages follows the legitimacy of reforming those: "Languages, after all, are humanly created, and it is not only a right, but a duty, to contribute to the best of poor ability to make them better for our fellows and for the generations to come" (Jespersen 1925, 112). Dissatisfied with the historical-descriptive limitations of the empirical science of linguistics, Carnap admired Jespersen as a linguist with a constructive interest in his subject despite the opposite inclination in his field.[15]

Language conservatism is often closely related to an organismic conception of language linked to eighteenth-century romantic thinkers such as Humboldt and Herder, who valued language as a national treasure, an expression of the soul of an ethnic community. This conception was targeted by Jespersen who rejected the accounts of language as an autonomous entity beyond the control of individual speakers: "Formerly languages were often spoken of as organisms whose natural growth was thought to be analogous to that of plants or even animals; but linguists have come to realize that this is a wrong view, because a language has no independent existence apart from those individuals who speak it" (Jespersen 1933/2010, 397). For Jespersen, postulating language as an entity beyond its concrete uses by individuals of a linguistic community is a metaphysical misconception. It is true that the individual speakers cannot change the language as they please if they cannot make themselves understood – in this sense they are well dependent on the linguistic community. But one should not forget that this dependency goes both ways, and the present day established language forms have all originated with the invention of individual speakers at some point, then spread little by little through the imitation of other speakers in the community, at which point they started to gain a collective presence. Jespersen compares

---

[15] "While a majority of linguists had been rather reluctant or strongly opposed to the idea of a synthetic international language, presumably because of their purely historical rather than constructive attitude toward languages, Jespersen was the first prominent linguist, also known to philosophers through his books on philosophy of language, who worked on the problem of language construction" (Carnap MA5: N21).

this dynamic to the emergence and adoption of folk tales. Stripped from its associated myths formed in the process of nation-building, language appears in its true function, as an instrument to communicate. Once we get over its associations with national identity and its role as a symbolic bearer of tradition and heritage, we can reduce language to an instrument built by humans for some practical purposes and strive to improve it instead of leaving it as it is. The instrumentalist conception of language leads the way to linguistic innovation in the name of pragmatism and progress: "From the fact that language is a means follows that a language and its components can be evaluated, altered, corrected, regulated, improved, and replaced by others and new languages and components of a language can be created at will" (Tauli 1974, 51).

Carnap's adoption of artificial languages to clarify the concepts of a more spontaneous language results from a similar striving for constructing better tools. His controversy with Wittgenstein on the subject of planned languages is best understood in terms of this fundamental difference between romanticism and instrumentalism. Wittgenstein explains his negative feelings toward Esperanto by appealing to tradition and cultural memory as the sole legitimate source for the genesis of languages. His criticism targets, in particular, its "invented" words and affixes and its "lacking in associations." The invented words are "cold" and such an invented language is not even a proper language – it just "plays at being 'language.'" Nyíri (1992) observes that Wittgenstein associates language intimately with a tradition rooted in a collective past of oral communication and relegates the written aspect to the second plan when it comes to genuineness ("A system of purely written signs would not disgust us so much."). Therefore, the heart of the conflict between Carnap and Wittgenstein on language construction is Wittgenstein's dismissal of the very notion of a language that could be transmitted non-traditionally: "At our very first meeting with Wittgenstein, Schlick unfortunately mentioned that I was interested in the problem of an international language like Esperanto. As I had expected, Wittgenstein was definitely opposed to this idea. But I was surprised by the vehemence of his emotions. A language which had not 'grown organically' seemed to him not only useless but despicable" (*IA*, 26). Wittgenstein did not separate language from tradition and conceived the formation of languages solely as a spontaneous, "organic" generation free from interventional impurities.[16] Löffler spots

---

[16] "The Junggrammatik combines, among others, the evolution idea of the 19th century with Romanticist ideas of Volksgeist and naturalness. Both points, the organism conception of

in these remarks "an argument against certain forms of PL [planned languages]," for, "if the tacit conventions needed for understanding everyday language are enormously complicated, then a PL, which must establish all those conventions artificially, is very likely to be shipwrecked" (Löffler 2004, 210). Wittgenstein's reaction against constructed languages reveals an organismic view of language as an autonomous being subject to spontaneous evolution in close contact with its community (Wittgenstein 1922, 4.002: "Everyday language is a part of the human organism and is no less complicated than it."). This organismic view condemns linguistic interventions as unwelcome disturbances that get in the way of the "natural" evolution of an ethnic language. It is characterized by a sharp distinction between natural and artificial, one questioned by Jespersen who suggests considering naturality and artificiality in language as a spectrum rather than a binary opposition.[17]

11.5 Neopositivist Criticism of Volk

The view of language as an organism is often associated with a similarly organismic conception of Volk that would be the bearer of a language. Both the community and its language are viewed as organic wholes of which the existence transcends the existence of their constituents (individuals in a community or speech forms uttered by individuals). In his essay on the historical roots of the Sapir-Whorf hypothesis that states the dependence of thought on language, Joseph distinguishes two opposite trends in the linguistic thought: the "metaphysical garbage" view represented by logicians and analytic philosophers and the "magic key" view that values language as an invaluable instrument in understanding a nation's world view:

> "Metaphysical garbage" is distinct from the Herder-Humboldt line in linguistics, which characterizes language not as a source of obstacles to

---

language and the primacy of spoken language, reappear in Wittgenstein, although in a prima facie strange coining: Wittgenstein sees all-day language as a part of the human organism" (Löffler 2004, 210).

[17] "It is customary to speak of such languages as English, French and German as natural, and such languages as Esperanto, Ido, Volapük, Occidental, Novial as artificial. It will be my task in this paper to show that this distinction is not exact, as the difference is one of degree rather than of species; very much in the so-called natural languages is 'artificial,' and very much in the so-called artificial languages is quite natural, at any rate in all those schemes that count; therefore it would be wise to choose more adequate terms. I shall consequently speak of the first class of languages as national languages, and of the second class as constructed or systematically planned languages" (Jespersen 1933/2010, 397).

universal logic, but as the embodiment of a national world-view, a kind of spiritual essence without which a culture cannot be adequately understood. Language is thus what we might call a *magic key*: for the claim or implication is that *studying the language of a people is the way to comprehend their minds or souls.* (Joseph 2002, 77; original emphasis)

It is important to note that these two viewpoints agree on the deterministic influence of language on thought – their divergence resides in their attitude toward this determinism: the "metaphysical garbage" line considers this influence as an obstacle to overcome by the study of universal logic while the "magic key" viewpoint values this power of language in shaping the world view of a nation and considers language as an essential part of collective identity. Jespersen contested the scientific value of such abstractions as Volk in linguistics and targeted theories of folk-mind that erected collective linguistic practices into a hypostasis above their concrete manifestations, for example, utterances by individual locutors: "A mystically assumed 'common mind' really explains nothing whatever in any department of life, any more than the assumption of a mystical 'common-stomach' would serve to explain how it is that people react in like manner to foods and poisons" (Jespersen 1925, 17).

The transcendent view of social wholes such as Volk was also targeted by the Vienna Circle in its resistance against the metaphysical trends that were gaining ground in German universities. For instance, in his lecture in Dessau Bauhaus, Carnap denied the existence of Volk in his empiricist dismissal of metaphysical realism.[18] Galison explains this attitude shared among logical positivists as a reaction to the political Nazi discourse in power: "Over the intervening years, much of what Carnap was opposing has lost its direct political significance. But in 1929 Carnap's four theses bore a manifest coherence in their opposition to powerful right-wing forces that sought to unify these ideas of Volk, metaphysics, the state, and God." (Galison 1990, 736) The International Congress of Philosophy that took place in 1934 in Prague witnessed a confrontation between the nationalist philosophy of Volk in its vitalistic metaphysics and its positivist opposition. Carnap and Reichenbach attacked Hans Driesch's organicism as mystical and unscientific whereas Schlick responded with a lecture "On

---

[18] "There are no social objects such as the state or the Volk" (Carnap's lecture "Der logische Aufbau der Welt," October 17, 1929, document dated 10 Oct. 1929, CP, PASP, document 110-07-45; Galison 1990, 736).

the Concept of Wholeness."[19] Recounting the congress in his account of logical empiricism, McGill credits the Vienna Circle with combating reactionary forces of their day using their anti-metaphysical position and states that "it was the logical positivists at the International Congress at Prague who provided the strongest counterpoise to the nationalism and mystagogy of fascist philosophy. Their logical analysis gave a clear challenge to the chauvinistic profundities of the National Socialists" (McGill 1936, 78).

Later, rather than dismissing the notion of community altogether in an empiricist skepticism over abstract entities, Carnap started to give it a more flexible interpretation contrasting with the monolithic view of Volk as organism. While arguing for the freedom of inventing new forms for clarifying concepts or improving international communication, Carnap does not actually deny the cultural function of language that goes beyond its mere instrumental function. But on the difference of language conservatists, he does not consider these two different functions as a conflicting pair. The thesis of linguistic relativity that states the cultural dependence of each language on the specific culture in which it has originated has frequently been used to discredit constructed languages, says Carnap. Yet, Sapir's activism in the IALA attests that the father of the thesis of linguistic relativity did not consider it incompatible with the creation and adoption of a constructed language. Carnap adds that the IALs of the twentieth century, too, are a product of a specific culture: the international culture of modern science and technology, which now extends to a global scale. Recognizing this connection, Carnap subverts the thesis of linguistic relativity in favor of IAL and gives a new meaning to culture that overcomes national boundaries:

> It is true that every living language uses a particular conceptual system for the description of the world, a system that has grown out of the specific cultural background of the language. This fact, which has been explained in detail by Whorf, is sometimes used as an objection against the possibility of a constructed international language. However, the existing international

---

[19] "For both sides, the debate over the totality concept [Ganzheitbegriff] was crucial. Carnap, Reichenbach, and Schlick denied the idea of a transcendent reality to the Deutschtum, Nation, or Volk and so threatened to undermine central tenets of right-wing ideology. According to Schlick, in sociological as well as physical or biological systems, one could build up higher levels of organization from an adequate understanding of constituent individuals. There simply was nothing further left to add about the 'totality' or 'whole.' To the Nazis and their allies, individuals had to be more than isolated entities; they were members of "higher totalities" whose full existence and whose cultural and spiritual acts could be understood only insofar as they were embedded in a larger inheritance, including their genetic material" (Galison 1990, 744).

language does possess a specific cultural background, as was emphasized by Gode. This background is the Western culture, more specifically, its modern science and technology, which originated in the Occident but which are now, together with their scientific terminology, the common property of many nations all over the world. (*IA*, 70)

11.6 Principle of Tolerance and Instrumentalism in Language Planning

From the rejection of organicism in linguistics follows the legitimacy of linguistic interventionism and the viability of language planning, as the individual practice becomes the constitutive factor in the making of languages in actual use inside the limits of de facto intelligibility and subsequent wider-scale acceptance instead of the conformity to some ideal norms defined by an essentialist view of language beyond the sum of its locutors' occurrences. The resulting instrumentalism centers the speakers, not the language, as an independent entity or a collective treasure: "A language is from this point of view only an instrument of communication, not a symbol of revelation, only a means, not an end" (Punya Sloka Ray quoted in Haugen 1971, 268). In a similar move, Carnap disconnects the theoretical field of ontology from the practical field of creating or choosing linguistic frameworks. Inside a given framework, questions concerning existence (for example, whether there are elephants, given the framework of physical things, or whether there are prime numbers greater than one hundred, given the framework of cardinal numbers) can be answered by relevant sciences. This implies experience and observation in physical sciences, logical reasoning in mathematics. In contrast, questions on the existence of the framework itself are not theoretical questions. A framework is not true or false, it does not conform to or contradict the real world; it is only a pragmatic choice of language use that may or not deliver fruitful results depending on our objectives.[20] Making the distinction between internal and external questions, Carnap disconnects the choice of framework from any ontological commitment:

> From the internal questions we must clearly distinguish external questions, i.e., philosophical questions concerning the existence or reality of the framework itself. Many philosophers regard a question of this kind as an ontological question which must be raised and answered before the

---

[20] These questions are dealt with by André Carus (Chapter 5), Vera Flocke (Chapter 2), and Erich H. Reck (Chapter 7) in this volume.

introduction of the new language forms. The latter introduction, they believe, is legitimate only if it can be justified by an ontological insight supplying an affirmative answer to the question of reality. In contrast to this view, we take the position that the introduction of the new ways of speaking does not need any theoretical justification because it does not imply any assertion of reality. (*ESO*, 31)

Liberating language forms from ontological charges enables Carnap to legitimize reference to abstract entities in science without committing to any sort of Platonism.

Later studies on Carnap in the historiography of logical empiricism have detailed Carnap's pragmatism (Richardson 2007; Creath 2012; Reck 2012). This pragmatism is shared by language reformers who often used the instrumental nature of language to justify deliberate intervention in it, in the same way Carnap justified the introduction of new linguistic forms. Here his opposition with Wittgenstein becomes clearer, as the latter stands for the tradition and the established system of meaning: "I wished to show that everyone is free to choose the rules of his language and thereby his logic in any way he wishes. This I called the 'principle of tolerance'; it might perhaps be called more exactly the 'principle of the conventionality of language forms'" (*IA*, 55). Accordingly, there is no question of truth when it comes to choosing linguistic forms, since this choice is a practical one by nature: "Strictly speaking, the question whether the solution is right or wrong makes no good sense because there is no clear-cut answer. The question should rather be whether the proposed solution is satisfactory, whether it is more satisfactory than another one, and the like" (*LFP*, 4). Reck (2012, 99) and Creath (2012, 172) ground the late Carnap's logical pluralism on the pragmatic nature of the task of coming up with or selecting among different possible linguistic conventions.

While Carnap's earlier systematizing approach to concepts positions him near early modern constructors of philosophical languages, this longing for systematization eventually leaves place to a defense of language construction in an instrumentalist spirit, following Carnap's turn to the principle of tolerance. Carnap's instrumentalism concerning the choice of theoretico-linguistic framework is comparable to the instrumentalism of language planners who argue for the possibility and legitimacy of creating new linguistic forms alongside established ones. With the principle of tolerance, Carnap justifies linguistic reconstruction as a fundamentally practical enterprise, reserving the theoretical to the "internal" questions. A linguistic framework is not true or false such as a cognitive theory could be, it can only be more or less adequate for the purposes it is being used for: "The acceptance [of a framework] cannot be judged as being either true or false because it is not an assertion. It can only be judged as being more or less expedient, fruitful, conducive to the aim for which the language is intended" (*ESO*, 31).

The late pragmatist Carnap insists on the instrumental nature of linguistic frameworks, leaving us with multiple possibilities regarding the adoption of one and the legitimate freedom to construct new ones to fulfil some specific purpose: "The acceptance or rejection of abstract linguistic forms, just as the acceptance or rejection of any other linguistic forms in any branch of science, will finally be decided by their efficiency as instruments, the ratio of the results achieved to the amount and complexity of the efforts required" (*ESO*, 40). The principle of tolerance opens the possibility for new linguistic forms, which should be evaluated based on their efficiency in accomplishing a pragmatic function, instead of their supposed adequacy with some external reality or some established tradition:

> Let us grant to those who work in any special field of investigation the freedom to use any form of expression which seems useful to them; the work in the field will sooner or later lead to the elimination of those forms which have no useful function. *Let us be cautious in making assertions and critical in examining them, but tolerant in permitting linguistic forms.* (*ESO*, 40; original emphasis)

11.7 Conclusion

Carnap's tendency for system construction and his vision of philosophy as explication of concepts with the use of formal languages oriented him toward language planning starting from his early years. The ideal language philosophy was open to create new linguistic forms alongside the ordinary language, an aspect of Carnap's thought that predisposed him to the idea of creating an interlanguage, preferably one satisfying the logical condition of regularity better than national languages. Even though we find no systematic connection between ideal language philosophy and interlinguistics, in the case of Carnap, overcoming the limits of ordinary language for philosophical analysis went hand in hand with a favorable view on languages crafted as a neutral medium between international speakers. The logical empiricist skepticism toward metaphysical entities in humanities (such as Volk) is another aspect of his philosophy that can be associated with his avowed internationalism. Furthermore, this values instrumentalism over romanticism concerning language, as it prevents concerns advanced by many people – linguists and nonlinguists alike – about the loss of an ethnic identity shared by an organic community and finding its most valuable expression in the traditional linguistics forms. Carnap's later liberalized empiricism with a pragmatic orientation (which starts with the explicit endorsement of the principle of tolerance) is a further move toward this instrumentalist position reclaimed by many language planners against conservative objections. Overall, Carnap's philosophy offers us many elements justifying the construction and active use of an IAL. The dynamics between found linguistic material and systematic construction or between the psychological principle of familiarity and the logical principle of regularity illustrate Carnap's multiple philosophical values that can be contradictory at times, but his values of criticism and tolerance permitted these to exist simultaneously in the service of creating the optimal interlanguage(s) without imposing a particular model from the top.

PART IV
Science and Theories

CHAPTER 12

Carnap on Theories and the Methods of Science

Lydia Patton[*]

12.1 Carnap as Philosopher of Science

With Hans Reichenbach and Moritz Schlick, Rudolf Carnap is among the scientific heavy hitters of logical positivism. Yet it can be surprisingly difficult to assess his contributions to the philosophy of science. Unlike Reichenbach and Schlick, Carnap did not write books devoted to relativity theory. His lectures on the philosophy of science were published as *An Introduction to the Philosophy of Science (IPoS)*, but they receive less press than the *Aufbau* or the *Logical Syntax of Language*.

There is a heavy emphasis in Carnap scholarship on the analysis of language and meaning. Carnap's analysis of science and its methods inclines toward analysis of languages involving syntax, semantics, and logic.[1] Carnap maintains positions along these lines throughout career, focusing on analyzing of languages, not through descriptive or "pragmatical" analysis alone but via the introduction and definition of formal languages.[2] While Carnap's positions on meaning and truth shifted throughout his career, this methodological tendency did not change.[3]

Carnap is a chief architect of logical positivism's distinction between theoretical and observational languages, maintaining a distinction in principle between analytic and synthetic statements. Further, Carnap thought we needed to find correspondence rules that connect theoretical statements to observational ones, allowing for translation between one

---

[*] Many thanks to the editors of this volume and to an anonymous reviewer for excellent comments on earlier drafts.
[1] His classic methods presented in "Testability and Meaning" involve the introduction of predicates through "reduction pairs" and "bilateral reduction sentences" (*T&M*, 443–446).
[2] In "Meaning and Synonymy in Natural Languages," a response to Quine's "Two Dogmas of Empiricism," Carnap argues that the "construction and semantical investigation of language systems is more important" than the "pragmatical investigation of natural languages" (1955a, 34).
[3] Because it focuses on a theme and not on analysis of any one text, the narrative of this chapter will have to elide the changes to Carnap's positions over time to some extent. In particular, it is not a complete account of the *Aufbau*, and explaining how this text fits in will have to wait for future work.

language and the other and thus for verification of theoretical claims by statements in the observation language.

Carnap's analysis of language is linked closely with the Received View of scientific theories, to which Carnap made fundamental contributions.[4] The Received View has come in for a thorough battering over time, losing ground on the empiricist side to Bas van Fraassen's account and elsewhere to various forms of structuralism. Even those who endorse some broadly Carnapian positions tend to disavow the Received View.[5]

The criticisms are familiar, alleging that Carnap's theory of science does not allow for a sophisticated entwinement of theory and observation, instead favoring heavy formalism and a brittle reductionism.[6] Saunders Mac Lane (1938), W. V. O. Quine (1951a), and Carl Hempel (1958) challenged Carnap's distinction between theoretical and observational languages.[7] They conceded that a practical working account of the difference could be maintained. But Hempel argued that the distinction is a continuum, that is, that there is no justification for a clear division between types of language. Quine argued that the analytic-synthetic distinction could not be made in principle.

The debates over these issues have been discussed thoroughly in the literature. Those discussions have centered on whether Carnap is right. The focus here, first, is on an independent understanding of Carnap's position. I will argue that Carnap's larger account of theoretical laws and scientific explanation, including prediction and testing, provide crucial context for Carnap's account of language.[8] Syntax and semantics are not only methods for linguistic analysis, they are also methods that allow us to

---

[4] As Sebastian Lutz (2012, 77–78) summarizes, the Received View found in, e.g., Carnap, Herbert Feigl, and Carl Hempel: "a scientific theory is formalized as a set of sentences (called theoretical sentences) of predicate logic that contain only logical or mathematical terms and the terms of the theory (*theoretical terms*). The theoretical terms are connected to terms that refer to observable properties (*observation terms*) through sets of correspondence rules, sentences that contain both theoretical and observation terms. The observation terms are given a semantic interpretation, which, through the correspondence rules and theoretical sentences, restricts the possible semantic interpretations of the theoretical terms."

[5] Recently, Lutz (2012, 80) has given a cogent defense of the Received View, arguing that its critics make "presumptions" that "are contentious or wrong, making the criticisms attacks on a straw man."

[6] See, e.g., Quine (1951a); Hempel (1958); Glymour (1980, 19–20). As Richardson (2003, 174) notes, Quine's objections presented Carnap as "the world's most technically able old-fashioned empiricist."

[7] I learned of Mac Lane's (1938) review of *Logical Syntax* from a talk by Steve Awodey.

[8] For analysis of similar themes in the early philosophy of Hans Reichenbach, see Richardson (2021, section 2).

analyze scientific results.[9] If we do not understand Carnap's account in this larger context, crucial linkages between and motivations for his views remain unexplained.

The account below will focus on Carnap's account of axiomatized theories as formal languages. Section 12.2 presents Carnap's view, controversial in the Vienna Circle, that axiomatized theories contain not only basic rules of logic but also a "specific calculus" that embodies the content of a particular theory. In this way, scientific laws can function as transformation rules in axiomatized theories. Section 12.3 explores the consequences of this position of Carnap's. Including scientific laws among the basic rules of a theory poses significant challenges, especially from an empiricist point of view. Scientific laws are introduced by postulation, and some of the theoretical terms they include cannot be defined, and can only be partially interpreted, in the observation language.[10] Section 12.4 briefly concludes, drawing out some implications of the reading in Sections 12.2 and 12.3 for Carnap's view of the relationship between philosophy and science.

12.2 The Role of Scientific Laws in Theoretical Languages

Reichenbach, Schlick, and Carnap wrestled with the question of how to construct an empiricist analysis of science in the 1920s and '30s.[11] Carnap's focus was on the "logical analysis of the concepts and sentences of the sciences" (*LSL*, xiii). Logical analysis constitutes an independent domain of philosophy, although philosophy is considered, nonetheless, to be continuous with the sciences.

The Received View of scientific theories to which Carnap contributed formalizes theories in predicate logic and then "the non-logical vocabulary is bipartitioned into *observational* and *theoretical* terms, where only the observational terms are directly interpreted. The interpretation of the theoretical terms is fixed only by the interpretation of the observation terms, the formalized theory, and additional sentences (*correspondence rules*) containing both observational and theoretical terms" (Lutz 2014b, 1475–1476). The Received View is often taken to imply a set of further

---

[9] *The Logical Syntax of Language* analyzes finitist and non-finitist systems of mathematics. The linguistic analysis is a tool, not the target.
[10] On the empirical significance of theoretical terms, see Lutz (2014a); on partial interpretation, see Friedman (2011).
[11] Referred to as *Wissenschaftslogik* or *Wissenschaftsanalyse*. For Reichenbach's project, see Richardson (2021). Andreas (2007) has written extensively on Carnap's *Wissenschaftslogik*.

claims. First, that the basic or "primitive" sentences of an axiomatized theory are all sentences with exclusively logical content. These sentences are considered to be true by linguistic convention. Second, that these basic sentences are analytic. On this reading, a translation into predicate logic renders a theory as a set of analytic purely logical sentences and their consequences.

Scholarship on the Received View (Ebbs 2011; Lutz 2014a, 2014b) has challenged both these assumptions, especially about Carnap.[12] According to a well-known "standard story," Carnap endorsed the claim that analytic sentences are "true by convention" and that the basic sentences of a theory are analytic.[13] On this reading of Carnap, the analytic sentences of a theory are co-extensive with its purely logical truths. And the logical truths are "true by convention," meaning that logical truths of a language system LS are true "*solely in virtue* of the linguistic conventions" of LS, and that the conventions "by themselves – that is, without presupposing any additional inference rules or logical truths in a metalanguage in which we specify the conventions for LS – logically imply all the logical truths of LS" (Ebbs 2011, 194). Analytic truth, on this account, is merely "truth by [linguistic] convention," whereas "genuine" truth must be synthetic.

There are several reasons to be suspicious of the standard story. Ebbs (2011, section 1) challenges the standard story overall, questioning the idea that Carnap endorsed the account of "truth by convention" above. Moreover, it is difficult to see why, given his other commitments, Carnap would support a thoroughgoing distinction between "real" or "genuine" truth and "truth by convention." That would require an account of "real truth" as something accessible outside the constitution and transformation rules of a formal language. But Carnap argues that trying to find an account of "genuine" or "real truth," external to any formal framework, is a pseudoproblem leading to pointless metaphysical speculation.[14]

Carnap's account of formal language systems throughout his career goes well beyond a reduction of theories to logical statements whose content is determined by linguistic convention. On the contrary, Carnap's approach was to analyze, using logic, how an axiomatized theory determines the meaning of its basic elements. By the time of *The Logical Syntax of*

---

[12] This "standard story" is perhaps more appropriately ascribed to early Wittgenstein.
[13] Ebbs (2011, 194) ascribes the "standard story" to Baldwin, Soames, Burge, and many others.
[14] Ebbs concludes (on distinct grounds) that Carnap did not endorse anything like the "truth by convention" view that is ascribed to him by the standard narrative.

Language, Carnap had developed a broader theory of how rules fix "syntactical form," that is, as he puts it, "any kind or category of expressions which is syntactically determined" (*LSS*, 16).[15] Carnap was able to extend the insight he had developed in the mathematical case, that rules or postulates introduced into a language can define terms of the language, to the case of the language of science more generally.[16] But his account of these rules was not limited to linguistic convention.

There are texts that, on the face of it, defend something like the standard story. In the "New Foundation of Logic" of 1929, Carnap attempts "to erect a Hilbertian axiomatic structure on a Wittgensteinian basis," using atomic sentences as "pictures of elementary facts" that are the basic propositions of the theory (Awodey and Carus 2009, 86). If the results of a theory are provable from its basic elements (e.g., axioms, terms, relations), then they are "true," which now means "provable within the system." Moreover, the act of axiomatizing the theory and showing how its results are proven ends up providing a logical analysis of the theory, showing the structural relations between the elements of the theory itself. Now, "Carnap distinguished the representational or meaning function of language from its purely combinatorial one, and now took the *latter*, rather than the former, as his starting point ... making the structure of language itself the object of logical study" (2009, 91).

The "New Foundation" account is prima facie consistent with the reading I have sketched above.[17] However, there are two reasons that Carnap should not be taken to defend the standard story in his mature work. The first is the influence of Gödel. In the 1920s, Carnap was indeed hopeful that a one-to-one correspondence could be established between an axiomatized theory and the observation language. That would yield a straightforward definition of analyticity. But Kurt Gödel pointed out to Carnap that, as Leitgeb and Carus (2021, section 4) put it, "it is impossible to define analyticity or logical truth in any metalanguage that can be

---

[15] Syntactic rules determine the conditions under which symbols and propositions are syntactically equivalent (*LSS*, 15).

[16] In 1934, Carnap is explicitly concerned with the question of the distinction between what he calls "definite" (LI) or "indefinite" (LII) languages. Definiteness involves the requirement of what Carnap would later call "finitism." LI is limited to predicates that can be ascribed to objects or not "in a finite number of steps according to a fixed method" (*LSS*, 11). In *LSL*, Carnap is careful to distinguish between finitist and non-finitist (definite and indefinite) languages.

[17] For this and other reasons, many have argued that Carnap retained some version of the standard story (Suppe 1974; Stegmüller 1979; Suppes 1992). Sebastian Lutz (2012, sections 2–3) has challenged this, as have Devidi and Solomon (1995), on distinct grounds. Awodey and Carus (2009) go on to track the changes Carnap made after realizing Wittgenstein had enclosed him in a "prison."

faithfully represented in the object language (e.g., by arithmetization); this is now familiar to us as Tarski's theorem on the indefinability of truth."[18] After his conversations with Gödel, Carnap abandoned this early definition of analyticity.[19]

The second reason to doubt the standard story is Carnap's inclusion of scientific laws in the basic sentences of an axiomatized theory. In his mature work, Carnap didn't require reduction of theories to a sole basis of first-order logic or primitive recursive arithmetic. An axiomatized theory can include propositions and even laws of mathematics and of physics among its basic or "primitive" statements, including among the definitions and transformation rules. To be sure, in Carnap's early logicism, basic mathematical propositions can be expressed logically. But even in the case of mathematics, Carnap helps himself to a richer structure than logic or primitive recursive arithmetic.[20]

Key to correcting the standard story is a richer understanding of Carnap's view of axiomatized theories. In *Foundations of Logic and Mathematics*, Carnap distinguishes between the logical *basic calculus* consisting of "the sentential calculus and a smaller or greater part of the functional calculus" and the *specific calculus*, for example, the "primitive sentences, called *axioms*," from which the results of that particular theory are derived (*FLM*, section 16). In both mathematics and physics, the specific calculus can go beyond first-order logic (see Lutz 2012, 89ff.). While the basic calculus must be assumed (often implicitly) and is often the same across theories, the specific calculus changes from theory to theory.

Even in the case of mathematics, Carnap broadens the axiomatic foundations to encompass considerations of generality and objectivity. In the 1920s, along with the mathematician Oskar Becker, Carnap was engaged in an investigation of the generality of mathematics and its relevance for "the problem of physical objectivity," starting with "the way in which an understanding of mathematics as a theory of manifolds or structures led to a particular sort of understanding of the generality and objectivity of mathematics" (Richardson 2003, 175). Carnap concludes that "Mathematical theories are, when fully precisely formed, axiomatic theories that determine the relations among the elements of a structure

---

[18] See also Awodey and Carus (2007, 2009). For critical analysis of Carnap's notion of "analytic-in-a-language" from *Syntax*, see Friedman (1988, 89ff.).
[19] For my view of Carnap on analyticity see Patton (2023).
[20] As Lutz (2012, 83) notes, he uses infinite type theory and modal operators.

and, in this way, also the identity of those elements themselves" (Richardson 2003, 176).[21]

In *Logical Syntax* (and even earlier), Carnap allowed scientific laws to function as basic sentences in axiomatized scientific theories. Wittgenstein had argued in the *Tractatus* (6.113) that basic or "primitive" sentences must be analytic and that it must be transparent whether they are logical or not. In contrast, Carnap argued that scientific laws (P-rules) can function as transformation rules, just as logical or L-rules could (*LSL*, section 51; Uebel 2009, 53). Ultimately, then, they function as basic sentences. This position brought him into conflict with his friend and fellow Vienna Circle member Moritz Schlick (Uebel 2009, section 5). Nonetheless, Carnap continued to argue to the end of his career that scientific laws can function as postulates that govern the translation theoretical sentences and allow us to learn the meaning of theoretical terms (1959/2000, 161 and throughout; 1956, 40–46). This position embeds scientific reasoning in his analysis of theories as formal systems.

12.3 Theoretical Terms and the Observation Language

From the 1930s onward, Carnap accepted that it may not be possible to define theoretical terms explicitly on the basis of observable "primitive" elements (*Basisphänomene*).[22] In subsequent work, Carnap focuses on broader methods for translating theoretical terms and relations into an observational language. Instead of giving a single method, building up theoretical concepts from the autopsychological, he allowed their meaning to be determined in different ways as well.

One of these methods was to specify the meaning of a term implicitly in terms of a formal axiomatization of a scientific theory. Carnap's developing view of axiomatized scientific theories deeply influenced his account of theoretical and observational languages. In *Foundations of Logic and*

---

[21] To be sure, these views can be consistent with considering the basic elements of mathematical theories to be expressible in terms of first-order logic. But I agree with Lutz that Carnap goes well beyond that.

[22] "Since Carnap's criteria of empirical significance are connected to the notion of meaning and the scientific language ... they are directly related to his positions on the semantics of scientific theories. As far as his explicit proclamations are concerned, this leads to a natural grouping of his positions up to 'Testability and Meaning'(*T&M*) on the one hand and of his later positions on the other. For in his earlier works, roughly those published while he was in Europe, Carnap relied on the assumption that it is possible to develop all the terms of science starting out from basic terms or sentences. His later works, published during his time in the United States, explicitly assume that this is not always expedient or even possible" (Lutz 2017, 221–222).

Mathematics (1939), Carnap explains his account of theoretical languages as "calculi":

> we can first construct a calculus and then lay down the interpretation intended in the form of semantical rules, yielding a physical theory as an interpreted system with factual content. The customary formulation of a physical calculus is such that it presupposes a logico-mathematical calculus as its basis, e.g., a calculus of real numbers ... To this basic calculus are added the specific primitive signs and the axioms, i.e., specific primitive sentences, of the physical calculus in question. (*FLM*, section 23, 56–57)

In Carnap's early constitution theory, theoretical language is translated into the autopsychological language of basic elements – that is, into a language that is by definition observational. In his account of axiomatized theories, as in the quotation above, the results of a theory are derived from basic elements that can include "primitive signs," "axioms," and other formal components. In the case of an axiomatized theory, the theory's empirical results are shown to be derivable from primitive or basic sentences. Translation into the observation language comes via correspondence rules that specify the empirical domain of theoretical terms, relations, and propositions. The relationship between the logico-mathematical and the physical calculus resembles that between mathematical and physical geometry or between "theoretical and experimental physics" (*FLM*, 57). The axiomatization of scientific theories allows for the embedding of facts in broader theoretical structures. Particular facts can be correlated with these structures via correspondence rules.

Including mathematical and scientific laws (P-rules) in the "specific calculus" of an axiomatized theory prompted Carnap to realize that his account faced a problem, which will be our main preoccupation here. Many of those laws require for their formulation theoretical terms that are too "rich," in Carnap's terms, to be observable (1959/2000, 159). But theoretical laws are essential to prediction in some domains (*IPoS*, 16)[23] and to the testing of scientific theories (*IPoS*, 230–231). Thus, they have an impact on the empirical basis of a theory.

Despite that, Carnap recognizes from early on that there is no straightforward way to define many theoretical terms by a direct translation

---

[23] In *The Logical Foundations of Probability* Carnap does say that "for predicting a future event on the basis of observations made, it is not necessary to make use of laws; the prediction can be inductively inferred directly from the observations" (*LFP*, 562). But that one instance is far from exhausting the roles for theoretical laws that Carnap defends elsewhere. The fact that one can make *some* predictions without laws does not necessarily mean that *all* scientific predictions can be made without laws.

between the theoretical and the observational language using correspondence rules. Such a rule would have to specify explicitly a class of observations that are correlated with the theoretical term. In the case of theoretical terms like molecules, fields, or continua, it is not straightforward to specify observational extensions explicitly.[24] Nonetheless, Carnap was committed to including physical laws (P-rules) in the stock of basic sentences of a theory.

Carnap was preoccupied throughout his career with the problem of how to give an account of theoretical terms in the observation language. As he puts it in "Methodological Character," the problem is to give "a criterion of significance for the theoretical language, i.e., exact conditions which terms and sentences of the theoretical language must fulfill in order to have a positive function for the explanation and prediction of observable events and thus to be acceptable as empirically meaningful" (1956, 38). Given his inclusion of P-rules in the specific calculus (e.g., the transformation rules) of a theory, he had to give an account of the empirical significance of theoretical terms that function in physical scientific laws. In his earlier work,[25] Carnap focused on the constitution of the meaning of theoretical terms in science from basic elements (Lutz 2017, 221–222). In the *Aufbau*, this took the form of the translation of theoretical sentences into an "autopsychological" language.[26] Translation does not necessarily mean equivalence. One language can be richer than the other. But as long as one can specify what one means by a theoretical term in the observation language, that satisfies Carnap's criterion that theoretical terms must have empirical significance (see Lutz 2014a for this latter concept).

---

[24] As Carnap remarks throughout his lectures on the philosophy of science and his writings on theoretical terms (*IPoS*, 1959/2000, 1958), science involves the formulation of theoretical laws governing "microprocesses" (*IPoS*, 228) and unobservable and inaccessible phenomena generally. In "Theoretical Concepts in Science," Carnap says that at first, he thought it was "impossible" to give "explicit definitions for all the theoretical terms in the observation language," but he has now changed his mind and attempts to do so in that talk (1959/2000, 168). Still, in his physics lectures, Carnap writes, "An empirical law may be justified by making observations of single facts. But to justify a theoretical law, comparable observations cannot be made because the entities referred to in theoretical laws are nonobservables" (*IPoS*, 229).

[25] One might be tempted to locate Carnap's discussion of the problem only after *Logical Syntax*, when he turned more explicitly to semantics. But the problem of how to specify the empirical meaning or significance of abstract concepts is in the *Aufbau* and in "Eigentliche und uneigentliche Begriffe."

[26] "In the *Aufbau*, Carnap (sections 38–39) describes how to translate every scientific sentence into a basic ("autopsychological") sentence. Translatability typically requires some background assumptions, which, for convenience of notation, I will treat as one long conjunction θ. Definition 1 Sentence σ is (non-trivially) translatable into language B by sentence θ if and only if there is a sentence β in B such that θ σ ↔ β (and θ β, θ ¬β)" (Lutz 2017, 222).

Thus, the question of how to specify the meaning of theoretical terms in the observation language came to take a central place in Carnap's account. In an axiomatized theory, facts can be ordered and terms defined by means of the axioms, used as rules to generate a complete system. In "Theoretical Concepts in Science" (1959/2000), "The Methodological Character of Theoretical Concepts" (1956), and "Beobachtungssprache und theoretische Sprache" (1958), Carnap explores a specific problem: the definition of theoretical terms and how they are related to observation. In the abstract for the latter text, Carnap writes,

> Among the non-logical constants of the language of science two kinds are distinguished, the observation terms (e.g., "blue") and the theoretical terms (e.g., "electric field"). *The latter terms are introduced, not by definitions, but by postulates of two kinds*, theoretical postulates, e.g., basic laws of physics, and correspondence postulates which connect the theoretical terms with observation terms. As Hilbert has explained, both mathematics and theoretical physics can in this way be constructed in the form of uninterpreted calculi. (Carnap 1958, 248, emphasis added)[27]

Carnap argues in this paper that theoretical terms are not defined but rather are "introduced" by means of two kinds of postulates. The theoretical postulates are the laws of physics: the P-rules discussed in the section above. Mathematical and physical theories can be axiomatized as "uninterpreted calculi" by specifying the theoretical postulates (physical laws) from which the results of the theory follow. The correspondence or C-rules contain both theoretical and observation terms, specifying relationships between them.

What does Carnap mean when he says that theoretical terms are introduced by postulates, not definitions? Carnap says explicitly that providing a correlation via correspondence rules does not provide a definition of a theoretical term in the observation language, writing: "it is, in

---

[27] There is some controversy in the literature over whether Carnap was a Hilbertian or not about axiomatized theories. Majer (2002, 213–217) argues no, observing that the logical empiricists did not fully grasp the extent of Hilbert's extension of axiomatic methods to physics. Demopoulous (2021, 195) argues yes: "The partial interpretation account sought to extend Hilbert's analysis to physics by providing an account of the empirical content of its theoretical statements that is based on the connections between theoretical terms and observation terms that are expressed by correspondence rules." Both can be right, if Carnap thought Hilbert had not extended his own method to physics and thus sought to fill that gap. Carnap (*T&M*, 459–460) cites Hilbert when laying out his own account of the testability of laws, and he uses Hilbert's epsilon operator in his analysis of theories via Carnap and Ramsey sentences (1959/2000). Carnap explicitly invokes Hilbert's metamathematics as a model for his own analysis of the language of science in *LSS* (§2).

general, not possible to give explicit definitions for theoretical terms on the basis of L_O" (1956, 42).[28] When he says, here and elsewhere, that one cannot define theoretical terms in the observation language, Carnap must mean that T-terms cannot be defined by specifying their extension.[29] One can define theoretical terms intensionally in the observation language by specifying the general type or domain of observations to which the T-term could apply, which does not require explicitly denumerating the set of observations to which the term applies. But Carnap remarks in the same text that "we take L_O as an extensional language" (1956, 42), so that, in general, definitions of terms in the observation language must be extensional. Carnap concludes that theoretical terms cannot be defined explicitly and extensionally on the basis of observational terms (1958, 237 and throughout).

According to this view, which Carnap held in the 1950s, the laws of physics do not necessarily define theoretical terms, even when used as postulates in an axiomatized theory.[30] In many cases, instead, they are used to "introduce" theoretical terms as elements of an "uninterpreted calculus" and to provide introduction and transformation rules that govern how these terms may be used and understood in formalized theories. The theoretical terms must be interpreted via correspondence rules that link theoretical to observational terms (1956, 46). For theoretical laws to have empirical significance means, in part, to use them – via correspondence rules – to make observable predictions.[31] But theoretical languages do not have intrinsic empirical meaning – the meaning of theoretical terms is revealed when we can derive a sentence in the observation language from a sentence or sentences in the theoretical language involving those terms (1956, 49–50).

---

[28] The issue of definition, interpretation, and postulation for Carnap will be discussed further below. My thanks to the editors for help in clarifying this question (they are not responsible for errors that remain).

[29] "Wir nehmen an, dass nur Terme, die nicht auf Grund der B-Terme [*Beobachtungsterme*] explizit definierbar sind, als T-Terme genommen werden" (Carnap 1958, 237). For his definitions of extensional and intensional languages, see (*M&N*, sections 11–12). Tuomela (1973, 95) writes, "Carnap's characterization of theoreticity allows for piecewise, and even explicitly defined concepts, provided that the definitions are not finitely applicable; that is, provided that the definienses include quantifiers so that one cannot ascertain in a finite number of steps whether the theoretical concept is applicable."

[30] Carnap (1959/2000) does attempt to define theoretical terms within a Ramseyfied theory using Hilbert's epsilon calculus. But as he says explicitly in that text, that was the first time Carnap had made such an attempt.

[31] "For an observer to 'accept' the postulates of T [the stock of theoretical laws], means here not simply to take T as an uninterpreted calculus, but to use T together with specified rules of correspondence C for guiding his expectations by deriving predictions about future observable events from observed events with the help of T and C" (Carnap 1956, 45).

Carnap's account of the "partial interpretation" of theoretical terms in axiomatized theories can be read in this context.[32] As Carnap remarks, theoretical terms are not defined by specifying their extension in the O-language, since this cannot be done. Instead, they are introduced by postulates that determine their role in a theory (P-rules) and their relationship to observation terms (C-rules). Then, they are interpreted – and only partially:

> One of the most important characteristics of the T-terms, and therefore of all sentences containing T-terms – at least if they occur not in a vacuous way – is that their interpretation is not a complete one, because we cannot specify in an explicit way by just using observational terms what we mean by the "electromagnetic field." We can say: if there is a distribution of the electromagnetic field in such and such a way, then we will see a light-blue, and if so and so, then we will see or feel or hear this and that. But we cannot give a sufficient and necessary condition entirely in the observational language for there being an electromagnetic field having such and such a distribution. Because, in addition to observational consequences, the content is too rich; it contains much more than we can exhaust as an observational consequence. (Carnap 1959/2000, 159)

Giving truth conditions for sentences with theoretical terms requires incorporating the scientific laws that function as P-rules, translation rules governing sentences that employ theoretical terms. The interpretation of scientific theories in particular requires scientific laws. As Carnap remarks in "Theoretical Concepts in Science,"

> we cannot simply point and say: by the "electromagnetic field' we mean this and that; or an electromagnetic field having an intensity of so and so much or a vector so and so. We cannot simply point and thereby learn it. We learn it by the postulates. These terms are introduced by the postulates; namely the T-postulates,[33] general laws of physics, which connect these terms among each other – which obviously is not sufficient to give any meaning to them – and then the second kind of postulates, the C-postulates, which connect these terms with those of the observation language. (1959/2000, 160–161)

---

[32] Carnap's account of theoretical terms is usually presented in terms of his "partial interpretation" view (Friedman 2011; Demopoulos 2021) and his account of empirical significance (Lutz 2014; "significance" is not Carnap's term). As Friedman notes (2011, 249–250, titles replaced with references), "the partial interpretation view of theoretical terms first emerges" in "his monograph Foundations of Logic and Mathematics (1939)" and "is further articulated in [Carnap 1956], and it is then connected with Carnap's use of the Ramsey sentence in [Carnap 1958] – through the mediation, as Stathis Psillos first documented, of [Hempel 1958]. Carnap continued to work on the Ramsey sentence representation of theories (and the closely related representation using Hilbert's ε-operator) throughout the late 1950s and early 1960s, culminating in [*IPoS*]."

[33] T-postulates here are what Carnap earlier called P-rules.

Carnap maintains throughout his career that scientific laws are basic statements of axiomatized scientific theories, necessary to learning the meaning of theoretical terms and to interpreting them. Laws are necessary but not sufficient: correspondence rules or postulates are also necessary to an interpretation. Beyond the "basic calculus" of logic, interpreting theoretical terms requires a "specific calculus" that includes scientific laws, even before the C-rules are applied (*LFP*, section 16).

Carnap's concepts of extensional definition and of interpretation may appear to be misleadingly similar in the case of theoretical terms. An explicit or extensional definition of a theoretical term is similar to what Carnap refers to as a complete interpretation of that term. If one can give a complete interpretation of a theoretical term in the observational language, for instance by providing a rule giving a one-to-one correspondence between the term and some set, that provides the basis for an extensional definition of the term in L_O. However, Carnap does not think that this is likely to happen in most cases: the extensions of interesting theoretical terms often can't be specified in terms of finite, discrete sets of observables. In other words, it is usually not possible to provide a one-to-one correspondence between a theoretical term and the set of observables to which it refers. That is precisely the problem Carnap is attempting to solve.[34]

12.4 Science, Philosophy, and Freedom

Carnap retained the use of theoretical laws and theoretical terms in his account of axiomatic theories throughout his career. This led to difficulties with defining theoretical terms in the observation language and contributed to the complexities of the partial interpretation view. These difficulties stem from Carnap's use of scientific laws as transformation rules in axiomatized theories. Embedding scientific laws in the axiomatic framework of a theory allows for their introduction via postulation (section 2), which also allows for theoretical terms to be postulated on the basis of scientific laws (section 3).

From an empiricist perspective, this may seem counterproductive. Why not simply put constraints on the language of science, requiring that it show its empirical credentials from the start? A prior commitment to empiricism might seem to motivate a set of requirements for theoretical languages: that they be finitist, that they refer only to observables, that we

---

[34] "Thus the structure can be uniquely specified but the elements of the structure cannot. Not because we are ignorant of their nature; rather, there is no question of their nature" (Carnap 1956, 46).

be able to define concepts in the observation language, and so on. It is striking, then, how explicitly Carnap rejects the requirements of finitism, observability, definability, nominalism, and the like for the theoretical language.[35] Carnap is clear that, while this move may seem at odds with empiricism, it is worth it, because it yields "freedom of expression" (1956, 42) and "much more freedom to the working scientist in the choice of his conceptual tools" (1956, 70).

Freedom in this case involves what might be called conventionalism but a kind that is very sensitive to the purposes of a given language. In "Methodological Character," Carnap remarks:

> For L_T [the theoretical language] we do not claim to have a complete interpretation, but only the indirect and partial interpretation given by the correspondence rules. Therefore, we should feel free to choose the logical structure of this language as it best fits our needs for the purpose for which the language is constructed. (1956, 46)

Two points are key to the final sentence. First, the *logical* structure of the language – what Carnap earlier called the "basic calculus" – can be freely chosen. But in the case of a scientific or mathematical theory, one must also take into account the "specific calculus" that includes the laws of that theory. That theory has been constructed for some purpose, and any adequate axiomatization of the theory must re-derive its essential results. Thus, the "free" choice afforded by partial interpretation is heavily constrained by the fact that theoretical languages are embedded in actual scientific theories. In most cases of interest, then, it is mistaken to attribute to Carnap an appeal to "arbitrary" convention in the constitution of meaning. The use of conventions is limited by the overarching requirements for providing an embedded analysis of scientific theories.

It might seem to be a barrier to my reading that Carnap himself responds to criticisms from Quine and Hempel by defending the distinction between theoretical and observational languages, and relatedly between analytic and synthetic propositions, in texts including "Meaning and Synonymy in Natural Languages" and "Theoretical Concepts in Science." In "Meaning and Synonymy," Carnap argues that Quine requires behavioral criteria for analyticity, otherwise the concept is "arbitrary." He good-naturedly responds to Quine by clarifying "the pragmatical concept of intension in natural languages" and outlining "a

---

[35] Carnap (*LSL*) explores finitist and non-finitist scientific languages. For an explicit rejection of wholesale requirements of finitism, nominalism, etc. in scientific languages see (1956, 41–46).

behavioristic, operational procedure for it" (1955a, 35). But in this paper, Carnap's agenda appears to be driven by Quine's criticisms, and he certainly defends nothing like the rigid analytic-synthetic distinction usually attributed to him. In "Theoretical Concepts," on the other hand, Carnap does propose a principled distinction between theoretical and observational languages and between analyticity and syntheticity. In this 1959 talk, Carnap presents a solution to a "big problem" posed by Hempel, namely, "how to define A-truth in the sense of analyticity or truth based on meaning ... for the theoretical language" (1959/2000, 162). And he does this in a paper called "Theoretical Concepts in *Science*."

In one of the last talks he ever gave, then, Carnap links his defense of analytic truth or A-truth closely to his account of scientific terms and laws. Indeed, throughout his career, Carnap's analysis of scientific theories is central to his account of the relationship between observational and theoretical languages.[36] In his "Intellectual Autobiography," Carnap writes about *Principia Mathematica*: "henceforth, the application of the new logical instrument for the purposes of analyzing scientific concepts and of clarifying philosophical problems has been the essential aim of my philosophical activity" (*IA*, 12).

The purpose of this chapter has been to show that Carnap's analysis of language and his account of axiomatic, linguistic frameworks is deeply embedded in his philosophy of science. His account of the rules used to constitute meaning includes, not only the general calculus of logic but also a specific calculus determined by the foundations of the scientific theory under consideration. Analysis of such theories may indeed identify which propositions are analytic and which synthetic, but that is done within an overall framework that takes particular scientific laws and mathematical structures to be fundamental to the theory itself. In that context, it is highly unlikely for the foundations of the theory to be reducible to analytic statements of logic. Understanding Carnap's account of how theories are embedded in frameworks thus requires more flexibility, and more knowledge of the relevant science, than is appreciated by some of Carnap's critics.

---

[36] Andreas (2021, section 1) notes that Carnap has two criteria for theoretical terms: that they refer to unobservables and that they exhibit semantic dependence on scientific theories.

CHAPTER 13

Carnap on Unity of Science

Bianca Crewe and Alan Richardson

13.1 Introduction

The phrases "unity of science" and "unified science" are firmly associated with logical empiricism. The *International Encyclopedia of Unified Science* was conceived by Otto Neurath in the early 1930s, edited by him, Rudolf Carnap, and Charles Morris, and partially completed over the course of the next few decades. The *Encyclopedia* was preceded by a series of short monographs under the series title *Einheitswissenschaft*, starting with Neurath's *Einheitswissenschaft und Psychologie* in 1933. Similarly, the final year of its initial run (1938), and in response to the fascist takeover in Germany and Austria, the journal *Erkenntnis* repackaged itself with an English title, *The Journal of Unified Science*. Moreover, the International Congress for the Unity of Science ran annually from 1935 to 1941.

Unity of science and unified science are, most particularly, within the logical empiricist domain associated with Otto Neurath, who conceived of the project of the *Encyclopedia* and wrote many essays in the 1930s introducing various audiences to the project of unified science. It is not too much to say that unified science really is, as Rainer Hegselmann (1992) once put it, the "positive paradigm" of logical empiricist philosophy for Neurath. Nonetheless, interpreting what the commitment to unified science is actually a commitment to in Neurath's own work is a nontrivial task. He deploys several characteristic but highly idiosyncratic notions – universal jargon, physicalism – and metaphors – encyclopedism, orchestration, mosaic – that require sorting through. One thing that is clear is that the physicalism of unified science not only binds the sciences together with one another but also, and at least as importantly, binds them to the evidence base of the common person engaged in the business of life.

The greatest service to our understanding of the philosophical significance of "unity of science" for the philosophical project of logical empiricism would, then, be to offer a comprehensive interpretation of Neurath's project.[1] But the mysteries of Neurath will not be unraveled here; our concern is primarily with Neurath's Vienna Circle colleague, Rudolf Carnap, and the significance of notions of unity of science within his work. We do this without presuming either that Carnap and Neurath agreed on the details of the unity of science nor that they disagreed.[2] Rather, we wish to offer a way into reading Carnap's work on unity of science that we also believe can be deployed interestingly in the case of Neurath, but we do not have the space to extend our reading to Neurath here. We cannot leave Neurath entirely to one side, of course, since the greatest flowering of essays concerned with unified science in the work of Carnap occurred precisely when he was deeply engaged with Neurath's views in the early 1930s, both in his work in the protocol sentence dispute and his writing on the universalism of the physicalist language. But Carnap did not first adopt the thesis of the unity of science from Neurath – he already articulated a version of a unity of science thesis in the *Aufbau* and held views one can find resonant with unity of science as far back as his dissertation, as we shall argue.

One might wonder, especially given the relative submergence of the theme of unity of science in Carnap's semantic period and in his work on the logical foundations of probability, whether unity of science was a central feature of Carnap's philosophy. One piece of evidence that it was is given in his "Intellectual Autobiography." The second main section of the "Intellectual Autobiography" is titled "Philosophical Problems." In it, Carnap discusses nine such problems in roughly chronological order by when he began thinking about them. "Physicalism and the Unity of Science" is the third problem he discusses (after pseudoproblems in philosophy and foundations of mathematics). In this section, he writes that "in our discussions [in the early 1930s in the Circle], chiefly under the influence of Neurath, the principal of the unity of science became one of the main tenets of our general philosophical conception" (*IA*, 52), and he dates his detailed engagement with unity of science concerns from the early 1930s through his Encyclopedia essay in 1938.

---

[1] There are such attempts; see, for example, Hegselmann (1992); Reisch (2005); Pombo (2011).

[2] Ouelbani (2005) and Pombo (2011) provide evidence that Carnap's vision of unity of science never aligned with Neurath's, not least in its organizational aspect given that while Carnap was happy to be an editor of the *Encyclopedia* he never really adopted encyclopedism as a vision for unity. See also Uebel (2013b) for unity of science and encyclopedism in Neurath.

13.2 Brief Summary of Carnap's Principal Unity of Science Interventions

Even before he arrived at Vienna, Carnap had committed to a version of a unity of science thesis in the *Aufbau* (written largely before 1926 but published in 1928). The most explicit version of the unity of science in the *Aufbau* is the claim that all the concepts of all the empirical sciences can be constituted within a single constitutional system. He first expresses this claim in section 4 as follows: "If a constitutional system of concepts or objects ... is possible in the manner indicated, then it follows that the objects of science do not come from several unrelated areas, but that *there is only one domain of objects and therefore only one science*" (*Aufbau*, section 4, original emphasis). (He justifies the slide between concepts and objects based on the idea that reading the constitutional system as constituting objects or as constituting concepts makes no material difference.) The universality of the constitutional system does not mean that the objects of science form an undifferentiated mass – different types of objects are constituted at different levels of the system – it merely means that there are no objects studied by any science whose being eludes constitution. By section 16, the thesis of the unity of the object domain of science has acquired enough importance to the project that Carnap dubs it "the fundamental thesis of constitution theory" (*Aufbau*, section 16). In section 16, the unity of the object domain is brought in to undergird Carnap's structuralist account of objectivity: through the processes of the constitutional system, each sentence of science is converted into a purely structural claim. The unity of the object domain means that there is no extra-systemic need to point to a specific domain of objects whose structure is being so described. There is only one domain of objects and thus each claim of science can be rendered purely structural.

It is clear in these early sections of the *Aufbau* that Carnap means these remarks on the unity of the object domain and structuralist objectivity to intervene in various ongoing arguments among philosophers and scientists on unity of science issues. This is most clear in his remarks in section 12 on structure descriptions. Whereas it would be impossible to capture the individuality of objects simply from property descriptions of those objects, Carnap argues that it is in principle possible (and necessary for science) that individual objects can be defined from their positions within structures of relations. He ties this claim in the methodology of constitution specifically to the ongoing arguments about the relations between the natural and cultural sciences in Germany:

Recently (in connection with idea of Dilthey, Windelband, Rickert), a "logic of individuality" has repeatedly been demanded; what is desired here is a method that allows a conceptual comprehension of, and does justice to, the peculiarity of individual entities, and which does not attempt to grasp this peculiarity through inclusion in narrower and narrower classes. Such a method would be of great importance for individual psychology and for all the cultural sciences, especially history ... I merely wish to mention in passing that the concept of structure as it occurs in the theory of relations would form a suitable basis for such a method. (*Aufbau*, section 12)

Here Carnap is siding against those who claimed that the natural and cultural sciences deployed fundamentally different methods of theorizing about fundamentally different sorts of things – a claim usually theorized as being due to the alleged inability of generalizing laws of natural science to comprehend individual objects in their full uniqueness. (He returns to this dispute briefly again in section 64, again siding with those who argue for unity of science.)[3]

There was, as already mentioned, a sort of unity of science thesis embedded already in Carnap's dissertation, *Der Raum*. It had a different form, however, from the *Aufbau*'s unity of the object domain. In the dissertation, what Carnap sought to do was distinguish different concepts of space that would allow scientists and philosophers to see that controversies over the nature of space between mathematicians, physicists, and philosophers were largely pseudo problems due to a conflation of topics. Through this process of disambiguation, scientists and philosophers could see that they were not engaged in intractable disagreements over the same objects of study – so there is no disunity of science in which mathematicians, physicists, and philosophers are understood to be approaching the very same objects but from incommensurable methodological viewpoints. More importantly, the discovery of different senses of space did not preclude there being interesting relations among the disambiguated objects. Carnap's account of conventionalist methodology in physics was presented as a question of how physicists came to coordinate fully determinate metrical mathematical spaces with the less structurally specified physical space – and he found a role for philosophical space in that process.

---

[3] Of course, Carnap's insistence on unity here does not answer all (or any, really) of the questions of the methods by which the object domain of the Geisteswissenschaften is constituted or how the reports and expressions of others augment the realm of the natural sciences. There is a robust debate about the resources Carnap deployed in the *Aufbau* for such matters, whether they violate the formal constraints of constitution, and what their scientific and/or philosophical provenience is. For some recent work on such topics see Dewulf (2017, 2021); Damböck (2022b); Tuboly (2022).

The fully mathematized structure of physics required that there be important relations among the various types of space, as he briefly outlines in section IV of the dissertation. He writes there that:

> From this it can now be seen why the different kinds of [intuitive space] – especially the different subspecies of [three dimensional metrical intuitive space] – and the corresponding types of [formal space] were constructed [aufgebaut]. The point and purpose of these constructions lies in [physical space]. The spatial relations of experience are brought into a consistent system [of physical space]; for this the more general form [of intuitive space] is constructed first, and for this, in turn, the still more general conceptual form [of formal space]. (*Raum*, 117)

This is a form of quasi-Kantian unity of science thesis: The goal is to explain the objective knowledge of the experiential world in physics and the philosophical role for intuitive and formal space is exhausted by the conceptual roles they play in rendering such empirical objectivity possible.

Within the context of the Vienna Circle in the early 1930s, the idioms within which Carnap discussed unity of science changed. Neurath had objected to the autopsychological starting point of the constitutional system of the *Aufbau* and Carnap's "methodological solipsism." Neurath found these views to be residues of philosophical idealism and argued that the protocol sentences that served as the ultimate evidence for scientific theories could, indeed had to be, formulated in a physicalist language that referred to objects and to persons. This is one form of the universalism of physicalist language for Neurath – no epistemological problem is solved by positing a language of pure experience that serves as the evidence base for science. Ultimately, on this matter Carnap took a conventionalist line: there is no fact of the matter about the sort of sentence used as the evidence base for science, but any logic of science must make a choice in the matter. On the choice itself, while not endorsing the specifics of Neurath's rather baroque protocol sentences, Carnap did agree that a choice within the physicalist language is the most apposite. This is one sense in which the physicalist language is "universal" for Carnap – and thus it is a sense in which there is unity of the language of science – no extrasystematic language of pure experience is requisite for the rational reconstruction of science.

The other main part of Carnap's work on unity of science in the 1930s is largely a matter not of theses but of research projects. Consider two sciences that have somewhat disjoint vocabularies, say, biology and physics. One can ask if the terms in the language of biology are definable in the language of physics. If so, one can ask whether a law stated in the language of biology is, as translated into the language of physics, derivable from physical laws. Suppose, as Carnap does by the mid-1930s, one gives up the idea that the terms of any science are in general definable in the protocol language but that nonetheless at least certain of the terms in the language of that science can be introduced via conditionals (Carnapian reduction pairs). Then there are any number of questions one can ask about the definability of the terms in one science in the terms of another. The entire articulated language structure of the various sciences can be investigated in this way. At various points, Carnap adopts certain theses as working hypotheses – for a while, for example, that the concepts of any proper science are definable in the observation language. But he had no compunction based on technical difficulties regarding giving up these theses or simply presenting the field as a field for technical projects in the logic of science.

After surveying various technical projects for defining concepts from one science in terms of another or of otherwise being able to derive sentences from one science from those of another, Carnap, in his *Encyclopedia* essay of 1938, ends with two specific claims. First, there was no unity of laws in the sciences current in 1938 and no plausible procedure for deriving the laws of the special sciences from the laws of physics had been discovered. However, there was, he claimed, a unity of language in science. This fact was enormously important, he claimed, specifically for the practical applications of theoretical knowledge – a claim he ends his essay on, while evoking without specifying the German debates about *Natur-* and *Geisteswissenschaft*:

> For very many decisions, both in individual and in social life, we need ... a prediction based upon a combined knowledge of concrete facts and general laws belonging to different branches of science. If now the terms of different branches had no logical connection between one another, such as is supplied by the homogeneous reduction basis, but were of fundamentally different character, as some philosophers believe, then it would not be possible to connect singular statements and laws of different fields in such a way as to derive predictions from them. Therefore, the unity of the language of science is the basis for the practical application of theoretical knowledge. (Carnap 1938, 62)

Now, many of Carnap's claims about the logical unity of the language of science have been criticized – some, as we have noted, by Carnap himself. He discarded definitional reduction of all the concepts of science to the terms of the observation language himself by 1936 at the latest, if for very different reasons from those raised against the *Aufbau* program by Quine. Both technical semantic objections as well as methodological objections to various other forms of reductionist projects among the special sciences have been raised. It is not our intention to rehearse or rebut those objections. Our interest lies elsewhere: across several decades of his career and many changes in the technical tools he brought forward to investigate the unity of science, Carnap was in some philosophically important sense committed to unity of science. What was this a commitment to and what motivated this commitment?

Some clues are relatively straightforward. Carnap was quite clear that he separated questions of the unity of science from metaphysical questions: "The question of the unity of science is meant here as a problem of the logic of science, not of ontology" (Carnap 1938, 49). That the question for Carnap is importantly not a metaphysical question seems a first principle of Carnap interpretation. Nonetheless, as we have seen, even in 1938, if implicitly and obliquely, Carnap took his unity of science project to intervene in a debate in German philosophy over whether cultural sciences differed in kind from natural science. In his retrospective remarks in 1963, Carnap brought up an even older philosophical dispute in German philosophy in discussing the Circle's interest in unity of science and physicalism – the debate between idealists and materialists from the early nineteenth century onward:

> Neurath admitted that the philosophical arguments of materialists, e.g., Ludwig Büchner and Ernst Haeckel, were often inadequate as measured by our logical standards. On the other hand, we [he explicitly mentions Schlick in this context-BC/AR] agreed with him that their general attitude and way of thinking was closer to sound scientific method than the thinking of Fichte, Schelling, and Hegel. (*IA*, 51)

We have already seen one other clue about the significance of unity of science for Carnap above, one that is less obvious: for Carnap the unity of science was of fundamental importance for practical decision-making since information from various sciences should flow into the decision-making process.

13.3 Carnap's Philosophical Commitment to Unity of Science

Having reviewed Carnap's various invocations of unity of science, we are in a better position to ask after its general philosophical significance. Rather than evaluating the above-mentioned proposals directly, we will use a technique of historical epistemology developed by Lorraine Daston and Peter Galison in their book *Objectivity* (2007).[4] Their account of the history of objectivity as an epistemic virtue situates it in relation to changing versions of the threat of dangerous forms of subjectivity. From this, we get a vision of objectivity as simultaneously "ethos and epistemology," a way of being and a way of knowing. An epistemological concern for objectivity, for Daston and Galison, induces a way of being that protects knowledge claims from the incursion of dangerous forms of subjectivity.

We look to apply the method of Daston and Galison to invocations of "unity." This approach enjoins us to look at unity discourse as aimed at the securing of proper knowledge by avoiding epistemologically and ethically dangerous forms of disunity. Reading the logical empiricist concern with unity of science this way speaks to several demands that have emerged in the secondary literature in recent years. On the one hand, in the matter of actors' categories, there is a contextualist project to think about how logical empiricism was engaged with its historical context and how specific work produced by logical empiricist philosophers is reflective of and responsive to that context. Then there is a methodological issue involving analysts' categories, arising especially in recent debates about the political and social dimensions of logical empiricism as a philosophical movement.[5] Such debates have prompted reflection about what the criteria should be for determining whether logical empiricism was "political."[6] Moreover, the question of where one should go to find the political commitments of a philosophical movement (for example, as features of external rather than internal history) has broader interpretive implications.

Using the above technique of historical epistemology to consider the nature of Carnap's philosophical commitment to the unity of science unites these demands. His invocations of unity showcase a general tendency in logical empiricism to link technical innovations to concrete social and political aims arising from the context of the early movement. This is especially true if we consider that unity concepts do not just serve Carnap when he is considering technical questions of reduction and the like; they serve as his motivating vocabulary. This is visible especially in Carnap's summary account of his philosophy in his "Intellectual Autobiography."

---

[4] For a more straightforward comparative evaluation of various Carnapian unity proposals from the *Aufbau* forward, see Klev (2016).
[5] This literature is extensive and includes Wartofsky (1982); Howard (2003); Reisch (2005); Uebel (2005), 2010, 2012a, 2020); S. Richardson (2009a, 2009b); Stump (2009); Romizi (2012); Richardson (2017); Damböck (2022a).
[6] See, for example, Reisch (2009); S. Richardson (2009a, 2009b); Uebel (2010, 2020).

Indeed, immediately after the comments on Haeckel and Hegel above, Carnap returns to a larger practical context, urged upon him by Neurath:

> The choice of a language form is a practical decision, [Neurath] argued ... He emphasized that all practical decisions are interconnected and should therefore be made from the point of view of a general goal. The decisive criterion would be how well a certain language form ... could be expected to serve the community which intended to use it. His emphasis on the interdependence of all decisions, including those in theoretical fields, and his warning against isolating the deliberation of any practical question, even that of the choice of a language form, made a strong impression upon my own thinking. (Carnap 1938, 51)

In this passage, we see a variety of unity concepts – interconnection, general goal, community, interdependence, non-isolation. It is these motivating unity concepts that we are most interested in. To help unpack them, we will have occasion to reflect on two other aspects of Carnap's summary account of his philosophy in his "Intellectual Autobiography"; his account of language planning and his understanding of scientific humanism, both of which combine scientific understanding with a concern for the betterment of the human estate.

Our interpretative approach demands that we look at unity discourse in Carnap as involving both an ethico-political and an epistemic program. But this simultaneously ethico-political and epistemic program surrounding the unity of science is not unique to Carnap. Indeed, the history of unity concerns in German philosophy and science stretch back to at least the middle of the nineteenth century and consistently reflect what Galison calls a "cultural politics" (Galison 2016, 20). For instance, in their efforts to establish physiology, medicine, and pathology as modern academic disciplines and sources of positive knowledge, figures like Emil Du Bois-Raymond, Rudolf Virchow, and Hermann Helmholtz articulated the call for the unified reduction of these fields to laws of classical mechanics in language reflecting a simultaneous demand for a unified German nation and constitution. Unity of laws was, in other words, both a liberal-nationalist political goal and a scientific-theoretical one (Anderton 1993; Galison 2016).

For Carnap, on the other hand, and for logical empiricism in the interwar period more generally, the unity of science reflects an explicitly internationalist agenda, as noted by Galison himself (2016). His essay and the collection it belongs to reflect growing scholarly attention to the question of why, in contrast with the contemporary emphasis on scientific disunity, scientists and philosophers held strongly to unity of science at this historical juncture.[7] We approach answering this question by examining various extant forms of politically and epistemically pernicious *disunity* in the immediate context, for which unified science was advanced as an antidote.

The First World War precipitated a tendency to subordinate science, philosophy, and politics to nationalist agendas. Prewar forms of scientific cooperation, characterized by Paul Forman (1973) as internationally competitive within a supranational framework after an analogy to the Olympic games, came to a halt virtually entirely. Existing scientific societies expelled members of enemy nations, and Germany and Austria were largely excluded from postwar reorganization of existing scientific institutions (Kevles 1971; Schroeder-Gudehus 1973). Even in left politics the situation was similar: in Germany, commitment to international solidarity among workers and shared opposition to a war fought over competing imperialist interests was excluded completely from parliamentary politics, and major socialist parties throughout Europe were largely supportive of the war efforts of their respective nations (Imlay 2016).

Perhaps more fundamentally, the cultural value placed in science and technology had been called into question in the minds of many people in the destruction wrought by modern warfare and industrialization. The credibility of Enlightenment accounts of the progress of science as an inherently moral progress had been damaged, if not destroyed (Richardson 2017). In much German philosophy and political theory, these were replaced by popular narratives of cultural pessimism and reactionary pastoralism, fond reminiscences of Greco-Roman classicism, and deep suspicions of social and political changes wrought by science, industrialization, and the tentative forays into liberal democratic social organization in the Weimar era.

These conditions, and the upheaval they wrought on philosophy as a discipline, can be distilled into demands that seem difficult to reconcile: on the one hand, there was a sense among those who resisted narratives of decline or anti-rationalism that philosophy should address and resolve a theoretical disunity resulting from the proliferation of positive knowledge in the nineteenth century and the continued growth and success of scientific work. This is visible across a range of work as varied as

---

[7] His essay appears in an edited volume devoted to investigating various manifestations of unity of science in connection with political aims between the First World War and the Cold War: see Kamminga and Somsen (2016).

Wilhelm Wundt's *System of Philosophy* (1919), in the developing field of sociology of knowledge, and, as we will see, Ernst Cassirer's later career philosophy of culture. In some instances, this intellectual and political upheaval was translated into a call for philosophy itself to become scientific in its methods and working conditions, though the details of what precisely this would entail varied significantly. On the other hand, there was a competing desire for a philosophy that would speak to the *emotional needs*[8] referenced in the preface of the *Aufbau* and make sense of the lived experienced of people in a society devasted by war and economic collapse, for whom science and its results were at best abstract and remote[9] and at worst a factor in their suffering.

The philosophical significance of the unity of science for Carnap lies somewhere within this tension: as Gottfried Gabriel notes, Carnap's invocation of *emotional needs* in the preface of the *Aufbau* is part of a larger effort to use the language of *Lebensphilosophie* to suggest that scientific philosophy is better equipped to fulfill the demands that *Lebensphilosophie* suggests are endemic to philosophy than *Lebensphilosophie* itself is (Gabriel 2004). Thus, for Carnap, science is a key to resolving both theoretical disunity and the disunity wrought by a view of philosophy as (inevitably) metaphysical, irrational, or preoccupied with a distinctive subject matter, be it *being, value,* or *Germanness.*

Indeed, the idea that philosophy would inevitably feature some irreducible and personal emotional-metaphysical expressions in the manner identified by *Lebensphilosophie* was one version of a problematic disunity Carnap's early philosophy sought to address. In this context, emphasis on the scientific attitude by the Vienna Circle implied a commitment to a common basis for the (re)construction of society on scientific and technical grounds. It was the language though which Carnap and his colleagues indicated a common cause with projects in art, architecture, planning, and education, as visible in documents like *The Scientific World-Conception*

---

[8] *Bedürfnisse des Gemüts.* "We, too, have 'emotional needs' in philosophy, but they are filled by clarity of concepts, precision of methods, responsible theses, achievement through cooperation in which each individual plays his part" (*Aufbau*, xvii). Both responsibility and cooperation are forms of social unity.

[9] The remoteness of science was especially acute given developments in physics such as relativity or quantum theory, both of which were profoundly nonintuitive in contrast to a Newtonian physics of medium-sized bodies. Hans Reichenbach's work in popular science education can likewise be understood as an attempt to reconcile the state of physics with the above demands for philosophy grounded on experience (Reichenbach 1930/1978). For an example of such efforts outside the scope of logical empiricism, see Wolfgang Pauli's correspondence and collaboration with Carl Jung.

(1929) and Carnap's preface to the *Aufbau* (1928).[10] Here we see unity as scientific attitude working as a kind of presupposition in Carnap's philosophy: in defiance of emphases on irreducible philosophical-conceptual differences between people (drawn often along national-historic-racial lines), Carnap gives us a view of science as a cultural good belonging equally to all.

One example of this can be found when Carnap explains his interest in language planning in his "Intellectual Autobiography."[11] Here, we see a commitment to science as uniquely capable of facilitating connections between people and branches of knowledge and of addressing and responding to troubling disunity. In this instance, the relevant and motivating threat of disunity is a version of linguistic relativism of the kind espoused by Benjamin Lee Whorf of the Sapir-Whorf hypothesis: language, on this view, rests on the unique conceptual backdrop of a given culture and is therefore always culturally specific. According to this argument, an artificial language like Esperanto is not expressive of any culture and will therefore not be equipped to displace natural languages or overcome divisions reinforced by their use.

Carnap responds by granting the first premise but goes on to argue that constructed international language is not without a specific cultural backdrop – this he says is "the Western culture" writ large, and particularly "its modern science and technology." Though originally Western cultural products, they have become, "together with their scientific terminology, the common property of nations all over the world" (*IA*, 70). Here unity is invoked as a presupposition: there is a unified culture of science that makes it a particularly apt basis for communication across the boundaries of nation or natural language. This cultural or attitudinal unity of science guides language planning despite the diversity of methods and disciplines in various scientific subfields.

Appeals to a shared scientific culture are also made in texts where Carnap and his colleagues introduce their methods and motivations and diagnose the problems of competing philosophical paradigms and the conditions of their execution. From these documents, we can see that Carnap's projects aimed at harmonizing investigation (for example, through a universal constructed language for the sciences or for everyday use) imply harmonizing investigators, with collaborative scientific work as a model for philosophy. In such instances, the connotations of unity have to do with reforms to philosophical practice, particularly the call to move

---

[10] On the relationship between logical empiricism and architecture, see Galison (1990).
[11] See further Başak Aray's chapter in this volume (Chapter 11).

away from philosophy as an individual and isolated venture to a communal task embedded in and responsive to the needs of a broader community.

The motivating disunity at stake here is therefore a competing or preceding way of doing philosophy, frequently invoked by the epithet *systematic* and associated most paradigmatically with Hegel. On this model, philosophy is the solitary work of an individual (genius) bent on constructing a system to encompass the totality of thought, which detractors considered to be invariably reflective of personal idiosyncrasies. A complaint emerging frequently in the public-facing texts introducing the attitudes and methods of logical empiricism and scientific philosophy is that this individualist, systematic approach resulted in the stagnation of philosophy relative to the empirical sciences, as well as its comparative lack of practical utility. Carnap presents this problem and its remedy with specific reference to unified science in the preface of the *Aufbau:* working in accordance with the scientific attitude,

> the individual no longer undertakes to erect in one bold stroke an entire system of philosophy. Rather, each works at his special place within the one unified science. For the physicist and the historian this orientation is commonplace, but in philosophy we witness the spectacle (which must be depressing to a person of scientific orientation) that one after another and side by side a multiplicity of incompatible philosophical systems is erected. If we allot to the individual in philosophical work as in the special sciences only a partial task, then we can look with more confidence into the future: in slow careful construction insight after insight will be won. Each collaborator contributes only what he can endorse and justify before the whole body of his co-workers. Thus stone will be carefully added to stone and a safe building will be erected at which each following generation can continue to work. (*Aufbau*, xvi–xvii)

The unity of science is therefore expressive of an ideal of shared labor for the reformation and modernization of philosophy. The unified, communal element of scientific research was a touchstone for addressing disunity conceived of as the various atomizing tendencies in philosophy and the broader culture in this period. But despite the practical successes resulting from embedding the sciences in industrial and institutional contexts in the nineteenth and early twentieth century, the relationship between their conventions, methods, theoretical terms, and their objects of study persisted as an open question. Thus, for Carnap, as for other philosophical approaches in this period, there is also a disunity concern that hinges on the lack of a clear relationship between distinct domains of knowledge.

On the face of it, the connection between the unity of scientific culture and the unity of science as a theoretical edifice is fairly weak, both conceptually and in Carnap's work. After all, one might well think that physicists and sociologists share a scientific culture and/or attitude without thinking that sociological laws are derivable from the laws of physics or even expressible in the language of physics. And, as we have seen, Carnap seems to leave such aspects of reduction as open questions. So, what help to unity of science is provided by stressing a community of scientists bound by a characteristic set of attitudes and justificatory processes?

The approach to the unity of science through the community of scientists does illuminate some characteristic aspects of Carnap's philosophy. For example, from the dissertation forward he seems to believe that if there is a dispute that appears to be stagnant or intractable then that is evidence that either (a) one or more participants is *not* exhibiting the proper attitude of science or (b) there is confusion among one or more participant about the nature of the discussion, that is, a confusion of the meaning of the terms under dispute. The latter is the argumentative procedure of the dissertation: confused, intractable arguments about space among mathematicians, philosophers, and physicists is itself evidence that these arguments are scientifically ill-formed. Carnap's intervention is to distinguish various meanings of "space" in order to show that the dispute is merely apparent. But this disaggregation of meanings does not mean that there are no connections among the various meanings of "space." To the contrary, the real contribution of the dissertation is precisely to find a way in which the mathematical, physical, and philosophical notions of space jointly operate in a proper understanding of the various forms of knowledge of space. So, here is a first interesting Carnapian principle of process around unity of science – distinguishing meanings can be useful in showing how concepts fit together and lead to an understanding of how a region of knowledge is indeed unified.

More generally, Carnap's anti-metaphysical stance seeks to eliminate only some of the problems generally thought metaphysical while clarifying and rendering tractable other such problems. We have seen that he grants genuine scientific interest in and content to questions of the reduction of laws and the translatability of languages for various branches of science. Unity of science questions maintain meaning but they are relocated from metaphysics to the logic of science. But the logic of science is the branch of philosophy that Carnap is seeking both to promote and render technically precise. It is in the project of the logic of science that the ethos of the scientific community finally finds full and adequate expression within philosophy. This allows us, for example, to illuminate the dual functions of the Principle of Tolerance. On the one hand, the Principle is a principle of practical freedom and permission – within certain limits a philosopher is free to propose any language they wish; but on the other hand, it is a principle that signals adoption of the characteristic attitudes of the scientific community – the constraints on philosophy are not moral or metaphysical; they are technical.

This aligns importantly with the end of Carnap's "Empiricism, Semantic, and Ontology," where on scientific and historical grounds he wishes to avoid Quinean philosophical dogmatism:

> To decree dogmatic prohibitions of certain linguistic forms instead of testing them by their success or failure in practical use, is worse than futile; it is positively harmful because it may obstruct scientific progress. The history of science shows examples of such prohibitions based on prejudices deriving from religious, mythological, metaphysical, or other irrational sources, which slowed up the developments for shorter or longer periods of time. Let us learn from the lessons of history. Let us grant to those who work in any special field of investigation the freedom to use any form of expression which seems useful to them; the work in the field will sooner or later lead to the elimination of those forms which have no useful function. *Let us be cautious in making assertions and critical in examining them, but tolerant in permitting linguistic forms.* (Carnap 1950, 40; original emphasis)

Here we see many aspects of the scientific attitude that Carnap was endorsing and expressing from the beginning of his career and made more precise with the metalogical turn: practical freedom in the adoption of linguistic forms, caution in asserting claims about the world, avoidance of non- and anti-scientific constraints on scientific theorizing, a functional and practical understanding of how proposed linguistic forms show their value in scientific contexts.

We can return now to the "Intellectual Autobiography," where Carnap invokes the unity of science in relation to the practical constraints supplied by the relevant community with respect to the choice of language form. His adoption of the physicalist language and his participation in the encyclopedia project further illustrate how a unified scientific attitude is brought to bear on universal and unified scientific language. Though we have noted that Carnap maintains a conventionalist line throughout his exchange with Neurath on protocol sentences, he does ultimately concede that it is important to be sensitive to the emotional and attitudinal connotations of a given language form. Thus, advantages of the physicalist language have much to do with attitudinal unity and the technical constraints on philosophy supplied by the unified and unifying scientific attitude rather than partisanship in the metaphysical debate between materialists and idealists.

This is especially visible in Carnap's "On Protocol Sentences" (1932/1987). Here, he writes that though both phenomenalism and physicalism can be applied effectively to the negative task of a logic of science – the elimination of absolutism and other "impurities" (Carnap, 1932/1987, 470) and more general the shift from philosophy as theory of knowledge to a logic of science – the physicalist language is more apt for the positive task. It is with reference to this that Carnap ends his article and indicates his future collaboration with Neurath: "now that we are working in a more positive and unified way, the philosophy of science will be developed even further" (Carnap, 1932/1987, 470). Thus, for Carnap, physicalism recommends itself on two counts: firstly, it does away with the autopsychological starting point of the constitution system of the *Aufbau* and with rules of translation (and therefore with the possibility of metaphysical interpretation and the connotation with idealism), and secondly, it promotes a more unified program of research in the philosophy of science.

As we have seen, this concern was at stake in methodological debates surrounding the relationship between the natural and cultural sciences in German philosophy in the nineteenth century and likewise motivated Cassirer's development of a philosophy of culture from his publication of first volume of *The Philosophy of Symbolic Forms* in 1923 until the end of his life in 1945.[12] The way the problem of disunity is construed and addressed in his work by contrast with Carnap's brings out the different meta-philosophical, stylistic, and cultural preoccupations of these respective paradigms. Cassirer retains systematicity as a philosophical ideal, his efforts toward a unity of knowledge spanning the symbolic forms of both the natural and cultural sciences.[13] Though they conceive of the dangers of disunity similarly,[14] the practice of science itself supplies an epistemic ideal for Carnap and his colleagues, whereas for Cassirer the diversity and mutual antagonism among various scientific accounts of humanity is part of the motivation for finding a higher unity in philosophy itself.

Carnap's commitment to the unity of the practice of science is evident in his discussion of the practical motivations for developing a unified scientific language: without such a language, there would be no way to amalgamate information to understand, predict, and control events, and no basis from which to make rational decisions. His delineation of the ways in which unity is and is not in question in his 1934 *The Unity of Science* speaks

---

[12] Matherne (2021) stresses the unity of culture as the primary *explanandum* of Cassirer's mature philosophy.
[13] Indeed, Cassirer writes in his preface to the third volume of the *Philosophy of Symbolic Forms* that his model is a Hegelian phenomenology of knowledge (Cassirer, 1929/1957, xiv).
[14] Cassirer's most explicit accounts of the political dimensions of this disunity threat are articulated in his work written in response to the Second World War; especially *The Myth of the State* (1946) and to a lesser degree *An Essay on Man* (1944).

to this: he is careful to note that the thesis of a universal language for science has nothing to say against the *practical* separation of scientific disciplines for the sake of division of labor, for as we have seen this practical separation is part of a unified scientific attitude that recommends the working practices of scientists as a model for philosophy.[15] Rather, it is in the potential of the physicalist language to unite distinct scientific fields that ensures the "thorough applicability of science" (Carnap 1934/2013, 101) to other domains of life. Ultimately, then, what is at stake in the development of a unified language for the sciences is the practical application of theoretical knowledge in a manner accessible to all. This is advanced in relation to the more general demand for experiential relevance on a universal basis – pressing given the historical and cultural context of the movement, and in some sense its retrospective hallmark, from Neurath's picture language to the *International Encyclopedia of Unified Science* itself.

This diagnosis of the practical problems of disunity in the sciences shows us the social function of philosophy as Carnap and his colleagues conceived it. The proposed solution – a unified scientific language – is framed not as an attempt to fulfill the historical task of philosophy but rather as a way of resolving certain debates or problems that had been of interest for the traditional discipline. This gesture of emphasizing the historical discontinuity of his research is carried through from Carnap's earliest publications to his mature works. Consistently, the break with past philosophical paradigms is made with reference to preceding understandings of the unity or disunity of knowledge, as we have seen in the case of section 12 of the *Aufbau* and in his encyclopedia essay of 1938. That Carnap and his co-conspirators framed the distinctiveness of their movement in relation to problems of unity and disunity reveals the significance of these concepts in relation to a broader cultural politics.[16]

---

[15] Of course, "The Unity of Science" was a title chosen for the translation of a 1932 essay whose original title (which can be rendered in English as "The Physical Language as Universal Language of Science") does not make the connection to "unity of science" nearly as directly.

[16] If the relevant and motivating notion of disunity shifted for Carnap in his move from Europe to America, this is not immediately apparent from his writing in connection with the *International Encyclopedia of Unified Science*. His 1938 "Logical Foundations of the Unity of Science" advances a unified scientific language in relation to decidedly old-world debates (as previously noted, the nineteenth-century problem of disunity between the various sciences) and figures (he refers to Freud and Adler as examples of psychology in relation to social science). That there is no significant shift here may reflect the fact that Carnap is consistently not the institutional liaison for the unity of science movement in either Europe or America. Though the fate of unified science in the American context has been the subject of some scholarly interest (see, for example, Galison 1998; Reisch 2005; Hollinger 2011), there is room for further research about how (and whether) Carnap himself conceived of his later-career work in relation to his new context.

For Carnap, then, the unity of science has much to do with efforts to update or modernize philosophy for the twentieth century and the break with the methods and paradigms of rationality of the previous one. This view of philosophy as a communal task organized around a shared attitude (rather than divisive metaphysical or doctrinal commitments) sheds light on Carnap's repeated emphasis on attitudinal influences in his "Intellectual Autobiography" and indeed his relationship to logical empiricism as a philosophical movement more generally: the unity implied by a shared scientific attitude does not stem from common adherence to doctrine. Rather, commonalities are expressed in terms of shared priorities and practical goals, against the backdrop of disunity as competing understandings of science, philosophy, and their political and epistemic implications.

CHAPTER 14

Carnap on Determinism and Free Will
Richard Creath

14.1 Introduction

The question of whether legal and moral responsibility and the freedom of the will that is said to be required for this is in any sense compatible with deterministic laws of nature has been one of the most widely discussed issues in metaphysics and ethics for thousands of years. It was certainly widely debated by the ancient Greeks (White 1985), probably ever since the very idea of exceptionless laws of nature was developed by the pre-Socratic philosophers (Vlastos 1975). So, it comes as a bit of a surprise that Rudolf Carnap, who famously rejected metaphysics (1932) and at one time treated ethics as a branch thereof (1935), included a whole chapter on determinism and free will in his philosophy of science text, *The Philosophical Foundations of Physics: Introduction to Philosophy of Science* (*IPoS*). In this chapter, I will examine this chapter and other relevant sections of Carnap's book both to understand his position on the issue and to attempt to reconcile the famously anti-metaphysical Carnap with his discussion of one of the prominent and enduring issues in the field of metaphysics.

Given that the arguments on these matters have continued unabated for thousands of years, it is hardly surprising that their central terms have been used in wildly different ways. Sometimes actions and the volitions that produce them are counted as free only when they are not subject to any causal influences whatsoever. Sometimes they are counted as free when they are not completely determined by outside events. Sometimes the will is counted as free when it can produce the act it intends or when the act thus produced has the outcome desired. Alternatively, an agent is sometimes said to be free or to act of his or her own free will when some specific list of "excusing conditions" (Hart 1968, 28ff.) is not in play. So, one of the first things to do (Section 14.2) is to clarify the notion of determinism itself. While it is Carnap's treatment of free will and determinism that will be our primary focus, Carnap's chapter is largely a response to a posthumous essay by Hans Reichenbach, "The Freedom of the Will" (1959), the broad outlines of which I will discuss in Section 14.3. Carnap's chapter on the topic is chapter 22, but the earlier portions of the book are an essential preliminary. They clarify what Carnap means by "laws of nature," "necessity," and "causality." And we will discuss Carnap's account of these matters in Section 14.4 and chapter 22 itself in Section 14.5. Finally, in Section 14.6, we return to the question of whether Carnap's account of free will in particular is a violation of his anti-metaphysical stance.

14.2 Preliminary Clarification: Determinism and Indeterminism

In 1814, Pierre-Simon de Laplace published *A Philosophical Essay on Probabilities* in which he vividly articulated the idea of determinism:

> We ought then to regard the present state of the universe as the effect of its anterior state and the cause of the one which is to follow. Given for one instant an intelligence which could comprehend all the forces by which nature is animated and the respective situation of the beings who compose it – an intelligence sufficiently vast to submit these data to analysis – it would embrace in the same formula the movements of the greatest bodies of the universe and those of the tiniest atom; for it, nothing would be uncertain and the future, as the past would be present to its eyes. (Laplace 1814/1951, 4)

Laplace was working from an understanding of Newton's laws according to which those laws are universal (nonstatistical), that is, that events can be explained by appeal only to such laws of nature (and, of course, suitable initial conditions). It makes no difference whether there is in fact or even could be such a vast intelligence. And it makes no difference for our purposes whether Newton's laws are correct. What is essential to determinism is that there is some set of universal laws of nature such that these laws together with any complete description of the universe at one moment, for example, the positions, masses, and velocities (speed and direction) of all elementary particles, logically implies every other event in the universe, past, present, and future. These laws and initial conditions need not be known, much less with certainty. But this is what is required for a system – universe – to be deterministic. Otherwise, it is indeterministic. Sometimes this idea of a logical implication is expressed by saying that all the events in the universe are predictable on the basis of these laws and initial conditions. This is a harmless rephrasing so long as "prediction" is understood to include the prediction of past events and does not suggest that such predictions could actually be carried out by even the vastest of intellects or by all of the computing power that the universe could contain.

Carnap would hasten to add that most scientists believe that our universe is not deterministic. In quantum mechanics there are statistical laws, and if these are among the most basic laws of nature, as is now widely believed to be the case, then the logical implication mentioned above would fail, and our universe would be indeterministic. Of course, whether quantum theory is correct is an empirical matter about which absolute certainty is impossible. Einstein never conceded that any basic laws are statistical. But Carnap is not asking whether our universe is deterministic. He and Reichenbach are asking whether a deterministic universe would have certain implications for human choice, free will, and such legal and moral consequences as those implications may have. And both take Newtonian laws and classical physics more generally to describe a deterministic system and quantum theory to describe an indeterministic one.

If our world is deterministic, then all our characters, choices, and actions are implied by a complete description of the events of a moment long before we are born together with a complete list of the laws of nature. For some, this suggests a version of fatalism, the idea that what we do or choose makes no difference. If fatalism is correct, we would get the same outcome, our fate, regardless of what we do. But determinism does not imply fatalism. There is no reason to think that in a deterministic system our choices do not affect what we do or that what we do does not affect what happens thereafter.

There are many concepts other than (in)determinism that need to be clarified in order to assess Carnap's discussion. And both Reichenbach and Carnap do so. But because they do this in different ways it will be convenient to postpone our clarifications and turn directly to Reichenbach's claims to which Carnap is responding.

14.3 Reichenbach's Claims on Free Will

The two most important conclusions that Reichenbach (1959) reaches are (1) that in a deterministic system there is no possibility of either free actions or free will, but (2) the indeterminacies of a world like that described in quantum mechanics makes both free action and free will possible. As he says in his final paragraph:

> The thesis that causality does not exclude free will has often been maintained, but it could not be made consistent so long as causality was identified with determinism. The present investigation shows that

determinism excludes complete freedom of will and action while probabilistic causality does not. And it shows, in addition, that the abandonment of causality as a consequence of quantum physics is also compatible with freedom provided that sufficiently high probabilities are left to permit us to regard volitions as causally relevant to our actions. (Reichenbach 1959, 192)

Reichenbach's definitions and the arguments he uses to reach these conclusions are rather complicated, and he is trying to showcase his probabilistic conception of causality and his new accounts of laws, conditionals-contrary-to-fact (counterfactuals), and necessity. These latter accounts were given in (Reichenbach 1954) and reprinted with an extensive discussion by Wesley Salmon in (Reichenbach 1954/1976). His conception of causality, in particular, is certainly well worth studying, but that is not possible here.

Reichenbach's account of free will received very little critical discussion. Clark Glymour and Frederick Eberhardt's treatment of it, in its entirety, is as follows:

> Reichenbach's discussion of free action and free will is an attempt to reconcile our judgments that some actions are done freely and others are not with a scientific and materialist conception of the world. An action is free if there is a prior circumstance in which a "volition" of the actor causes the action, and in that, otherwise the same, circumstance a volition to act otherwise would with high probability have brought about a different action. Reichenbach goes to some lengths to explain just how the volition must cause the action in order to be free, but the conditions are open to fairly simple counter-examples. He also makes no attempt to relate free action to moral responsibility, or its absence to innocence. (Glymour and Eberhardt 2008/2021, section 6)

Glymour and Eberhardt are right that Reichenbach's formal definitions ignore moral responsibility or innocence but probably because Reichenbach took the relation between them and free will to be obvious, as we will see in a moment. If the relation between freedom and responsibility is obvious in practical, everyday contexts, however, it is not at all obvious for Reichenbach's technical definitions of freedom. And he does nothing to show that one should be held legally or morally responsible for decisions or acts that are free in his technical sense.

One of the most striking features of Reichenbach's discussion of free will is that he divides the issues into a theoretical problem and a practical problem, saying that the latter is not too difficult to solve:

> It appears plausible that the practical problem [of free will] has centered mainly around the concept of responsibility as faced in ordinary life and specifically in legal decisions. Age, illness, and various situations are sometimes regarded as extenuating circumstances which absolve a person from the responsibility for his actions. The legal profession seems to be increasingly aware of these considerations; this is borne out by the fact that, due to psychiatric influence, the notion of punishment is being replaced by the notion of rehabilitation or cure, and help or therapy is given with the aim of making the person morally free. The law formulates the general conditions for responsibility (freedom) and non-responsibility (lack of freedom), and empirical evidence determines which rules apply in a particular instance. The practical problem, therefore, is not in principle too difficult to solve. (Reichenbach 1959, 153)

What Reichenbach describes here as "extenuating circumstances" is further spelled out by H. L. A. Hart under the heading of "excusing conditions":

> It is characteristic of our own and all advanced legal systems that the individual's liability to punishment, at any rate for serious crimes carrying severe punishment, is made by law to depend on certain ... *excusing* conditions: the individual is not liable to punishment if at the time of his doing what would otherwise be a punishable act he was unconscious, mistaken about the physical consequences of his bodily movements or the nature or qualities of the thing or persons affected by them, or, in some cases, if he was subjected to threats or other gross forms of coercion or was the victim of certain kinds of mental disease. This is a list, not meant to be complete ... If an individual breaks the law when none of the excusing conditions are present he is ordinarily said to have acted "of his own free will," "of his own accord," "voluntarily" ... (Hart 1968, 28)

He goes on to say that he thinks that "the core of the problem of free will must be sought in the practical problem" (1959, 153) and that "the theoretical problem of free will can be solved along lines of reasoning that start with the practical problem" (1959, 153). In fact, however, Reichenbach's formal treatment of the theoretical problem of free will does not follow the lines of reasoning that he has just outlined for the practical problem. If it had, it would discuss how the circumstances regarded as extenuating bear on freedom or responsibility, and it does not. If the practical problem is not difficult to solve by formulating the general conditions for responsibility, then it is puzzling why, to anyone like Reichenbach sympathetic to some form of pragmatism, there should be any theoretical problem at all. Instead, the idea that in a deterministic universe decision and freedom make no sense seems to be a preliminary assumption of Reichenbach's that his formal apparatus is designed to explicate.

Turning then to that formal apparatus, Reichenbach's fundamental idea is that: "*An action B is free* in the situation A if it is possible for the action B to have been preceded by a causally relevant volition and B is not physically impossible in the situation A" (1959, 189). A causally relevant volition concerning B is one such that if one wills B, then B occurs with a probability close to 1, and if one wills not-B, then not-B occurs instead with a probability close to 1. The conditionals in this last sentence are those of counterfactuals, and both volitions and both the occurrence of B and the nonoccurrence of B must not be physically impossible in situation A. The situation is not some partial description of the facts at that time. Nor is it some minimally modified version of the context as in the Stalnaker and Lewis accounts of counterfactuals. Situation A is in effect what Laplace's vast intelligence knows about the circumstances at a time as close as you like before the willings take place.

This means that if the world is deterministic, then either the volition that B or the volition that not-B must be, in Reichenbach's sense, physically impossible in situation A. If the world is indeterministic, then each of those willings can be physically possible. Thus, determinism is incompatible with free action, and indeterminism is compatible with it.

The case is extended to the will by treating decisions (willings) as actions. An act of will is free in situation A if it could have been preceded by a causally relevant volition, and that act of will is not physically impossible in that situation. Again, this has the consequence that free action is possible in an indeterminist world but not in a determinist one. Thus, Reichenbach captures his initial thought that decision and free will make no (consistent) sense in a deterministic world.

It is worth noting that Reichenbach's account of freedom, whether of action or of willing, is framed in terms of its causal antecedents. If those antecedents make alternative actions physically impossible, in Reichenbach's sense, then one is not free. And because the account of freedom depends on the causal antecedents, his account is in this sense backward-looking.

There remains one area of conflict between Reichenbach and Carnap that bears on the forgoing machinery and that is on what is physically possible. Both tie their accounts of this to a prior notion of laws. And both take laws to be supported only inductively rather than a priori. In these respects, their accounts are similar. As we shall see, however, for Carnap something is physically possible if and only if it is consistent with the totality of laws of nature. Reichenbach's account is more elaborate, but in essence it says that an event type is physically possible at a time if and only if it is logically consistent with the totality of laws and the initial conditions at that time.

This seems very much more restrictive than Carnap's definition, and in a deterministic world it is. In such a world, everything other than its initial condition, should there have been such a state, would be physically necessary. Where the basic laws are statistical, however, that is, in an indeterministic world, Reichenbach's definition above is broader. This is because the laws in such a world are statistical frequencies, and any particular event is logically consistent with the laws and initial conditions, no matter how physically improbable that particular event may be.

On this basis, Reichenbach thinks that in an indeterministic world he can give a satisfactory account of contrary-to-fact conditionals where the antecedents thereof are physically possible. And he thinks, moreover, that in a deterministic world no such account of counterfactuals can be given: the determinist account would be restricted to using material conditionals, and no account based on these, however elaborate, will be satisfactory.

I see no reason to think that these last claims about what accounts the determinist can or cannot give are true. But my intent is not to evaluate Reichenbach's account or even to explore all its details.

It is plain, however, that Reichenbach's account of free will involves a lot of interrelated machinery. One way of challenging this account would be to challenge either the formal adequacy of the background machinery or to show that it is open to serious counterexamples. But this is not what Carnap does. He does give his own preliminary accounts of laws, necessity, and causality. But as we shall see in Section 14.4, this is not presented as a direct challenge to Reichenbach. Perhaps Carnap thought that the similarities between these accounts outweighed their differences or that any real differences could be worked out. Or perhaps Carnap thought that the best way to counter Reichenbach's conclusions was to sketch an alternative concept of free will that is exhibited where we ordinarily think it is and that is not dependent on whether the universe is deterministic.

14.4 Carnapian Preliminaries

Carnap does not reject Reichenbach's definitions or arguments as formally defective, but he does think that we need not accept Reichenbach's conclusions on free will and determinism. Carnap's discussion of such conclusions in (*IPoS*, chapter 22) presupposes his views of causality, laws, and modality, which he outlines in chapters 1 and 19–21. These issues have, of course, generated an enormous literature. We can sidestep the controversies, however, because our discussions here are aimed at seeing what Carnap's position is, evaluating his response to Reichenbach, and asking whether that response violates Carnap's own anti-metaphysical principles.

We said that Reichenbach wanted to showcase his probabilistic account of causation. Carnap does not reject Reichenbach's account but sketches a broader account that is nevertheless largely compatible with Reichenbach's. After some discussion of the difficulties of ordinary conceptions of causality Carnap says: "What is meant when it is said that event B is caused by event A? It is that there are certain laws in nature from which event B can be logically deduced when they are combined with a full description of event A" (*IPoS*, 194). This would have to be modified slightly for probabilistic causation. But the fundamental point is that the place to begin one's discussion is with laws because they are central to causation.

The view of laws that Carnap outlines in (*IPoS*) would now be called a regularity view. Laws of nature are of two sorts: universal laws, exemplified by Newton's laws and indeed by all of classical physics, and statistical laws, exemplified by the regularities described in quantum mechanics. Universal laws can be expressed by sentences of the form $(x)(Fx \supset Gx)$, where the quantifier "(x)," is that of classical first-order predicate logic and the connective, "$\supset$," is a material conditional. These simple material conditionals underwrite predictions, where "prediction" is taken widely enough to include inferences to both current and past events.[1] But even among universal conditional statements, not all are laws. Some generalizations will be purely accidental. Carnap *believes* that the difference between laws and accidental generalization is semantical: laws have "nomic form." He does not say what this form is, saying only that it is an unresolved problem for philosophy of science. (*IPoS*, 212–213)

Carnap insists that the laws of nature, whether universal or statistical, are not necessary or modal truths, where the necessity involved is presumably logical or metaphysical necessity. In the universal case, he makes the

---

[1] Statistical laws of nature, when understood as both Carnap and Reichenbach do, as statistical frequencies also underwrite predictions, though the logic of such predictions is more complicated. Carnap does not exhibit the logical form of such statistical laws, so the connective, "$\supset$," might not appear. Even so the connection should be counted as a material rather than a modal one. (Cf. next paragraph.)

argument that if the phrase "and this holds with necessity" were to be added to the merely contingent regularity, "(x)(Fx⊃Gx)" to yield "(x)(Fx⊃Gx) and this holds with necessity," the result would make no difference whatsoever about any observable feature of any predicted event and therefore adds nothing of any significance (*IPoS*, 199–201).

Carnap is in no way hostile to the notion of necessity. He is after all the author of *Meaning and Necessity* (*M&N*). Thus, for him to say that the laws of nature are not themselves necessary truths is not to say that some form of necessity cannot be involved. Carnap then proceeds to define nomic or causal necessity in terms of what is implied by the laws. Since the laws imply themselves, the laws can be called nomically necessary. So Carnap's point here must be twofold: First, laws of nature are at bottom inductively supported, that is, they are not a priori in any traditional sense. Second, necessity is not presumed in the definition of laws, but laws are presumed in the definition of nomic necessity. The difference is in the order of definition and the kind and status of the necessity involved. On these two points, Carnap and Reichenbach agree.

As we said, there are differences over physical or nomic possibility. And this generates further differences downstream. But the accounts of causation, laws, and necessity held respectively by Reichenbach and Carnap are sufficiently similar that they are not the primary source of their differences over free will. It is to the latter, discussed in Carnap's chapter 22 of *IPoS*, that we now turn.

14.5 Chapter 22, Determinism and Free Will

We come at last to Carnap's own treatment of determinism and free will.[2] Reichenbach's discussion had been highly intricate and formal and filled with detailed definitions and arguments. Uncharacteristically, Carnap's discussion was not. This is by design. He says: "No detailed discussion of this question [free will] will be given here, because, in my opinion it is not affected by any of the fundamental concepts or theories of science"

---

[2] Carnap claims no originality for his general position here and cites (California Associates 1938) and Schlick (1930/1939), presumably, as giving fuller statements of it. He might also have cited, and does in the bibliography, (Russell 1914, 211–242), which parallels one part of his argument. There are, of course, other writers in the empiricist tradition who have taken somewhat similar positions, such as found in (Ayer 1946/1954). Given the age of the issue, none of these works could claim to be unprecedented either. And, of course, none could be a response to (Reichenbach 1959). Also given the age of the issue, a full literature review would have been both impossible for Carnap and inappropriate for the context for which his chapter was written.

(*IPoS*, 218). Yet Carnap is very clear that he rejects both of Reichenbach's main theses: (1) that if the world is deterministic in the Laplacean sense, then free choice is impossible and (2) that if the world is indeterministic, as in quantum mechanics, the possibility of free choice, free action, and meaningful decisions is thereby restored. Carnap will argue against these two theses and for a different conception of the relation between choice and causality, but he will do so informally, drawing on examples and analogies. His argument goes beyond this to undermine the idea that causality is somehow a threat to our making meaningful decisions.

Carnap begins by saying that he plans to use the expressions "causality" and "causal structure of the world" in a wide sense in which it is the totality of laws that describe the causal structure of the world. He is fully aware that ordinarily we would say that the cause must temporally precede the effect. The footprint in the sand is never thought to be the cause of the person who walked along the beach. Carnap proposes to use the expression "causal law" widely because the inference from footprint to moving foot is nonetheless a causal inference. As he says: "There is no reason why the term 'causal law' cannot be used in a comprehensive way that applies to all the laws by which certain events are predicted and explained on the basis of other events regardless of whether the inferences go forward or back in time" (*IPoS*, 217). This verbal decision makes no substantial difference to his argument with respect to determinism and free will. But it does call attention to his conception of laws as grounds for inference from one event to another, rather than as showing some sort of metaphysical compulsion between them. One can hardly think that the footprint compelled the foot to precede it.

Determinism then becomes a special thesis about the causal structure of the world, namely, that the laws of the universe are such that they together with a complete description of the world at any one time logically imply every other event in the whole history of the universe, whether in the past or the future. He says that this is the view held by Newton and analyzed in detail by Laplace.[3] Carnap is not saying that the universe *is* deterministic in this sense. He knows that most physicists believe that it is not. They believe that some of the basic laws of nature are probabilistic, and if so, the world is not deterministic.

Reichenbach's first claim, that strict determinism rules out choice and free will, is widely held, but it involves, Carnap thinks, a confusion

---

[3] Actually, in requiring that all of the events of the past be implied, this formulation is slightly stronger than Laplace's, who required only that events after the temporal cross-section be implied. But if the laws are temporally symmetric, as Newton's were, then the two formulations are equivalent.

between *predictability* on the basis of observed regularities and *compulsion*. Carnap then gives three cases of genuine compulsion: (1) a prisoner, locked in a cell, cannot do what he or she wants; (2) a case where you are holding a gun and I, who am stronger, overpower you and force your finger to depress the trigger, something you do not wish to do; and (3) one person compelling a second to do something that the second does not want to do by making threats of terrible consequences. No doubt all three cases need to be fleshed out, but there clearly can be cases of compulsion of these sorts.

The three cases of compulsion have something in common: the persons being compelled are being forced to do something *against their wills*. Moreover, in these three cases, the persons are being forced to do something against their will by outside agents. Predictability on the basis of regularities of nature is not like that. Consider a case of choice where there is great regularity and predictability provided, for example, by settled character traits. Carnap says:

> I have a friend who is very fond of certain musical compositions by Bach that are seldom performed. I learn that a group of excellent musicians are giving a private performance of Bach, at the home of a friend, and that some of these compositions are on the program. I am invited and told I may bring someone. I call my friend, but before I do this, I am almost certain that he will want to go. On what basis do I make this prediction? I make it, of course, because I know his character traits and certain laws of psychology. Suppose that he actually comes with me, as I had expected. Was he compelled to go? No, he went of his own free will. He is never freer, in fact, than when he was given a choice of this sort …
>
> The free choice of this man is surely compatible with the view of Laplace. Even if total information about the universe, prior to his decision, made it possible to predict that he would attend the concert, it could still not be said that he went under compulsion. It is compulsion only if he is forced by outside agents to do something contrary to his desire. (*IPoS*, 219)

Of course, character is molded by education and experience, but if the choice springs from character, it is free.

In the first three cases above, we get compulsion without free will because the persons were forced to do something against their desires. The case of the Bach lover involved as much predictivity as you like, but there the choice was freely made and there was no compulsion. This is Carnap's argument against the idea that determinism is incompatible with free will, that is, against the first of Reichenbach's claims.

We noted earlier that on Reichenbach's conception what makes an act or willing free or not are the causal antecedents thereof. Reichenbach's concept of freedom is therefore backward-looking. Carnap's conception of freedom looks forward. It is put in terms of whether we can act as we desire and obtain the outcome we would wish. When we do what we have chosen, we are free in Carnap's sense.

There are, of course, hard cases. One could say of a psychotic that this abnormality compelled his or her action. But the word "compelled" can be used only because in such a case the psychotic is prevented from seeing or understanding the choices and incapable of rational deliberation. The boundaries of such cases are always vague, but this does not damage the general point that a free choice is one made by a person capable of foreseeing the consequences of alternative courses of action and choosing a preferred set of consequences (*IPoS*, 221).

But Carnap wants to do more than make a negative argument against the incompatibility thesis; he wants to make a positive argument for the importance of causal regularities in free choice. A choice involves deliberating about alternatives and for this one must know the causal consequences of one's actions. And this could not be done unless there was a sufficiently high degree of regularity in the world, though this need not be deterministic. Such knowledge is uncertain even in a deterministic world. Carnap mentions explicitly only the regularities that go from our actions to the world. But such knowledge requires that the world have impact on us that partly causes our observation reports. And our settled habits of inference are causal dispositions as well. Our choices are parts of the world's causal chains (*IPoS*, 221). The regularities involved in all this are essential to anything we would care to call choice. Without a fairly high degree of causal regularity, and again this need not be deterministic, there could be no legal or moral responsibility, and there would be no point to education or moral or legal responsibility. Again, "if no compulsion is involved, which means that the choice is based on his own preference, arising out of his own character, there is no reason for not calling it a free choice ... There is no reason to say that his character *compelled* him to act as he did." (*IPoS*, 221).

That the world is a causally structured place and that our characters are the product of many causes are often thought to be threats to our free will. Carnap's second argument is that a high degree of causal structure is not a threat to free will but essential to it. To make meaningful decisions we must know the causal consequences of our actions. And that knowledge of the world requires a causal engagement with it.

Carnap wants to make a third point, and this one is relevant to Reichenbach's second claim: that the indeterminism of a world like that described in quantum mechanics makes both free action and free will possible. Carnap agrees that a microevent like a quantum jump may have a macroeffect, perhaps even in human beings. But this is *not* a source of the relevant sort of freedom to allow moral or legal responsibility. Suppose that there is such a quantum event at the point of a decision and that the quantum event makes the decision go one way rather than another. Remember, however, that that quantum event is *random*, so the decision that results would be random as well. This is hardly the sort of thing for which one should be praised or blamed. Now the range of indeterminacy in quantum mechanics is extremely small, but if it were made substantially larger it would *reduce* the possibility of responsible choice rather than enhance it. The uncertainties involved in quantum mechanics are very much smaller than the uncertainties in ordinary life arising from the limitations of our knowledge. Indeed, that range of indeterminacy in quantum mechanics is so small that on the practical level there is no difference between strict determinism and modern quantum physics.

To summarize: First, Carnap argues that there is no reason not to call an action or choice free if it proceeds from the agent's character and preferences. Such freedom is entirely compatible with even the strictest determinism. This is an argument against the first of Reichenbach's claims. Second, Carnap argues that a high degree of causal structure is essential to rational deliberation and choice. Third, Carnap argues that quantum indeterminacy does not make free choice or free will possible. This is because, insofar as random quantum events make the difference between one choice and another, those choices are random as well. And no one should be praised or blamed for acts that arise randomly.

14.6 Does Carnap Violate His Own Anti-metaphysical Stance?

It will seem obvious to many philosophers that in exploring causation and free will in the way we have described, Carnap is doing metaphysics. After all, both free will and causation are among the oldest topics in the field. The same philosophers will no doubt be aware that Carnap famously rejected metaphysics in the strongest terms possible. And so Carnap's remarks on these topics are puzzling. How can Carnap reject what he himself is doing? Is Carnap being hypocritical in discussing these topics?

Or was his call in the early 1930s to "overcome"[4] metaphysics just a passing phase that he eventually outgrew?

In rejecting metaphysics, Carnap is using the term "metaphysics" as other European philosophers of the early twentieth century used it – not for a field of study but for a certain kind of philosophic activity. He mentions few such philosophers by name. One of them was Henri Bergson, an enormously popular French philosopher and author of *Introduction to Metaphysics* (1903/1913/1973). There Bergson contrasts metaphysics with ordinary empirical science. Such science can only compare individual objects of the world using abstract concepts. It thus produces a static picture of the world that necessarily distorts it. Metaphysics, by contrast, eschews concepts to directly apprehend the essence of things in all their Heraclitan glory. It is thus in a position to correct the distortions of empirical science. Ordinary empirical science is fine as far as it goes, and Bergson is not hostile to it. But metaphysics goes further and deeper than ordinary empirical science ever can.[5]

Carnap's quarrel with Bergson and others is not over the meaning of the word "metaphysics" but over whether metaphysics in that sense is an appropriate thing to do or to aspire to do. Carnap rejects it as an enterprise. In the very early thirties, Carnap's anti-metaphysical crusade targeted its claims to be yielding substantive truths about the world that are deeper or go beyond what ordinary empirical science can find. For Carnap, the way to win the battle against the pretentions of metaphysics was by very careful logical clarification of what was being said – in the expectation that the metaphysicians were in fact saying nothing at all.

I have no intention here of evaluating Carnap's argument, but it is plain that by "metaphysics" Carnap does not mean a subject area or a sub-discipline of philosophy but a certain conception of philosophy. Metaphysics is to provide a deeper knowledge of the world than science can provide, so it can then correct the distortions of science. So just because Carnap is discussing topics that are traditionally within the subject area of metaphysics, this should not imply that Carnap is conceiving of his own work in Bergson's way or trying to acquire knowledge beyond the reach of ordinary science.[6]

---

[4] Carnaps famous paper of that time, 1932, is known to most English speakers as "The Elimination of Metaphysics through the Logical Analysis of Language" (Carnap 1932/2004). A better translation of the title would be "Overcoming Metaphysics through the Logical Analysis of Language."
[5] For a fuller discussion of Carnap and Bergson on metaphysics, see Creath (forthcoming).
[6] Carnap spends some time in *IPoS* (187–190) distinguishing what he takes to be the proper work of a philosophy of science from an older "metaphysics of nature."

When in the mid-thirties Carnap developed his mature philosophy with its hallmark Principle of Tolerance, Carnap's understanding of metaphysics and rejection of it did not change. But it could be differently expressed. By this point, Carnap had come to the idea that what seem to be different and incompatible philosophical claims are best understood as various proposals for structuring the language of science. There is no uniquely correct language, so no theoretical question can arise as to which is in fact the correct one. Instead, there is only the practical question as to which is the most useful or useful for a particular purpose. We need not all use the same language, but we do need to be as explicit as possible about what are the rules of our language or of any language under discussion. Only then can we evaluate claims within it. Ultimately, it is the empirical scientists who will decide for themselves what conceptual structures, that is, what languages, they find most useful. Philosophers will in no sense be able to "correct" them. Thus, someone who proposes to say what the correct language is and moreover to do so from a nonconceptual philosophic standpoint (as a Bergson might) would be doing metaphysics in much the same sense of that term that Carnap was using a few years earlier.

But this is precisely what Carnap is *not* doing in the discussion of causality and free will in *IPoS*. He does not say that he has the correct conception of free will. His repeated phrase, and I quoted several occurrences, was "there is no reason why we cannot say." There is no theoretical reason why we cannot adopt Carnap's concept of free will because there is no such theoretical reason to be had. Nor does he say that Reichenbach's definitions are wrong. Carnap says only that we don't have to accept them. Presumably, Carnap thinks that his own concepts are good explications of our ordinary ones and that they draw useful distinctions for moral and legal evaluations. Such questions would be pragmatic ones and might not admit of a unique answer.

My suspicion is that Carnap would not consider Reichenbach's essay on free will (Reichenbach 1959) to be an example of metaphysics either. Reichenbach sometimes conveys the impression that he has found the right answer to the particular problem he is working on. But this is not the way that Carnap would interpret him. In another, but similar, context Carnap took Reichenbach to be trying to turn a traditional metaphysical question, the existence of theoretical entities, into an empirical question that because it was suitably clarified as an empirical question would have a correct answer (*RSE*, 870).

So our original puzzle about whether Carnap is violating his own antimetaphysical stance evaporates. Carnap's notion of metaphysics is not as a subject area within philosophy but as the idea that metaphysicians can achieve by philosophic means a substantive knowledge of the world that goes deeper or beyond what empirical science can achieve. Metaphysics would thus be in a position to correct that science. Carnap certainly had no such pretentions. Nor is he claiming that he has found the uniquely correct concept of freedom. The fact that Carnap addressed issues that are traditionally included in the subject area of metaphysics does not show that he was doing what he called metaphysics or addressing these issues in a way that he consistently rejected.

14.7 Summary

In his *Philosophical Foundations of Physics: An Introduction to the Philosophy of Science* (*IPoS*) Carnap spent a whole chapter on one of the oldest issues in the field of metaphysics: the issue of whether free will of a sort that legal and moral responsibility depends on is compatible with strict determinism. Such a determinism is roughly the idea that all our decisions, actions, etc. are caused in full detail by events before we were born. In that chapter, Carnap is challenging some claims of Reichenbach: that such a determinism would make choice and freedom meaningless and that indeterminism would make free will and action possible after all. Carnap argued that we do not need to accept either of these claims by Reichenbach. Carnap argued further that a high degree of causal structure in the world does not threaten our ability to choose freely. Instead, such a causal structure and our causal engagement with the world is essential for rational deliberation and free choice about what to do. Carnap's discussion of this age-old problem from metaphysics is puzzling to some because it seems to violate his own well-known anti-metaphysical stance. As we saw, however, once we understood more clearly what Carnap's rejection of metaphysics is about, the puzzle evaporates. In doing so, a clearer understanding of his discussion of free will emerges as well.

Bibliography

Works of Carnap

Carnap, R. (1926/2019). "Physikalische Begriffsbildung/Physical Concept Formation." In *CW1*, 339–424.
  (1927). "Eigentliche und uneigentliche Begriffe." *Symposion: Philosophische Zeitschrift für Forschung und Aussprache* 1: 355–374.
  (1929). *Abriss der Logistik*. Vienna: Springer.
  (1929/2004). "Von Gott und Seele. Scheinfragen in Metaphysik und Theologie." In Th. Mormann (ed.), *Scheinprobleme in der Philosophie und andere metaphysikkritische Schriften*. Hamburg: Felix Meiner Verlag, 49–63.
  (1930/2004). "Die Alte und die Neue Logik." In Th. Mormann (ed.), *Scheinprobleme in der Philosophie und andere metaphysikkritische Schriften*. Hamburg: Felix Meiner Verlag, 63–80.
  (1931/1983). "The Logicist Foundations of Mathematics." In P. Benacerraf and H. Putnam (eds.), *Philosophy of Mathematics: Selected Readings*. Cambridge: Cambridge University Press, 41–52.
  (1932/1987). "On Protocol Sentences." *Nous* 21 (4): 457–470.
  (1932/2004). "Überwindung der Metaphysik durch logische Analyse der Sprache." In Th. Mormann (ed.), *Scheinprobleme in der Philosophie und andere metaphysikkritische Schriften*. Hamburg: Felix Meiner Verlag, 81–110.
  (1934). *Logische Syntax der Sprache*. Vienna: Springer. (*LSS*)
  (1934). "Theoretische Fragen und praktische Entscheidungen." *Natur und Geist* 2: 257–260.
  (1934/2013). *The Unity of Science*. Translated by Max Black. London; New York: Routledge.
  (1935). *Philosophy and Logical Syntax*. London: Kegan Paul, Trench, Trubner, & Co.
  (1935/1937). "Ein Gültigkeitskriterium für die Sätze der klassischen Mathematik." *Monatshefte für Mathematik und Physik* 42: 163–190. Translated into English in *LSL*, §34a–i.
  (1936). "Testability and Meaning." *Philosophy of Science* 3 (4): 419–471; 4 (1): 1–40. (*T&M*)
  (1936). "Über die Einheitssprache der Wissenschaft. Logische Bemerkungen zum Projekt einer Enzyklopädie." *Acte du Congrès international de philosophie*

scientifique, Sorbonne, Paris 1935, 2. Unité de la science. Actualités scientifiques et industrielles 389: 60–70.
(1936/1949). "Truth and Confirmation." In H. Feigl and W. Sellars (eds.), Readings in Philosophical Analysis. New York: Appleton-Century-Crofts, 119–127.
(1937). "Logic." In E. Douglas et al. (eds.), Factors Determining Human Behavior. Cambridge, MA: Harvard University Press, 107–118.
(1937). Logical Syntax of Language. London: Routledge & Kegan Paul. (LSL)
(1938). "Logical Foundations of the Unity of Science." In R. Carnap, Ch. Morris, and O. Neurath (eds.), International Encyclopedia of Unified Science. Chicago: University of Chicago Press, 42–62.
(1939). Foundations of Logic and Mathematics. Chicago: University of Chicago Press. (FLM)
(1942). Introduction to Semantics. Cambridge, MA: Harvard University Press. (IS)
(1943). Formalization of Logic. Cambridge, MA: Harvard University Press. (FoL)
(1944). "The Problem of a World Language." Books Abroad 18 (3): 303–304.
(1945a). "The Two Concepts of Probability." Philosophy and Phenomenological Research 5: 513–532.
(1945b). "On Inductive Logic." Philosophy of Science 12 (2): 72–97.
(1947a). "Probability as a Guide in Life." Journal of Philosophy 44: 141–148.
(1947b). "On the Application of Inductive Logic." Philosophy and Phenomenological Research 8 (1): 133–148.
(1947/1956). Meaning and Necessity. Chicago: University of Chicago Press. (M&N)
(1950). "Empiricism, Semantics, and Ontology." Revue International de Philosophie 4 (11): 20–40. (ESO)
(1950). Logical Foundations of Probability. Chicago: University of Chicago Press. (LFP)
(1952). The Continuum of Inductive Methods. Chicago: University of Chicago Press. (CIM)
(1952). "Meaning Postulates." Philosophical Studies 3: 65–73.
(1955a). "Meaning and Synonymy in Natural Languages." Philosophical Studies 6 (3): 33–47.
(1955b). "On Some Concepts of Pragmatics." Philosophical Studies 6: 89–91.
(1956). "The Methodological Character of Theoretical Concepts." In H. Feigl and M. Scriven (eds.), The Foundations of Science and the Concepts of Psychology and Psychoanalysis. Minneapolis: University of Minnesota Press, 38–76.
(1958). "Beobachtungssprache und theoretische Sprache." Dialectica 12 (3–4): 236–248.
(1959/2000). "Rudolf Carnap's Theoretical Concepts in Science." Studies in History and Philosophy of Science 31 (1): 151–172.
(1962). "The Aim of Inductive Logic." In E. Nagel et al. (eds.), Logic, Methodology, and Philosophy of Science. Stanford: Stanford University Press, 303–318.

(1962). *Logical Foundations of Probability*. 2nd ed. Chicago: University of Chicago Press. (*LFP2*)
(1963). "Intellectual Autobiography." In P. A. Schilpp (ed.), *The Philosophy of Rudolf Carnap*. LaSalle, IL: Open Court, 3–84. (*IA*)
(1963). "Replies and Systematic Expositions." In P. A. Schilpp (ed.), *The Philosophy of Rudolf Carnap*. LaSalle, IL: Open Court, 859–1013. (*RSE*)
(1966). *An Introduction to the Philosophy of Science*. New York: Basic Books. (*IPoS*)
(1967). *Der logische Aufbau der Welt*. Berlin-Schlachtensee: Weltkreis-Verlag [1928]. Quoted from the English translation, *The Logical Structure of the World*. Translated by R. A. George. Berkeley: University of California Press. (*Aufbau*)
(1970). "Notes and News." *The Journal of Philosophy* 67 (24): 1026–1029.
(1971). "A Basic System of Inductive Logic." In R. Carnap and R. C. Jeffrey (eds.), *Studies in Inductive Logic and Probability, Volume I*. Berkeley; Los Angeles: University of California Press, 35–165.
(1972). "Notes on Semantics, 1955, Los Angeles." *Philosophia* 2: 3–54.
(1977). *Two Essays on Entropy*. Berkeley; Los Angeles: University of California Press.
(1990). "Quine on Analyticity [orig. 1952]." In R. Creath (ed.), *Dear Carnap, Dear Van. The Quine-Carnap Correspondence and Related Work*. Berkeley; Los Angeles: University of California Press, 427–432.
(2000). *Untersuchungen zur allgemeinen Axiomatik*. Edited by Th. Bonk and J. Mosterín. Darmstadt: Wissenschaftliche Buchgesellschaft.
(2017). "Value Concepts (1958)." *Synthese* 194: 185–194.
(2019). *The Collected Works of Rudolf Carnap, Volume 1: Early Writings*. Edited by A. W. Carus, M. Friedman, W. Kienzler, A. Richardson, and S. Schlotter. Oxford: Oxford University Press. (*CW1*)
(2019). *Der Raum: Ein Beitrag zur Wissenschaftslehre / Space: A Contribution to the Theory of Science*. In A. W. Carus, M. Friedman, W. Kienzler, A. Richardson, and S. Schlotter (eds.), *The Collected Works of Rudolf Carnap, Volume 1: Early Writings*. Oxford: Oxford University Press, 21–171. (*Raum*)
(2022a). *Tagebücher 1908–1919*. Herausgegeben von Christian Damböck, unter Mitarbeit von Brigitta Arden, Brigitte Parakenings, Roman Jordan und Lois M. Rendl. Hamburg: Felix Meiner Verlag.
(2022b). *Tagebücher 1920–1935*. Herausgegeben von Christian Damböck, unter Mitarbeit von Brigitta Arden, Brigitte Parakenings, Roman Jordan und Lois M. Rendl. Hamburg: Felix Meiner Verlag.
(in preparation). *Tagebücher 1936–1970*. Herausgegeben von Christian Damböck, unter Mitarbeit von Brigitta Arden, Philipp Bauer und Brigitte Parakenings. Hamburg: Meiner Verlag.
Carnap, R., and Bachmann, F. (1936/1981). "On Extremal Axioms." *History and Philosophy of Logic* 2: 67–85.
Carnap, R., and Hochkeppel, W. (1993). "Interview mit Rudolf Carnap (1964)." In *Rudolf Carnap: Mein Weg in die Philosophie. Übersetzt und mit einem*

Nachwort sowie einem Interview herausgegeben von Willy Hochkeppel. Stuttgart: Reclam, 133–148.

Carnap, R., and Jeffrey, R. C. (eds.). (1971). *Studies in Inductive Logic and Probability, Volume I*. Berkeley; Los Angeles: University of California Press.

Carnap, R., Hahn, H., and Neurath, O. (1929/2012). *Wissenschaftliche Weltauffassung: Der Wiener Kreis*. Edited by F. Stadler and Th. Uebel. Vienna; New York: Springer.

Secondary Literature

Abi, B. et al. (2021). "Measurement of the Positive Muon Anomalous Magnetic Moment to 0.46 ppm." *Physical Review Letters* 126: 141801.

Anderton, K. M. (1993). *The Limits of Science: A Social, Political, and Moral Agenda for Epistemology in Nineteenth Century Germany*. Cambridge, MA: Harvard University.

Andreas, H. (2007). *Carnaps Wissenschaftslogik*. Paderborn: Mentis.

(2021). "Theoretical Terms in Science." In E. N. Zalta (ed.), *The Stanford Encyclopedia of Philosophy*. https://plato.stanford.edu/entries/theoretical-terms-science/.

Aray, B. (2019). "Louis Couturat, Modern Logic, and the International Auxiliary Language." *British Journal for the History of Philosophy* 27 (5): 979–1001.

Awodey, S. (2007). "Carnap's Quest for Analyticity. The *Studies in Semantics*." In M. Friedman and R. Creath (eds.), *The Cambridge Companion to Carnap*. Cambridge: Cambridge University Press, 226–247.

Awodey, S., and Carus, A. W. (2001). "Carnap, Completeness, and Categoricity: The *Gabelbarkeitssatz* of 1928." *Erkenntnis* 54 (2): 145–172.

(2007). "Carnap's Dream: Gödel, Wittgenstein, and Logical, Syntax." *Synthese* 159 (1): 23–45.

(2009). "From Wittgenstein's Prison to the Boundless Ocean. Carnap's Dream of Logical Syntax." In P. Wagner (ed.), *Carnap's Logical Syntax of Language*. Basingstoke: Palgrave Macmillan, 79–106.

Awodey, S., and Reck, E. (2002). "Completeness and Categoricity, Part 1: 19th Century Axiomatics to 20th Century Metalogic." *History and Philosophy of Logic* 23: 1–30.

(2004). *Frege's Lectures on Logic: Carnap's Student Notes 1910–1914*. LaSalle, IL: Open Court.

Ayer, A. J. (1946). *Language, Truth and Logic*. 2nd ed. New York: Dover.

(1946/1954). "Freedom and Necessity." In *Philosophical Essays*. London: Macmillan & Co. Ltd., 271–284.

(1957). "The Conception of Probability as a Logical Relation." In S. Korner (ed.), *Observation and Interpretation in the Philosophy of Physics*. New York: Dover, 12–17.

Ayer, A. J. et al. (1968). "Repression in Mexico." *New York Times*, December 25.

Baccarat, L. (2024). "Neurath's Anticorrespondentism and Avenarius." In Ch. Damböck, J. Friedl, and U. Höfer (eds.), *Ways of the Scientific World-Conception. Rudolf Carnap and Otto Neurath*. Amsterdam: Brill-Rodopi.

Beaney, M. (2013). "The Historiography of Analytic Philosophy." In M. Beaney (ed.), *The Oxford Handbook of the History of Analytic Philosophy*. Oxford: Oxford University Press, 30–60.
    (2016). "Historiography, Philosophy of History and the Historical Turn in Analytic Philosophy." *Journal of the Philosophy of History* 10: 211–234.
    (2020). "Two Dogmas of Analytic Historiography." *British Journal for the History of Philosophy* 28: 594–614.
Bentley, J. (2023). *Logical Empiricism and Naturalism. Neurath and Carnap's Meta-theory of Science*. Cham: Springer.
Bergson, H. (1903/1913/1973). *An Introduction to Metaphysics*. Translated by T. E. Hulme. Houndsmills; Basingstoke: Palgrave Macmillan.
Bernays, P. (1967). "Hilbert, D." In P. Edwards (ed.), *Encyclopedia of Philosophy*, vol. 3. New York: Macmillan, 496–505.
Boghossian, P. (1996). "Analyticity Reconsidered." *Nous* 30: 360–391.
Bohnert, H. G. (1975). "Carnap's Logicism." In J. Hintikka (ed.), *Rudolf Carnap: Logical Empiricist*. Dodrecht: Reidel, 183–216.
Borsanyi, S. et al. (2021). "Leading Hadronic Contribution to the Muon Magnetic Moment from Lattice QCD." *Nature* 393 (April 7): 51–55.
Bright, L. K. (2017). "Logical Empiricists on Race." *Studies in History and Philosophy of Biological and Biomedical Sciences* 65: 9–18.
    (2018). "Du Bois' Democratic Defence of the Value Free Ideal." *Synthese* 195 (5): 2227–2245.
Brozek, A. (2022). "Jan Lukasiewicz's Program of the Logicization of Philosophy: Its Genesis, Content and Realizations." *Synthese*. https://link.springer.com/article/10.1007/s11229-022-03699-7.
Brun, G. (2016). "Explication as a Method of Conceptual Re-engineering." *Erkenntnis* 81: 1211–1241.
    (2020). "Conceptual Re-engineering: From Explication to Reflective Equilibrium." *Synthese* 197: 925–954.
Burgess, A., Cappelen, H., and Plunckett, D. (eds.) (2020). *Conceptual Engineering and Conceptual Ethics*. Oxford: Oxford University Press.
Burke, Ch., Kindel, E., and Walker, S. (eds.) (2013). *Isotype: Design and Contexts, 1925–1971*. London: Hyphen Press.
Cappelen, H. (2018). *Fixing Language: An Essay on Conceptual Engineering*. Oxford: Oxford University Press.
Carnap, A. (1897). *Friedrich Wilhelm Dörpfeld. Aus seinem Leben und Wirken*. Gütersloh: Druck und Verlag von C. Bertelsmann.
Carus, A. W. (1999). "Carnap, Syntax, and Truth." In J. Peregrin (ed.), *Truth and Its Nature (If Any)*. Dordrecht: Springer, 15–35.
    (2007). *Carnap and Twentieth-Century Thought: Explication as Enlightenment*. Cambridge: Cambridge University Press.
    (2013). "History and the Future of Logical Empiricism." In E. Reck (ed.), *The Historical Turn in Analytic Philosophy*. London: Palgrave, 261–293.
    (2017). "Carnapian Rationality." *Synthese* 194: 163–184.

(2019). "Neurath and Carnap on Semantics." In J. Cat and A. T. Tuboly (eds.), *Neurath Reconsidered: New Sources and Perspectives*. Cham: Springer, 339–361.

(2021). "Werte beim frühen Carnap: Von den Anfängen bis zum Aufbau." In Ch. Damböck and G. Wolters (eds.) *Der junge Carnap in historischem Kontext: 1918–1935*. Cham: Springer, 1–18.

(2022). "Die religiösen Ursprünge des Nonkognitivismus bei Carnap." In Ch. Damböck, G. Sandner, and M. Werner (eds.), *Logischer Empirismus, Lebensreform und die deutsche Jugendbewegung / Logical Empiricism, Life Reform, and the German Youth Movement*. Cham: Springer, 143–161.

Cassirer, E. (1929/1957). *The Philosophy of Symbolic Forms: Volume Three: The Phenomenology of Knowledge*. New Haven; London: Yale University Press.

(1946). *The Myth of the State*. New Haven; London: Yale University Press.

Castelvecchi, D. (2021). "Is the Standard Model Broken? Physicists Cheer Major Muon Result." *Nature* (April 7). www.nature.com/articles/d41586-021-00898-z.

Church A. (1943). "Review of Carnap's *Introduction to Semantics*." *The Philosophical Review* 52 (3): 298–304.

Cohnitz, D., and Rossberg, M. (2006). *Nelson Goodman*. Chesham: Acumen.

Comandon, A., and Ong, P. (2020). "South Los Angeles since the 1960s: Race, Place, and Class." *The Review of Black Political Economy* 47 (1): 50–74.

Cote-Meek, S. (2014). *Colonized Classrooms – Fernwood Publishing*. Winnipeg, MB: Fernwood.

Cournot, A. A. (1843). *Exposition de la theorie des chances et des probabilités*. Paris: Hachette.

Couturat, L. (1901). *La Logique de Leibniz*. Paris: Alcan.

(1910). *Etude sur la Derivation dans la Langue Internationale*. Paris: Delagrave.

Couturat, L., and Léau, L. (1903). *Histoire de la Langue Universelle*. Paris: Hachette.

Creath, R. (1990a). *Dear Carnap, Dear Van. The Quine-Carnap Correspondence and Related Work*. Berkeley; Los Angeles: University of California Press.

(1990b). "The Unimportance of Semantics." In A. Fine, M. Forbes, and L. Wessels (eds.), *PSA 1990*, vol. 2. East Lansing, MI: Philosophy of Science Association, 405–415.

(1996). "Languages without Logic." In R. N. Giere and A. W. Richardson (eds.), *Origins of Logical Empiricism*. Minneapolis: University of Minnesota Press, 251–265.

(1999). "Carnap's Move to Semantics: Gains and Losses." In J. Wolenski and E. Köhler (eds.), *Alfred Tarski and the Vienna Circle*. Dordrecht: Kluwer, 65–76.

(2003). "The Linguistic Doctrine and Conventionality: The Main Argument in 'Carnap and Logical Truth.'" In G. L. Hardcastle and A. Richardson (eds.), *Logical Empiricism in North America*. Minneapolis: University of Minnesota Press, 234–256.

(2012). "Before Explication." In P. Wagner (ed.), *Carnap's Ideal of Explication and Naturalism*. Basingstoke: Palgrave MacMillan, 161–174.

(forthcoming). "What Was Carnap Rejecting When He Rejected Metaphysics?" In J. Baxter, W. Bausman, and O. Lean (eds.), *Biological Practice to Scientific Metaphysics*. Minneapolis: University of Minnesota Press.

Dahms, H.-J. (2004). "*Neue Sachlichkeit* in the Architecture and Philosophy of the 1920s." In S. Awodey and C. Klein (eds.), *Carnap Brought Home: The View from Jena*. Chicago: Open Court, 357–376.

(2016). "Carnap's Early Conception of a 'System of the Sciences': The Importance of Wilhelm Ostwald." In Ch. Damböck (ed.), *Influences on the Aufbau*. Cham: Springer, 163–185.

Damböck, Ch. (ed.) (2016). *Influences on the Aufbau*. Cham: Springer.

(2022a). "The Politics of Carnap's Non-cognitivism and the Scientific World-Conception of Left-Wing Logical Empiricism." *Perspectives on Science* 30 (4): 493–524.

(2022b). "Carnap, Reichenbach, Freyer. Non-cognitivist Ethics and Politics in the Spirit of the German Youth-Movement." In Ch. Damböck, G. Sandner, and M. Werner (eds.), *Logischer Empirismus, Lebensreform und die deutsche Jugendbewegung / Logical Empiricism, Life Reform, and the German Youth Movement*. Cham: Springer, 163–180.

(2022c). "Carnap's Non-cognitivism and His Views on Religion, against the Background of the Herbartian Philosophy of His Grandfather Friedrich Wilhelm Dörpfeld." In E. Ramharter (ed.), *The Vienna Circle and Religion*. Cham: Springer, 23–39.

(2024). "Entscheidungstheoretische, modallogische und metaethische Gesichtspunkte in Carnaps 'Value Concepts (1958).'" In E. Ficara et al. (eds.), *Revisiting the History and Philosophy of Logic and Mathematics*. London: College Publications.

Damböck, Ch., and Wolters, G. (2021). (eds.) *Der junge Carnap in historischem Kontext: 1918–1935*. Cham: Springer.

Damböck, Ch., Sandner, G., and Werner M. (eds.) (2022). *Logischer Empirismus, Lebensreform und die deutsche Jugendbewegung / Logical Empiricism, Life Reform, and the German Youth Movement*. Cham: Springer.

Daston, L., and Galison, P. (2007). *Objectivity*. Princeton: Princeton University Press.

De Morgan, A. (1847). *Formal Logic: Or the Calculus of Inference Necessary and Probable*. London: Taylor and Walton.

Dea, S. (2019). "Academic Freedom, Scholarly Responsibility and the New Gender Wars." *University Affairs* (blog). August 2, 2019.

(2021). "The Evolving Social Purpose of Academic Freedom." *Kennedy Institute of Ethics Journal* 31 (2): 199–222.

Demopoulos, W. (2013). *Logicism and Its Philosophical Legacy*. Cambridge: Cambridge University Press.

(2021). "The Partial Interpretation of Scientific Theories." In Ch. Limbeck-Lilienau and Th. Uebel (eds.), *The Routledge Handbook of Logical Empiricism*. New York: Routledge, 194–202.

Devidi, D., and Solomon, G. (1995). "Tolerance and Metalanguages in Carnap's *Logical Syntax of Language.*" *Synthese* 103 (1): 123–139.
Dewey, J. (1971). "Theory of Valuation." In O. Neurath, Ch. Morris, and R. Carnap (eds.), *Foundations of the Unity of Science II.* Chicago: University of Chicago Press, 379–447.
Dewulf, F. (2017). "Rudolf Carnap's Incorporation of the *Geisteswissenschaften* in the *Aufbau.*" *HOPOS* 7 (2017), 199–225.
  (2021). "Carnap's Opposition to Logic of the Geisteswissenschaften." In Ch. Damböck, and G. Wolters (eds.), *Der junge Carnap in historischem Kontext: 1918–1935.* Cham: Springer, 55–73.
Donaldson, Th. (2017). "The (Metaphysical) Foundations of Arithmetic?" *Noûs* 51 (4): 775–801.
Dörpfeld, F. W. (1895). *Zur Ethik.* Gütersloh: Druck und Verlag von C. Bertelsmann.
Dreben, B. (1994). "In Mediis Rebus." *Inquiry* 37: 441–447.
Dutilh Novaes, C. (2018). "Carnapian Explication and Ameliorative Analysis: A Systematic Comparison." *Synthese* 197: 1011–1034.
  (2020). "Carnap Meets Foucault: Conceptual Engineering and Genealogical Investigations." *Inquiry.* www.tandfonline.com/doi/full/10.1080/0020174X.2020.1860122.
Dutilh Novaes, C., and Reck, E. (2017). "Carnapian Explication, Formalisms as Cognitive Tools, and the Paradox of Adequate Formalization." *Synthese* 194: 195–215.
Ebbs, G. (2011). "Carnap and Quine on Truth by Convention." *Mind* 120 (478): 193–237.
  (2017). "Carnap on Ontology." In *Carnap, Quine, and Putnam on Methods of Inquiry.* Cambridge: Cambridge University Press, 44–54.
Edmonds, D. (2020). *The Murder of Professor Schlick: The Rise and Fall of the Vienna Circle.* Princeton: Princeton University Press.
Einstein, A. (1921). *Geometrie und Erfahrung.* Berlin: Springer.
Falk, J. (1999). *Women, Language and Linguistics. Three American Stories from the First Half of the Twentieth Century.* London; New York: Routledge.
Feigl, H. et al. (1970). "Homage to Rudolf Carnap." In *PSA: Proceedings of the Biennial Meeting of the Philosophy of Science Association,* XI–LXVI.
Feldbacher-Escamilla, Ch. (2021). "Carnap's Conditions of Adequacy for Explications and Conceptual Engineering." *Logique et Analyse* 256: 487–509.
Flocke, V. (2019). "Carnap's Defense of Impredicative Definitions." *The Review of Symbolic Logic* 12 (2): 372–404.
  (2020). "Carnap's Noncognitivism about Ontology." *Noûs* 54 (3): 527–548.
Forman, P. (1973). "Scientific Internationalism and the Weimar Physicists: The Ideology and Its Manipulation in Germany after World War I." *Isis* 64 (2): 151–180.
Fox Keller, E. (1982). "Feminism and Science." *Signs* 7 (3): 589–602.

Frege, G. (1884/1980). *The Foundations of Arithmetic.* Edited and translated by J. L. Austin. New York: Northwestern University Press.
Freyer, H. (1926). *Der Staat.* Leipzig: Ernst Wiegandt Verlagsbuchhandlung.
　(1930). "Ethische Normen und Politik." *Kant-Studien* 35: 99–114.
Fricker, M. (2007). *Epistemic Injustice: Power and the Ethics of Knowing.* New York: Oxford University Press.
Friedman, M. (1988). "Logical Truth and Analyticity in Carnap's Logical Syntax of Language." In W. Aspray and P. Kitcher (eds.), *History and Philosophy of Mathematics.* Minneapolis: University of Minnesota Press, 82–94.
　(1999). *Reconsidering Logical Positivism.* Cambridge: Cambridge University Press.
　(2000). *A Parting of the Ways: Carnap, Cassirer, and Heidegger.* Chicago: Open Court.
　(2001). *Dynamics of Reason.* Stanford: CSLI Publications.
　(2006). "Carnap and Quine: Twentieth-century echoes of Kant and Hume" *Philosophical Topics* 34: 35–58.
　(2010). "Synthetic History Reconsidered." In M. Domski and M. Dickson (eds.), *Discourse on a New Method: Reinvigorating the Marriage of History and Philosophy of Science.* LaSalle, IL: Open Court, 571–814.
　(2011). "Carnap on Theoretical Terms." *Synthese* 180: 249–263.
　(2018). "Carnap's Philosophy of Logic and Mathematics." In E. Reck (ed.), *Logic, Philosophy of Mathematics and Their History: Essays in Honor of W. W. Tait.* London: College, 141–170.
Friedman, M., and Creath, R. (eds.) (2007). *The Cambridge Companion to Carnap.* Cambridge: Cambridge University Press.
Gabriel, G. (2004). "Carnap Brought Home." In S. Awodey and C. Klein (eds.), *Carnap Brought Home: The View from Jena.* LaSalle, IL: Open Court, 3–20.
Galison, P. (1990). "Aufbau/Bauhaus: Logical Positivism and Architectural Modernism." *Critical Inquiry* 16 (4), 709–752.
　(1998). "The Americanization of Unity." *Daedalus* 127 (1): 45–71.
　(2016). "Meanings of Scientific Unity: The Law, the Orchestra, the Pyramid, the Quilt and the Ring." In H. Kamminga and G. Somsen, (eds.), *Pursuing the Unity of Science: Ideology and Scientific Practice from the Great War to the Cold War.* London; New York: Routledge, 12–29.
Gandon, S. (2012). *Russell's Unknown Logicism: A Study in the History and Philosophy of Mathematics.* Basingstoke: Palgrave Macmillan.
George, A. (1986). "Whence and Whither the Debate between Quine and Chomsky?" *Journal of Philosophy* 83: 489–499.
　(2011). "Quine's Philosophical Legacy." *American Philosophical Quarterly* 48: 301–304.
　(2014). "Quine's Indeterminacy" *Harvard Review of Philosophy* 21: 41–55.
Gibbard, A. (1990). *Wise Choices, Apt Feelings. A Theory of Normative Judgment.* Cambridge, MA: Harvard University Press.
　(2003). *Thinking How to Live.* Cambridge, MA: Harvard University Press.
Glymour, C. (1980). *Theory and Evidence.* Princeton: Princeton University Press.

Glymour, C., and Eberhardt, F. (2008/2021). "Hans Reichenbach." In E. N. Zalta (ed.), *Stanford Encyclopedia of Philosophy*. https://plato.stanford.edu/archives/sum2021/entries/reichenbach/.
Goldfarb W. (1997). "Semantics in Carnap. A Rejoinder to Alberto Coffa." *Philosophical Topics* 25 (2): 51–66.
Goldfarb, W., and Ricketts, Th. (1992). "Carnap and the Philosophy of Mathematics." In D. Bell and W. Vossenkuhl (eds.), *Science and Subjectivity. The Vienna Circle and 20th Century Philosophy*. Berlin: Akademie Verlag, 61–78.
Goldsmith, J., and Laks, B. (2019). *Battle in the Mind Fields*. Chicago: University of Chicago Press.
Good, I. J. (1966). "On the Principle of Total Evidence." *British Journal for the Philosophy of Science* 17 (4): 319–321.
Goodman, N. (1977). *The Structure of Appearance*. 3rd ed. Dordrecht: D. Reidel. (1990). *A Study of Qualities*. New York: Garland.
Grattan-Guinness, I. (2000). *The Search for Mathematical Roots 1870–1940. Logics, Set Theories and the Foundations of Mathematics from Cantor through Russell to Gödel*. Princeton: Princeton University Press.
Gray, J. (2008). *Plato's Ghost: The Modernist Transformation of Mathematics*. Princeton: Princeton University Press.
Greimann, D. (2007). "Das korrekte Explizieren von Begriffen." *Zeitschrift für Philosophische Forschung* 61: 261–282.
  (2012). "A Typology of Conceptual Explications." *Disputation* 4 (34): 645–670.
Grelling, K. (1929). "Realism and Logic: An Investigation of Russell's Metaphysics." *Monist* 39: 501–520.
Habgood-Coote, J. (2021). "What's the Point of Authors?" *The British Journal for the Philosophy of Science*. www.journals.uchicago.edu/doi/10.1086/715539.
Hacking, I. (1975). *The Emergence of Probability*. Cambridge: Cambridge University Press.
Hamami, Y. (2018). "Mathematical Inference and Logical Inference." *The Review of Symbolic Logic* 11 (4): 665–704.
Hanson, S. O., and Hendricks, V. F. (eds.) (2018). *Introduction to Formal Philosophy*. New York: Springer.
Harding, S. (1991). *Whose Science? Whose Knowledge? Thinking from Women's Lives*. Ithaca: Cornell University Press.
Harman, G. (1996). "Analyticity Regained?" *Nous* 30: 392–400.
Hart, H. L. A. (1968). "Legal Responsibility and Excuses." In *Punishment and Responsibility*. New York: Oxford University Press, 28–53.
Hartimo, M. (2021). *Husserl and Mathematics*. Cambridge: Cambridge University Press.
Haslanger, S. (2000). "Gender and Race: (What) Are They? (What) Do We Want Them to Be?" *Noûs* 34 (1): 31–55.
Haugen, E. (1971/2019). "Instrumentalism in Language Planning." In J. Rubin and B. Jernudd (eds.), *Can Language Be Planned? Sociolinguistic Theory and*

Practice for Developing Nations. An East-West Center Book. Honolulu: The University Press of Hawaii, 267–276.

Hegselmann, R. (1979). Normativität und Rationalität. Zum Problem praktischer Vernunft in der Analytischen Philosophie. Frankfurt: Campus Verlag.

(1992). "Einleitung. Einheitswissenschaft: Das positive Paradigma des Logischen Empirismus." In J. Schulte and B. McGuinness (eds.), Einheitswissenschaft. Frankfurt: Main Suhrkamp, 7–23.

Heidelberger, M. (2024). "Between Pietism and Herbartianism: Archaeological Vestiges in Carnap's Thought." In Ch. Damböck, J. Friedl, and U. Höfer (eds.), Ways of the Scientific World-Conception. Rudolf Carnap and Otto Neurath. Amsterdam: Brill-Rodopi.

Hempel, C. G. (1958). "The Theoretician's Dilemma." In H. Feigl, M. Scriven and G. Maxwell (eds.), Minnesota Studies in the Philosophy of Science, vol. II. Minneapolis: University of Minnesota Press, 37–98.

(1973). "Rudolf Carnap, Logical Empiricist." Synthese 25 (3/4): 256–268.

Hilbert, D. (1899). Grundlagen der Geometrie. Leipzig: Teubner.

Hirsch, E. (2011). Quantifier Variance and Realism: Essays in Metaontology. Oxford: Oxford University Press.

Hiz, H., and Swiggers, P. (1990). "Bloomfield the Logical Positivist." Semiotica 79: 257–270.

Hofweber, Th. (2016). Ontology and the Ambitions of Metaphysic. Oxford: Oxford University Press.

Hogben, L. (1943). Interglossa. A Draft of an Auxiliary for a Democratic World Order, Being an Attempt to Apply Semantic Principles to Language Design. Harmondsworth, NY: Penguin.

Hollinger, D. A. (2011). "The Unity of Knowledge and The Diversity of Knowers: Science as an Agent of Cultural Integration in the United States between the Two World Wars." Pacific Historical Review 80 (2): 211–230.

Huttegger, S. M. (2017). The Probabilistic Foundations of Rational Learning. Cambridge: Cambridge University Press.

(2019). "Analogical Predictive Probabilities." Mind 128 (509): 1–37.

Hylton, P. (2007). Quine. Abingdon: Routledge.

(2014). "Quine's Naturalism Revisited." In G. Harman and E. Lepore (eds). A Companion to W. V. O. Quine. Hoboken, NJ: Wiley-Blackwell, 148–162.

(2019). "Carnap and Quine on Analyticity: The Nature of the Disagreement." Nous 55: 445–462.

Hylton, P., and Kemp, G. (2019). "Willard Van Orman Quine." In E. N. Zalta (ed.), Stanford Encyclopedia of Philosophy. https://plato.stanford.edu/entries/quine/.

Imlay, T. C. (2016). "International Socialism at War, 1914–1918." In T. Imlay (ed.), The Practice of Socialist Internationalism: European Socialists and International Politics, 1914–1960. Oxford: Oxford University Press, 17–48.

"Interim Report of the Committee on Academic Freedom to the Academic Senate, Northern Section, of the University of California." 1951. University of California.

"It's Official – The Harper Government Muzzled Scientists. Some Say It's Still Happening." 2018. CBC. March 22. www.cbc.ca/news/health/second-opin ion-scientists-muzzled-1.4588913.
Isaacson, D. (2002). "Carnap, Quine and Logical Truth." In D. Bell and W. Vossenkuhl (eds.), *Science and Subjectivity*. Berlin: Akademie Verlag, 100–130.
Jansen, A. (1996). "ISOTYPE and Infographics." In E. Nemeth and F. Stadler (eds.), *Encyclopedia and Utopia: The Life and Work of Otto Neurath (1882–1945)*. Dordrecht: Kluwer, 143–156.
Jeffrey, R. C. (ed.) (1980). *Studies in Inductive Logic and Probability*, vol. II. Berkeley; Los Angeles: University of California Press.
  (1990). *The Logic of Decision*. 2nd ed. Chicago: University of Chicago Press.
  (1992). *Probability and the Art of Judgement*. Cambridge: Cambridge University Press.
  (1994). "Carnap's Voluntarism." In D. Prawitz, B. Skyrms, and D. Westerståhl, eds. *Logic, Methodology, and Philosophy of Science IX*. Amsterdam: Elsevier, 847–866.
  (2004). *Subjective Probability: The Real Thing*. Cambridge: Cambridge University Press.
Jespersen, O. (1925). *Mankind, Nation and Individual from a Linguistic Point of View*. Oslo: H. Aschehong.
  (1933/2010). "Nature and Art in Language." In *Selected Writings of Otto Jespersen*. London: Allen & Unwin, 387–399.
Johnson, W. E. (1924). *Logic, Part III: The Logical Foundations of Science*. Cambridge: Cambridge University Press.
  (1932). "Probability: The Deductive and Inductive Problems." *Mind* 41: 409–423.
Joseph, J. (2002). *From Whitney to Chomsky. Essays in the History of American Linguistics*. Amsterdam; Philadelphia: John Benjamins.
Kamminga, H., and Somsen, G. (eds.) (2016). *Pursuing the Unity of Science: Ideology and Scientific Practice from the Great War to the Cold War*. London; New York: Routledge.
Kemeny, J. G. (1948). "Models of Logical Systems." *Journal of Symbolic Logic* 13: 16–30.
  (1955). "Fair Bets and Degree of Confirmation." *The Journal of Symbolic Logic* 20: 263–273.
  (1956). "A New Approach to Semantics." *Journal of Symbolic Logic* 21: 1–21, 149–161.
  (1963). "Carnap's Theory of Probability and Induction." In P. A. Schilpp (ed.), *The Philosophy of Rudolf Carnap*. LaSalle, IL: Open Court, 711–738.
Kevles, D. J. "'Into Hostile Political Camps': The Reorganization of International Science in World War I." *Isis* 62 (1): 47–60.
Koellner, P. (2009). "Carnap on the foundations of logic and mathematics." https://citeseerx.ist.psu.edu/viewdoc/summary?doi=10.1.1.645.5922.

Kuhn, Th. (1962). *The Structure of Scientific Revolutions*. Chicago: University of Chicago Press.
Laplace, P.-S. de. (1814/1951). *A Philosophical Essay on Probabilities*. New York: Dover.
Lavers, G. (2004). "Carnap, Semantics and Ontology." *Erkenntnis* 60: 295–316.
  (2008). "Carnap, Formalism, and Informal Rigour." *Philosophia Mathematica* 3 (16): 4–24.
  (2019). "Hitting a Moving Target: Gödel, Carnap, and Mathematics as Logical Syntax." *Philosophia Mathematica* 27 (2): 219–243.
Leitgeb, H. (2013). "Scientific Philosophy, Mathematical Philosophy, and All That." *Metaphilosophy* 44: 267–275.
Leitgeb, H., and Carus, A. W. (2021). "Rudolf Carnap." In E. N. Zalta (ed.), *The Stanford Encyclopedia of Philosophy*. https://plato.stanford.edu/entries/carnap/.
Lenin, V. I. (1927). *Materialismus und Empiriokritizismus. Kritische Bemerkungen über eine reaktionäre Philosophie*. Vienna: Verlag für Literatur und Politik.
Leonard, H., and Goodman, N. (1940). "The Calculus of Individuals and Its Uses." *Journal of Symbolic Logic* 5: 45–55.
Limbeck-Lilienau, C. (2022). "The First Vienna Circle and the Erlangen Conference." In Th. Uebel and C. Limbeck-Lilienau (eds.), *The Routledge Handbook of Logical Empiricism*. London; New York: Routledge: 99–108.
Löffler, W. (2004). "'Esperanto. The Feeling of Disgust': Wittgenstein on Planned Languages." In J. C. Marek and M. E. Reicher (eds.), *Papers of the 27th International Wittgenstein Symposium 8–14 August 2004. Erfahrung und Analyse – Experience and Analysis*. Kirchberg am Wechsel: ALWS, 209–211.
Longino, H. (1983). "Beyond 'Bad Science': Skeptical Reflections on the Value-Freedom of Scientific Inquiry." *Science, Technology, & Human Values* 8 (1): 7–17.
  (1990). *Science as Social Knowledge: Values and Objectivity in Scientific Inquiry*. Princeton: Princeton University Press.
Lutz, S. (2012). "On a Straw Man in the Philosophy of Science." *HOPOS* 2 (1): 77–120.
  (2014a). "Carnap on Empirical Significance." *Synthese* 194 (1): 217–252.
  (2014b). "What's Right with a Syntactic Approach to Theories and Models?" *Erkenntnis* 79: 1475–1492.
  (2017). "Carnap on Empirical Significance." *Synthese* 194 (1): 217–252.
MacBride, F. (2021). "Rudolf Carnap and David Lewis on Metaphysics." *Journal for the History of Analytical Philosophy*, 9 (1): 1–31.
MacLane S. (1938). "Carnap on Logical Syntax." *Bulletin of the American Mathematical Society*, 44: 171–176.
Majer, U. (2002). "Hilbert's Program to Axiomatize Physics and Its Impact on Schlick, Carnap and Other Members of the Vienna Circle." In M. Heidelberger and F. Stadler (eds.), *History of Philosophy Science: New*

Trends and Perspectives. Vienna Circle Institute Yearbook 9. Dordrect: Springer, 213–224.

Marr, D. (1982). *Vision: A Computational Investigation into the Human Representation and Processing of Visual Information.* Cambridge, MA: MIT Press.

Marschall, B. (2022). "Carnap's Philosophy of Mathematics." *Philosophy Compass.* https://compass.onlinelibrary.wiley.com/doi/full/10.1111/phc3.12884.

Matherne, S. (2021). *Cassirer.* New York; London: Routledge.

Maxwell, G., and Feigl, H. (1961). "Why Ordinary Language Needs Reforming." *The Journal of Philosophy* 58 (18): 488–498.

McElvenny, J. (2013). "International Language and the Everyday: contact and collaboration between C.K. Ogden, Rudolf Carnap and Otto Neurath." *British Journal for the History of Philosophy* 21 (6): 1194–1218.

  (2018). *Language and Meaning in the Age of Modernism: C. K. Ogden and His Contemporaries.* Edinburgh: Edinburgh University Press.

McGill, V. J. (1936). "An Evaluation of Logical Positivism." *Science & Society* 1 (1): 45–80.

McLeod, S. (2019). *Modality and Anti-metaphysics.* New York; London: Routledge.

Menger, K. (1928). *Dimensionstheorie.* Leipzig: Teubner.

  (1934/1974). *Morality, Decisions, and Social Organization: Towards a Logic of Ethics.* Dordrecht: D. Reidel.

  (1994). *Reminiscences of the Vienna Circle and the Mathematical Colloquium.* Dordrecht: Kluwer.

Mormann, Th. (2007). "Geometrical Leitmotifs in Carnap's Early Philosophy." In M. Friedman and R. Creath (eds.), *The Cambridge Companion to Carnap.* Cambridge: Cambridge University Press, 43–64.

Morris, S. (2018). "Carnap and Quine: Analyticity, Naturalism, and the Elimination of Metaphysics." *The Monist* 10: 394–416.

Muller, J. Z. (1987). *The Other God That Failed. Hans Freyer and the Deradicalization of German Conservatism.* Princeton: Princeton University Press.

Neurath, O. (1936/1983). "Encyclopedia as 'Model.'" In R. S. Cohen and M. Neurath (eds.), *Otto Neurath: Philosophical Papers 1913–1946.* Dordrecht: Reidel, 145–458.

Nittle, N. (2019). "Operation Bootstrap: Empowering the African American Community through Entrepreneurship." KCET. November 19. www.kcet.org/shows/lost-la/operation-bootstrap-empowering-the-african-american-community-through-entrepreneurship.

Nyíri, J. C. (1992). *Tradition and Individuality: Essays.* Dordrecht: Kluwer.

O'Connor, C. (2019). *The Origins of Unfairness: Social Categories and Cultural Evolution.* Oxford: Oxford University Press.

Ogden, C. K. (1936/1994). "Basic English and Grammatical Reform." In T. W. Gordon (ed.), *From Bentham to Basic English.* London: Routledge, 187–226.

Ouelbani, M. (2005). "Carnap und die Einheit der Wissenschaft." In E. Nemeth and N. Roudet (eds.), *Paris–Wien: Enzyklopädien im Vergleich*. Dordrecht: Springer, 205–219.

Overbye, D. (2021). "A Tiny Particle's Wobble Could Upend the Known Laws of Physics." *New York Times*, April 7.

Patton, L. (2023). "Whose Dogmas of Empiricism?" In S. Morris (ed.), *The Philosophical Project of Carnap and Quine*. Cambridge: Cambridge University Press, 114–131.

PBS SoCal. (n.d.). "Lost LA: Operation Bootstrap." PBS SoCal. Accessed October 26, 2021. www.pbssocal.org/shows/lost-l-a/clip/operation-bootstrap.

Pincock, Ch. (2005). "A Reserved Reading of Carnap's *Aufbau*." *Pacific Philosophical Quarterly* 86: 518–543.

Pombo. O. (2011). "Neurath and the Encyclopaedic Project of Unity of Science." In J. Symons, O. Pombo, and J. M. Torres (eds.), *Otto Neurath and the Unity of Science*. Dordrecht: Springer, 59–70.

Potochnik, A., and Yap, A. (2006). "Revisiting Galison's 'Aufbau/Bauhaus' in Light of Neurath's Philosophical Projects." *Studies in History and Philosophy of Science* 37: 469–488.

Price, H. (2007). "Quining Naturalism" *Journal of Philosophy* 104: 375–402.

  (2009). "Metaphysics after Carnap: The Ghost Who Walks?" In D. Chalmers, D. Manley, and R. Wasserman (eds.), *Metametaphysics. New Essays on the Foundations of Ontology*. Oxford: Oxford University Press, 320–346.

  (2013). *Expressivism, Pragmatism, and Representationalism*. Cambridge: Cambridge University Press.

Putnam, H. (1962). "The Analytic and the Synthetic." In H. Feigl and G. Maxwell (eds.), *Minnesota Studies in the Philosophy of Science*, vol. 3. Minneapolis: University of Minnesota Press, 358–397.

Queloz, M. (2021). *The Practical Origins of Ideas: Genealogy as Conceptual Reverse-Engineering*. Oxford: Oxford University Press.

Quine, W. V. O. (1948). "On What There Is." *Review of Metaphysics* 2: 21–38.

  (1951a). "Two Dogmas of Empiricism." *The Philosophical Review* 60 (1): 20–43.

  (1951b). "On Carnap's Views on Ontology." *Philosophical Studies* 2: 65–72.

  (1953/1976). "Mr. Strawson on Logical Theory." In *The Ways of Paradox and Other Essays*. 2nd ed. Cambridge, MA: Harvard University Press, 137–157.

  (1958). "Speaking of Objects." In *Ontological Relativity and Other Essays*. New York: Columbia University Press, 1–25.

  (1960). *Word and Object*. Cambridge, MA: MIT Press.

  (1963). "Carnap and Logical Truth." In P. A. Schilpp (ed.), *The Philosophy of Rudolf Carnap*. LaSalle, IL: Open Court, 385–406.

  (1969a). "Ontological Relativity." In *Ontological Relativity and Other Essays*. New York: Columbia University Press, 26–68.

  (1969b). "Epistemology Naturalized." In *Ontological Relativity and Other Essays*. New York: Columbia University Press, 69–90.

(1974). *The Roots of Reference*. LaSalle, IL: Open Court.
(1978/1981). "On the Nature of Moral Values." In *Theories and Things*. Cambridge, MA: Harvard University Press, 55–66.
(1986). "Reply to Morton White." In E. Hahn and P. A. Schilpp (eds.), *The Philosophy of W. V. Quine*. LaSalle, IL: Open Court, 663–665.
(1987). *Quiddities*. Cambridge, MA: Harvard University Press.
(1991/2008). "Two Dogmas in Retrospect." In D. Føllesdal and D. B. Quine (eds.), *Confessions of a Confirmed Extensionalist and Other Essays*. Cambridge, MA: Harvard University Press, 390–400.
(2001/2008). "Confessions of a Confirmed Extensionalist." In D. Føllesdal and D. B. Quine (eds.), *Confessions of a Confirmed Extensionalist and Other Essays*. Cambridge, MA: Harvard University Press, 498–506.
Quine, W. V. O. (2004). *Quintessence: Basic Readings from the Philosophy of W. V. Quine*. Edited by R. Gibson. Cambridge, MA: Harvard University Press.
Ramsey, F. P. (1931). "Truth and Probability." In R. B. Braithwaite (ed.), *The Foundations of Mathematics and Other Logical Essays*. London: Routledge and Kegan Paul, 156–198.
Reck, E. H. (2004). "From Frege and Russell to Carnap: Logic and Logicism in the 1920s." In S. Awodey and C. Klein (eds.), *Carnap Brought Home: The View from Jena*. LaSalle, IL: Open Court, 151–180.
(2005). "Frege's Natural Numbers: Motivations and Modifications." In M. Beaney and E. Reck (eds.), *Gottlob Frege, Critical Assessments*, vol. III. London: Routledge, 270–301.
(2007a). "Frege-Russell Numbers: Analysis or Explication?" In M. Beaney (ed.), *The Analytic Turn*. London: Routledge: 33–50.
(2007b). "Carnap and Modern Logic." In M. Friedman and R. Creath (eds.), *The Cambridge Companion to Carnap*. Cambridge: Cambridge University Press, 176–199.
(2012). "Carnapian Explication: A Case Study and Critique." In P. Wagner (ed.), *Carnap's Ideal of Explication and Naturalism*. Basingstoke: Palgrave MacMillan, 96–116.
(2013). "Hempel, Carnap, and the Covering Law Model." In N. Milkov and V. Peckhaus (eds.), *The Berlin Group and the Philosophy of Logical Empiricism*. Berlin: Springer, 311–324.
Reck, E. H., and Schiemer, G. (eds.), (2020). *The Prehistory of Mathematical Structuralism*. Oxford: Oxford University Press.
Reichenbach, H. (1930/1978). "The Philosophical Significance of Modern Physics." In M. Reichenbach and R. S. Cohen (eds.), *Hans Reichenbach: Selected Writings*, vol. 1. Dordrecht: Reidel, 304–323.
(1954). *Nomological Statements and Admissible Operations*. Amsterdam: North-Holland.
(1954/1976). *Laws, Modalities, and Counterfactuals*. Reprinting of *Nomological Statements and Admissible Operations* with Foreword by W. C. Salmon. Berkeley: University of California Press.

(1959). "Free Will." In M. Reichenbach (ed.), *Modern Philosophy of Science: Selected Essays*. London: Routledge and Kegan Paul, 151–192.

Reisch, G. (1991). "Did Kuhn Kill Logical Empiricism?" *Philosophy of Science* 58: 264–277.

(2005). *How the Cold War Transformed Philosophy of Science. To the Icy Slopes of Logic*. New York: Cambridge University Press.

(2009). "Three Kinds of Political Engagement for Philosophy of Science." *Science and Education* 41: 191–197.

Richardson, A. W. (1998). *Carnap's Construction of the World: The Aufbau and the Emergence of Logical Empiricism*. Cambridge: Cambridge University Press.

(2003). "The Geometry of Knowledge: Lewis, Becker, Carnap and the Formalization of Philosophy in the 1920s." *Studies in History and Philosophy of Science* 34 (1): 165–182.

(2007). "Carnapian Pragmatism." In M. Friedman and R. Creath (eds.), *The Cambridge Companion to Carnap*. Cambridge: Cambridge University Press, 295–315.

(2010). "Ernst Cassirer and Michael Friedman: Kantian or Hegelian Dynamics of Reason?" In M. Domski and M. Dickson (eds.), *Discourse on a New Method: Reinvigorating the Marriage of History and Philosophy of Science*. LaSalle IL: Open Court, 279–294.

(2013). "Taking the Measure of Carnap's Philosophical Engineering: Metalogic as Metrology." In E. Reck (ed.), *The Historical Turn in Analytic Philosophy*. London: Palgrave, 60–77.

(2017). "'Neither a Confession Nor an Accusation': Michael Polanyi, Hans Reichenbach, and Philosophical Modernity after World War One." *Historical Studies in the Natural Sciences* 47 (3): 423–442.

(2021). "On the Empirical Refutation of Epistemological Doctrine in Hans Reichenbach's Early Philosophy." In S. Lutz and A. T. Tuboly (eds.), *Logical Empiricism and the Physical Sciences: From Philosophy of Nature to Philosophy of Physics*. New York: Routledge, 157–178.

Richardson, S. (2009a). "The Left Vienna Circle, Part 1." *Studies in History and Philosophy of Science Part A* 40: 14–24.

(2009b). "The Left Vienna Circle, Part 2. The Left Vienna Circle, Disciplinary History, and Feminist Philosophy of Science." *Studies in History and Philosophy of Science* 40 (2): 167–174.

Ricketts, Th. (1996). "Carnap: From Logical Syntax to Semantics." In R. N. Giere and A. W. Richardson (eds.), *Origins of Logical Empiricism*. Minneapolis; London: University of Minnesota Press, 213–250.

(2003). "Languages and Calculi." In G. L. Hardcastle and A. W. Richardson (eds.), *Logical Empiricism in North America*. Minneapolis: University of Minnesota Press, 257–280.

(2004). "Frege, Carnap, and Quine: Continuities and Discontinuities." In S. Awodey and C. Klein (eds.), *Carnap Brought Home: The View from Jena*. LaSalle, IL: Open Court, 181–202.

(2007). "Tolerance and Logicism: Logical Syntax and the Philosophy of Mathematics." In M. Friedman and R. Creath (eds.), *The Cambridge Companion to Carnap*. Cambridge: Cambridge University Press, 200–225.

Romizi, D. (2012). "The Vienna Circle's 'Scientific World-Conception': Philosophy of Science in a Political Arena." *HOPOS* 2: 205–242.

Rosen, G. (2010). "Metaphysical Dependence: Grounding and Reduction." In B. Hale and A. Hoffman (eds.), *Modality: Metaphysics, Logic and Epistemology*. Oxford: Oxford University Press, 109–136.

Russell, B. (1903). *Principles of Mathematics*. Cambridge: Cambridge University Press.

(1919). *Introduction to Mathematical Philosophy*. London: George Allen & Unwin.

(1924/1958). "Logical Atomism." In D. Pears (ed.), *The Philosophy of Logical Atomism*. LaSalle, IL: Open Court, 157–181.

Russell, B., and Whitehead, N. A. (1910–1913). *Principia Mathematica*, 3 vols. Cambridge: Cambridge University Press.

Schiemer, G. (2012). "Carnap's Untersuchungen: Logicism, Formal Axiomatics, and Metatheory." In R. Creath (ed.), *Rudolf Carnap and the Legacy of Logical Empiricism*. Vienna: Springer, 13–36.

(2013). "Carnap's Early Semantics." *Erkenntnis* 78 (3): 487–522.

Schiemer, G., and Reck, E. (2013). "Logic in the 1930s: Type Theory and Model Theory." *The Bulletin of Symbolic Logic* 19: 433–472.

Schiemer, G., Zach, R., and Reck, E. (2017). "Carnap's Early Metatheory: Scope and Limits." *Erkenntnis* 194 (1): 33–65.

Schilpp, P. A. (ed.) (1963). *The Philosophy of Rudolf Carnap*. LaSalle, IL: Open Court.

Schlick, M. (1925/1974). *General Theory of Knowledge*. 2nd ed. Translated by A. E. Blumberg. New York: Vienna: Springer-Verlag.

(1930/1939). *Problems of Ethics*. Translated by David Rynin. New York: Prentice-Hall.

Schlimm, D. (2013). "Axioms in Mathematical Practice." *Philosophia Mathematica* 21 (1): 37–92.

Schroeder-Gudehus, B. (1973). "Challenge to Transnational Loyalties: International Scientific Organizations after the First World War." *Science Studies* 3 (2): 93–118.

Schwartzkopff, R. (2011). "Numbers as Ontologically Dependent Objects: Hume's Principle Revisited." *Grazer Philosophische Studien* 82 (1): 353–373.

Shapiro, S. (1997). *Philosophy of Mathematics: Structure and Ontology*. New York: Oxford University Press.

Sher, G. (2008). "Tarski's Thesis." In D. E. Patterson (ed.), *Alfred Tarski: Philosophical Background, Development, and Influence*. Oxford: Oxford University Press, 300–339.

Shieh, S. (2017). "Pragmatism, Apriority, and Modality: C. I. Lewis against Russell's Material Implication." In P. Olen and C. Sachs (eds.),

Pragmatism in Transition: Contemporary Perspectives on C. I. Lewis. London; New York: Palgrave, 103–145.

Shimony, A. (1955). "Coherence and the Axioms of Confirmation." *The Journal of Symbolic Logic* 20: 1–28.

Siegetsleitner, A. (2014). *Ethik und Moral im Wiener Kreis. Zur Geschichte eines engagierten Humanismus.* Vienna: Böhlau Verlag.

Simon, H. (1969). *The Sciences of the Artificial.* Cambridge, MA: Harvard University Press.

Skyrms, B. (1990). *The Dynamics of Rational Deliberation.* Cambridge, MA: Harvard University Press.

  (1995). "Strict Coherence, Sigma Coherence and the Metaphysics of Quantity." *Philosophical Studies* 77: 39–55.

Stadler, F. (1997). *Studien zum Wiener Kreis. Ursprung, Entwicklung und Wirkung des Logischen Empirismus im Kontext.* Frankfurt/Main: Suhrkamp.

Stegmüller, W. (1979). *The Structuralist View of Theories.* New York: Springer.

Stein, H. (1992). "Was Carnap Entirely Wrong, After All?" *Synthese* 93: 275–295.

Strawson, P. F. (1954/1974). "Wittgenstein's Philosophical Investigations." In *Freedom and Resentment and Other Essays.* London: Methuen, 133–168.

  (1959). *Individuals: An Essay in Descriptive Metaphysics.* London: Methuen.

  (1963). "Carnap's Views on Constructed Systems versus Natural Languages in Analytic Philosophy." In P. A. Schilpp (ed.), *The Philosophy of Rudolf Carnap.* LaSalle, IL: Open Court, 503–518.

  (1986). "Reference and Its roots." In L. Hahn and P. A. Schilpp (eds.), *The Philosophy of W. V. Quine.* 2nd ed. LaSalle, IL: Open Court, 519–532.

Strawson, P. F., and Grice, H. P. (1956). "In Defense of a Dogma." *Philosophical Review* 65: 141–158.

Stump, D. (2009). "Pragmatism, Activism, and the Icy Slopes of Logic in George Reisch's Portrait of Philosophy as a Young Field." *Science and Education* 18: 169–175.

Suppe, F. (ed.) (1974). *The Structure of Scientific Theories.* Urbana: University of Illinois Press.

Suppes, P. (1992). "Axiomatic Methods in Science." In M. Carvallo (ed.), *Nature, Cognition and System II.* Heidelberg: Springer, 205–232.

Sznajder, M. (2018). "Inductive Logic as Explication: The Evolution of Carnap's Notion of Logical Probability." *The Monist* 101 (4): 417–440.

  (2022). "Janina Hosiasson-Lindenbaum on Analogical Reasoning: New Sources." *Erkenntnis.* https://link.springer.com/article/10.1007/s10670-022-00586-y.

Táíwò, O. O. (2021). "Joining Team Positivism." *The Sooty Empiric* (blog). February 1. http://sootyempiric.blogspot.com/2021/02/joining-team-positivism-by-olufemi-o.html.

Tarski A. (1936/1956). "The Establishment of Scientific Semantics." In J. Woodger (ed.), *Logic, Semantics, Metamathematics.* Oxford: Oxford University Press, 401–408.

  (1936/2002). "On the Concept of Following Logically." *History and Philosophy of Logic* 23: 155–196.

(1954–1955). "Contributions to the Theory of Models." *Indagationes mathematicae* 16: 572–588; 17: 56–64.

(1933/1956). "The Concept of Truth in Formalized Languages." In J. Woodger (ed.), *Logic, Semantics, Metamathematics*. Oxford: Oxford University Press, 152–278.

Tauli, V. (1974). "The Theory of Language Planning." In J. A. Fishman, *Advances in Language Planning*. The Hague: Mouton & Co., 49–67.

Thomasson, A. L. (2015). *Ontology Made Easy*. Oxford: Oxford University Press.

Tomalin, M. (2009). *Linguistics and the Formal Sciences*. Cambridge: Cambridge University Press.

Tuboly A. T. (2017). "From 'Syntax' to 'Semantik' – Carnap's Inferentialism and its Prospects." *Polish Journal of Philosophy* 11 (1): 57–78.

(2022). "The Constitution of geistige Gegenstände in Carnap's Aufbau and the Importance of Hans Freyer." In Ch. Damböck, G. Sandner, and M. Werner (eds.), *Logischer Empirismus, Lebensreform und die deutsche Jugendbewegung / Logical Empiricism, Life Reform, and the German Youth Movement*. Cham: Springer, 181–204.

Tuomela, R. (1973). *Theoretical Concepts*. Wien: Springer.

Uebel, Th. (2005). "Political Philosophy of Science in Logical Empiricism: The Left Vienna Circle." *Studies in History and Philosophy of Science Part A* 36 (4): 754–773.

(2009). "Carnap's Logical Syntax in the Context of the Vienna Circle." In P. Wagner, (ed.), *Carnap's Logical Syntax of Language*. Basingstoke: Palgrave Macmillan, 53–78.

(2010). "What's Right about Carnap, Neurath and the Left Vienna Circle Thesis: A Refutation." *Studies in History and Philosophy of Science Part A* 41 (2): 214–221.

(2012a). "Carnap, Philosophy and 'Politics in the Broadest Sense.'" In R. Creath (ed.), *Carnap and the Legacy of Logical Empiricism*. Vienna: Springer, 133–148.

(2012b). "On the Production History and Early Reception of The Scientific Conception of the World. The Vienna Circle." In Carnap, R., Hahn, H., and Neurath, O. (1929/2012). *Wissenschaftliche Weltauffassung: Der Wiener Kreis*. Edited by F. Stadler and Th. Uebel. Vienna; New York: Springer, 291–314.

(2013a). "Pragmatics in Carnap and Morris and the Bipartite Metatheory Conception." *Erkenntnis* 78: 523–546.

(2013b). "Neurath's Unity of Science and the Encyclopedia Project." In B Kaldis (ed.), *Encyclopedia of Philosophy and the Social Sciences*, vol 2. London: Sage: 659–662.

(2015). "Three Challenges to the Complementarity of the Logic and the Pragmatics of Science." *Studies in History and Philosophy of Science* 53: 23–32.

(2020). "Intersubjective Accountability: Politics and Philosophy in the Left Vienna Circle." *Perspectives on Science* 28 (1): 35–62.

(2021). "Was bedeutet Carnaps 'Reinigung' der Erkenntnistheorie?" In Ch. Damböck, G. Sandner, and M. Werner (eds.), *Logischer Empirismus, Lebensreform und die deutsche Jugendbewegung / Logical Empiricism, Life Reform, and the German Youth Movement*. Cham: Springer, 127–147.

(2022). "The Bipartite Metatheory Conception of Philosophy." In Th. Uebel and C. Limbeck-Lilienau, (eds.), *The Routledge Handbook of Logical Empiricism*, Abingdon: Routledge, 361–370.

(ms.) "Carnap and the Indeterminacy of Translation." Talk given at the Conference "60 Years of Quine's *Word and Object*" at the University of Campinas, Brazil in August 2021. Unpublished Manuscript.

UN News. (2021). "IPCC Report: 'Code Red' for Human Driven Global Heating, Warns UN Chief." UN News. August 9. https://news.un.org/en/story/2021/08/1097362.

Verhaegh, S. (2018). *Working from Within: The Nature and Development of Quine's Naturalism*. Oxford: Oxford University Press.

(2020). "Coming to America: Carnap, Reichenbach and the Great Intellectual Migration. Part I: Rudolf Carnap." *Journal for the History of Analytical Philosophy* 8 (11): 1–23.

Vlastos, G. (1975). *Plato's Universe*. Seattle: University of Washington Press.

Wagner, P. (ed.) (2009). *Carnap's Logical Syntax of Language*. Basingstoke: Palgrave Macmillan.

(ed.) (2012). *Carnap's Ideal of Explication and Naturalism*. Basingstoke: Palgrave MacMillan.

(2017). "Carnapian and Tarskian Semantics." *Synthese* 194: 97–119.

Wartofsky, M. (1982). "The Vienna Circle as a Social Movement." *Grazer Philosophische Studien*, 16–17 (1): 79–101.

Weber, M. (1919). *Wissenschaft als Beruf*. Munich: Duncker und Humblot.

Weiner, J. (2021). *Taking Frege at His Word*. Oxford: Oxford University Press.

Weir, A. (2014). "Quine's Naturalism." In G. Harman and E. Lepore (eds.) *A Companion to W. V. O. Quine*. Hoboken, NJ: Wiley-Blackwell, 114–147.

Werner, M. (2003). *Moderne in der Provinz. Kulturelle Experimente im Fin de Siècle Jena*. Göttingen: Wallstein Verlag.

White, M. J. (1985). *Agency and Integrality: Philosophical Themes in the Ancient Discussions of Determinism and Responsibility*. Dordrecht: D. Reidel.

Wieman, H. N. (1937). "Review of 'Factors Determining Human Behavior by Harvard Tercentenary Publications.'" *The Journal of Religion* 17 (3): 321–324.

Williamson, T. (2013). *Modal Logic as Metaphysics*. Oxford: Oxford University Press.

Wilson, M. (2022). *Imitation of Rigor. An Alternative History of Analytic Philosophy*. Oxford: Oxford University Press.

Wittgenstein, L. (1922). *Tractatus Logico-Philosophicus*. Translated by C. K. Ogden. London: Routledge & Kegan Paul.

Wolters, G. (2004). "Styles in Philosophy: The Case of Carnap." In S. Awodey and C. Klein (eds.), *Carnap Brought Home: The View from Jena*. Lasalle, IL: Open Court, 25–39.
Yablo, S. (1998). "Does Ontology Rest on a Mistake?" *Australian Society Supplementary* 72 (1): 229–283.
Yap, A. (2010). "Feminism and Carnap's Principle of Tolerance." *Hypatia* 25: 437–454.
Zabell, S. L. (1982). "W. E. Johnson's Sufficientness Postulate." *The Annals of Statistics* 10 (4): 1091–1099.
  (1991). "Ramsey, Truth, and Probability." *Theoria* 57 (3): 211–238.
  (1997a). "The Continuum of Inductive Methods Revisited." In J. Earman and J. D. Norton (eds.), *The Cosmos of Science: Essays of Exploration*. Pittsburgh; Konstanz: University of Pittsburgh Press; Universitäts Verlag-Konstanz, 351–385.
  (1997b). "Confirming Universal Generalizations." *Erkenntnis* 45: 267–283.
  (2007). "Carnap on Probability and Induction." In M. Friedman and R. Creath (eds.), *The Cambridge Companion to Carnap*. Cambridge: Cambridge University Press, 273–294.
  (2008). "Philosophy of Inductive Logic: The Bayesian Perspective." In L. Haaparanta (ed.), *The Development of Modern Logic*. Oxford: Oxford University Press, 725–774.
  (2011). "Carnap and the Logic of Inductive Inference." In D. Gabbay, S. Hartmann, and J. Woods (eds.), *Handbook of the History and Philosophy of Logic, Volume 10: Inductive Logic*. Amsterdam: Elsevier, 265–309.

Index

a priori
 relativized, 63
 synthetic, 15, 26, 63, 135
abstract entities, 40, 49, 229, 231
academic freedom, 81–85
academic responsibility, 85
Adler, Friedrich, 25
Adler, Max, 25
ameliorative analysis, 127, 142, 145–146
analytic philosophy, 1, 51, 127, 146, 217
 historiography, 51–54
 of language, 138
analyticity, 41, 42, 43, 98, 99, 101, 169, 238, 240, 250
 explication, 112–113
 questions of law, 101–102
 semantic, 110, 111
Austro-Marxism, 25
Avenarius, Richard, 29
Ayer, A. J., 202, 278

Basic English, 215, 220
Bauch, Bruno, 3, 18, 173
Bauer, Otto, 25, 29
Bauhaus, 13, 23, 24, 29, 71, 79, 228
Beaney, Michael, 51–54, 68
Becker, Oskar, 242
Bergson, Henri, 283
Beth, Evert, 89
bipartite metatheory, 126
Boghossian, Paul, 112
Brentano, Franz, 16, 20

Carnap, Rudolf
 deflationism to philosophy, 108, 113
 family background, 18
 FBI investigation, 79
 intellectual development, 18, 74–78
 loyalty oath, 79
 Mexican professors, 80–81
 on metaphysics, 282–285
 on space and geometry, 176, 255
 semantical turn, 155, 157, 159, 161, 164, 166, 168, 170
 wartime essay, 74
Carus, André W., 7, 65–67, 68, 124, 223
Cassirer, Ernst, 53, 63, 128, 146, 262, 267
causality, 279, 281
Chomsky, Noam, 93, 96
Church, Alonzo, 156, 167, 197
civil rights, 83
Cohn, Jonas, 3, 18
Comte, August, 5
conceptual engineering, 46, 127, 129, 142, 145
conceptual scheme, 90, 91, 103
constitution theory, 65, 177, 179, 244, 254, 255
continental philosophy, 6
conventionalism, 4, 239–243, 250, 255–256, 266
 in logic, 167, 169
correspondence rules, 237, 239, 244, 246, 247, 249
Couturat, Louis, 214, 216, 217
Craig, Edward, 128
Creath, Richard, 94

Daston, Lorraine, 259
Davidson, Donald, 96, 98, 138
decision-making, 29, 30
Dennett, Daniel, 93
Dewey, John, 16, 20
dialectical materialism, 26
Dilthey, Wilhelm, 5, 6
Dingler, Hugo, 4
Dörpfeld, Friedrich Wilhelm, 16, 18–21
Dörpfeld, Wilhelm, 18
Dreben, Burton, 90, 94
Driesch, Hans, 6, 228
Du Bois, W. E. B., 75
Du Bois-Raymond, Emil, 260
Dummett, Michael, 138

Eberhardt, Frederick, 273
Einstein, Albert, 99, 101, 134, 272

empiriocriticism, 13, 28
Enlightenment, 4, 65–67, 142, 223, 261
epsilon calculus, 247
Erkenntnis, 76, 252
Esperanto, 76, 214, 217, 220
expertise, 17
explication, 41, 66, 99, 100, 112, 126, 194, 196, 221–224
    definition, 129–132
    practical agenda, 143
extensionalism, 123

fallibilism, 107
fatalism, 272
Fechner, Gustav Theodor, 18
Feigl, Herbert, 223, 238
Flitner, Wilhelm, 16, 20
Forman, Paul, 261
Foucault, Michel, 128
framework, 41, 42, 91
    of numbers, 42–43
Frank, Philipp, 79, 115, 193
Frege, Gottlob, 3, 5, 18, 121, 132, 133, 139, 141, 146, 218
    on descriptions, 137–139
    on numbers, 135–137
Freyer, Hans, 3, 5, 6, 21–25
Friedman, Michael, 7, 61–63, 64, 65, 67, 68, 82, 175

Galison, Peter, 72, 259, 260
Gätschenberger, Richard, 6
Geisteswissenschaften, 4, 255
general axiomatics, 180–183, 188–191
general relativity, 99
George, Alexander, 94, 96
German Youth Movement, 13, 18, 23, 75
Glymour, Clark, 273
Goldscheid, Rudolf, 25
Goodman, Nelson, 5, 56–59, 64, 67, 68, 127, 148, 193, 209
Gödel, Kurt, 33, 37, 133, 154, 183, 186, 193, 241
Grelling, Kurt, 54–56, 67, 68
Grice, Paul, 98
grounding, 48
Guérard, Albert L., 220

Haeckel, Ernst, 18, 260
Hart, H. L. A., 274
Hegel, G. W. F., 260, 264
Heidegger, Martin, 82
Helmholtz, Hermann, 260
Hempel, Carl G., 76, 148, 193, 221, 238, 250
Herder, Johann Gottfried, 225
Hertz, Paul, 3
Hilbert, David, 133, 154, 174, 175, 248

historical epistemology, 259
Hogben, Lancelot, 215, 221
Humboldt, Alexander von, 225
Husserl, Edmund, 3, 5, 6, 128
Hylton, Peter, 107, 120, 126

Ido, 214
inductive logic, 31, 165, 195
intensionality, 98, 114, 247
Interglossa, 215, 221
Interlingua, 214, 216, 220
internal/external questions, 38, 44, 109, 120, 230
International Auxiliary Language Association, 215, 229
International Encyclopedia of Unified Science, 76, 252, 268
intersubjective accountability, 72–73, 85
intersubjectivity, 64, 73, 78, 85
Isotype Institute, 73
ISOTYPE, 73, 215

Jespersen, Otto, 214, 223, 224, 225, 227
Jung, Carl, 262

Kant, Immanuel, 51, 104, 135, 136, 173, 194
Kaplan, David, 77
Kemeny, John, 119, 156, 197, 198, 201, 210
Kemp, Gary, 107, 120, 126
Korsch, Karl, 25
Köhler, Wolfgang, 3
Kraus, Oskar, 16, 20
Kuhn, Thomas, 125

language change, 115–116
Laplace, Pierre-Simon de, 271–272, 275, 279
Latino sine Flexione, 216
laws of nature, 117, 270, 271–272, 276, 277, 278, 279
Leibniz, G. W., 216, 217, 218
Leitgeb, Hannes, 124
Lenin, V. I., 25
Leonard, Henry S., 56–58
Lewin, Kurt, 3
logicism, 115, 136, 186, 242
Lutz, Sebastian, 238
Lvov-Warsaw School, 140

Mac Lane, Saunders, 161, 238
Mach, Ernst, 5, 18, 29, 134
Marxism, 25, 26, 29
Maxwell, Grover, 223
meaning
    criterion of, 13
    postulates, 98
    and reference, 154

Mehlis, Georg, 3
Meinong, Alexius, 138, 141
Menger, Karl, 134
meta-ethics, 20
metalanguage, 157
metalogic, 63, 139, 266
metaphysics
  Aufbau, 35–36
  and frameworks, 45–46
  Methodological Interpretation, 33, 37, 38, 42, 49
  non-scientific meaning, 36
  Subject Matter Interpretation, 33, 37, 38–43, 49
Mill, John Stuart, 135
Moholy-Nagy, László, 3
Moore, G. E., 136
moral discourse, 20
Morris, Charles, 193, 252

Natorp, Paul, 18
naturalism, 16, 102, 103, 106
  epistemology, 123–125
Necessitism, 47
necessity, 277
neo-Kantianism, 4, 62, 173
Neurath, Marie, 73
Neurath, Otto, 25, 28, 70, 73, 76, 79, 142, 146, 148, 193, 215, 217, 220, 222, 252, 256, 260, 266, 267, 268
Newton, Isaac, 279
Nietzsche, Friedrich, 5, 128
Nohl, Herman, 3, 18
nominalism, 58, 250
noncognitivism, 122, 123
  definition, 19
  disagreement, 21
  fascism, 21, 23
  impartiality, 20, 30
  as political, 16
Nyíri, Kristóf, 226

objectivity, 64, 68, 78, 259
observational terms, 239, 243–249, 251, 257
Occam's Razor, 136
Ogden, Charles K., 215, 220
ontology, 141
  deflationism, 39
ordinary language, 92, 94, 100
Ostwald, Wilhelm, 4, 18

Pauli, Wolfgang, 262
Peano, Giuseppe, 216
philosophy
  ideal language, 127
  mathematical, 127, 137, 140, 145
  ordinary-language, 91, 216
  political engagement, 71
philosophy of science
  feminist, 75
  political neutrality, 28
physicalism, 29, 217, 222, 252, 256, 258, 266
Poincaré, Henri, 4, 18, 104, 134
Popper, Karl, 74
pragmatics, 90, 110–111, 115, 120, 124
  of science, 115
pragmatism, 147, 226, 231, 232, 274
Price, Huw, 103
principle of tolerance, 104, 107, 108, 109, 123, 166–170, 230–232, 265, 284
probability, explication, 114
protocol-sentence debate, 28, 266
P-rules, 117–119, 243, 244, 246, 248
Putnam, Hilary, 116

quantum mechanics, 272, 282
quasi-analysis, 57, 58, 59
Quine, W. V. O., 4, 5, 59, 63, 64, 65, 67, 68, 77, 98, 108, 127, 141, 148, 193, 237, 238, 250, 258, 266
  on obviousness, 94–95
  ontology, 96

racism, 82–84
Ramsey sentence, 118, 248
Ramsey, Frank, 138, 186, 195, 198, 201
rational reconstruction, 60, 66, 129, 216
Received View, 238, 239
regimentation, 95
Reichenbach, Hans, 3, 23, 75, 177, 193, 228, 237, 239, 262, 271, 272–276, 277, 279, 281, 282, 284, 285
Reichenbach, Maria, 77, 85
Reisch, George, 79
Richardson, Alan, 7, 63–65, 66, 67, 68
Rickert, Heinrich, 3, 6, 18
Romizi, Donata, 26, 71, 74
Rosenberg, Ethel, 79
Rosenberg, Julius, 79
Russell, Bertrand, 5, 51, 54, 56, 60, 121, 129, 132, 133, 139, 142, 146, 174, 175, 177, 193, 216, 218
  on descriptions, 137–139
  on numbers, 135–137

Salmon, Wesley, 273
Sapir-Whorf hypothesis, 227, 263
Schleyer, Johann, 214
Schlick, Moritz, 18, 71, 74, 178, 217, 226, 228, 237, 239, 243, 278
scientific humanism, 17, 31, 260

scientific world-conception, 18, 25, 28, 71, 73, 75
Sellars, Wilfrid, 93
semantical system, 41
semantics, 113
　model-theoretic, 119
sense data, 5, 29, 60
Shimony, Abner, 83, 198, 199, 202
social engagement, 2
social engineering, 142
state description, 163
Stegmüller, Wolfgang, 83
stipulation, 101
Strawson, Peter, 91, 92, 93, 97, 146, 147, 148, 222
　critique of Carnap, 92, 100, 223
structure theory, 176–180
synonymity, 98

Tarski, Alfred, 133, 139–140, 141, 146, 148, 153, 155, 162, 167, 183, 186, 193
tautology, 36, 41, 129, 177, 181, 183
theoretical terms, 243–249, 251
　partial interpretation, 248
type theory, 177, 179, 182, 183, 191, 242

Uebel, Thomas, 26, 70–73, 85
Unity of Science movement. *see* unified science
use/mention distinction, 39

Vaihinger, Hans, 6
value, 14
　function, 29, 30

van Fraassen, Bas, 238
Verein Ernst Mach, 25
verificationism, 35, 37, 44, 56
Vienna Circle, 34, 71, 73, 82, 134, 140, 142, 144, 156, 186, 217, 228, 229, 239, 243, 256, 262
　left wing, 26, 70, 74, 79
　manifesto, 25, 71, 78, 262
　political agenda, 27, 70, 259
Virchow, Rudolf, 260
Volapük, 214
Volk, 227–230, 232
voluntarism, 104

Waismann, Friedrich, 165
Weber, Max, 17
Whitehead, Alfred N., 56, 177
Wieman, Henry Nelson, 16
Wien, Max, 3
Williams, Bernard, 128
Williamson, Timothy, 47–48
Windelband, Wilhelm, 53
Wittgenstein, Ludwig, 5, 41, 91, 92, 94, 121, 129, 138, 164, 165, 177, 185, 186, 217, 226, 227, 231, 243
Wolters, Gereon, 78
Wundt, Wilhelm, 18, 262
Wyneken, Gustav, 23

Zamenhof, Ludwik Lejzer, 214, 219
Ziehen, Theodor, 6

For EU product safety concerns, contact us at Calle de José Abascal, 56–1°, 28003 Madrid, Spain or eugpsr@cambridge.org.

www.ingramcontent.com/pod-product-compliance
Ingram Content Group UK Ltd.
Pitfield, Milton Keynes, MK11 3LW, UK
UKHW020909120825
461685UK00043B/1388